FORSYTH LIBRARY
FORT HAYS STATE UNIVERSITY

The Brownings and France

The Brownings and France

A CHRONICLE WITH COMMENTARY

Roy E. Gridley

THE ATHLONE PRESS
London

First published 1982 by The Athlone Press Ltd
90–91 Great Russell Street, London WC1B 3PY

© Roy E. Gridley 1982

Distributor in the USA and Canada
Humanities Press Inc
New Jersey

British Library Cataloguing in Publication Data

Gridley, Roy E.
  The Brownings and France.
  1. Browning, Elizabeth Barrett –
  Knowledge – France   2. Browning, Robert
  – Knowledge – France   3. France –
  Civilization
  I. Title
  821'.8   PR4197.F/
  ISBN 0-485-11231-0

All rights reserved. No part of this publication may be reproduced,
stored in a retrieval system, or transmitted in any form or by any
means, electronic, mechanical, photocopying or otherwise, without
prior permission in writing from the publisher.

Typeset by Preface Ltd, Salisbury, Wilts.

Printed in Great Britain by
The University Press, Cambridge

Contents

This book is for my sons
Karl and Mark

Acknowledgments

I am grateful for the financial support this study has received from the General Research Fund of the University of Kansas. Scholarly support in the form of advice and encouragement came from many of my colleagues in nineteenth-century literary studies at the University of Kansas; I wish to thank especially Peter Casagrande, Edward F. Grier, Bernard Hirsch, Harold Orel, Max K. Sutton and George J. Worth. Particular thanks, also, to Dorothy Douglass Leidig, Brian Southam and Sheila Traill.

The following publishers have kindly granted me permission to quote from editions of the Brownings' letters: Barnes and Noble for *Browning to His American Friends*, ed. Gertrude Reese Hudson; University of Texas Press for *Dearest Isa*, ed. Edward C. McAleer, © John Murray Ltd, who also grant permission for *Elizabeth Barrett to Miss Mitford*, ed. Betty Miller, and for *Elizabeth Barrett Browning: Letters to Her Sister*, ed. Leonard Huxley; Yale University Press for *Elizabeth Barrett to Mr. Boyd*, ed. Barbara P. McCarthy, and for *New Letters of Robert Browning*, eds William C. DeVane and Kenneth L. Knickerbocker; Harvard University Press for *Learned Lady*, ed. Edward C. McAleer, and for *The Letters of Robert Browning and Elizabeth Barrett Barrett*, ed. Elvan Kintner; University of Illinois Press for *Letters of the Brownings to George Barrett*, eds Paul Landis and Ronald E. Freeman; and Ohio University Press for *Diary by E.B.B.*, eds Philip Kelley and Ronald Hudson.

This investigation was supported by University of Kansas research allocations nos. 3171–2038, 3494–0038, and 3672–0038.

Note on Editions and the Text

For Robert Browning's work from *Pauline* up to and including the first volume of *Men and Women*, I cite *The Complete Works of Robert Browning*, eds Roma A. King, Jr., *et al.* (Athens: Ohio University Press, 1969–81). For his subsequent poems I cite *The Works of Robert Browning*, ed. F. G. Kenyon (London: Smith, Elder, 1912). For Elizabeth's poems, I cite *Complete Works of Elizabeth Barrett Browning*, eds Charlotte Porter and Helen A. Clarke (New York: George D. Sproul, 1901).

Both Brownings, but especially Elizabeth in her letters, were irregular and erratic in spelling, punctuation, placing of French accents, etc. To correct silently these deviations from modern usage would both mislead the reader and destroy the flavour of the Brownings' epistolary styles; to place a [sic] each time an irregularity occurs would be extremely cumbersome. I have, then, tried to reproduce faithfully texts of their letters as given in the standard editions. English translations from the French, except when otherwise noted, are my own.

Abbreviations of Frequently Cited Titles

American Friends	*Browning to his American Friends: Letters between the Brownings, the Storys and James Russell Lowell*, ed. Gertrude Reese Hudson (New York: Barnes and Noble, 1965).
Dearest Isa	*Dearest Isa: Robert Browning's Letters to Isabella Blagden*, ed. Edward C. McAleer (Austin: University of Texas Press, 1951).
EB to Miss Mitford	*Elizabeth Barrett to Miss Mitford: The Unpublished Letters of Elizabeth Barrett Barrett to Mary Russell Mitford*, ed. Betty Miller (London: John Murray, 1954).
EB to Mr. Boyd	*Elizabeth Barrett to Mr. Boyd: Unpublished Letters of Elizabeth Barrett Barrett to Hugh Stuart Boyd*, ed. Barbara P. McCarthy (New Haven: Yale University Press, 1955).
Irvine and Honan	William Irvine and Park Honan, *The Book, the Ring, and the Poet: a Biography of Robert Browning* (New York: McGraw-Hill, 1974).
Learned Lady	*Learned Lady: Letters from Robert Browning to Mrs. Thomas FitzGerald, 1876–1889*, ed. Edward C. McAleer (Cambridge: Harvard University Press, 1966).
Letters, ed. Hood	*Letters of Robert Browning Collected by Thomas J. Wise*, ed. Thurman L. Hood (New Haven: Yale University Press, 1933).

Letters, ed. Huxley	*Elizabeth Barrett Browning: Letters to her Sister, 1846–1859*, ed. Leonard Huxley (London: John Murray, 1929).
Letters, ed. Kenyon	*The Letters of Elizabeth Barrett Browning*, ed. Frederic G. Kenyon, 2 vols (New York: Macmillan, 1897).
Letters to George	*Letters of the Brownings to George Barrett*, eds Paul Landis and Ronald E. Freeman (Urbana: University of Illinois Press, 1958).
Letters to Ogilvy	*Elizabeth Barrett Browning's Letters to Mrs. David Ogilvy, 1849–1861*, eds Peter N. Heydon and Philip Kelley (New York: The Browning Institute, 1973).
New Letters	*New Letters of Robert Browning*, eds William C. DeVane and Kenneth L. Knickerbocker (New Haven: Yale University Press, 1950).
RB and EBB	*The Letters of Robert Browning and Elizabeth Barrett Barrett, 1845–1846*, ed. Elvan Kintner; 2 vols (Cambridge: Harvard University Press, 1969).
RB and Julia Wedgwood	*Robert Browning and Julia Wedgwood: A Broken Friendship as Revealed in their Letters*, ed. Richard Curle (New York: Frederick A. Stokes Co., 1937).

Foreword

France – more than Italy and often more than England – was for Elizabeth Barrett and Robert Browning the scene of what was most interesting and significant in their contemporary culture. From childhood onwards, both displayed a lively interest in and wide appreciation of France: her language, literature, history, politics, her rivers and railways, her seaside and mountain villages. Paris – with its "fountains of living literature," its "brilliant civilization," and its "life, and mobility, and above all that continual beat of mind" – was especially attractive to the Brownings. Early in their marriage, they hoped to live permanently in Paris. That dream faded after two sojourns there convinced them that Parisian winters were too harsh for Elizabeth. They continued to hope that France could be their home: Paris in the warmer months; somewhere in the South of France during the winter. They were *en route* from Rome to Paris in June of 1861 when Elizabeth was stricken and subsequently died at Florence. For the next twenty-two years after her death, Robert Browning spent some three months of nearly every year in France. This chronicle records the Brownings' early study of French and early reading in French literature and history, their delight in the new French writing, their sojourns in and travels across France, their close observation of mid-century French politics, and, after 1861, Robert Browning's pleasure in the quiet coastal and mountain villages in Brittany, Normandy, Haute-Savoie and Isère.

To this narrative of the Brownings' experience of France I have added brief sketches of the intellectual, literary, political or religious milieu of France in the middle decades of the century. Such sketches may clarify the Brownings' complex attitudes towards, for example, the Revolution of 1848 and towards Louis-Napoleon's transformation of the Second Republic into the Second Empire. Sketches of the literary milieu of Paris may also provide some perspective on the

xi

nature of Robert Browning's realism and even naturalism. A few other British Victorians enter the narrative – Dickens, Carlyle, Rossetti, Thackeray, Arnold, Tennyson; they appear but briefly and are there to piece out the record the Brownings have left us, to provide responses to France different from those of the Brownings, and to remind us that France was an important part of the Victorian experience.

Because the Brownings' experience of French culture enriched not only their lives but also their art, the chronicle is interspersed with commentary upon a number of their poems. French themes, setting, subjects and even modes entered scores of their poems: from Elizabeth's *Essay on Mind* (1826) through *Aurora Leigh* (1856) to *Poems Before Congress* (1860) and from Robert's *Pauline* (1833) through his "French trilogy" of *Prince Hohenstiel-Schwangau* (1871), *Fifine at the Fair* (1872) and *Red Cotton Night-Cap Country* (1873). The commentary supplements existing criticism of the Brownings' poetry and provides a different context in which to view individual poems. In hope of enriching the reading of their poetry, I have introduced into the narrative, for example, discussion of the French analogues to *Pauline* or of the influence of Balzac, Sue, Sand or Soulié on *Aurora Leigh*, and suggestions of similarities between "Apparent Failure" and certain Baudelaire poems, or between *Red Cotton Night-Cap Country* and emerging French naturalism; there are also comments on Bishop Blougram's admiration for Balzac, on the importance of Breton topography to *Fifine at the Fair* or that of Haute-Savoie to *La Saisiaz*. These French contexts might also adjust a bit the persisting emphasis in Browning studies upon historic Italy, Italian politics, or the notion that Robert Browning was largely indifferent to his contemporary world. Indeed, contemporary French culture entered his poetry and letters with frequency and fullness.

The testimony recorded in their letters and poems is rich and diverse and filled with vignettes of French culture: the colourful life along the Champs-Élysées, the sounds of cannonading near Porte St. Denis on the night of December 4, 1851, the illusory pastoral quiet of Calvados, a crowded tour of La Grande Chartreuse, a Pardon near Pointe du Raz, the impotent rage of Parisian journalists after Louis-Napoleon's *coup d'état*, the confusion at channel ports when the Prussians drove with unexpected suddenness across France, the discomfort of jarring rides in provincial diligences and

the luxury of first-class travel on the new Marseille-Paris railway, a
netted dolphin at Arcachon, a stopped watch in Rousseau's room
near Chambéry, the "ragged Red diluted with the lower theatrical"
of George Sand's salon, Béranger "in his white hat wandering along
the asphalte," the rustic peace of Le Croisic in late summer after a
winter in the "black rainy beastly-streeted London world." After the
dullness of Florence, Parisian salons – "the shop windows of the
world" Elizabeth called them – were exhilarating to the Brownings.
During their first extended stay in the French capital in 1851–52,
Elizabeth determined to leave Robert "no peace till he gets into
acquaintance with all the delightful scamps of feuilletonistes and
artists in Paris." Some acquaintances were made during this and
subsequent visits: Lamartine, Sand, Mérimée, Cousin, Thierry,
Michelet, François Buloz, Gavarni, Rosa Bonheur and Ary Scheffer, Paul but not Alfred de Musset, Ristori but not Rachel; in later
years Robert met Doré, Gérôme, Rodin, Renan, perhaps Taine.

More important than literary and artistic society, however, were
French books, journals and newspapers through which they could
"look through a loophole at the world." Balzac was an early and
lifelong favourite; so, too, was Stendhal's *Le Rouge et le noir*. Robert
preferred Dumas' plays and memoirs; Elizabeth devoured his endless stream of novels and was convinced that Dumas did "write his
own books, that's a fact." Though Robert read even into old age a
good deal of Sand's work, he never shared Elizabeth's enthusiasm
for "Sand*ism*." They also had "great wars" about the merits of
Soulié, Sue, and even Hugo. *Madame Bovary* became "'Robert's
favourite book,'" but he was disappointed by the weak historical
verisimilitude of *Salammbô*. He was also surprised by the scholarly
weakness of Renan's *Vie de Jésus*. They wept along with the rest of
the Vaudeville audience at Dumas *fils' La Dame aux camélias*, but
they were impatient with Italian lending libraries that stocked plenty
of books by Dumas *fils* while *Le Cousin Pons* or an instalment of *Les
Splendeurs et misères des courtisanes* had to be sought out with the
greatest diligence. Their letters and poems offer a perspective on the
availability of books, modes of publication, problems of press censorship. Their writings also give us some idea of what it was like to
depend from afar on newspapers to inform one about the course of
the Revolution of 1848 and the Second Republic, or to watch at first
hand the establishment and collapse of the Second Empire. Four

years before her death Elizabeth wrote to her sister Henrietta, whose first child had just been born, to urge her sister not to neglect the child's education in foreign languages: "the world is *thrown open* now," she wrote, "and an intelligent man mustn't be simply an Englishman or a Frenchman but a citizen of all countries." This chronicle is, finally, a portrait of what two of the more informed, intelligent and articulate British Victorians found of value and interest in France.

1

An Early Acquaintance with Things French

i

EB's Journey to Paris in 1815 – Her Sojourn at Boulogne – Early Reading and Tutoring in French – Her Judgment of Corneille and Racine – Madame de Staël's Corinne *– Lamartine, "a poet too – tho' he is a frenchman."*

ii

RB's Family Interest in France – His Early Reading and Study under M. Loradoux – French Analogues to Pauline: *Rousseau, Senancour, de Staël, Amiel and Balzac.*

iii

EB Becomes a "complete and unscrupulous" Reader of New French Fiction – Her Desire to Live in Paris – Hugo Better than Boz or Scott – Sand's "eloquence and passion" – EB's Praise of Balzac's Genius.

i

In the autumn of 1815 after the allied victory at Waterloo, Edward Moulton Barrett, like many other citizens of nations long in conflict with revolutionary and Napoleonic France, determined that he and his wife should visit Paris. At the last moment, Mr. Barrett's impetuous and rather indulged nine-year old daughter Elizabeth also determined that she would accompany her parents. "I was very much delighted when I set off for France," Elizabeth wrote at the opening of the "Notes" she compiled upon her return from the

1

journey, "and have never repented my resolution to go."[1] The month-long sojourn was Elizabeth's first introduction to the land she would, in her mature years, consider the bright and stimulating centre of contemporary intellectual, literary, and political life. The crossing from Dover on October 18, 1815, further introduced her to an inconvenience Robert Browning and she would often suffer together during their many journeys to France – sea-sickness. At Calais, however, the tide was out and the water calm; shoeless and shirtless men, looking "more like monkeys than men," waded into the surf to carry the passengers onto the sands. From her arrival at Calais until she sailed back to Dover from Boulogne, Elizabeth noted carefully the sights, sounds, tastes and smells of France: a good supper with champagne at Calais; the early morning harnessing of tired horses to a "nodding Cabriolet" in the yard of the inn of "Monsr. Quillac"; the fine dishes and wine at the Hôtel de l'Europe in Abbeville; the cathedral at Amiens; Prussian troops crowding around Clermont; breakfast and a visit to the destroyed château of the Prince de Condé at Chantilly.

Finally, after four days' travel in a four-horse barouche, came the sight of "the superb Church of St. Denis where the King was buried." Thoughts of Louis XVI's martyrdom gave way to the "very disagreeable smell" of the streets of central Paris and to a wearying search for accommodation commodious but not *trop cher*." The new king, Louis XVIII, could be seen daily at the Tuileries from the windows of the rooms the Barretts finally found on the fifth floor of the Hôtel de Rivoli. Like the thousands of other foreign visitors crowding into the capital of the restored Bourbons, the Barretts made excursions to the places made famous and infamous by the turbulence of recent French history: the Place de la Bastille; Josephine's chambers at Malmaison; the site of the Tower of the Temple, which Napoleon had razed in 1808 to halt royalist pilgrimages to the place of Louis XVI's and Marie-Antoinette's imprisonment. They took a day's excursion to Versailles and another to the Jardin des Plantes; twice Elizabeth saw Talma at the theatre, and she spent a third night at the Opéra-Comique watching a ballet. The Louvre was open but in some disarray as the representatives of allied governments culled the collection for works stolen by Napoleon. At the Panthéon it was to the rationalist Voltaire's tomb rather than the romantic Rousseau's or the revolutionary Mirabeau's that Elizabeth directed her interest. Into these three weeks the Barretts also crowded a good deal of shopping and visits to factories where goods long denied the English were made – Parisian carpets, china and glass. The journey from Paris held less delight and fascination for Elizabeth than had the journey to Paris. The carriage lost a wheel; beds were damp; the food was no longer so uniformly good; the Hôtel de France in Rouen was dirty and the cathedral there "scarcely worth seeing." By late November, the young Elizabeth was glad to be back "by a good comfortable English fireside."[2]

During the next five years Elizabeth became a competent student of the French language. For some three years she shared a French tutor with her brother Edward, who was preparing for admission to Charterhouse. And during these years before she turned fifteen she returned to France to live for seven months "at Boulogne, for masters, which are excellent there, and for the acquirement of that habit of talking French, which comes at a call."[3] The months at Boulogne were apparently very pleasant ones. She remembered she was "always laughing and joking," as she told Hugh Stuart Boyd later: "I well recollect that when we were in France, and when a woodfire was smoking in a disagreeable manner, a gentleman observed – 'I am very glad about this smoke. Now I can say I have seen the tears in Mademoiselle Barrett's eyes.'"[4] It was probably at Boulogne that she became friends with the young French girl to whom she addressed the brief epithalamium "To Victoire, On Her Marriage," published in 1833:

> Victoire! I knew thee in thy land,
>   Where I was strange to all:
> I heard thee; and were strange to me
>   The words thy lips let fall.
> I loved thee – for the Babel curse
>   Was meant not for the heart:
> I parted from thee, in such way
>   As those who love may part.[5]

The convention of the poem requires that language – like the "sea [which] doth rush between" and like marriage – also separates the poet from her "Gallic friend." Yet at Boulogne Elizabeth learned the French tongue well enough so that after nearly thirty years without

3

visiting France and after living a very secluded life in England, her French still came "at a call."

After her return from Boulogne, Elizabeth began to read widely in French literature and history. Mr. Barrett forbade her to read books from the section of library containing Gibbon and *Tom Jones*. In the uncircumscribed section she found Voltaire and Rousseau, probably the *Dictionnaire philosophique portatif* and *Les Confessions*. At the age of twelve she judged the French of Madame de Sévigné "excellent"; she remembered Sévigné's gossipy, amusing letters about seventeenth-century court and country life well enough more than a decade later to quarrel in her diary with the generally cheerful French-woman who had asserted that "the thoughts early in a morning, are couleur de rose."[6] Probably at twelve or so she began to read some Racine and Corneille; and, perhaps in imitation, she wrote a number of French "tragedies" of which only an eleven-page Roman drama in rhymed French hexameters has survived.

Régulus opens with the Roman general's daughter Orphille plead-ing with her mother Marcia against a dangerous attempt to retrieve the captured Régulus from the Carthaginians. "Votre dessin est folle," cries Orphille, "Cherchez Régulus/Captif dans la Carthage!" Finish-ing off the hexameter with an appropriate rhyme, the mother replies: "N'en parlez plus." Scene ii finds a disguised and soliloquizing Régulus. Orphille (*en pleurant*) recognizes his voice: "Juste ciel, c'est mon Père!" Orphille and her mother are unable to dissuade Régulus from his determination to remain captive so Rome can remain free. With this noble resolve, he rushes away leaving wife and daughter to die – in one another's arms – of disappointment. In the epilogue the young author steps forward to comment upon her "farce"; she insists that although she is not a Tory, she, like Régulus, loves her country:

Messieurs et Mesdames, je souhaite finir notre comédie
Avec un peu d'explanation touchant ma tragédie;
J'ai voulu la faire, sur la conduite de Régulus
Qui me semble toujours aussi noble que généreuse.
Vous en devinerez peut-être que je ne suis pas *Tory*,
Et avouez Messieurs, que j'aime bien ma patrie. . . .[7]

(Ladies and Gentlemen, I wish to end our Comedy
With a small explanation touching my Tragedy;

Wherein I wished to treat the conduct of Regulus
Which always seems to me as noble as generous
From it you will divine that I'm no *Tory*
And, Gentlemen confess that well I love my Country.)

(EB's translation)

Elizabeth's study of French was, of course, subsidiary to her study of Greek and Latin. But by 1820 when she was fourteen, she had developed a lively, idiomatic style she displayed in three epistolary exercises that combine her classical learning with her knowledge of French. The exercises are three letters written in French to Homer, Socrates and Pindar. Homer is addressed as "Seigneur Homère, Les Champs Elyseès, Pres du Palais de Pluton, L'Enfers." In this chatty letter Elizabeth revealed to Homer her preference for him over his Roman imitator Virgil, whom she calls "un lurion, un coquin, un lache, un poltron."[8]

Elizabeth's reading in French during the next decade – 1820 to 1830 – appears to have been largely in the service of her classical studies or as an aid to her philosophical studies preparatory to her writing of *An Essay on Mind* (1826). To the blind Greek scholar Hugh Stuart Boyd, who himself had written Latin verse, she rather daringly approved Voltaire's strictures against any Latin poetry since the Augustans and endorsed Voltaire's "summary criticism of Du Fresnoy's elegant *Ars Graphica*." At the same time she delights in Lucan's *Pharsalia* despite "the classical *growl* against it, given vent to, by most critics – with that Cynic of Criticism, Scaliger, at their head." Nor does she approve Scaliger's *"Mantuamaniacal"* preference for Virgil over Homer.[9] French philosphers, too, had caught her attention. In her *Essay on Mind* she asserts that "Buffon err'd" in his materialism; so, too, did Condillac in his reduction of ideas and ideals to mere sensation. In a note she cites, from Condillac's *Traité des sensations* (1754), his assertion "que la réflection n'est dans son principe que la sensation même", but she denies the truth of it.[10] Elizabeth was a Christian idealist: though the mode of her *Essay* is that of Pope, the sentiments are closer to, say, those of Chateaubriand, whom she had not yet read, than to the French rationalists. It is not surprising, then, that her single reference to Descartes is to his early visionary experience when "The whispered sound . . . stole on Descartes' ear,/ Hallowing the sunny visions of his youth/ With that eternal mandate, 'Search for Truth!' "[11] Although she could appreci-

5

ate the "clever and animated" common sense of Voltaire arguing in his preface to *Histoire de Charles XII* (1731) for biased writing of history, she thought excessive rationalism had marred French drama:

> Hence, let our Poets, with discerning glance,
> Forbear to imitate the stage of France.
> What though Corneille arouse the thrilling chords,
> And walk with Genius o'er th' inspirëd boards;
> What though his rival bring, with calmer grace,
> The classic unities of time and place, –
> All polish, and all eloquence – 'twere mean
> To leave the path of nature for Racine;
> When Nero's parent, 'midst her woe, defines
> The wrong that tortures – in two hundred lines:
> Or when Orestes, madden'd by his crime,
> Forgets life, joy, and everything – but rhyme. (II, 1061–72)

Elizabeth's youthful judgment of French neo-classical drama reflects her careful study of the French translation of A. W. Schlegel's *Cours de littérature dramatique* (three volumes, Paris and Geneva, 1814). During the 1820's, while she was reading Wordsworth, Byron, Shelley and Keats with enthusiasm, she continued to think of French poetry as continuing the manner of Racine. Writing to Mr. Boyd in 1829 she announces that she had been re-reading Racine. She prefers Shakespeare, with all his "extravagancies," to Racine who had originally "disgusted" her and whom she now finds "intolerable." From Racine she generalizes, with the help of a metaphor drawn from landscape gardening:

> The French have no part or lot in poetry. I am more and more convinced that they have *none*. A gentleman in this neighbourhood has been justly criticised for having the borders of a pond near his house levelled & rolled, by which he of course destroyed every picturesque roughness & undulation. The French do just the same with the banks of their Helicon. They are all made smooth & neat & clean & uninteresting. Every neighbouring spot is worked into a parterre. Even sublime & terrible subjects are cultivated with much the same attention to preciseness – laid out, like the burial ground near Paris, with trim shrubs, mown grass, & gravel walks![12]

Elizabeth's was not an uninformed opinion, however commonplace it might have been in 1829. She had read and re-read Racine and Corneille and perhaps Molière; she was thoroughly familiar with classical drama and Shakespeare; she had, herself, written a number of tragedies in French. Her careful reading of Lamartine two years later moderated her general distaste for French poetry, but her bias against it remained throughout her life. In 1844, to the discredit of English fiction and especially Dickens, she praised the fiction of Hugo, Balzac, Sand, Sue and "even the Soulies, and the grade lower"; but in a postscript she added that the "French have no rhythmetic poetry, from a defect in the language: and their poetry finds issue in prose. . . ."[13] In 1853, while admitting she didn't "know as much about French modern poetry" as she should, she nevertheless reiterated to her close friend, the novelist and play-wright Mary Russell Mitford, that the "French essential poetry seems to me to flow out into prose works into their school of romances, and to be least poetical when dyked up into rhythm."[14] In the same year, to another correspondent, she commented: "Balzac convinced me that the French language was malleable into poetry."[15] It was not Balzac who originally convinced her; it was Madame de Staël.

In June of 1832 Elizabeth was working her way through *Genesis* in the Hebrew. Tired of "fagging" over Hebrew grammar, she stopped and read, for the third time, Madame de Staël's *Corinne*. "It is an immortal book," she told Mr. Boyd, "and deserves to be read three score and ten times – that is, once every year in the age of man."[16] If she had taken her own counsel to read *Corinne* once a year, she would have first read that romance while she was re-reading Racine. She probably first became acquainted with the work of Madame de Staël when she read an English translation of the *Considérations sur les principaux événements de la révolution française* (1818). Elizabeth read a number of such contemporary *mémoires* in translation during the 1820's. Among them were Las Cases' *Mémorial de Sainte-Hélène* (1822–23), Madame de Campans' *Mémoires sur la vie privée de Marie-Antoinette* (1823), and the *Mémoires* of Comtesse de Genlis (1825), a work she read a second time in 1831. Published posthumously in 1818, de Staël's *Considérations* was an early work filled with enthusiasm for Rousseau and republican ideals. The book did not have, as did *Corinne* (1807), so many of those attitudes Elizabeth would share with de Staël: anti-Napoleonism and anti-clericalism;

frequent praise for cosmopolitan living fused with near stereotyping of national characteristics; the figure of the isolated woman of genius pursuing alone her poetic muse; the evocation of feeling and moral precept from land, city and sea. Elizabeth's letter to Boyd suggests that by 1832 she was conversant with de Staël's life as well as her work; the letter also reveals that she was a careful reader, alert to the influence de Staël had had on others: "Lord Byron hated Madame de Staël," she told Boyd, "because she was always prominent in conversation and used to lecture him, – but I believe he estimated her Corinne, and am sure that his writings were the better for his readings. . . . Harold has often spoken with the voice of Corinne, and often when he has spoken with the most passion and eloquence."[17] (Byron's translation in stanzas 179–82 of *Childe Harold* from Book I, Chapter IV of *Corinne* would have been perhaps but one of many influences Elizabeth noted.)

In her diary for 1831 she also noted that the Byronic pose had become verbose and ineffective when imitated in French verse by Lamartine. Reading Lamartine's "Last sons of Childe Harold," she confided to her diary that the *"dernier* chant wants the Byronic character (– an inevitable want for a French composition) and is not quite equal [even to] Lamartine."[18] Elizabeth found wanting in French poetry what she found admirable in French prose. A diary entry a few months later suggests something of what she had found so attractive in the romance of intrigue, mystery, passion and travel of Madame de Staël. A neighbour, Miss Baker, had objected "to such books as Corinne," Elizabeth notes, "because they lead the mind to expect more in life than can be met in life. Well! – allow that they do! – The expectation brings more happiness than any reality, – as realities go, – c[oul]d do. Romance of spirit is a far rarer fault than worldiness of spirit." She concludes rather testily: "I wish I knew a few people who had been 'spoilt' by reading Corinne. I know nobody."[19]

She did know someone with whom she could talk of Lamartine – another neighbour, Miss Steers, with whom in the summer of 1831 she read and discussed the best known of the new French poets. Elizabeth read several volumes of Lamartine's poems that summer. The reading seems to have been almost a test of the question she posed in her diary: *"Can any good poetry come out of Paris?"* Her answer was ambivalent after reading *Méditations poétiques* (1820), *Le*

Dernier Chant du Pèlerinage d'Harold (1825) and the two recently
published volumes, *Harmonies poétiques et religieuses* (1830). She preferred the nostalgic reminiscences of the early poems to the mixture
of political and religious meditation in the later volumes. "Milly, ou
la Terre natale" and "Le Tombeau d'une mère" she picked out for
special praise, although in the former she found "much lengthiness
together with much picturesqueness & *Goldsmith.* . . ." Both poems
hark back to Lamartine's earlier mode, though they appeared in the
second volume of *Harmonies*. Lamartine's ruminations on faith and
politics in the second volume she found inferior: "He certainly Pros-
crustianizes."[20] Just as Lamartine lacked the power of Byron, he
lacked the lyric intensity of Shelley's *Adonais*, a poem she praised
extravagantly the same day she noted in her diary: "Finished Lamartine who is a poet too – tho' he is a frenchman."[21] A serious and fairly
systematic reading of Lamartine had caused her to modify somewhat
her judgment of two years before when she had asserted to Boyd that
"The French have no part or lot in poetry."

Elizabeth's preference for English contemporary poetry over that
of the French was, at this time, matched by her preference for
English political life over that of France. She would reverse radically
this political stance in the 1840's and 1850's; however, during
1830–32, while both nations were undergoing important governmental reform, Elizabeth remained staunchly British. The news of
"the cannonading which has been going on in Paris" reached her at
the Barretts' Herefordshire home, Hope End, in early August 1830.
Though she could have had no sympathy for the ultra-royalist
regime of Charles X, she had read enough memoirs and histories of
the first revolution to fear revolutionary violence. To Mr. Boyd she
expressed her hope that Charles X would "not pay for his madness,
the price which poor Louis the 16th paid for his weakness."[22] But
she approved any punishment short of execution. She was, by and
large, indifferent to the events which a few days after she wrote this
letter would bring Louis-Philippe and the republican tricolour to the
Hôtel de Ville. "The French nation is not an interesting nation," she
commented coolly; yet she thought that one should watch the course
of events to make sure French repression did not threaten English
liberties: "No English ear ought to like hearing [the French] chain
clanking over our sea."[23] During the next two years the English
nation worked in parliamentary fashion to remove some of its own

aristocratic chains. The passage of the Reform Bill in June of 1832 coincided with renewed violence in Paris, sparked by Louis-Philippe's support of the Bourbon regime of Don Carlos. Elizabeth's reaction to the two events was one of smug complacency: "I do not wonder at the French being surprised at our bill having been passed by the people and without bloodshed," she wrote to Boyd. "We think before we fight, – and they fight before they think: exempli gratia, what do *you* decide about the fighting which is now going on in Paris, where the fighters are still undetermined as to whether they would be republicans or Carlists?"[24]

ii

By 1832 Robert Browning had received an education in languages quite similar to that of Elizabeth Barrett: early instruction in Latin and Greek; some tutoring in Italian; then, from the age of fourteen to sixteen, daily study of French and regular tutoring by Auguste Loradoux, "*Professeur de Langues*, Walworth." For these two years – 1816–18 – "French and French literature were Browning's primary occupation," says John Maynard in his excellent and thorough recreation of Browning's childhood and youth.[25] These were the years of Browning's intense and crucial discovery of Shelley; but he also read a good deal of Voltaire as well as Le Sage's *Gil Blas*, lyrics of Marot and Ronsard, some of Molière, Corneille and Racine.[26]

The multi-volume *Biographie universelle* became, in the 1830's and 1840's, Browning's source for facts, details, general biographical outlines, references to other books on subjects like Paracelsus, Sordello, King Charles-Emmanuel II or Victor-Amédée. He may have merely consulted the *Biographie* at the British Museum, but students of Browning have long accepted the "surmise" of his early biographer W. Hall Griffin that the encyclopaedic work was in Mr. Browning's large private library and that, in William C. DeVane's words, the "fifty volumes seem to have been read *in toto* by the poet."[27] Had the *Biographie* been "easily available in his father's library," the young Browning would have had access to thousands of relatively brief accounts of "the public and private life of all men who have attracted attention because of their writings, actions, talents, virtues or crimes," as the subtitle announces. Begun in 1811

10

during Napoleon's reign, the *Biographie* was largely completed under the Bourbon Restoration. Napoleon, whose actions and crimes should have been recited in volume 30 (1821), was excluded altogether; the omission was amply corrected by a 230-page entry in the supplementary volume of 1844. The diverse authors were not drily objective. Had the young Browning come across the 1824 entry on Robespierre, he would have been informed in the opening sentence that Robespierre was "the leader of the popular tyranny, the deadliest and the bloodiest who has ever tormented the human race. . . ." Reading the *Biographie* would certainly have been a convenient and effective way for the young Browning to extend his knowledge of the French language and of French and universal history; it may have contributed to his lifelong distrust of the Bonapartes; it may have helped form his sense that history is best rendered in a mixture of the public and private lives of individual human beings.

Other training in French included exercises in translating from Greek poetry into the French, which provided a mixture of classical and French study similar to that in Elizabeth's French epistles to Homer, Socrates and Pindar. Less laborious reading may have come with Madame de Staël, one of whose chants in *Corinne* Browning drew upon for an epigram for his juvenile "Dance of Death." Another of his "juvenile performances" bore the title "On Napoleon." His father found the poem "remarkably beautiful" and secretly saved it for many years; after his father's death in Paris in 1866, Browning apparently burned the poem along with so many other family letters and papers. We cannot know if, as he was wont to do in later years, Browning early in his life associated Napoleon with the other scourges of mankind, but he may well have shared Madame de Staël's attitude towards the usurper of republican ideals. The Browning family doubtless welcomed the restoration of relations between France and England after the fall of Napoleon. Robert's two favourite uncles, William and Reuben, took positions with the Rothschild bank, Reuben in the London office and William, for twenty years, in the Paris office. Both uncles were fluent in French and often conducted their mutual correspondence in French. William, during his long tenure in Paris, took an active interest in French scholarship and literature. In 1829 he published his two-volume *The History of the Huguenots during the Sixteenth*

11

Century. Later he published two historical novels based on French history and in the mode not just of Scott but of Balzac's *Les Chouans* or Hugo's *Notre-Dame de Paris*. Reuben's *Hoel Morvan; or the Court and Camp of Henry V* (London, 1844) with its French settings and large cast of French characters complementing the English scenes and characters, and his *The Provost of Paris, a Tale of the Court of Charles VI* (Paris, 1833) reveal wide knowledge of French history.

Robert's father was equally erudite in French history. He had been fortunate enough in his youth to attend the progressive school of Reverend Bell at Cheshunt where not only classical but modern languages, including French, were taught. That early instruction was useful in his studies throughout his life, and especially when he moved to Paris in 1852 to live there the last fifteen years of his life delightedly visiting the Parisian bookstores and libraries, drawing caricatural histories of the French nation, or instructing visitors on the history of Paris. Although Browning did not, as did Elizabeth Barrett, travel and live in France as a child, he must have developed early a sense of French as the language of a living, contemporary culture. Elizabeth, living a relatively secluded and provincial life at Hope End, relied on French books sent from London or borrowed from the library of a father who knew no French and who had had to rely on his wife's French when he made his short journey to France in 1815. Elizabeth could discuss Lamartine with Miss Steers or she could argue in her diary with those who thought French romances harmful. Her most intimate intellectual acquaintance, however, was Mr. Boyd, who was almost exclusively and most pedantically interested in the Greek Christian Fathers. The milieu of the London suburb of Camberwell was decidedly more cosmopolitan. And for the Browning family the focus of that cosmopolitanism was France. "At a time when Paris was as clearly the world centre of fashion and culture as London was of finance and trade," Maynard has argued convincingly, "Browning followed the cultural and literary life of France with a real and immediate involvement."[28]

Browning's first published poem, *Pauline: a Fragment of a Confession* (1833), reflects his involvement with things French. Here the poet speaks intimately to a young woman who writes in French and whose home seems to lie in the mountains of Switzerland or Savoy. He struggles to "tell the past," to describe the history of his spiritual crisis, and to analyse and define the sense of self and vocation which

has led him back to a reaffirmation of "God and truth/And love."
Early he had turned from the outside world "into the dim orb/Of
self" where he eventually discovered a "clear idea" of his identity:

> Existing as a centre to all things,
> Most potent to create and rule and call
> Upon all things to minister to it;
> A principle of restlessness
> Which would be all, have, see, know, taste, feel, all –
> This is myself. . . .

Such intense absorption with self, he recognized, might have led to
psychic disintegration had he not retained "A need, a trust, a yearn-
ing after God" and a capacity to "trust in signs/And omens" and see
"God everywhere." When during a "pause, and long restraint" he
lost that sense of his creative self, "cunning, envy, falsehood, all the
world's wrong" stained him. He sought relief in the solitary pursuit
of song and poetry and eventually in affirmation of the revolutionary
hopes for mankind hymned by Shelley: "I threw myself/To meet it,
I was vowed to liberty,/Men were to be as gods and earth as heaven."
Commitment to human liberty led to his determination to turn from
preoccupation with self "to look on real life . . . to look and learn/
Mankind, its cares, hopes, fears, its woes, and joys." But when
suddenly and inexplicably he recognized that such a search was but
another delusion, the young poet's moral collapse was swift: "First
went my hopes of perfecting mankind,/Next – faith in them, and
then in freedom's self/And virtue's self, then my own motives,
ends/And aims and loves, and human love went last." Turning away
from the world to inspect the condition of his inner self, he found
paradoxically that nothing and yet everything had changed: "My
powers were greater: as some temple seemed/My soul, where naught
is changed and incense rolls/Around the altar, *only God is gone*/And
some dark spirit sitteth in his seat." When shadowy troops within
the temple hail the poet himself as king, he smilingly accepts this
"vanity of vanities." The crisis is over; new power and resolve
flood into him; and restoration of his confidence in self and his belief
in God begin through the agency of Pauline's human love, through
his patriotic love of England, through his empathetic powers to live
the lives of the smallest of natural creatures, and through his persis-

13

tent "hunger" after God. With the love of Pauline, whom he urges to return with him to her mountain home, and with Shelley to bolster and encourage him, the poet achieves a state that is "happy, free from doubt/Or touch of fear."

Pauline is at one and the same time a personal if not autobiographical confession and an attempt by a precocious young poet to explore and define the role of the poet in the England and Europe of his day. As Morse Peckham has argued recently, "insofar as the poem is autobiographical, Browning was identifying himself as an exemplification of the primary Romantic figure or role."[29] The poem's relationship, indeed its explicit indebtedness, to the great English Romantics, especially to Shelley but also to Wordsworth, Byron and Keats, has long been recognized. A half-century ago, Henri-Léon Hovelaque concisely surveyed a number of French confessional works which resemble *Pauline*. They are works in which "the hazards of existence," Hovelaque says, "have provoked from the depths of each author, according to his particular temperament, diverse anxieties, and it is the internal drama of their personalities that they invariably have sought to tell."[30] He further notes the emphasis in these works upon passionate love, upon musings about human destiny and moral suffering. Rousseau is an obvious antecedent to *Pauline*. But not, I think, his *Julie, ou la Nouvelle Héloïse* (1761), to which Hovelaque directs us. There the strong narrative set amid domestic scenes broken by an occasional outburst of passion or of rage against social privilege sets a tone and creates a mode far different from *Pauline*. It is *Les Confessions* (1781, 1788), of course, which suggests itself to the reader of *Pauline*; however, in making this point recently Maynard reminds us that it was not until 1835 that Browning mentioned Rousseau in any known document and then the reference is to *Du contrat social* (1761).

Hovelaque offers other French prototypes, among them Chateaubriand's *René* (1801). René's passion, his love of solitude and his introspective musing about himself and God are qualities shared by Browning's young poet. The strong narrative of René's frustrated incestuous love for Amélie, however, scarcely resembles the rather confident self-analysis and affirmation of love in *Pauline*. Chateaubriand's *Le Génie du christianisme* (1802), into which the tale of René was interpolated, is closer in mode, sentiment, and tone. Chateaubriand's meditations on the moral and poetic beauty of a religion that he believed had fostered and would foster human liberty correspond rather closely to *Pauline*. The note in French that Pauline appends to the poem and the long descriptions of her Alpine home would support Hovelaque's choice of Senancour's epistolary confession *Obermann* (1804) as an antecedent work. Were Senancour's persistent melancholy and scepticism ever relieved and were his Alpine valley ever invested with the beauty and delight Browning's speaker imagines for Pauline's native mountains, *Obermann* would be a strong candidate as a direct influence on Browning's first poem. Browning probably had read some of another work Hovelaque mentions: Madame de Staël's *Corinne*. Certainly Lord Nevil's redemption from obscure remorse by his love for Corinne finds an echo in *Pauline* as it does in scores of romantic works. *Corinne*, however, is markedly different from Browning's poem. It is not just that *Corinne* is a crowded novel turned travelogue, but that its narrator and its heroine especially are given to analysing human behaviour in quite lucid, rational, and even social terms; this contrasts sharply with the introspective searching in *Pauline*. If any of *Corinne* got into *Pauline* it is in the young Frenchwoman's analysis of the "songe et confusion" of the poem itself. A similar protest should be registered against Hovelaque's suggestion of Benjamin Constant's fictionalized version of his liaison with Madame de Staël in *Adolphe* (1816). Constant's careful scrutiny of motive and feeling as he describes a passion turned irksome is intellectual and rational. When Browning, in Hovelaque's phrase, "dissèque son propre moi," he renders that dissection of himself poetically.

Of all the French authors Hovelaque proposes to be closely akin to the Browning of *Pauline* the most appropriate may be two more immediate contemporaries, one he probably never heard of and another he definitely began to read very soon after the publication of *Pauline* – Henri-Frédéric Amiel (1821–81) and Honoré de Balzac (1799–1850). Amiel was nine years younger than Browning, and nothing of his *Fragments d'un journal intime* was published until the final years of Browning's life. Amiel's painfully objective self-analysis of his sense of futility, of irresoluteness, and of creative sterility is carried on in a manner that has its counterpart in *Pauline*. In the intimacy of his journal, Amiel was able to look at himself as though he were an object outside himself. Although Amiel was to remain throughout his life an idealist sharply critical of the literary realism of his century, he had developed a process or mental stance necessary to such realism. Amiel, unlike the poet of *Pauline*, was never able to exorcise his despair; nevertheless, as Hovelaque says, "he knows well how to note, with singular keenness, the diverse forms and successive phases of his moral sickness."[31] Amiel writes:

> Was there ever any one so vulnerable as I? If I were a father how many griefs and vexations a child might cause me. As a husband I should have a thousand ways of suffering, because my happiness demands a thousand conditions. I have a heart too easily reached, a too restless imagination; despair is easy to me, and every sensation reverberates again and again within me. What might be, spoils for me what is. What ought to be consumes me with sadness. So that reality, the present, the irreparable, the necessary, repel and even terrify me. I have too much imagination, conscience, and penetration, and not enough character.[32]

Such acute self-observation was already apparent in Browning's first published poem and was the distinctive contribution of *Pauline* to the genre of the romantic confession. As Morse Peckham has shown, Browning completely synthesizes and recapitulates much of what had preoccupied his immediate confessional predecessors; but he also extended their mode by a special quality Peckham calls the "de-subjectification of the personality."[33] The young poet's ability to look at himself with at least some objectivity was an early important step towards the more dramatic and realistic poetry that would become Browning's characteristic manner. Throughout his career, Browning would reveal in his art preoccupations and modes congruent to, but not influenced by, the work of his French contemporaries and near contemporaries. *Pauline* may not be so thoroughly "dramatic in principle" as Browning claimed when he reissued the poem in 1868. He had, however, tried to "assume & realize" in it just one of "many different characters" he was contemplating for a series of works – a poem, a novel, a speech, an opera. The speaker in *Pauline* was "the *Poet* of the batch," as Browning said in his note on the John Stuart Mill copy of the poem; and the persona was, he continued, the character "who would have been more legitimately *myself*." Browning tried a number of rhetorical strategies by which the self might be examined as a character. His inclusion of Pauline as an auditor to the confessional self-analysis is the most crucial of these strategies; the elaboration of the auditor's role into the French note that analysed the poetic utterance adds a bit of ironic detachment to the poem as do the epigrams from Marot and Agrippa and the theatrical adieux to the audience in the closing lines. John Maynard, recently examining these various devices, frequently describes their effect as "realistic," the mode as "dramatic realism," and the particular significance of *Pauline* to be its "movement toward a greater sense of reality and a fuller psychological realism" than is to be found in Browning's romantic predecessors.[34]

By 1830 Honoré de Balzac had transformed the romantic novel into a fiction in which, by amassing carefully observed and recorded prosaic details of financial transactions, street scenes, gesture, physiognomy, and speech, the author provided a convincing illusion of contemporary life. This novel was *Les Dangers de l'inconduite* (1830), later entitled *Gobseck*. Two years later Balzac returned, one might say reverted, to the confessional novel in his semi-autobiographical *Louis Lambert* (1832). Hovelaque finds numerous similarities between this novel and *Pauline*: the extraordinary self-consciousness of the young Louis, his confidence in his special genius, his youthful studies, and his alienation from his fellows relieved only by his passionate love for Pauline de Villenois. These and other similarities to *Pauline* lead Hovelaque to think that "Browning has managed to read – and at times imitate – Balzac's novel. . . ."[35] Direct influence is possible. Balzac finished *Louis Lambert* in July of 1832, and published it later that year; Browning finished *Pauline* in October of 1832 but did not publish it until March of 1833. Maynard's study of Browning's correspondence with his young French friend Amédée de Ripert-Monclar, however, casts doubt upon the probability of any direct borrowing from *Louis Lambert*. Further, Balzac's *La Peau de chagrin* (1831), with its romantic egoist Raphael de Valentin seeking redemption through love for his Pauline, provides equally strong analogues; this earlier novel even provides a long Alpine sojourn and a closing scene with Pauline cradling the head of the hero in her arms. That scene might be a fit prelude for the opening scene of *Pauline*:

Pauline, mine own, bend o'er me – thy soft breast
Shall pant to mine – bend o'er me – thy sweet eyes,
And loosened hair and breathing lips, and arms,
Drawing me to thee. . . .

17

Unfortunately Balzac's Raphael, like Louis Lambert after him, dies in Pauline's arms; Browning's poet is alive and well. *La Peau de chagrin*, with its magic talisman which has the power to fulfil Raphael's desires while it steadily draws his life from him, is far from the realistic fiction of the earlier *Gobseck* or of later Balzac novels. Still, Balzac felt it necessary in a preface to the first edition to warn the reader that this was not a subjective, confessional work and not to confuse the author with the work: "readers can never remain impartial between a book and its maker,' he admitted with some complaint. "Involuntarily they project, in their thought, a figure: they create a man and suppose him young or old, large or small, friendly or disagreeable." He recognizes that the degree of affinity between the work and the author is quite close when the author is Byron or Maturin or even Rabelais. They are among the "authors whose personal character is vividly reproduced by the nature of their compositions and in which the work and the man are one and the same thing." There are, however, other works, such as *Le Peau de chagrin* presumably, written by "writers whose spirit and manner strongly contrast with the form and depth of their works."[36]

Balzac's caution against confusing the assumed narrator with the author is very close in intention to the various protestations Browning made about *Pauline* and his later assertion that his poems were "utterances of so many imaginary persons, not mine." When Balzac reissued *La Peau de chagrin* later in 1831, he dropped the preface and relied upon an epilogue to establish the narrator as a rather cynical, ironic, worldly man who wittily deflates the romantic illusion of redemption through Pauline's love. Pauline was but "the queen of illusions"; he describes to an unnamed listener the nature of that illusion and how one wakes from it:

> . . . there is a magical power in her light breathing that draws your lips to hers; she flies and you follow; you feel the earth no longer beneath you. . . . Every nerve in you is quivering; you are filled with pain and longing. O joy for which there is no name! You have touched the woman's lips, and you are awakened at once by a horrible pang. Oh! ah! yes, you have struck your head against the corner of the bedpost. . . .[37]

In Browning's poem the French note by Pauline provides a similar ironic distance between the poet and his work, albeit without the humorous deflation. Within the year after the publication of *Pauline* Browning began to read Balzac regularly, and by the late 1830's he had become Browning's favourite contemporary novelist, a position he retained until Browning read *Madame Bovary* some twenty years afterwards. Later, readers like Swinburne and Hopkins would recognize the similarity of Balzac's realistic fiction and Browning's realistic poetry. Already at the beginning of his career the young Browning shared an impulse towards realism with the older Balzac, who was turning his back on the hack romances he had written in the 1820's and beginning to build his *Comédie humaine*. Coincidentaly, when Balzac removed his original preface from *La Peau de chagrin* another preface by Philarète Chasles was substituted. Chasles would review Browning's *Paracelsus* in 1840 for the *Revue des Deux Mondes*, and in his lectures at the Collège de France in 1852 on her life and work, Chasles would cause Elizabeth Barrett and her husband considerable embarrassment and pain.

iii

In 1839, some six years before she met Robert Browning, Elizabeth Barrett complained to Miss Mitford that she felt "a hundred miles behind everybody as to French literature of the present day – knowing scarcely anything except of Lamartine and Victor Hugo – and Edgar Quinet, by grace of the Athenaeum, – and the Athenaeum's own Rhapsodist in criticism (Jules Janin). . . ."[38] If Elizabeth was behind, she soon caught up with and passed most of her contemporaries in knowledge of recent French literature. By 1845 she could describe herself with wit and justice as "the most complete and unscrupulous romance reader within your knowledge. . . . On my tombstone may be written '*Ci-gît* the greatest novel reader in the world,' and nobody will forbid the inscription."[39] Scores of those novels were written by Hugo, Sand, Sue, Soulié, de Kock, Charles de Bernard, Stendhal, and Balzac. Her bias in favour of French fiction remained, but she also read the poetry not only of Lamartine, Hugo, and Quinet but also of Béranger and Delavigne. She marched through a "long dynasty of French memoirs," read Victor Cousin, became familiar with Chateaubriand's *Le Génie du christianisme*, and read works of such forgotten writers as Michel Raymond, Camille

Bodin, Madame Charles Reybaud, Louis de Queihle, and "a French
authoress yclepped Madme Amable Tastu." In this latter's *Proses*
(1836) Elizabeth found "a good deal of beauty and sweetness and not
a bit of naughtiness." She was, at the same time, reading the new
book of poems called *Dramatic Lyrics* by Robert Browning, but had
not made up her mind about them.[40]

Elizabeth read omnivorously the work of her English contemporaries. However, as she wrote to Richard Hengist Horne while
helping him prepare his assessment of present British literary
figures, *A New Spirit of the Age* (1844), it was "melancholy to look
round and see no such bloom of intellectual glory on our own literature" as she saw everywhere evident in the literature of "La Jeune
France."[41] When the July Monarchy had come to power in 1830,
Elizabeth had commented: "The French nation is not an interesting
nation." By 1844 "the King of the French – that right kingly king,
Louis-Philippe" had become for her the noblest monarch in Europe
because of his encouragement of art and literature. "Let a young
unknown writer accomplish a successful tragedy, and the next day
he sits at the king's table – not in metaphor, but face to face," she
asserts while comparing Louis-Philippe's reign to that of the young
Victoria. "See how different the matter is in our own court, where
the artists are shown up the back stairs, and where no poet (even by
the back stairs) can penetrate, unless so fortunate as to be a banker
also. What is the use of kings and queens in these days, except to
encourage arts and letters."[42] Everything about the French nation
was now of interest to her: Guizot's latest illness, Louis Daguerre's
"wonderful invention," the trial of Marie Cappelle for the murder of
her husband, Delphine Gay's satiric attack, *L'École des journalistes*
(1839).[43] And Elizabeth began to think of returning to France. She
could "see in the books and traditions" that life had "a livelier sap"
in France; she admired "all the Parisian glories and rationalities"
which made the English seem by comparison "just social bar-
barians."[44] About the time her closed room on Wimpole Street was
redecorated with painted foliage which reminded her of the arcadian
"pays tendre" of Madame de Scudéry, she also began to think of
living "in the warmer south of France."[45] The intellectual and artistic life of the French capital was equally as attractive as the health-
restoring South. Had she the "strength and liberty," she told Miss
Mitford, she "would go tomorrow" to live two or three years on the

Continent dividing her time between Germany, Italy and France:

> France, I say, – but it should rather be Paris – because I should
> care for the insight into men, nearly as well as for the prospects
> from mountains. What help it would give to the mind, – what help
> in versatility and aptitude, and variety of association . . to any
> thinking active mind, alive to clasp, with both hands, the advan-
> tages on every side! Is it not true that change in the sensations, and
> in those ideas more closely connected with the external world, . .
> must react strongly, deeply, and freshly on the inner Being, –
> conducing to the fuller development of the Imaginative and
> Reflective powers? I think so.[46]

Paris as an arena of heightened and enriching thought and feeling,
especially of stimulating intellectual and literary life, would become
a recurrent theme in Elizabeth's correspondence during her married
life.

Elizabeth Barrett read widely and incessantly in the new French
fiction, but she did not read indiscriminately. She sometimes playfully described herself in her drive for the title of " 'the greatest
novel reader in the world' " as being able to read any work so long as
either the story or a character was interesting; she was "not fastidi-
ous," she said, in her choice. During her married life she would also
draw humorous vignettes of Robert Browning throwing down in
boredom some new *roman-feuilleton* which she already had read or
soon would read from beginning to end: "he takes too high a standard, I tell him," she wrote during their first year in Italy, "and
won't listen to a story for a story's sake. I can bear to be amused, you
know, without a strong pull on my admiration. So we have great
wars sometimes, and I put up Dumas' flag, or Soulie's, or Eugene
Sue's . . . and carry it till my arms ache."[47] Such self-portraits of
herself as an uncritical female bibliophagist are misleading. She
knew, as she wrote before her marriage, that there "is the love of
literature, which is one thing, and the love of fiction, which is
another."[48] She followed suggestions and hints given by Jules Janin
in his essays, especially "Literature of the Nineteenth Century –
France" which had appeared in the *Athenaeum* in May of 1837. But
Elizabeth soon sorted out what was "literature" and what was mere
"fiction."

Victor Hugo, all of whose romances she "went regularly through"

around 1841, had early become her favourite.[49] Soon George Sand
was twinned with Hugo, and by the end of 1842 Balzac, "the most
powerful writer of the French day next to Victor Hugo and George
Sand!"completed her "triumvirate."[50] Well below these three she
began to place in decreasing degrees of merit, Sue, Soulié, Charles
de Bernard and Paul de Kock. She enjoyed the "broad farce" and
"impulsive gaiety" of de Kock, and his *Mon Ami Piffard* (1844) set
her "laughing most cordially"; she knew, however, that it was only
"farce rolled out into narrative form, – neither more nor less." She
taunted Miss Mitford with the possibility – if only de Kock's grisettes
could be morally redeemed – of translating de Kock "into excellent
moral reading for 'prude Angleterre.'"[51] Miss Mitford was further
chided for preferring de Kock and Bernard to Balzac and Sand
because in the latter the "'taint' of both stank in [Miss Mitford's]
nostrils." With similar detached amusement she can summarize
Soulié's *Les Deux Cadavres*: "begins with a violation and a murder,
and ends consistently with a murder and a violation, – the hero who
is the agent of this 'just proportion' being shut up at last and starved
in a premature coffin, after having his eyelids neatly sewed up by the
fair fingers of his lady-love."[52] Elizabeth's tone here is similar to
Robert Browning's when in 1840 he assured W. C. Macready that
his new tragedy would be more stageable: "There is *action* in it,
drabbing, stabbing, et autres gentillesses. . . .[53]

Elizabeth always placed Eugène Sue well below her triumvirate
but well above Soulié or de Kock. She preferred his *Mystères de Paris*
to his historical romance, *Jean Cavalier* (1840). *Mystères*, too, has the
sensational elements of rape, murder, and scenes of the Parisian
demi-monde, but these elements are leavened by the philanthropy
and reformist zeal of M. Rudolphe. When Elizabeth read *Mystères*
she was also studying the government reports on the conditions of
the English working poor; about the same time, 1843, she published
"The Cry of the Children." When she read *Mystères* as it came out as
roman-feuilleton in the *Journal des Débats* (1842–43), she was apparently attracted by its reformist sentiment. When *Mystères* was repub-
lished in two volumes she re-read it twice; but when Sue became
more openly the didactic socialist in *Les Sept Péchés capitaux*
(1847–49), Elizabeth's admiration cooled. Hugo, Sand and Balzac
were the writers Elizabeth most admired; Stendhal's *Le Rouge et le
noir* was – as we shall see – the single work which most deeply

22

affected her. She was aware of the deficiencies of the lesser writers, but she recognized them as a part of the exceptional creativity going on in contemporary France: "why the whole literature looks like a conflagration – and my whole being aches with the sight of it, – and when I turn away *home*, there seems nothing to be seen, it is all so neutral tinted and dull and cold by comparison. Full indeed of power and caprice and extravagance is this new French literature – a kind of practical palinodia to the Louis quatorze glories."[54]

When Elizabeth began to read Victor Hugo regularly in the early 1840's, he had already entered that hiatus in his creative work which would last for nearly fifteen years. The pause in Hugo's career as a novelist was even greater: he had published nothing in that genre since *Claude Gueux* (1834) and would not return to extended prose romance until *Les Misérables* (1862), one year after Elizabeth's death. Her decided bias towards prose fiction, combined with Hugo's silence in that genre while Sand and Balzac continued regularly to publish novels, may partly explain why Hugo was soon the least prominent of her triumvirate of French writers. She had read some of "Hugo Victor's" [*sic*] poetry while studying Lamartine in the summer of 1831. Those two poets were the only ones of the second generation romantic French writers with whom she acknowledged familiarity in 1839. Three years later she assured Miss Mitford that she held Hugo "long before, for a wonderful genius."[55] She had just gone "regularly through the romances of the gifted Frenchman," and an immediate effect of reading Hugo was that English fiction looked "paler and paler" to her.[56] Dickens, whom she admired "absolutely and gratefully," fell in her estimation a "good furlong" when she read Hugo. Dickens' "tenderness" and "humour" could not compensate for his lack of powerful seriousness: her sense of Boz's "power and genius grew grey and weak 'in a single night' with reading Hugo."[57] To a number of correspondents she compared particularly Hugo's *Le Dernier Jour d'un condamné* (1829) to Fagin's condemnation in *Oliver Twist*. She was convinced that in that instance Dickens had silently but unsuccessfully imitated Hugo. Hugo's *Le Dernier Jour* is fiction in the service of social reform. So was *Oliver Twist*. Hugo, however, was the more profound; and he was also a worthy successor to Scott in the historical novel. Admitting that she thought his historical drama *Le Roi s'amuse* (1832) to be "very great," Elizabeth considered that *Notre-*

Dame de Paris revealed the true "greatness, par excellence, of its . . *poet.*" "Is not Nôtre Dame a more wonderful work, a more sublime *poem,*" she asked, "than anything which our Scott ever performed or imagined, or saw in a dream when he rested from his Ivanhoe?"[58]

Hugo's extravagances, exaggerations, and grotesqueries, to which the playwriting Miss Mitford objected, were for Elizabeth evidence of his genius for infusing into his work a deeper philosophical and poetical portrait of human nature. In this Hugo was akin to Shakespeare and superior to Scott: "I honour Walter Scott for so much," she said while defending Hugo, "but never for *his knowledge of human nature*. It seems to me [Scott] *paints* human nature – that he looks at it pictorially and conveys it to his canvas in its attitude and garment of picturesqueness – thinking at least as much of the setting of the folds, as of the beating of the heart. He is more a painter than a poet or philosopher."[59] With *Notre-Dame de Paris*, Hugo now supplied a contemporary polarity to the "smooth & neat & clean & uninteresting" classicism, especially of Racine, which she had so disliked earlier. Rather surprisingly, Elizabeth's burgeoning enthusiasm for Hugo was accompanied by a deeper appreciation of Racine. Knowledge of both made it possible for her to judge more severely the hybrid romantic-classicism of Casimir Delavigne, whose plays she found *"without the extenuating perfection of Racine's style, and without the glory of Victor Hugo's genius.* We have in him [Delavigne] neither the perfect execution, nor the inspired conception – and the 'juste milieu' does therefore, to my mind, savour of mediocrity."[60] Elizabeth praised Hugo for his "style"; but it was his "genius" for powerful, poetic conceptions that she most admired. However, with no new work forthcoming from Hugo, Elizabeth's interest in him began to flag. When Louis-Napoleon drove him from the barricades in 1851, Elizabeth was in Paris to observe but not to sympathize with the poet turned politician; Hugo's counter-attack in *Napoléon le petit* (1852) she judged a scurrilous lie. Her admiration returned only when he returned to his earlier poetic mode in *Les Contemplations* (1856).

"Victor Hugo stands first of all in genius, I think," Elizabeth wrote in 1842, "– and I should say so distinctly if I could make up my mind to call George Sand *second* to any genius living." While her interest in Hugo waned, enthusiasm for Sand grew. From the very beginning of her reading of Sand, Elizabeth judged her superior in "eloquence and passion" not only to Hugo and lesser novelists but even to Rousseau, whom she thought "cold, lifeless, loveless, deaf and dumb to her!"[61] This high estimate was neither eccentric nor exaggerated in the early 1840's; it was shared by Balzac, Chateaubriand, Sainte-Beuve, by Heine, by the young Dostoievski, by Arnold. Sand's *"womanhood,"* as Elizabeth immediately recognized, was of crucial importance to her admiration, but it was also the source of some ambivalence towards Sand. Elizabeth had pondered the mystery of the infrequency of great women writers, and she apparently felt that the scarcity of women predecessors hampered her own development as a poet. She had a deep appreciation for those she called the "grandfathers" of literature; however, she looked "everywhere for grandmothers" and found only Sappho and Madame de Staël. Sand became not merely a worthy successor but the "first female genius of any age or country."[62] Edgar Allan Poe in his dedication of *The Raven and Other Poems* (1845) called Elizabeth Barrett "The Noblest of Her Sex"; Elizabeth had already given that honour over to Sand.

Only two years Elizabeth's senior, Sand had by the early 1840's achieved worldwide fame for her literary achievement and her personal notoriety. More than just a great novelist, Sand used her eloquence in the service of Saint-Simonianism, feminism, and utopian socialism, and was viewed by a wide range of European intellectuals as a revolutionary force. To Matthew Arnold and Arthur Hugh Clough, still at Oxford, Sand was "the incarnation of a new spirit of revolt and renovation."[63] "During the 1840's," Dostoievski was to write, "George Sand's glory was so high and the faith in her genius so great that we, her contemporaries, all expected of her in the near future something immense and unheard of, not to say definitive solutions."[64] Elizabeth, too, expected "something immense" from Sand. The two sonnets she wrote to Sand at this time display her almost suppliant adoration of the Frenchwoman's successful challenge to the world of men:

> Thou large-brained woman and large-hearted man,
> Self-called George Sand! whose soul, amid the lions
> Of thy tumultuous senses, moans defiance
> And answers roar for roar, as spirits can. . . . ("A Desire")

The second sonnet, "A Recognition," begins with a rhetorical question which denies that Sand has exchanged her "woman-heart" while exercising the masculine vigour of her genius:

True genius, but true woman! dost deny
The women's nature with a manly scorn,
And break away the gauds and armlets worn
By weaker women in captivity?

Once Sand's genius has been praised in the opening of each sonnet, Elizabeth turns to exhort Sand to move beyond defiance, scorn, and "that revolted cry." Sand has the power to bring a "holier light" into the world; both sonnets close with a petition to Sand to let her genius bring sanctity, purity and grace to others. Sonnets that began as paeans to Sand's genius end with rather self-righteous urgings for her to work for a more "stainless fame" and to more "purely aspire." Small wonder that Sand did not particularly care for the sonnets. In her letter to Amédée Pichot, who had sent her translations of Elizabeth's sonnets, Sand wrote: "The most magnificent eulogies are not deserved, and I cannot say how much they amaze me. I am no longer at an age to pay much attention to lions roaring within me, and I do not recall that they have ever made so great an uproar."[65] Sand's notoriety caused Elizabeth to hesitate sending her the sonnets. Her anxiety, however, derived in no way from her fear that Sand might be offended: Sand was "kind, generous, noble," she told Miss Mitford, and "would meet *us* in a generous spirit." She simply saw no reason, after she had already published the sonnets, to subject herself to "any stress of conventional opinion" by opening a correspondence with Sand. And there was, of course, Mr. Barrett: "As to Papa, if we *do* send, I won't tell him that the 'French authoress' who is to be the recipient, smokes cigars and is discontented with the decencies of life. I shall keep that among the 'Mysteries of Paris.' "[66]

Elizabeth to some extent kept her love of the new French fiction "hidden in our sleeves for the sake of propriety," but she was not especially prudish. She admired the frankness and honesty of the French writers, and she often railed at British hypocrisy and the "squeamishness of this Age . . this Ostrich Age . . which exposes its own eggs, and then hides its head in the sand."[67] She was, as she described herself, "more a latitudinarian in literature than it is generally thought expedient for women to be." And while granting what her friend Chorley called the " 'perilous stuff' " in Sand's fiction, she still liked "George Sand's wickedness better" than she liked Dickens, Disraeli, or Bulwer. Like Meredith after her, she knew that some books weren't for little people and fools. *Les Maîtres Mozaïstes* (1837) was an exception which but for the damning name of George Sand on the title-page "may be read aloud by the most proper of governesses to her pupils."[68] The novel is a tale of rivalry, intrigue and revenge between two families of Venetian mosaic craftsmen: the detestable Bianchini family which prostitutes its art for profit and the idealistic Zuccati brothers who retain their artistic integrity in the search for beauty in their medium. The action is interwoven with expository passages endorsing the social and moral value of strict dedication to one's art. These are ideas Elizabeth would echo in her ambitious *roman*-poem *Aurora Leigh*.

Elizabeth was also reading *Lélia* (1833), Sand's painful and despairing confessional novel of a woman grown cold and indifferent but still submitting to the carnal passion of her lover Stenio. Mixed in are attacks on monogamy and marriage, attacks often voiced by the freely promiscuous Pulchérie, who claims a woman must sell herself either into the slavery of prostitution or of marriage. To Lélia's religious doubts are added the erotic dreams of the Irish monk, Magnus. Some comic exaggeration informs Elizabeth's description of how she was both repelled and fascinated by this sensational novel: " '*Lelia*' again, made me blush in my solitude to the ends of my fingers – blush three blushes in one . . . for *Her* who could be so shameless – for her sex, whose purity she so disgraced – and for myself in particular, who could hold such a book for five minutes in one hand while a coal-fire burnt within reach of the other."[69] Despite her entrancement, Elizabeth found "*Lelia* a serpent book both for language-colour and soul-slime and one which I could not read through for its vileness."[70] Unable to finish *Lélia*, she turned to *Indiana* (1832), the novel which had first and suddenly established Sand's fame. The novel had, as Sand's would-be mentor Hyacinthe de Latouche wrote to her, placed Sand "at one leap, at the head of contemporary writers."[71] The sexual encounters in the novel are less explicit than in *Lélia*: the noble Raymond de Ramière's seduction of the Creole servant Noun – while fantasizing that he is making love to Indiana – is the most sensual scene. Noun's pregnancy, her awareness that marriage to Raymond is socially impossible, her suicide, all provide a moral dénouement to the novel which is absent in *Lélia*. Do Raymond and Indiana consummate their love in his Paris apartment? That is left to the reader and to Indiana's husband to ponder. To Sand the night in Paris is not a sensual pleasure but an assertion of Indiana's personal freedom from her dictatorial old-soldier husband. Elizabeth thought *"Indiana less revolting as a whole"* than *Lélia*: the novel revealed "the bent of the author's peculiar womanhood, to the sensual and physical – and yet that work does appear to me very brilliant and powerful, and eloquent beyond praising."[72] *Jacques* (1834), by comparison, lacked similar "high qualities of rhetoric and language."

Elizabeth felt herself to be very sensitive to prose style, and she could, as she said, read with pleasure a treatise upon walking sticks were it well written. Along with her "genius" then, it was Sand's style that attracted her: the French of "this brilliant monstrous woman Madme Dudevant, is french *transfigured*. . . . It is not french – it is french no more. We recognize nothing like it in Voltaire – and the previous (so called) classic writers. It is too sweet for french, – and too strong – and above all, too numerous."[73] The novels of Sand reinforced Elizabeth's long-held opinion that prose not verse was the appropriate medium for French literary genius. Her enthusiasm for Sand's prose style was widely shared. Latouche, who feared that the hasty publication of *Indiana* would result in a pastiche as bad as Balzac, found to his surprise the "simplicity, the brilliance and the firmness of the style" which, in their turn, Sainte-Beuve, Flaubert and Proust would also admire.[74] If Elizabeth could not, "for all its eloquence," finish *Lélia*, she could read almost anything else by Sand both for its style and for what she called its "noble elevations both intellectual and moral." In 1844, after two years of reading Sand, she told Miss Mitford that she would "not be ashamed before the whole world, to confess" her belief in Sand's greatness: "If I had a reputation like her own, I would do it the next moment."[75]

Shortly before Christmas 1842, Elizabeth sent Miss Mitford three Sand novels and a copy of *Le Père Goriot*. Elizabeth had not previously mentioned Balzac, but already she ranked him with Hugo and Sand; and she had read enough of his various *Scènes* to recognize *Le Père Goriot* as the best of Balzac: "It appears to me the most powerful work of its writer, I have read – and also the most open to tenderness. I like it best – and also admire it the most." Balzac she thought "less a poet . . less ideal – less eloquent – nearer to the ground . . deeper in the mire" than either Hugo or Sand; but with *Le Père Goriot* he became the third of her triumvirate of French authors. As with Sand, Elizabeth was simultaneously attracted to and repelled by Balzac: attracted by the powerful realism, repelled by the ugliness and corruption he so realistically portrayed. *Le Père Goriot*, though a "very painful book," was nevertheless "full of moody reckless power." Unlike Sand, whose artistic sin was her excessive portrayal of physical, sensual passion, Balzac perhaps too greatly emphasized the "influence of social corruptions." Hence there were elements in Balzac she found "very revolting – cold and bitter with a sight and slough of evil . . to be shrunk from, as at the touch of a worm."[76] Elizabeth often adopts the epistolary persona of a shocked female when writing to Miss Mitford, who never shared her enthusiasm for Sand and who at this time continued to prefer among French novelists Charles de Bernard to Balzac and Sand.

A few days after Christmas, Elizabeth wrote again noting that Miss Mitford had remained silent on *Goriot* and wondering whether she had thrown the book into the fire. Her advice to Miss Mitford is a Victorian version of William Carlos Williams' advice to the first readers of Allen Ginsberg's *Howl*: "Lift up your skirts, ladies, we're going through hell." She urges her friend to keep her composure and read *Goriot*, "a very powerful work – altho' the road through it is muddy, and noxious to the nostrils. And after all – we talk loudly and aright . . with a rightous indignation, – against this and similar works. . . ." If Miss Mitford wants some measure of how disgustingly sensual books can be, she should look into Marivaux or Crébillon *fils*, whose lewd and lascivious oriental tale *La Sopha* (1745) Elizabeth had – after fifteen minutes – dropped "like a burning iron." Compared to such eighteenth-century *romans*, "the books of La jeune France are clean and holy. . . ."[77] Over a year later Miss Mitford remained unconverted, but Elizabeth continued to insist she "make way through" Balzac's novels. She asked Miss Mitford to note especially Balzac's descriptive passages in which he amasses minute details as might a Dutch painter and "yet comprehends wholeness and unity. You touch, taste, and handle everything he speaks to you of – yet he can write withal such eloquent sentiment" as to produce also a novel like *Le Lys dans la vallée*, which Elizabeth now recommended.[78]

A reluctant Miss Mitford began to read carefully, among other Balzac works, *Illusions perdues* and *La Femme supérieure*. Elizabeth rather heatedly rejected Mitford's comparison of Dickens to Balzac – "*He* is fathoms below *him* as an artist" – but both followed with interest the fates of David Séchard and Lucien de Rubempré in *Illusions perdues*. Elizabeth thought this early version of the novel ended inconclusively. Séchard had too passively accepted his defeat by his unscrupulous commercial rival, le grand Cointet, whom Elizabeth had hoped Balzac would kill off. And the fate of Lucien remained a mystery: "Did the Spaniard adopt him in order to make a *mouchard* of him – or what?" Elizabeth could not have discovered from *Illusions perdues* that the Spanish priest was the Jacques Collin-Vautrin-Dodgedeath of *Le Père Goriot*; only when Elizabeth sought out in a Florentine lending-library Balzac's *Une Instruction criminelle*, Part IV of *Les Splendeurs et misères des courtisanes*, was that common identity and the fate of Lucien made clear. Miss Mitford complained that the obsessive attention to detail made for a "heaviness and slowness" in Balzac. Elizabeth offered a "counter-thought" which reveals her intelligent appreciation of Balzac's realism. The seemingly extraneous details, she argued, added to the "subtlety and deepness of the *life*" in Balzac's characters. Balzac, she goes on, does not amass details as might "a costume-writer with scenic intentions," as might, she said, Scott or his imitator G. P. R. James, or, as she commented elsewhere, Charles de Bernard. Balzac's use of details comes from "seeing in them with that subtle power of apprehension and combination peculiar to him, the outward expression and sacramental sign of the inward man." Just as the ancients divined mysteries from the viscera of animals, Balzac revealed inward character by attention to houses, furnishings, dress and physiognomy. She ends by citing a particular example from *La Femme supérieure*: "Now just look at the catalogue raisonné of the Rabourdin clerks – and grant the wonderfulness of the characteristic emphasis which comes in the dress. We do not so much see the men the more for it – we *know* them better for it!"[79]

By the spring of 1845 Elizabeth had won Miss Mitford over to Balzac. She had also made the acquaintance of another convert to Balzac – Robert Browning. Miss Mitford had earlier characterized Browning as a young dandy addicted to "'silver forkism'" and compared him to Balzac's Lucien. Elizabeth had not yet met Browning in person, but from his poetry and letters she was convinced that he was "a very masculine writer and thinker, and as remote as possible from Balzac's type of the *femmelette*, Lucien de Rubempré. . . ."[80]

2

A Mutual Admiration for *La Jeune France*

i

RB's Knowledge of Hugo – Friendship with Count Amédée de Ripert-Monclar – Early Appreciation of Balzac – A French Review of Paracelsus *– EB, RB and Stendhal.*

ii

RB and EB Discover Their Common Interest in New French Writing – French Language, Literature, News and Gossip Reflected in Their Love Letters – Comments on Soulié, Sue, Dumas and Balzac – RB Declines to Share EB's Enthusiasm for "Sandism."

iii

RB and EB Discuss Napoleon I – Some Early Poems on French Subjects: "Crowned and Buried," "Incident in the French Camp," "Nationality in Drinks" — Ronsard and Marot in RB's "The Glove."

---

i

Robert Browning, like Elizabeth Barrett, had read Lamartine and Hugo in the early 1830's. More interested in dramatic literature than Elizabeth, Browning could by the year of its publication entertain acquaintances with improvised translations of scenes from Hugo's *Lucrèce Borgia* (1833). He could speak "with levity" of Hugo's volume of lyrics, *Les Feuilles d'automne* (1831);[1] but he doubtless read with admiration *Notre-Dame de Paris* (1831) not long after its publication. He valued that novel sufficiently to make it one of two books

32

he sent in 1842 to his friend Alfred Domett, who had emigrated to New Zealand; the other book was *Sordello*. The early works of Sand and Sue, along with some Soulié, he apparently had read some years before Elizabeth had begun her reading of those authors. In a letter to her in 1846 he speaks of having "let this reading drop some ten years ago."[2] More practical use of his knowledge of French would have come with his quasi-diplomatic journey to St. Petersburg in 1834 and his brief sojourn in Paris in 1837. And sometime before 1835 he had helped his "old French master" Auguste Loradoux prepare an instructional text of *Gil Blas*.[3]

Most important to Browning's awareness of contemporary French intellectual and literary life was the three-year friendship he began in 1834 with Count Amédée de Ripert-Monclar. Monclar was an intelligent and knowledgeable young Parisian who was with Browning a good bit during Monclar's visits to London; they again saw each other in Paris in 1837 when Browning visited his Uncle Reuben there. John Maynard, who has studied the correspondence between Monclar and Browning, surmises that because Browning's French was better than Monclar's English, much of their conversation, like the letters, was carried on in French. With Monclar, and possibly through the influence of Monclar's historian uncle Fortia, Browning officially if not actively became a part of the Parisian intellectual scene when he and Monclar were enrolled as original members of the Institut Historique, founded in Paris in 1834. More important, Browning could write to Monclar of his own work or comment on English contemporaries like Bulwer or Disraeli. In return, Maynard writes, "Monclar gave Browning a firsthand report on the literary and intellectual world of Paris. Browning would make Monclar draw pictures of French writers he had seen in Paris such as Hugo or George Sand. His letters to Monclar are full of references to Hugo, Dumas *père*, or Lamartine."[4] The inclusion of Dumas suggests Browning's interest in French theatrical literature; it was an interest never shared by Elizabeth, whose enthusiasm for Dumas came with her reading of *Le Comte de Monte-Cristo* (1844–45). Except for that novel, Robert consistently showed impatience with the novels Dumas had begun to write after 1839. Nevertheless, his response to the new French fiction was quite similar to Elizabeth's. Like her, he immediately recognized French superiority over contemporary English novelists. "I entirely agree with you in your estimate of the comparative value of French & English Romance-writers," he told Elizabeth in 1846. "I bade the completest adieu to the latter on my first introduction to Balzac, whom I greatly admire for his faculty, whatever he may choose to do with it."[5]

What works provided Browning's "first introduction" to Balzac is not clear. He may have known *Louis Lambert* or *La Peau de chagrin* by the time he published *Pauline* in 1833. As late as the summer of 1835, however, he told Monclar he knew little of Balzac. And Maynard reports that when "Browning spoke slightingly of Balzac, Monclar knew enough to correct him and perhaps stimulated Browning to the more serious considerations he would give the Promethean novelist in the next few years."[6] If at Monclar's urging in 1835 Browning began to read more recently published Balzac, *Le Père Goriot* may have provided his first truly enthusiastic reading. In his letter of April 27 to Elizabeth, Browning specifically mentions two characters, Rastignac and Despleins, who first make their appearances in *Le Père Goriot*. Balzac originally published the novel as a *roman-feuilleton* in *La Revue de Paris* in the autumn of 1834; five other editions came out in 1835. The other specific reference in the letter to Elizabeth is to *La Messe de l'athée*, which came out in *La Chronique de Paris* on January 3, 1836. He may, of course, have read these and other works in any number of editions or the various collected *Scènes* or even the first edition of the *Comédie humaine* (1844). At least as early as 1839 he read *Béatrix* "in the feuilleton of the *Siècle*, day by day";[7] he may well have begun earlier the practice of following the initial serial publication of Balzac's fiction. When he read any given Balzac novel would be of consequence only were there evidence of any direct influence by or borrowing from Balzac. There is not. What is more significant is that Browning early recognized Balzac as the master novelist of his day; further, such recognition came when Browning himself was experimenting with ways of writing more objective, realistic poetry. He found "so delightful" the opening detailed descriptive passages of *Béatrix*; he admired Balzac's characters because "they keep alive, moving."[8]

Summing up their discussion of Balzac, Elizabeth emphasized Balzac's realism but also the poetic intensity of his language:

> For Balzac, I have had my full or overfull pleasure from that habit you speak of, . . & which seems to prove his good faith in the life & reality of his creations, in such striking manner. He is a writer

of most wonderful faculty – with an overflow of life everywhere – with the vision & the utterance of a great seer. His French is another language – he throws new metals into it . . malleable metals, which fuse with the heat of his genius.[9]

Balzac is, as it were, a writer who had succeeded where Sordello had failed to create a new "Language, – welding words into the crude/ Mass from the new speech around him." This was the quality of Balzac that Maynard thinks was most important to the young Browning: "Balzac's larger, almost visionary concern for the entire scope of human life and his vigorous language, bringing poetic strength and freedom of expression to a portrayal of reality, [this] was immensely important as a general influence on the man who would move poetry in the direction of the novel, just as Balzac had moved the novel in the direction of modern poetry."[10] Often the heightened language of Balzac occurs most forcefully in those set speeches – Vautrin to Rastignac or to Lucien, Benassis to Genestas – passages which E. J. Oliver in his *Honoré de Balzac* notes in passing "come close to the dramatic monologues of Browning, who equally adopted masks that were not his own to express the views of a Blougram or a Sludge."[11]

Browning was already experimenting with such set speeches to reveal the inner psychological reality of character in *Paracelsus* (1835). He had tried, he wrote in the preface, "to reverse the method usually adopted by writers whose aim it is to set forth any phenomena of the mind or the passions, by the operation of persons and events; and that, instead of having recourse to an external machinery of incidents to create and evolve the crisis I desire to produce, I have ventured to display somewhat minutely the mood itself in its rise and progress. . . ." By such an experiment Browning had moved beyond the confessional mode of *Pauline*. In March of 1836 John Forster hailed that achievement: "Mr. Browning has the power of a great dramatic poet; we never think of Mr. Browning while we read his poem; we are not identified with him, but with the persons into whom he has flung his genius."[12] In the same month that Forster praised Browning's new objectivity, Balzac published *Facino Cane*, the novella in which the narrator meets and studies the aged Venetian musician obsessed with lost treasure. At the beginning the narrator extends Balzac's earlier insistence (in the preface to *La Peau de chagrin*) that author and character should not be confused. "With me observation had become intuitive," the narrator begins; "it did not neglect the body, but penetrated further, into the soul or rather it grasped the outer details so completely that it at once passed beyond them. It gave me the ability to live the life of another, substituting myself for him. . . ."[13] Balzac's narrator, more openly and rather boastfully, describes a process of literary creation towards which Browning was moving in *Paracelsus*, in "Johannes Agricola" and in "Porphyria's Lover." In *Strafford* (1836) Browning's strategy to submerge the author and reveal "Action in Character, rather than Character in Action" included formal dramatic rendering, historical scholarship, and incidentally a Venetian song which heightens the pathos of Strafford's death. Browning's Sordello briefly welded together a language by which he "took/An action with its actors, quite forsook/Himself to live in each. . . ." Sordello failed, but Browning succeded in creating through language an illusion of psychological reality within characters diverse from himself. Balzac, too, had so succeeded; and Browning recognized and admired that success.

Until he read *Madame Bovary*, Browning found no other contemporary author so capable of making his characters seem to live. Browning doubtless would have been pleased, had he known, that Philarète Chasles, friend and early champion of Balzac, devoted several pages of a review of recent English drama in the *Revue des Deux Mondes* in 1840 to *Paracelsus*, a work whose merit Chasles wrongly claims "has passed almost unnoticed in England." Chasles called special attention to the "interior drama which is at play in all great and famous men, and which takes on a quality of frenetic beauty in such a character as Paracelsus. . . ." Though Chasles found fault with "the verbosity, the incoherence, the vagueness of details" in certain scenes, and though the action was blurred by "the dissertations of a hazy aesthetic" and by "the long-windedness of a prolix style," the French critic believed *Paracelsus* "must be considered, however, as a very beautiful moral and psychological analysis." *Paracelsus* contained "toutes les traces d'un esprit supérieur" and of an intelligence "subtile et profonde."[14]

Stendhal's *Le Rouge et le noir* (1830) found relatively early and appreciative readers in Elizabeth Barrett and Robert Browning in the mid-1840's when the novel was not widely known even in France, although *La Chartreuse de Parme* had received wider recognition and was the occasion of Balzac's praise in the ephemeral *La Revue parisienne* in 1840. Not until 1856, in an article in the *Edinburgh Review*, was the British public alerted to Stendhal's achievement; the cult of Beylisme began to grow only after Taine's praise in *Essais de critique et d'histoire* (1866) and the biography by Mark Patton in 1874. Elizabeth apparently came upon *Le Rouge* by chance and without preconceptions in the early spring of 1845. Normally when writing about contemporary French authors, she reveals some knowledge of the author's career and general reputation. In April of 1845 she begged her friend Miss Mitford "to order and read 'le rouge et le noir' by a M. de Stendhal . . a 'nom de guerre' I fancy. I wish I knew the names of any other books written by him." Although the author was a literary cipher to her, Elizabeth was profoundly moved by his novel: "so dark and deep is the colouring," she told Miss Mitford, *Le Rouge* "is very striking and powerful and full of deep significance." She was apparently never to become aware of any "other books" by Stendhal, but in her initial enthusiasm for *Le Rouge* she applied what for her had become the test of contemporary literary genius – comparison to Balzac: "Balzac could scarcely put out a stronger hand. It is, as to simple power, a first-class book – according to my impression – though painful and noxious in many ways. . . . It has ridden me like an incubus for several days."[15] Elizabeth's somewhat equivocal reaction to *Le Rouge* remained when she re-read the novel with Robert towards the end of their first winter in Italy.

From Pisa in February of 1847 Elizabeth announced to Miss Mitford that "Robert is a warm admirer of Balzac and has read most of his books"; however, he was impatient with Dumas, Soulié and Sue because Robert held to "too high a standard" and, unlike Elizabeth, would not "listen to a story for a story's sake." A day or two before they had read together "the 'Rouge et Noir', that powerful book of Stendhal's (Beyle), and he [Robert] thought it very striking, and observed – what I had thought from the first and again and again – that it was exactly like Balzac *in the raw*, in the material and undeveloped conception. What a book it is really, and so full of pain and bitterness, and the gall of iniquity!"[16] Elizabeth's syntax and diction here are tantalizingly vague – all the more so because this is the last time either Browning or she would make any direct statement about Stendhal's art. Robert seems to have been struck by the nearly documentary "material" drawn from contemporary French life; yet he found the novel undeveloped and *"raw."* The sense of rawness might refer to the spare, reportorial, often brusque style which Stendhal himself, in his deliberate attempt to avoid the pretentious phrasing of Chateaubriand and his imitators, thought "trop haché" (too chopped).[17] André Gide, that great admirer of Browning, found that in "Stendhal no phrase evokes the one after it or takes life from the preceding one."[18] But where Gide found Stendhal's pen traced "the most delicate line," the Brownings, who admired the poetic fullness of Balzac's style, may have found rawness in Stendhal's. If *"raw"* and "undeveloped" are to be taken in a larger sense than style, the Brownings may have been thinking of the relatively sparse and economical *mise en scène* of *Le Rouge*. The village of Verrières, the embankment of the Doubs, the grounds of the Rênals' residence, the library of the Hôtel de La Mole – Stendhal creates them all in sufficient detail; *Le Rouge*, however, does not have the Balzacian abundance of description of streets, buildings, furniture, clothing, even physiognomy. Robert, who was impatient with a "story for a story's sake" and who would become a master of the detailed *mise en scène*, had been attracted to such long, detailed Balzacian passages ever since he had read the opening chapters of *Béatrix* in 1838. Finally, "raw" might refer to the tone of *Le Rouge*, the attitude Stendhal takes towards his characters. Perhaps it was in his tone that Elizabeth found "bitterness," "gall," and "noxious" qualities. Certainly in *Le Père Goriot, Illusions perdues*, or *Les Mystères de Paris* there is more that is sordid, ugly and brutal than there is in *Le Rouge*.

Balzac and Sue, however, are decidedly more sympathetic to their deserving characters than is the ironic, detached, sardonic Stendhal. A couple of years later, Elizabeth would comment upon Balzac's compassion for fallen humanity in *Le Cousin Pons*: what other author, she asks, "could have taken such a subject, out of the lowest mud of humanity, and glorified and consecrated it?"[19] To her Balzac was a kind of M. Rudolph from *Les Mystères* who sought, found and restored to the paths of virtue and piety a Fleur-de-Marie or a Slasher. Stendhal was, of course, little interested in such rescue work from "the lowest mud of humanity"; he was interested, as Harry Levin notes, in "the psychology of delusion, the mechanism of self-deception, the eternal quixotry of the human mind."[20] Often in brief internal monologues Stendhal reveals such self-deception:

Julien accepting as "ses moments d'action les plus intéressants" the pious routine of the seminary where, as in Robert's "Spanish Cloister," there was "a way of eating a boiled egg which announces progress made in the pious life"; Madame de Rênal confusing her brief respite from the boredom of provincial marriage with perfect happiness; Mlle. Mathilde giving herself to Julien and the next morning justifying herself because her seducer was a keen student of politics and "un homme de mérite"; even the wise and admirable Father Pirard reveals his parvenu taste for the "architecture magnifique" of the Hôtel de La Mole, which the author steps in to inform us is abominable.[21]

Stendhal often deflates such delusions by commenting upon his characters' foibles in sardonic asides to his dear reader. These intrusions, which F. W. J. Hemmings describes as "humorous *persiflage*," create for *Le Rouge* an authorial persona similar to the quizzical, bantering persona Robert would adopt in the epilogue to "Bishop Blougram," in "Apparent Failure," *The Ring and the Book* and *Red Cotton Night-Cap Country*. In Balzac, such authorial intrusions tend towards more effusive didacticism; in Sue they descend to sentimental bathos and melodramatic bombast. Stendhal's characters are crisply, sharply judged; yet, as in Robert's mature monologues, even the judgments of rogues and fools are balanced by some sympathy, a balance necessary to the revelation of psychological complexity. Stendhal may be less tolerant of the foibles of Julien or Mathilde than is Browning of Cleon, Fra Lippo, even such special-pleaders as Mr. Sludge or Prince Hohenstiel-Schwangau. Still, *Le Rouge* does balance sympathy and judgment; and the careful reader must end "liking Julien Sorel," as Robert M. Adams has argued so well. To do so, however, the reader must participate in what Adams describes as a "rather complicated game, an *intrigue intérieure*, expectations of the average . . . reader. Whatever can be predicted of that reader in the way of passive expectation, softness for rhetoric, innocence of intrigue, and conventional moral stances, Stendhal is ready to take advantage of."[22]

Browning, like Stendhal, made strenuous and similar demands upon his readers; few were willing to participate patiently in his complex presentation of the minds of unconventional and often morally reprehensible characters. Not until the 1860's, when Stendhal's reputation too began to rise, did Browning find enough sufficiently hardy readers to bring him wide appreciation. Their art was in many ways similar: great compression of language, fondness for irony and interest in restricted points of view, a penchant for intellectual argumentation, a strong tendency towards analysis of motive. They shared also a wide knowledge and appreciation of Italian painting, sculpture and music; each took delight in the colourful life of Italian towns and countryside; each searched Italian libraries in their enthusiasm for Renaissance history and found documentary material to be used in their realistic art.

The similarity of literary interest between Stendhal and Browning is perhaps nowhere more strongly revealed than in their common interest in the old Roman murder of Pompilia Comparini by her husband Guido Franceschini. Stendhal had discovered and made transcripts of several "historettes" in a Roman library in 1833 or 1835. Three of these – *Vittoria Accoramboni, La Duchesse de Palliano* and *Les Cenci* – he translated along with some editorial intrusion and published in the *Revue des Deux Mondes* in 1837 and 1838. A fourth of these *Chroniques italiennes, San Francesco à Ripa*, was published by François Buloz in the *Revue* in 1853 at a time when Browning, having met Buloz and others associated with the *Revue*, was reading it with some regularity. Stendhal's "historette" entitled "Accuse processo et morte del Signor Guido Franceschini," however, remained unpublished in manuscript at the Bibliothèque Nationale where, having been refused by the British Museum, it had been deposited in 1851. None of these "historettes" became fictions using documentary sources in the manner of *Le Rouge et le noir*, though he did think of turning the Vittoria Accoramboni narrative into a fiction. *"I thought in March 1833 of making this story as that of* Julien," Stendhal wrote in the margin of the Accoramboni manuscript, "But where is 1) the interest, 2) the satire, the bases *of every novel*? I am scarcely after a vulgar success. But where can the author who is not an antiquarian find details which are true and in unlimited numbers?" For the Franceschini murder case, Stendhal had even less novelistic material available to him: only a single moralistic account by one of the members of the Confraternita della Misercordia, who had accompanied the condemned to the scene of execution. That edifying recitation of Guido's death Stendhal found a "crime plat," too dull and narrow to be worked even into a *chronique* like *Les Cenci*. [23] The Florentine lawyer Cencini compiled soon after the executions a fuller set of documents about the Franceschini case into an Old Yellow Book. There Browning found "détails vrais et en nombre illimité," sufficient satiric material, and almost obsessive interest. From it he was to create the most masterly *roman*-poem of the century.

The Brownings' response to *Le Rouge et le noir* is directly if briefly and ambiguously recorded. They were, it seems clear, unaware of Balzac's own public appreciation of *La Chartreuse de Parme* (1839), a novel which apparently did not show up on the shelves of the various subscription libraries of Pisa, Florence, Siena or Rome in which they constantly sought out French novels. Nor apparently did Stendhal's early volumes on his Italian travels or his *Histoire de la peinture en Italie* (1817). At various times the Brownings became acquainted with people who had known Stendhal. Elizabeth once and Robert several times visited the Roman campagna with Jean-Jacques Ampère, whom Stendhal had earlier guided in an archaeological tour of the campagna. In Paris in 1855 at the salon of a friend of Stendhal, Madame Mohl, they met Stendhal's old travelling companion, Prosper Mérimée. Vague suggestions that Robert knew other works of Stendhal occur. *De l'Amour* (1822) – along with Balzac's *Physiologie du mariage* (1830) – has been unconvincingly proposed as the "French book" Bishop Blougram cites on the origin of the human desire for privacy while making love.[24] In a letter Robert wrote to his longtime friend, the novelist Isa Blagden, from Rome in 1861 there is a hint that he may have read *La Chartreuse de Parme*. He politely praises Isa's new novel *Agnes Tremorne*, a novel in which the hero Herbert is confined, much like Fabrice del Dongo, in a prison fortress. He praises his friend's novel "for much observation of character & picking up of 'petits faits vrais' which other gleaners in the same field have overlooked. . . ." The phrase, as Edward McAleer points out, appears in a letter from Stendhal to Balzac in 1840.[25] But the phrase was in common use by mid-century, and it was soon part of the standard vocabulary for those who wished to speak of realistic literature. In old age Browning would quote from Stendhal's *Armance* (1827) when he wrote from Venice in 1885 to assure Mrs. Thomas FitzGerald that he looked forward to a visit to her home when he returned to England: Mrs. FitzGerald will, he thinks, "understand what Stendhal insists upon as one of the best results of travel – 'l'étonnement du retour.'"[26]

ii

The letters Browning exchanges with Elizabeth Barrett from January of 1845 until September of 1846 are crowded with French phrases, quotations from French authors, lively discussions of contemporary French writing, and frequent reference to French news or gossip. The portrait that emerges is of two cosmopolitan people, witty, alert to and familiar and at ease with things French. That familiarity and ease is apparent when they frequently have recourse to a French quotation or phrase because it seems the most apt or allows scope for some playfulness. Such is the case when Elizabeth closes a long letter with "Am I not 'femme qui parle' today?" or when she coyly begs pardon for correcting a bad line in one of Robert's poems then blots out her own correction and announces that " 'quand je m'efface il n'y a pas grand mal, (it is no great harm when I blot out myself.)" A particularly bad headache Robert describes as "mauvaise, mauvaise, mauvaise"; and, while despairing of proper critical attention to one of his plays, he cries out *"Ces Misères!"* This tragic phrase he intones just before he describes arrangements he has made to take his sister to see Rachel play Hermione in Racine's *Andromaque*, arrangements that will keep him from calling on Elizabeth.[27] Or he can refer to Jules Janin's canard against Rachel's grammar. In the *Journal des Débats* (September 10, 1838) Janin had quoted Rachel as saying that before she came to classical acting in the Théâtre Français she had acted at the more popular Gymnase: " 'C'était moi que j'était au Gymnase,'" Browning via Janin quotes Rachel as blurting out. To this, Browning says, Janin should have replied, " 'Je le savions!' "[28]

Often they can turn a French quotation to quite unusual purposes: broaching the subject of marriage, a subject Elizabeth had forbidden, Robert begins a letter questioning whether she did "in the prosecution of her studies, get a book on the forb . . . no *un*forbidden shelf – wherein Voltaire pleases to say that 'si Dieu n'existait pas, il faudrait l'inventer (if God did not exist, it would be necessary to invent him).' I feel, . . . that if *marriage* did not exist, I should infallibly *invent* it."[29] Elizabeth, too, sometimes finds an odd and complex application for a French phrase. Discussing the straightforward, comfortable relations she has with several friends and the complex and ambivalent feelings she has towards her dictatorial father, she refers to François de Malherbe's strictures against the facile imitators of Ronsard – " 'Cela se peut facilement' (That is easily possible)" – to describe her relationship to certain friends. "But for another relation," she goes on, "it was all different – & rightly so – & so very different – 'Cela ne se peut nullment' (That is not at all possible) – as in Malherbe."[30] Only once does Elizabeth shift to French to solemnly declare her love, closing a letter with "May God bless you . . 'très bon'! – tres cher, pour cause. Toute à toi – pour toujours."[31] Once she quotes sentimental French verses:

> "Si l'âme est immortelle
> L'amour ne l'est-il pas?"

However, she prefaces the quotation with a childhood recollection of two women discussing the pain of watching their lovers become, in the first year of marriage, husbands. The sentimental verses are "Beautiful verses," but she quotes them "just to prove to you that I do not remember *only* the disagreeable things . . only to tease you with. . . ."[32] There is a similar qualification of sentiment, a kind of verbal hedging around phrases that might seem excessively romantic, when she applies to herself – "not fretfully, I hope – not complainingly, I am sure" – words by Madame de Staël: "*jamais je n'ai pas été aimée comme j'aime.*' (I have never been loved like I love.)" She lingers for a while over that self-analysis, but soon turns merrily to complain of one of Frédéric Soulié's characters "who, in the course of an 'emotion,' takes up a chair . . *unconsciously*, & breaks it into very small pieces, & then proceeds with his soliloquy. Well! – the clearest idea this excites in *me*, is the low condition in Paris of moral government and of [Parisian] upholstery." Pressing his suit in subsequent letters, Robert incidentally concurs with her "appreciation of Parisian *meubles*."[33]

A light, humorous tone invests the Brownings' use of French; they seem at home in the language. The merging of that tone with, for example, Elizabeth's reading of Dumas suggests something of the intelligent critical distance she could maintain. Dumas was "a right good storyteller when he is of a mind for storytelling; – telling, telling, telling, & never having done." But Dumas had distressed Elizabeth by hanging the hero of *La Guerre des femmes* after only four volumes. She preferred that romance writers keep their heroes alive for at least six volumes: "Yet oh . . to see one's hero, the hero of four volumes, & not a bad hero either in some respects, hung up before one's eyes? . . it wrongs the natural affections to think of it!

– it made me unhappy for a full hour! – There should be a society for the prevention of cruelty to romance-readers against the recurrence of such things!"[34] Two months later, glad to see it was six full volumes, she began *Le Comte de Monte-Cristo*. She weaves into her letter, by delightful counterpoint, Dumas' narrative and her growing love for Browning:

> Now that the hero is safe in the dungeon (of the Château d'If) it will be delightful to see how he will get out – somebody knocks at the wall already. Only the narrative is not always very clear to me, inasmuch as, when I read, I unconsciously interleave it with such thoughts of you as make very curious cross readings . . . j'avais cru remarquer quelques infidélités (I thought I noticed some infidelities) . . . he really seems to love me – l'homme n'est jamais qu'un homme (man is never just a man) . . . never was any man like him – ses traits étaient bouleversés (his features were disordered) . . . the calmest eyes I ever saw. . . .[35]

For his part, Robert could read a new Balzac novel (probably in this case *Les Comédiens sans le savoir*), then write Elizabeth a brief complaint about someone who disliked the unintelligibility of his poetry. He slips into a French locution to express his hurt vanity:

> My love, I send you things, with exactly as much vanity as . . . no comparison will serve! it is the French vulgarism – comme . . . n'importe quoi! Celui me pousse à la vanité comme – n'importe quoi! (like . . . no matter what! It impels me to vanity like – no matter what!)
>
> Will you have a significative 'comme' of another kind? 'je me trouve bête ce matin comme . . trente-six oies!' (I am as silly – this morning as . . thirty-six geese) – (I assure you this is no flower culled from Balzac this morning – but a little *'souvenir'* of an old play.)
>
> Now, if I were to say to myself something is dear as 'thirty-six Ba's' – I should be scared. . . .[36]

Familiarity with general French culture is also apparent in their letters. Elizabeth could jokingly recommend Thiers as the appropriate person to review a new history of France for young people by an American lady; or she could turn the name of the director of the French Royal Observatory, Dominique Arago, into a metaphor for the wise man who remains silent while fools prattle. With a dig at the literary sterility of Victoria's court, she passes on gossip that Isidore, the queen's French hairdresser, reads Béranger and is hence "the most literary person at court."[37] Robert could recognize Mary Shelley's reliance on Alexis Rio's *De la poésie chrétienne* (1836) for her *Rambles in Germany and Italy* (1844) or note that Parisian publishers found it necessary to thicken a volume by Dickens by adding some humorous sketches by Thackeray.[38] Once he named two rose bushes he recently planted "Brennus," after the old Gallic resister to the Romans, and the other "Madame Laffarge," after the young Frenchwoman recently found guilty of poisoning her elderly husband. The names, he thought, were "very characteristic of Old Gaul and young France."[39] Another French murder trial attracted the attention of both Robert and Elizabeth. Alexandre Dujarier, manager of *La Presse*, and a M. de Beauvallon had quarrelled in a Parisian cafe; subsequently Dujarier was killed in a duel, and Beauvallon was tried for his murder. Dumas was among the witnesses. Browning refers to the affair while arguing that one's "genius" does not exculpate one's immorality. He did not consider those French journalists geniuses, but he was upset that their literary prominence seemed to set them above common cafe quarrellers in Paris: "go to-night into half the *estaminets* of Paris, and see whether the quarrels over dice and sour wine present any more pleasing matter of speculation *au fond*."[40]

The trial interested Elizabeth because the *Athenaeum* had commented that the affair bore out the truth of Balzac's "frightful delineation of the literary world of Paris." She saw in the *Athenaeum* article some hypocrisy on the part of the London literary world, although she did think that Balzac's satiric attack on "his literary brothers" and Parisian journalists in *Un Grand Homme de province à Paris* (1839) was an unfortunate blemish on Balzac's greatness.[41] The English reporting of the the affair was to her another instance of the "crass ignorance" existing between the French and English literary worlds. She hoped that to overcome that mutual ignorance someone would found a "European review" which would direct itself to "the intelligent readers of all the countries of Europe, & take all the rising reputations of each, with the national light on them as they rise, into observation & judgment." Such a journal, she thought, might end that habit of English reviewers "to snatch up a French book, & say something prodigiously absurd of it. . . ."[42] One English "ignoramus" had praised the novels of Madame Charles Reybaud, "who is in fact a hack writer of romances third & fourth rate . . ." A Frenchman like Jules Janin could be just as foolish. Elizabeth had for several years relied upon Janin's suggestions for her readings of French novels, but she decried Janin's denial of Balzac's greatness in *Illusions perdues*. She was hardly surprised, then, to find Janin refer foolishly to the great friendship between Byron and Robert Southey.

The note of surprised and delighted common agreement on most subjects punctuates the letters Robert and Elizabeth wrote to each other. Only Elizabeth's great admiration for George Sand provoked any serious demur by Robert. Though long an enthusiast for Sand's writing, Elizabeth first mentioned Sand rather casually some five months after Robert began the correspondence. Commenting that she, like Robert, believes in a kind of literary inspiration, she quotes Sand's *Spiridion* (1838) to define more closely what she means by inspiration: " 'Tout ce que l'homme appelle inspiration, je l'appelle aussi revelation. . . .' (All that man calls inspiration I also call revelation)[43]" A bit later, after solemnly pledging Browning not to reveal her secret thoughts to two strong-minded, independent women writers, Anna Jameson and Harriet Martineau, Elizabeth confesses that she believes women lack the power of artistic inspiration, that "there is a natural inferiority of mind in women. . . ." George Sand, however, was the exception:

> [Sand] I regard with infinitely more admiration than all other women of genius who are or have been. Such a colossal nature in every way – with all that breadth & scope of faculty which women want – magnanimous, & living the truth & loving the people – and with that 'hate of hate' too, which you extol – so eloquent, & yet earnest as if she were dumb – so full of a living sense of beauty, & of noble blind instincts toward an ideal purity – & so proving a right even in her wrong.

She ends this outburst of praise for Sand by commenting that Robert's description of François Vidocq's museum of criminal artifacts reminds her of certain "masonic trial scenes" in Sand's *Consuelo* (1842–43).[44] Robert had quite enjoyed the French detective's London exhibition and commentary on various weapons of mayhem and murder; he remembered specifically a small "dessert-knife" with which a young man stabbed his mother fifty-two times, and he appreciated Vidocq's lively account of the murderer Lacenaire, a "jeune homme d'un caractère fort avenant – mais c'était un poète. . . . (a young man with a strong, pleasing character – but he was a poet)"[45] Vidocq, one of the originals for Balzac's Vautrin, interested Browning more than did *Consuelo*, which he soon began to read. The reading provoked two long critical comments from Browning. In the first he objected strongly to the easy omniscience of the novelist-narrator:

> Do you know, "Consuelo" wearies me – oh, wearies – and the fourth volume I have all but stopped at – there lie the three following: but who cares about Consuelo after that horrible evening with the Venetian scamp, (where he bullies her, and it does answer, after all she says) as we say? And Albert wearies too – it seems all false, all writing – (not the first part, though). And what easy work these novelists have of it! a Dramatic poet has to *make* you love or admire his men and women – they must *do* and *say* all that you are to see and hear – really do it in your face, say it in your ears, and it is wholly for *you*, in *your* power, to *name*, characterize and so praise or blame, *what* is said and done . . if you don't perceive of yourself, there is no standing by, for the Author, and telling you: but with these novelists, a scrape of the pen – out blurting of a phrase, and the miracle is achieved – "Consuelo possessed to perfection this and the other gift" – what would you more?[46]

A few days later Browning finished the last three volumes despite his impatience with the novel and despite Elizabeth's taunting him about his complaint at Sand's "want of art" while he continued to admire Hans Christian Andersen. "There lies Consuelo – done with!" he wrote. "I shall tell you frankly that it strikes me as precisely what in conventional language with the customary silliness is styled a *woman's*-book, in its merits & defects, – and supremely timid in all the points where one wants, and has a right to expect, some *fruit* of all the pretence and George Sand*ism*. . . ." He found the plot illogical, Consuelo's set speeches unconvincing, and the characters of Count Christian, Baron Frédéric, Albert, and Porpora, inadequately portrayed. In trying to account for Consuelo's fascination with the handsome, indolent Anzoleto, Sand had, Browning thought, turned "over the leaves of a wrong dictionary, seeking help from Psychol-

ogy, and pretending to forget there is such a thing as Physiology."
Sand had talent, not genius; she was capable of some eloquence but
with finality Browning concluded: "I am not George Sand's – she
teaches me nothing – I look to her for nothing – . . . ."⁴⁷

Elizabeth feigned agreement with "nearly all" these strictures
against *Consuelo*; she countered, however, that it was unfair to
depreciate Sand because of the defects of one novel. And, as if to try
Robert's patience to the limit, she reminded him that it was difficult
to judge even *Consuelo* without reading its three-volume sequel *La
Comtesse de Rudolstadt* (1843). That admonition came in her letter of
August 16, 1845. Both remain silent on the subject of George Sand
until the following spring when their mutual friend Henry Chorley
published in the *Athenaeum* a review of a number of French novels
including Sand's *Le Meunier d'Angibault* (1844) and *Le Péché de
Monsieur Antoine* (1845). In the former, the *nouveau riche* capitalist is
frequently indicted by the narrator and other characters for his
exploitation of the poor, and is accused, with echoes from Proudhon,
of having amassed his property by theft. The capitalist's economic
sins are compounded by the domestic tyranny he exercises over his
daughters. *Le Péché de Monsieur Antoine* continues the combined
themes of utopian communism and domestic tyranny. Here Émile
Cardonnet spurns the ill-gotten fortune of his capitalist father and
marries a humble craftsman's daughter. Fortunately, Émile soon
inherits a fortune from an aristocrat sympathetic to utopian communism so that his dream of a Fourieristic commune can be realized.
Émile Cardonnet is an early prototype for Elizabeth's Romney
Leigh. By the time *Aurora Leigh* was published in 1856, however,
Elizabeth had come to think of the utopian communism Sand extol-
led as a tragic delusion. In 1846 she apparently considered Sand's
politics as simply part of her "earnestness of aim" which she had
displayed from the beginning of her career in *Rose et Blanche* and
Indiana. Angry that Chorley had dared compare Sand to the didactic
English writer Sarah Ellis, Elizabeth points to Sand's recent novella
Tévérino (1845). Free of socialist moralizing, *Tévérino* celebrates the
freedom and gaiety of a wandering songster-horsetrainer who brings
some colour and delight into the lives of bored and respectable
Italian burghers. Elizabeth apparently considered *Tévérino* evidence
of Sand's imaginative versatility, and she found "insufferable" Chorley's "digging & nagging at a great reputation' like Sand's.⁴⁸ Robert,

too, was rather surprised at Chorley's article: "I read it, and quite wonder at him. – I suppose he follows somebody's 'lead' – writes as he is directed," Robert comments in partial defence of Chorley. Chorley had, it seems, greater admiration for Sand when he had earlier loaned to Robert a copy of her first overtly socialist novel *Le Compagnon du tour de France* (1840).[49] Overtly *Christian* socialist is perhaps a better description of this picaresque tale of the journeyman carpenter Agricol Perdiguier and his Christ-like comrade Pierre Huguenin, who travel about France establishing communal homes for workmen, preach their particular brand of guild socialism and, inevitably, inspire the love of high-born ladies and the ire of aristocratic fathers.

Neither Robert nor Elizabeth reveal what they thought of Sand's growing political radicalism, but it is probable that it was through her novels that they became familiar indirectly with the sociopolitical ideas of Lamennais and Pierre Leroux or the more radical Proudhon. These were ideas they would examine more closely – and generally reject – during the turmoil of the Second Republic. During their courtship Elizabeth and Robert express almost no interest in French politics except for a passing, nearly opaque reference to Thiers' surprising support of French and British friendship, or to the most recent attempt to assassinate Louis-Philippe. Both references are turned by Elizabeth to very personal purposes. Her hope that Robert will always "care for" her, she likens to the seemingly "charmed life" of the French king. Once they had decided to elope, Robert hoped Elizabeth would come to New Cross to meet his parents, but she advises against the meeting and claims they must be as Machiavellian in their marital plans as is Monsieur Thiers in his politics.[50] Robert's final reference to George Sand is similarly personal and surprisingly sympathetic to Sand: not wanting to be dependent upon Elizabeth's income once they have gone to Italy, Robert declares that he hopes they will live simply "in one room like George Sand in 'that happy year'" she spent with Jules Sandeau and which she described in *Lettres d'un voyageur* (1834–36).[51]

iii

Casting about for a way to make some money, Robert rather early in the correspondence comments that Charles Kean once offered him £500 for a suitable play and that the publisher Colburn told him "confidentially that he wanted more than his dinner 'a novel on the subject of *Napoleon*' *!!!* So one may make money. . . ."[52] The italics and exclamation marks indicate that Browning considered absurd the suggestion that he write a novel on Napoleon. Mr. Colburn doubtless had wished to take advantage of the swell of interest in Napoleon after the return of the Emperor's ashes to Paris in 1840. Elizabeth, whose physician at Torquay recommended "the subject as a noble one," had memorialized "Napoleon's Return" in the *Athenaeum* on July 4, 1840.[53] The British warship *Bellerophon*, aboard which Napoleon had surrendered after Waterloo and on which his ashes were transported from St. Helena, lay at anchor in Tor Bay as she wrote. The twenty-eight-stanza poem, later entitled "Crowned and Buried," sings Napoleon's great military victories and his destruction of ancient European monarchies, but it scorns the transformation of the Republic into Empire when the hands of the French people "toward freedom stretched" only to drop "Paralyzed/ To wield a sword or fit an undersized/King's crown to a great man's head." Napoleon – a rapacious, autocratic tyrant – gave France glory but destroyed the "vision of her liberty." The poem ends in ambivalence towards its subject:

> I think this nation's tears thus poured together,
> Better than shouts. I think this funeral
> Grander than crownings, though a Pope blessed all.
> I think this grave stronger than thrones.
>   But whether
> The crowned Napoleon or the buried clay
> Be worthier, I discern not: angels may.

When Elizabeth sent Hugh Stuart Boyd a copy of the poem, she said decisively: "Napoleon is no idol of *mine*."[54] Nevertheless, "Crowned and Buried" reveals something of that "immoral sympathy with power" of which John Kenyon had accused her.[55] That sympathy she soon would extend to Louis-Napolean. Robert's poetic response to the renewed interest in Napoleon is rather characteristic of his bias towards lesser known or even obscure historical anecdote or personages. "Incident in the French Camp" (1842) has as its speaker an unnamed French soldier who remembers watching an anxious Napoleon the day Lannes stormed Ratisbon. Napoleon is presented as the troubled but profoundly thoughtful field tactician:

With neck out-thrust, you fancy how,
   Legs wide, arms locked behind,
As if to balance the prone brow
   Oppressive with its mind.

The focus shifts to the mortally wounded boy who rides from Ratisbon to Napoleon's station to bring news of Lannes' success. Upon
hearing the good news, Napoleon's eye, like that of a rapacious eagle,
"flashed; his plans/Soared up again like fire." But when Napoleon
noticed the boy's wound, fiery ambition turns to maternal tenderness as his eye "Softened itself, as sheathes/A film the mother-
eagle's eye/When her bruised eaglet breathes." Here Browning celebrates not the Emperor's martial glory but his occasional tenderness;
more obviously, however, he celebrates not Napoleon but the
admirable loyalty of the common French soldier, courier and narrator alike.

Neither Elizabeth nor Robert admired Napoleon unreservedly,
but like the rest of their generation they were familiar with a good bit
of Napoleonic lore. Some of that lore is rather obscure. Elizabeth
cites with disapproval Napoleon's definition of poetry as "*'science
creuse'*"; and upon sending a ring to Robert she warns that it is
small and probably will not fit him "as it would not Napoleon before
you."[56] Sometimes the Napoleonic legend is given witty personal
application. In October of 1845 Robert made a hasty journey to Paris
and back on his uncles' business. Leaving London on Monday and
returning on Wednesday, he had been excessively anxious lest he be
unable to negotiate railway and ferry timetables well enough to keep
his Wednesday appointment with Elizabeth. Proud of his success, he
comments: "What you fear, precisely that, never happens, as
Napoleon observed and grew bold."[57] In January of 1846 Elizabeth
counted the number of letters Robert had sent during the past year's
campaign to win her love: "A hundred letters I have, by this last,
. . to set against Napolean's Hundred Days."[58] Their mutual
friend Richard Hengist Horne had been quick to offer the public a
work on Napoleon, his two-volume lavishly illustrated *A History of
Napoleon* (1841). To Horne Elizabeth had written how much she had
enjoyed his book; to Robert she confided that Horne had had to hire
someone to study the subject of Napoleon for him.[59] When Horne
sought Elizabeth's collaboration on another book of his, *A New
Spirit of the Age* (1844), she was able to supply him with some

anti-Napoleon anecdotes by another friend she shared with Robert –
Walter Savage Landor. Landor, she told Horne, had been to Paris to
witness the ceremony that made Napoleon First Consul for life.
From that event Landor dated his hatred of Napoleon for his destruction of republican ideals; and so Landor was rather pleased to
catch sight of Napoleon in Tours after his abdication in 1814, his
entourage reduced to a single servant.[60] She also translated for Horne
Landor's Greek epigram on Napoleon:

> Napoleon! thy deeds beyond compeers,
>> Who shall write, thrillingly? –
> The Father of Years!
> And – with the blood of children – willingly.[61]

Napoleon's subversion of republican ideals was compounded,
especially for Robert, by the great carnage his wars had brought to
Europe. Napoleon's motives were obscure if admirable, but the
effects of his actions were obvious enough, as Robert's Bishop
Blougram would later say: plain to see were "the blown up millions –
spatter of their brains/And writhing of their bowels and so
forth. . . ." The violent suicide in 1846 of a once ardent Napoleon-
ist, Benjamin Haydon, occasioned some further discussion of
Napoleon between Robert and Elizabeth. For some time Haydon
had corresponded with Elizabeth, and he had recently given her his
diary with the ingenuous, egotistical request that she edit it. On the
day of Haydon's suicide she had gone to Samuel Rogers' house
where she had seen a copy of Haydon's painting *Napoleon at St.
Helena*. When Elizabeth reported the tragic event and the coincidence to Robert, he rather callously commented that he preferred
Blake's painting to Haydon's grandiose historical canvases depicting
such things as "Napoleon and the world's surprize"; but he was glad
to learn that Haydon's most recent essay was "a dissertation on
respective merits of Napoleon and Wellington – how wrong Haydon
felt he had been to prefer the former . . and the why and the
wherefore."[62] Haydon's recantation of his worship of Napoleon and
his recognition of Wellington's greatness pleased Robert. It confirmed his own preference for the English hero which he had with
spirit expressed in "Nationality in Drinks" (1844):

> – Here's to Nelson's memory!
> 'T is the second time that I, at sea

Right off Cape Trafalgar here,
Have drunk it deep in British Beer.
Nelson forever – any time
Am I his to command in prose or rhyme!

France, represented in the poem by a "laughing little flask" of claret, has no comparable hero. When, sadly, the flask is empty it is dropped into the ocean as though it were the corpse of "some gay French lady."

The interest in France in the letters of Elizabeth and Robert rarely enters the poetry Elizabeth wrote in the early 1840's. Her poem on Napoleon is the only work given completely to a French subject. Her two sonnets to George Sand make no mention of Sand's nationality. In "A Vision of Poets" (1844), "soft Racine" and "grave Corneille" share but three lines in her roll call of poets from Homer to Keats. "Lady Geraldine's Courtship" (1844) she apparently thought of as an attempt to bring into poetry contemporary scenes and manners in the mode of Sand. It was, she told Boyd, "a 'romance of the age,' treating of railroads, routes, and all manner of 'temporalities,' and in so radical a temper that I expect to be reproved for it by the Conservative reviews around."[63] The favoured Sand theme of love between rich and poor here ends happily. The contemporaneity is established when "palpitating engines snort in steam" across Geraldine's estate, when she controls votes in the Commons, and when she and her peasant-born lover read Tennyson and Browning. Elizabeth herself did not think highly of the poem, but it did set her immediately to planning "a longer poem of a like class – a poem comprehending the aspect and manners of modern life, and flinching at nothing of the conventional."[64] That *roman-poem*, *Aurora Leigh*, with its clear indebtedness to de Staël, Sand, Balzac, Sue and other French novelists, would not be completed for over a decade. Her hesitation in writing that "novel-poem," she told Robert in February of 1845, came because "I am waiting for a story, & I won't take one, because I want to make one, & I like to make my own stories. . . ."[65]

Robert was as likely to *take* a story as to *make* one. That of *Paracelsus* he had taken from the *Biographie universelle*. The massive research for *Sordello* probably also began with the *Biographie*. He returned to that work in 1842 for his play *King Victor and King Charles*. The *Biographie* led him to Condorcet's commentary on Voltaire's brief account of the Victor-Charles story. Yet another source, as Browning acknowledged in his advertisement for the play, was the Abbé Roman's *Récit*. The *Biographie* would also supply him with information about the Breton crusader family, Dreux, upon which he could base his apparently imaginary Loys de Dreux in *The Return of the Druses* (1843); the encyclopaedia also contains an entry on Hakem-Biama-Allah and cites Silvestre de Sacy's *Chrestomathie arabe* (Paris, 1806). Sacy's two-volume *Exposé de la religion des Druzes* (Paris, 1838), William DeVane suggests, may also have been known to Browning.[66] Both plays offer evidence of Robert's reliance upon French historical scholarship, but neither reveals any particular attitude he may have held about France and its history.

The short poem "Count Gismond" (1842) Browning must originally have thought of as a representation of something essential in the French character. When it first appeared in *Dramatic Lyrics*, it carried the title "France" and was paired with another poem entitled "Italy," subsequently to be known as "My Last Duchess." Browning's renaming "France" "Count Gismond" suggests he soon wished to emphasize the particular character of the chivalric knight in Provence rather than any national characteristic the anecdote of love and honour might carry. Gismond's challenge to Count Gauthier's slur upon the lady's honour is no more typical of France than is the murderous envy of the lady of the *ancien régime* in "The Laboratory," or the arbitrary choice of Paris as the city in which the young Duke in "The Flight of the Duchess" is taught to try to revive feudal ways in the middle of the industrial 1840's. The Duke might have more easily learned such foolishness in London or his native Germany. The Germanic pedantry of the Duke's revival of medieval "usages thoroughly worn out" has its counterpart in the crabbed dullness of Sibrandus Schafnaburgensis' tome, which the poet lets moulder in the stagnant rainwater of his garden while he

> went in-doors, brought out a loaf,
> Half a cheese, and a bottle of Chablis;
> Lay on the grass and forgot the oaf
> Over a jolly chapter of Rabelais.[67]

If, as William DeVane suggest, some of these poems "attempt to catch the spirit of France in a small incident," this brief celebration of the robust humour of Rabelais catches that spirit as well as does the comic paean to claret in "Nationality in Drinks."

More ambitous is Browning's dramatization of two strains of French poetic practice in "The Glove." Two poets, Pierre Ronsard and Clément Marot, observe the scene on the Parisian streets during the time of Francis I when a lady tested Sir De Lorge's love by tossing her glove near a captive lion. The story of De Lorge retrieving the glove, then unexpectedly throwing it into the face of the vain lady, had already been versified by Leigh Hunt, who doubtless relied upon Schiller's story and on Saint Foix' *Essais historiques sur Paris*. [68] Browning's elaboration of the narrative – an elaboration inspired, DeVane thinks, by his reading of the *Mémoires* of the Marquis de Lassay – shifts the emphasis away from the didactic narrative of a woman's vanity to a dramatization of how two poets might respond to a single event. Ronsard is made into the narrator, and twice he characterizes Marot as a poet incapable of observing nature – human or animal. His first verbal thrust at Marot comes when, trying to describe the fierce lion, Ronsard comments that Marot, the pastoral versifier of the Psalms "Whose experience of nature's but narrow," would doubtless engage in Latin periphrasis to describe the brute as *"Illum Juda Leonem de Tribu."* In contrast, Ronsard describes the lion in some detail including even a brief memory – by the lion – of his African home. Once the glove was thrown, the lady reproved and De Lorge approved by King Francis and his court, Marot is allied with the imperceptive court and its acceptance of the superficial appearances of the incident. Ronsard, however, curious about the secret motive behind the lady's action, followed the lady as she fled the "hooting and laughter" of the crowd:

> Clement Marot stayed; I followed after,
> And asked, as a grace, what it all meant?
> If she wished not the rash deed's recallment?
> "For I" – so I spoke – "am a poet:
> Human nature, – behoves that I know!"

Ronsard's keen interest in the obscure springs of human action is rewarded when the lady explains that she dropped the glove to test De Lorge's conventional language against action, to find what all his courtly protestations about his willingness to die for her "Really

55

mean." Ronsard is hero and Marot villain in this drama of how language must be adjusted to reality. The two poets were contemporaries in the court of Francis I, but Browning's own bias towards psychological realism is here projected onto Ronsard without any special appropriateness. When she read the poem, Elizabeth drew attention to that personal element within the poem and to Browning's penchant for putting his own ideas and feeling into the mouth of a dramatic character: "for your 'Glove,' all women should be grateful, – & Ronsard, honoured, in this fresh shower of music on his old grave . . though the chivalry of the interpretation as well as much beside, is so plainly yours, . . could only be yours perhaps."[69]

3

Watching France from Italy, 1846–51

i

The Wedding Journey to Paris – By Train and Diligence to Lyon –
A Voyage Down the Rhône to Avignon – A Visit to Petrarch's
Vaucluse – On to Marseille and Pisa.

ii

Boredom in Italy – Searches for New French Books and Attendant
Difficulties of Being "exiles from Balzac" – Re-reading Sue,
Dumas, and Stendhal – A Growing Interest in French Politics but
Concern that Politics May Harm French Literature.

iii

RB and EBB Disillusioned by Italian Politics – They Watch
Closely the 1848 Revolution in France – Both are Ambivalent towards
the French Radical Reds: the Fourierists, Blanc, Proudhon, Ledru-
Rollin, Sand and Sue – Suppression of the Parisian Workers in June
of 1848 – RB Still Hopes for a Republic – EBB Looks to a Strong
Leader Such as Louis-Napoleon.

i

During the summer before their marriage, Robert and Elizabeth
began to consider a journey through France to Italy. At first Robert
preferred a sea-voyage to Italy because travel by water would be less
difficult for Elizabeth; however, a route across France gradually
became more attractive. In June, Elizabeth's Uncle Hedley and his

57

family came from Paris to London for a visit. They advised the
French route and urged a stay in Paris. Friends – Henry Chorley and
Anna Jameson – were planning summer excursion to Paris. By late
June, Elizabeth was beginning to think of a water route across
France – "the Seine, the Soane[*sic*], the Rhone" – to avoid jarring
and fatiguing travel by coach. In mid-July she sent Robert an advertisement clipped from the *Daily News* and asked him to "observe
that the land journey, or river-voyage, is very much cheaper than the
sea-voyage by the steamers. . . ." By the end of July Robert had
consulted maps and devised a rather uncertain itinerary:

I find by the first map, that from Nevers the Loire proceeds S.E.
till the *Arroux* joins it, and that just below it communicates with
the Canal du Centre, which runs N.E. from *Paray* to *Chagny* and
thence to Châlons sur Saône. It is a roundabout way, but not more
so than the post-road by Autun – the Canal must be there for
something, & in that case, you travel from Orleans to Leghorn by
water and with the least fatigue possible. I observe that steamboats
leave St. Katherine's Wharf every Thursday and Sunday morning
at 8 o'clock for Havre, Rouen & Paris – would that way be advis-
able? I will ascertain the facts about Nevers & Châlons by the time
we meet.[1]

The Brownings followed, in general, this itinerary, but they would
never discover the purpose of that canal that Robert thought "must
be there for something." Their first journey through France
together would call for several exhausting rides in the diligence along
provincial French roads.

Robert had successfully negotiated ferry, diligence and railway
timetables during his brief visit to Paris the previous October, and
he was confident of his skills as a traveller. Elizabeth had not been to
France since her childhood sojourn at Boulogne. Through her reading, however, Paris had become for her the focus of civilized life:
"Parisian rationalities and glories" and the city's active and varied
social and intellectual life led her to think of Paris as a city conducive
"to the fuller development of Imaginative and Reflective powers."[2]
Still, she did not wish to linger long in France during the wedding
journey. She thought they should "go quick, quick, & not stop
anwhere within hearing of England . . not stop at Havre, nor Rouen,

nor at Paris – *that* is how I decide.'[3] Robert agreed and wrote back that he "should hate to be seen at Paris by anybody a few days after our adventure. . . ."[4] His study of railway timetables convinced him that they could "reach Havre early in the morning and get to Paris by four o'clock, perhaps, in the afternoon . . . in time to leave for Orleans and spend the night there, I suppose."[5] He was too confident. An exhausting night-crossing from Southampton forced them to rest the day in Le Havre, from which they took the night-diligence to Rouen. That journey evokes something of the phantasmagoria of De Quincey's mailcoach ride, for Elizabeth remembered "now five horses, now seven . . . wild and loosely harnessed . . . some of them white, some brown, some black, with manes leaping . . . a fantastic scene it was in the moonlight."[6] Once they had arrived in Paris from Rouen by rail, Robert sought out Anna Jameson, who found Elizabeth "nervous, frightened, ashamed, agitated, happy, miserable."[7] The Brownings took apartments at Mrs. Jameson's Hôtel de la Ville de Paris, where they remained a week to rest and make plans to continue the journey to Pisa in company with Mrs. Jameson and her niece, Gerardine Bates.

Apparently much of the week in Paris was spent quietly at the hotel, resting and talking or "watching the stars rise above the high Paris houses. . . ."[8] But they went out to restaurants, and during the visit to the Louvre from their hotel in the rue de l'Évêque they would have seen something of the life of the boulevards, passing doubtlessly by l'Église de la Madeleine, the Place de la Concorde, and the Tuileries gardens and palace. Writing to Miss Mitford from Moulins a few days after leaving Paris, Elizabeth blamed Paris itself for her failure to write sooner:

You can understand now, ever dearest Miss Mitford, how the pause has come about writing. The week in Paris! Such a strange week it was, altogether like a vision. Whether in body or out of body I cannot tell scarcely. Our Balzac should be flattered beyond measure by my thinking of him at all. Which I did, but *you* more. I will write and tell you more about Paris. You should go there indeed. And to our hotel, if at all. Once we were at the Louvre, but we kept very still of course, and were satisfied with the *idea* of Paris. I could have borne to live there, it was all so strange and full of contrast. . . .[9]

Paris would become less strange during the Brownings' extended visits there in the 1850's, but their enthusiasm for the French capital never left them during their life together in Italy. Could Elizabeth "have borne to live there," especially through the winters, they hoped that Paris rather than Florence would be their home. Writing to Miss Mitford seven years later, in March of 1853, Elizabeth complained of the intellectual and literary dullness of Florence: ". . . we don't absolutely moulder here in intellect, only Robert has (but indeed I have too) tender recollections of 'that blaze of life in Paris,' and we both mean to go back to it presently. No place like Paris for living in. Here one sleeps, 'perchance to dream,' and praises the pillow."[10] The quiet and repose of Florence and Tuscany frequently contrast in Elizabeth's thoughts with "'that blaze of life in Paris.'" The pastoral calm and solitude of the Tuscan hills become the setting for the concluding books of her *Aurora Leigh* (1857). In her evocation of the colour and excitement of Paris, as first seen by Aurora, however, we catch something of Elizabeth's own delight:

> . . . the terraced streets,
> The glittering boulevards, the white colonnades
> Of fair fantastic Paris who wears trees
> Like plumes, as if man made them, spire and tower
> As if they had grown by nature, tossing up
> Her fountains in the sunshine of the squares,
> As if in beauty's game she tossed the dice,
> Or blew the silver-down-balls of her dreams
> To sew futurity with seeds of thought
> And count the passage of her festive hours.
>
> The city swims in verdure, beautiful
> As Venice on the waters, the sea-swan.
> What bosky gardens dropped in close-walled courts
> Like plums in ladies' laps who start and laugh:
> What miles of streets that run on after trees,
> Still carrying all the necessary shops,
> Those open caskets with the jewels seen!
> And trade is art, and art's philosophy,
> In Paris.[11]

The Brownings and Mrs. Jameson planned, as she told Lady Byron, to leave Paris on September 28 and go to Orléans via

Chartres, thence on to Bourges, to Lyon, and to Avignon, to catch a steamer from Marseille to Leghorn on October 4. The journey would take a week longer than planned; but, except for the visit to Chartres which would have required a ten-hour diligence ride from Chartres to Orléans, the party held to its itinerary. They left on Monday evening, the 28th, from the railway terminus in the Boulevard de l'Hôpital near the Jardin des Plantes and went directly to Orléans where they spent the day and night of the 29th. Mrs. Jameson and, presumably, Robert "wandered the streets of this old city";[12] Elizabeth rested at the hotel and read the first letters received since they had left London: congratulations and approval of the marriage came from, among others, John Kenyon, Miss Mitford, Carlyle, Barry Cornwall, and Monckton Milnes; there were also "very hard letters" from her brother George and her father, who thought she had married "for *genius* . . mere genius."[13] Two night-diligence rides, first to Bourges then to Roanne, caused, Elizabeth told her sisters, "a good deal of fatigue which has done me no essential harm. I am taken such care of; so pillowed by arms and knees. . . ."[14]

Even hardier travellers might have complained of fatigue from provincial French diligence rides in the 1840's. In his *Pictures from Italy* (1846), which Mrs. Jameson read during the trip, Dickens gives a lively description of this mode of travel: "the Diligence," he wrote of his journey to Chalon two years before, "with the dusty outsides in blue frocks, like butchers; and the insides in white nightcaps; and its cabriolet head on the roof, nodding and shaking like an idiot's head. . . ." Dickens saw the diligences two or three times a day as they passed his own private carriage; however, even "an English travelling-carriage of considerable proportions" such as Dickens' could be noisy, dusty, jolting and exhausting:

Crack, crack, crack, crack. Crack-crack-crack. Helo! Hola! Vite! Voleur! Brigand! Hi hi hi! En r-r-r-r-r-route! Whip, wheels, driver, stones, beggars, children, crack, crack, crack; helo! hola! charité pour l'amour de Dieu! crick-crack; round the corner, up the narrow street, down the paved hill on the other side; in the gutter; bump, bump; jolt, jog, crick, crick, crick; crack, crack, crack; into the shop-windows on the left-hand side of the street, preliminary to a sweeping turn into the wooden archway on the right; rumble, rumble, rumble; clatter, clatter, clatter; crick,

crick, crick; and here we are in the yard of the Hôtel de l'Ecu d'Or; used up, gone out, smoking, spent, exhausted. . . .[15]

Mrs. Jameson would complain from Avignon that Dickens had "so exagerated [*sic*]" some things in his account that she tended to "distrust him as a describer." In the same letter she provides her own description of the effect of the diligence rides upon Elizabeth: ". . . the suffering has been very great. Not only we have had to carry her fainting from the carriage but from her extreme thinness & weakness, every few hours journey has bruised her all over, till movement became almost unbearable."[16] Elizabeth was strong enough at Bourges to climb up and visit the Cathedral of St. Étienne. *Murray's Handbook* warned mid-century English travellers that Bourges was a city of "streets of dead walls"; however, the cathedral was recommended as "one of the finest in France," one of its chief attractions being "the quantity, excellence, and good preservation of the *painted glass* of windows of the choir and chapels."[17] Murray was confirmed when the party entered St. Étienne's and found, in Elizabeth's phrase, "all the sunsets of time had stained the wonderful painted windows."[18] At Roanne on the Friday, they planned the next day to "take the railroad to Lyons, and next day embark on the Rhone."[19] The Roanne-Lyon railway was the first constructed in France, and it still used horses rather than locomotives. Although "passenger trains traverse it in about 6 hours," it was "*not* recommended to English travellers" by Murray as late as 1854.[20] It is likely that the Brownings continued by diligence to Lyon; they fell yet another day behind in their schedule.

Lyon was then a city of nearly two hundred thousand people, the second city in France and the chief French manufacturing centre. Murray advised that there "are few more stately cities, in external aspect, in striking situation, seated as it is on two great rivers, the Rhône and the Saône, or in the lively air of bustle and commerce diffused through its interior."[21] Dickens, who had come with his carriage on a steamboat from Chalon, thought "Every manufacturing town, melted into one, would hardly convey an impression of Lyons as it presented itself to me: for all the undrained, unscavengered qualities of a foreign town, seemed grafted, there, upon the native miseries of a manufacturing one. . . ." Both Murray and Dickens warn the English traveller about "all the little streets whose name is legion" that led away from the quais up the steep hillsides.[22] "The interior is one stack of lofty houses, penetrated by lanes so excessively narrow and nasty," cautions Murray, "as not to be traversed without disgust."[23] Dickens seems to have ventured away from the more fashionable boulevards along the quais, and he was disgusted by

> houses, high and vast, dirty to excess, rotten as old cheeses, and as thickly peopled. All up the hills that hem the city in, these houses swarm; and the mites inside were lolling out of the windows, and drying their ragged clothes on poles, and crawling in and out at the doors, and coming out to pant and gasp upon the pavement, and creeping in and out among huge piles and bales of fusty, musty, stifling goods; and living, or rather not dying till time should come, in an exhausted receiver.[24]

Perhaps it is just as well that we do not know what the Brownings thought of Lyon. They must have spent at least the day of October 5 there before boarding, early on the morning of October 6, one of the "steamboats [which] profess to descend to Avignon in 7 hours. . . ."[25]

The voyage down the Rhône must have been very disappointing. The vineyards, olive groves, villages, ruined castles clinging to the slopes and heights, the Alps in the distance and, above Avignon, Petrarch's Mont Ventoux, all should have been seen through what Murray called "the superior transparency of a southern atmosphere. . . ."[26] That scenery on a sunny July day led Dickens to one of his few lyric paragraphs as he forgot the "very dirty vessel full of merchandise" and described "the noble river, bringing at every winding turn, new beauties into view."[27] The Brownings had to watch from the windows of the "hot crowded cabin" of what Mrs. Jameson called "a dirty confined steamboat, the rain pouring in torrents."[28] After eleven hours they disembarked above the old broken bridge outside the walls about a mile from the Hôtel de l'Europe in the centre of Avignon. It would have been dusk by then; and, like other steamboat passengers, they probably found themselves "in the hands of the *porters* of Avignon, who are a notoriously brutal set, whose exactions and insolence ought to be repressed by the police."[29] The next day the weather cleared: they were "in the *South* here, olive trees, figs, vines at every step; the silk harvest going on, groves of mulberries. . . ."[30] While Elizabeth rested at the hotel, Robert and Mrs. Jameson visited the Palace of the Popes, then given over largely to a prison and barracks. They saw the old woman who had pointed out to Dickens the various horrors of the rooms used by the Inquisition. To Dickens the woman was a She-Goblin who "shrieked as if she were on the rack herself; and had a mysterious, hag-like way with her forefinger, when approaching the remains of some new horror. . . ."[31] To Lady Byron Mrs. Jameson complained that Dickens saw things "under so peculiar an aspect"; she and Browning had seen only a "poor consumptive woman."[32]

The following day the entire party, including Elizabeth's spaniel, Flush, made an excursion to Vaucluse to honour the memory of Petrarch. They walked out of the village along the Sorgues to the Fountain of Vaucluse. Normally at this time of year "the exquisitely limpid waters are dried up near the head . . . and instead of bursting out exuberantly from the cavern, filtrate underground, and issue out, some hundred yards lower down . . ."[33] Mrs. Jameson found the "scenery more *savage* and barren" than she had expected. The recent rains, however, had made "the fountain a most tumultuous torrent."[34] It was here that the "most celebrated episode of the wedding trip took place," as Gardner Taplin, the most restrained of Elizabeth's biographers, says.[35] A less restrained Frances Winwar presents the episode through the eyes of young Gerardine Bates and Flush:

> There at the source of those *dolci acque* which the Italian poet had sung, she saw Browning take up his wife in his arms and, wading through the shallow waters, seat her upon a rock in the middle of the stream. From the bank Flush watched apprehensively. Seeing his mistress in peril of death, he gallantly plunged, determined to rescue her, and was laughingly baptized in the name of Petrarch. Life glowed with adventure for the happy pair.[36]

Virginia Woolf, in her biography of Flush, held the point of view more rigorously canine:

> At last the light broadened; the rattling stopped. He heard birds singing and the sigh of trees in the wind. Or was it the rush of water? Opening his eyes at last, he saw – the most astonishing sight conceivable. There was Miss Barrett on a rock in the midst of rushing waters. Trees bent over her; the river raced around her.

She must be in peril. With one bound Flush splashed through the
stream and reached her.[37]

Back at the Hôtel de l'Europe the next morning, Mrs. Jameson
wrote rather drily to Lady Byron: "We were at the Vaucluse yesterday of which I spare you all description at present. . . . On the
whole a very pleasant day. . . . E. B. is tolerably well this morning. . . ."[38]

Late on October 9 or early on the 10th, they left Avignon by
diligence for Aix and were in Marseille in time to board the coastal
steamer *L'Océan* late on the "Burning, glaring afternoon" of
October 11. Dickens had found Marseille "a dirty and disagreeable
place . . . a compound of vile smells perpetually arising from a
great harbour full of stagnant water, and befouled by the refuse of
innumerable ships with all sorts of cargoes: which, in hot weather, is
dreadful to the last degree."[39] As so often, Murray echoes Dickens:
"the port becomes the sewer of the city, and is offensive from filth
which, flowing into it, is allowed to stagnate in its tideless sea."[40]
The Brownings only passed through Marseille on the way to the
port, but Elizabeth retained a rather sharp memory of it when nine
years later she wrote to her brother Alfred who was in Marseille,
perhaps on War Office business connected with shipment of troops
and *matériel* to the Crimea: "Do you like Marseilles? I only know it
by passing through. It's fashionable not to like it. But I like the very
scenery, . . that wild, rugged, desolate, stretchy landscape & the
picturesque, coloured population – Still, as a residence, the agree-
ableness may be left in doubt."[41] Sailing out of the harbour of
Marseille and along the coast, they sat "upon the deck . . . and had a
vision of mountains, six or seven deep, one behind the other."[42]
They were soon in Pisa.

ii

The Brownings would not return to France for five years. After the
winter in Pisa, they settled in Florence where the apartment in Casa
Guidi became "a residence, that is, a *pied à terre* – in Italy, all but
free when we wish to use it; and when we care to let it, producing
eight or ten pounds a month in help of travelling expenses."[43] During those years France and things French were much in their

thoughts and became a constant source of comparison to the life around them in Italy. Barbara Melchiori has recently argued that there has been a mistaken emphasis upon Browning's life in Italy: the "Italy which really mattered to Browning," she says rightly, "was the Italy he found in his library, the Italy of the past."[44] For both Brownings, the measure of the contemporary world was in France. It offered those modern "French fountains of living literature"; its politics and political theories were to be followed and carefully studied; it had a capital which, as Elizabeth said, "combines so much . . . one lives there in the midst of brilliant civilization. . . ."[45] But the Brownings were initially pleased with Pisa. After the arduous journey across France, Elizabeth found Pisa restful and peaceful, qualities she would always associate with Italy: "Oh, it is so beautiful and so full of repose, yet not *desolate*: it is rather the repose of sleep than of death." But repose could be something else; Pisa had, Elizabeth admitted, "its dulnesses."[46]

The difficulty of getting contemporary French books contributed to the dullness, as did the almost total vacuum of interesting contemporary Italian literature. Perhaps Elizabeth did not quite expect to find "a literary and artistic renaissance" in Italy, as Gardner Taplin suggests.[47] However, both she and Robert had a strong preference for the realistic novel, then so rich a genre in France. G. M. Carsaniga in "Realism in Italy" describes the literary poverty of Italy in the middle of the nineteenth century in this way:

> The tendency was, then, for Italian writers to form a restricted, elitist caste of intellectuals, using an artificial language, cut off from the rest of the population and therefore insensitive to their needs. Deprived of the rich cultural nourishment provided by a broadly based audience drawn from every level of society, they were faced with a limited number of options. They could pretend that their small *coterie* of intellectuals represented the whole of the society; or they could turn elsewhere – to the past, or to foreign cultures – for stimulation. . . .[48]

The effect of this condition, Carsaniga says, was a literature marked by "extreme inbreeding and parochialism, but also overdependence on cultural imports from abroad. . . ." It is not surprising then to find the Brownings, a month after their arrival in Pisa, "yawning over the dreary state of Italian fiction."[49]

Elizabeth's account of a November evening in their apartment at Collegio Ferdinando captures quite well the cultural milieu described by Carsaniga. Professor Ferucci, who had arranged for them to use the university library, came to call and found them "reading, sighing, yawning over" *Niccolò dé Lapi*, a novel by Massimo d'Azeglio, Manzoni's son-in-law, published at Milan in 1841. Ferucci, who insisted on speaking French, pronounced the novel "'excellent, très beau.'" Elizabeth declared the book "the dullest, heaviest, stupidest, lengthiest." Manzoni himself was but an imitator of Scott; and for his son-in-law to then imitate him, Elizabeth thought, compounded the dullness. Not wishing "to offend the Professor's literary and national susceptibilities," and in his "zeal for Italy," Robert defended d'Azeglio and apparently even compared him favourably to Eugène Sue. After Ferucci's departure, Robert took up *Niccolò dé Lapi* again, but "the dullness grew too strong for even his benevolence, and the yawning catastrophe . . . overthrew him."[50] The booklist from the local subscription library offered little relief. It was, rather, "a most melancholy insight into the actual literature of Italy. Translations, translations, translations from third and fourth and fifth rate French and English writers, chiefly French; the roots of thought, here in Italy, seem dead to the ground. It is well that they have great memories – nothing else lives".[51] (She adds, perhaps a bit enviously, 'Dickens is going to Paris for the winter. . . .") By mid-December they had read more, but the charge still holds: "What is purely Italian is, as far as we have read, purely dull and conventional. There is no breath or pulse in the Italian genius."[52] The Italian winters were, perhaps, superior to those of Paris: but as she told her sister Arabel, the Italians "have the sun, and no light."[53] In their search for recent fiction, the Brownings were thrown "back on the memory of Balzac with reiterated groans."[54]

By February they had discovered another subscription library with a "tolerable supply of French books . . . though Balzac appears very imperfectly. . . ." Elizabeth intended to dun the library for Balzac's recently published "Instruction Criminelle," for she was particularly eager to find out how Balzac would treat the character of Lucien Chardon (*dit* de Rubempré). Elizabeth had analysed at length the "poor 'femmelette'" Lucien in a letter to Miss Mitford in 1844. Now she wished to discover whether Balzac "discharges"

Lucien "as a 'forçat' [yet] neither man nor woman – and true poet, least of all."[55] A bit of the publishing history of *Une Instruction criminelle* may reflect something of the difficulties the Brownings encountered in their attempt to keep up with Balzac. Lucien de Rubempré is an important character, but he appears significantly only in two of Balzac's completed novels: first in *Illusions perdues* (1837), then in *Splendeurs et misères des courtisanes* (December, 1846). Robert probably read *Illusions perdues* soon after its publication; Elizabeth read it very carefully in 1844. Between 1838 and December of 1846 Balzac published, in various forms, parts of the long fiction which would become *Splendeurs et misères des courtisanes*. The Brownings could, for example, have followed some of Lucien's adventures in *Esther, ou les Amours d'un vieux banquier* published as a *feuilleton* in *Le Parisien*, May 21 – July 1, 1843. What Elizabeth refers to as "Instruction Criminelle" became the third part of *Splendeurs et misères* in December, 1846, under the title "Ou mènent les mauvais chemins." Under the title *Une Instruction criminelle* it had run as a *feuilleton* in *L'Époque* in July of 1846. In effect, the Brownings were trying to find the Parisian newspaper version, or perhaps a pirated Belgian version of a part of a novel, when the entire novel had been published a month or two before. The problems of keeping up with Balzac increased. By the summer of 1848, Elizabeth urged Miss Mitford to send "the list of Balzac, *after* 'Les Miseres de la Vie Conjugale,' I mean. I left him in the midst of 'la Femme de Soixante Ans.' " The latter had been published in August of 1846, the former in 1845. "When Robert and I are ambitious," Elizabeth continues, "we talk of buying Balzac in full some day, to put him in our bookcase from the convent, if the carved-wood angels, infants and serpents, should not finish mouldering away in horror at the touch of him."[56] Robert would transfer this dream to his Bishop Blougram, who thinks of fitting out his ideal "cabin of life" so that

All Balzac's novels occupy one shelf,
The new edition fifty volumes long. . . .

The urbane Bishop is thinking of the 1855 Houssiaux edition. In the late 1840's and in Italy, the Brownings were falling behind: "Balzac is six or seven works deep from us," Elizabeth complains to Mrs. Jameson in July of 1848.[57] They were fortunate that in March of

1850 Robert had "exhumed" in Florence a three-year-old copy of *Le Cousin Pons*.[58]

Balzac clearly was the Brownings' favourite author during this period, but Elizabeth's letters reveal somewhat less clearly the grounds for their admiration. Her comments on Balzac normally occur in the context of discussion of a number of contemporary writers, and he becomes the assumed standard against whom others – with the exception, for Elizabeth, of George Sand – are to be measured. Miss Mitford was the correspondent most favoured with accounts of the Brownings' literary discussions or "great wars," as Elizabeth called them. With the library subscription that first winter in Pisa came a daily copy of *Le Siècle*, in which Frédéric Soulié was then publishing a *roman-feuilleton, Saturnin Fichet*. Robert had started it, but had left Elizabeth to persevere alone. She soon found it, with its crowd of indifferent characters and familiar *doppelgänger* motif, "deplorably dull." This was the letter in which she announced to Miss Mitford "Robert is a warm admirer of Balzac and has read most of his books, but certainly – oh certainly – he does not in a general way appreciate our French people quite with our warmth. . . ." Elizabeth was good-naturedly aware that she could tolerate almost any French novel so long as it contained an interesting character or an exciting plot. She upheld the virtues of Dumas, Soulié, and Sue. Robert, though "properly possessed" by Sue's *Les Mystères de Paris*, dissented.

Sue's *Mystères*, of course, had plenty of story. Hardly a chapter goes by without the introduction of some new intrigue by the Countess MacGregor, the Screech-Owl and the Schoolmaster, or the infamous Dr. Polidori; numerous disguises and intricate counterplots are necessary if M. Rudolph is to foil such wickedness. Frequent and prolonged flashbacks are necessary to explain the presence – and the extraordinary loyalty to our hero – of Mrs. George, the faithful Murphy, the black physician David. The episodic plot formed by coincidence, intercepted letters, overheard conversations, must also be interrupted to account for Rudolph's mastery of all the manly arts or his fluency in the argot of Parisian criminals. When the crippled Hoppy is lessoned in that argot, however, we have something more than a "story for a story's sake": we have virtual disquisition on the nature of the secret language of the French criminal classes. Such digressions abound and are rivalled by excessive if conventional description of life high and low. There are also the periodic returns to the pastoral world of Rudolph's model farm where the reader, along with the by now terrified and blinded Schoolmaster, must listen to lengthy discourse by honest old Père Châtelain on the economic and social organization of utopian agriculture. Sue has turned his sensational *roman* into an anatomy which ranges widely if unrealistically over contemporary French life. Perhaps for that reason, both Robert and Elizabeth placed Sue above other sensational novelists, though well below Balzac. Sue rivals Balzac in the abundance of his fictional world. Such abundance may have been in Robert's mind when he commented that, in comparison to Balzac, there was an "undeveloped" quality to *Le Rouge et le noir*, a novel he and Elizabeth were now reading together.[59]

In 1838 in his first recorded comment on Balzac, Robert was attracted to the long opening *mise en scène* of *Béatrix* and would remember it vividly thirty years later when he visited the novel's setting in Brittany; but once Balzac had finally moved on to the plot, "the story of Guérande in Bretagne," Robert thought "the going on of it all is naught."[60] He would make a similar complaint about George Eliot's *Romola* when the author turned, in the third volume, from the "minutenesses" carefully detailing the setting in historical Florence to her hero and plot.[61] This preference for descriptive detail and novelistic material nearly extraneous to plot may further explain why the Brownings regretted Balzac's attempts at drama, for which Elizabeth said "he has no faculty whatever. In fact, the faculty he has is the very reverse of the dramatic, ordinarily understood."[62] It was in his novels, not his plays, that Balzac explored "the great garden of life . . . absolutely and exactly in the guise of the great garden of France, a subject vast and comprehensive," as another novelist who failed as a playwright, Henry James, would say.[63] Elizabeth especially regretted that the scarcity of Balzac's novels in Italy limited her access to his world. "Isn't it hard on us?" she complained after three years there, "Exiles from Balzac!"[64]

The exclamation marks and diction in Elizabeth's complaints that in Italy they were as on "a desert island so far as modern books go"[65] may suggest to the modern ear a tone excessively serious and inflated. Normally the tone is playful and humorous. But for her, and to a lesser extent for Robert, access to French books and newspapers was of great importance: they were the means by which the

Brownings could "look through a loophole at the world."[66] In *Le Siècle*, *La Presse*, or Galignani's *Messenger* – published in Paris – they could read the latest *feuilletons*, the reviews and announcements of new books, or literary gossip about Dumas or Sand or even about themselves. In *La Presse* they read with amusement an article which "mentioned with regret" Elizabeth's blindness.[67] The printed gossip supplemented that of visitors like Margaret Fuller, who reported on her return from Paris that George Sand was a " 'magnificent creature' " but that her *soirée* was " 'full of rubbish' "; or that Balzac, a lion whom Miss Fuller did not find, "went into the world scarcely at all, frequenting low cafes, so that it was difficult to track him out."[68] Elizabeth believed neither charge. They tried to keep up on George Sand: Robert was "in an enthusiasm about" *André*; Elizabeth could not find a copy of *Lucrézia*. "Blessed is the man," she writes characteristically in this letter, "who reads Balzac, or even Dumas."[69] They passed the time, while awaiting Dumas' new novel, re-reading *Le Comte de Monte-Cristo*. While on holiday at Siena they were happy to find a rather good subscription library, "though Dumas fils seems to fill up many of the interstices where you think you have found something."[70] It was necessary to fall back on – "see how *arrière* we are in French literature" – Charles de Bernard's *Gentilhomme campagnard* or Chateaubriand's *Mémoires d'outre-tombe*, which turned out to be "curiously uninteresting," written as it were about his "youth with a grey goose quill . . . he must have more to tell than he tells."[71]

By the spring of 1848 the "new French revolution" had begun to compete with the French novelists for the Brownings' interest. The blending of fictional art with contemporary politics and social conditions was a marked feature of the writers whom the Brownings most admired: Balzac, Sand, Stendhal. It was against the background of their reading of the realistic novelists and the novels of more popular novelists – Sue, Soulié, Karr – that, stimulated by the events of 1848, they began a closer study of French politics and political and social theory. On May 1, 1848, Elizabeth wrote an eloquent letter to their benefactor John Kenyon in which she moves from a defence against the charge that she and Robert sympathize with the French communists to a description of how important a part the novelists have played in forming her love of France:

Do you know how I love France and the French? Robert laughs at me for the mania of it, or used to long before this revolution.

When I was a prisoner, my other mania for imaginative literature used to be ministered to through the prison bars by Balzac, George Sand, and the like immortal improprieties. They kept the colour in my life to some degree and did good service . . . through reading the books I grew to love France, in a mania too . . . yes, and am guilty of thinking more of Paris than of Lombardy itself, and try to understand financial difficulties and social theories with the best will in the world. . . .[72]

Apart from the vast panorama of French life in their favourite Balzac, scores of novels displayed, with increasing obviousness, interest in social and political conditions and in various reformist theories. Even as early as *Notre-Dame de Paris* (1830) Hugo had infused his historical romance with anti-clericalism and broad humanitarianism which he had begun in *Le Dernier Jour d'un condamné* (1829) and continued in *Claude Gueux* (1834). In 1834 George Sand's *André*, for which Robert expressed enthusiasm, broadened the pleas for sexual freedom in *Indiana* (1832) and *Lélia* (1833) to include the symbolic marriage between the poor and the rich, the Venetian flower-girl and her noble lover. By 1837 Sand's admirable character in *Mauprat*, Patience, advises Bernard: "Follow my advice . . . Love the people; hate those who hate the people . . . make yourself the friend of the people."[73] The social message of Sand became more insistent in *Le Compagnon du Tour de France* (1840), *Consuelo* (1842), *Le Comtesse de Rudolstadt* (1843) and *Le Meunier d'Angibault* (1844). Often in these novels Sand, who had scorned the restrictions of marriage, arranges her plot so that marriage between members of estranged social classes becomes, at least symbolically, a panacea for social and economic injustice. Elizabeth would adopt and adapt the convention in her *Aurora Leigh*.

Another favourite, Eugène Sue, had in the early 1840's turned from dandyism to sensationally document the lives of the lower and criminal classes in his *Les Mystères de Paris* (1842–43). Elizabeth's attitude towards the progress of Sue's career during the 1840's reflects something of both Brownings' attitudes towards the relationship between imaginative literature and immediate social and political issues and especially reformist theory. Robert's own work had, with some important exceptions, quite studiously avoided overt or direct comment on contemporary issues. One of the important exceptions would be the only work he produced during this first

Italian sojourn: *Christmas Eve and Easter Day*, an analysis of contemporary religious practice, written in a mode Donald Smalley calls
"stark realism".[74] Elizabeth's major work during these years was her
hymn to Italian freedom, *Casa Guidi Windows*. She had, earlier,
drawn upon documentary reports of labour conditions for her "Cry
of the Children." Both she and Robert had greatly admired Sue's
documentation of the suffering of impoverished Parisian working
classes in *Les Mystères*. But in *Les Sept Péchés capitaux* (1847–48) and
Les Mystères du peuple (1849–56), Sue's didactic message began
to crowd his documentary art. His *romans–feuilletons* became
propagandist tracts.

Unable to get any new work by Sue and others, Elizabeth won-
dered in 1849 if Sue and other writers had been "struck dumb by the
revolution." "Do you mean," she asks Miss Mitford, "that they
have left off writing – those French writers – or that they have tired
you out with writing that looks faint beside the rush of facts, as the
range of French politics show those? Has not Eugène Sue been
illustrating the passions? Somebody told me so."[75] Not until 1850
did she read Sue's *Les Sept Péchés* – at about the same time she had
heard of Balzac's death. The death of "one of the greatest and (most)
original writers of the age" saddened the Brownings. Sue, however,
drew Elizabeth's ire because he had died creatively: "Indeed, there
seems to be fatality just now with the writers of France. Soulié,
Bernard, gone too; George Sand translating Mazzini; Sue in a
socialistic state of decadence – what he means by writing such trash
as the 'Péchés' I really can't make out; only Alexandre Dumas keeping his head up gallantly. . . ."[76] Only Dumas, with his *Vingt Ans
après* (1845), *Fronde* (1848), *Les Quarante-cinq* (1848) and other historical romances of intrigue and escape, *l'action et l'amour*, kept the
artist's head above contemporary politics. A year earlier Elizabeth
had feared that George Sand was "probably writing 'banners' for the
'Reds,' which, considering the state of parties in France, does not
really give me a higher opinion of her intelligence or virtue."[77] Now
Sand was translating Mazzini. A couple of months later, with Sue's
"Les Enfants de l'Amour" before her, Elizabeth found the earlier
favourite novelist "in decided decadence . . . since he has taken to
illustrating Socialism!"[78]

73

iii

This anger and exasperation with Sue for "illustrating Socialism" carries a double emphasis: Sue has compounded the sin of didacticism by preaching or "illustrating" the wrong doctrine. From Florence the Brownings closely followed the progress of the "new French revolution" from early March of 1848 onwards. By 1850 the socialist doctrine of Sue, of Louis Blanc and the Fourierists was, for Elizabeth, "the most desecrating and dishonouring to humanity of all creeds." With self-conscious exaggeration she announced to Miss Mitford that she would rather "live under the absolutism of Nicholas of Russia than in a Fourier machine, with my individuality sucked out of me by a social airpump."[79] It is worthwhile, I think, for a number of reasons, to follow in some detail the Brownings' intensified interest in politics during these years. Most important, in Elizabeth's correspondence during 1848–50 unfolds an articulate and thoughtful set of political attitudes informed by knowledge of political events and political theory. Further, Robert – about whose political ideas we know so little – did, I believe, share many of his wife's attitudes. Also, neither of the Brownings ever really changed the political attitudes they formulated during these years. Finally, it was the French political arena – not the Italian – which most intensely formed their attitudes. Because commentators have so often stressed the importance of Italian politics in their life, it is perhaps best to begin with this latter point.

The first important political event the Brownings witnessed in Italy occurred on their first wedding anniversary, September 12, 1847, when the Florentines celebrated with colourful pageantry the Grand Duke's establishment of a *consulta* and a Tuscan civic guard. For three hours the Brownings watched the procession, and in the evening they walked to the Arno to see the illuminations and the festive, patriotic scenes which Elizabeth would describe in the first part of *Casa Guidi Windows*. "The people were embracing for joy. It was a state of phrensy and rapture, extending to the children of two years old," Elizabeth wrote to her sister Henrietta the next day, "several of whom I heard lisping *vivas* . . ."[80] A bit later, Robert, watching the newly constituted and brightly uniformed civic guard parade about the streets, remarked: "Surely, after all this, they would *use* those muskets? It's a problem, a 'grand peut-être.' "[81]

Robert's slight sarcasm at the Tuscan love of pageantry but lack of serious political intent was soon adopted by Elizabeth. In early February, 1848, the Grand Duke granted a constitution, and by March the rising in Milan bred hopes that Tuscany like Lombardy might try to throw off the Austrian authority. Florence did not rise, and Elizabeth's interest began to flag. Elizabeth was already "guilty of thinking far more of Paris than of Lombardy itself." By October she explains how it is that she and Robert have grown "gradually cooler and cooler on the subject of Italian patriotism, valour, and good sense. . . ." The Tuscan revolution was turning into comic opera: "Every now and then a day is fixed for a revolution in Tuscany, but up to the present time a shower has come and put it off. Two Sundays ago Florence was to have been 'sacked' by Leghorn, when a drizzle came and saved us."[82] Eventually the Leghornese did invade and drive the Grand Duke into temporary exile at Gaeta, but by the spring of 1849 a counter-revolution had returned the Duke and the Austrian troops. Having become "altogether *blasée* about revolutions and invasions," Elizabeth sharpened her sarcasm: "The counter-revolution was strictly *counter*, observe. I mean that if the Leghornese troops here had paid their debts at the Florentine coffee houses, the Florentines would have let their beloved Grand Duke stay at Gaeta to the end of the world."[83] She was impatient with "revolutions made by boys and *vivas*, and unmade by boys and *vivas*."[84] The Tuscans, she came to feel, lacked not only patriotism but a steadfast manliness necessary for effective political action: "The people are gentle, courteous, refined, and tender-hearted. What Balzac would call 'femmelette.' All Tuscany is 'Lucien' himself."[85]

Fortunately for their political education the Brownings could watch other revolutions than the comic-operetta one in progress at Florence that they could watch, as it were, from the balcony at Casa Guidi. The one being staged by the "dear heroic French" had to be followed through the newspapers and journals. Although they often received *Le Siècle*, *La Presse* and occasionally *The Times* at Casa Guidi, the other papers – especially any ephemeral revolutionary ones – had to be seen at the reading room of Galignani's or Vieusseux's, both of which refused to admit women. As a result Elizabeth, as she complained, could "read only the newspapers through Robert's eyes." At first he apparently provided rather full accounts of what he read: "Every morning as Robert goes to the post and to look at the newspapers, I say 'Bring me back news of a revolution!' And generally he brings me back news of two! Since the creation there never was such a succession of moral earthquakes." But Robert also could, as the confusion and turmoil in France continued, gruffly but still good-naturedly refuse to regurgitate the latest news; at such times Elizabeth felt "suspended over a hiatus" in information about the progress of events in Paris, as she questioned and he replied brusquely: "M. Thiers speech – 'Thiers is a rascal; I make a point of not reading one word said by M. Thiers.' M. Prudhon [*sic*] – 'Prudhon is a madman; who cares for Prudhon?' The President – 'The President is an ass; he is not worth thinking of.' "[86] This spirited exchange between Robert back from the reading room and Elizabeth anxious for news should not be taken as evidence that Robert deliberately ignored the "moral earthquakes" rumbling in Paris. He would continue, it is true, to think President Louis-Napoleon an ass, but he watched the man's career closely; and he would soon write a brief but incisive commentary on the ideas of M. Proudhon.

So in the newspapers that came to Florence, towards whose political events the Brownings had "cooled," they watched with serious interest the events in France, where "there is every noble aspiration, there are men of splendid talents and virtues. . . ." Instead of festive illuminations as in Florence, in Paris "the ideas go up like rockets, and, in the midst of our acclamation and admiration, drop down in ashes."[87] Some of those ideas – those they admired and those they rejected – are revealed in a letter Elizabeth wrote less than two weeks after the Republic had been declared on February 24, 1848. She approved the abolition of hereditary titles: "Let the notion of privileged orders perish, as it ought." The granting by the state of titles in recognition of distinctive service, however, should be retained. The right of equal opportunity for all to advance according to their talents and industry should be encouraged; however, the goal of total equality Elizabeth thought impractical, "absurd and iniquitous." "Every man should have the right of climbing – ", she thought, "but to say that every man should equally climb, (because the right is equal) is a wrong against the strong and industrious." The new government's confiscation of the Orleans' properties seems "unhappy and unworthy"; but, then, whatever "touches upon

property is wrong." Elizabeth ends this section of the letter by saying that "Robert and I agree nearly on all these points, but here and
there we have plenty of room for battles."[88] The disagreements –
"domestic 'émeutes,'" she would call them later – turned largely on
Elizabeth's early disillusionment with the Republic and her desire to
see more forceful leadership in the person of Louis-Napoleon. That
was a battle which would continue through their married life and
indeed after Elizabeth's death. But there does seem to be a great deal
on which they did agree.

As Republicans "by profession," both Robert and Elizabeth were
made anxious by many of the proposals being put forward by "the
theorists in Paris." Among the theorists was Louis Blanc, who had
been put in charge of a committee to organize public employment in
ateliers nationaux along the lines he had advocated in his pamphlet
L'Organisation du travail (1839). What workshops were set up did not
follow very closely Blanc's ideas and became little more than places
where the unemployed could register for the dole or be harangued
by Blanc. But in April in Florence the Brownings did not know
that, and they associated Blanc's ideas with a part of "communism"
they did not approve. "As to communism," Elizabeth wrote to Miss
Mitford, "surely the practical part of *that* . . . is attainable simply by
the consent of individuals who may try the experiment of associating
their families in order to [gain] the cheaper employment of the
means of life, and successfully in many cases." What they approved,
then, was voluntary association for both production and consump-
tion. What they disapproved and feared was a "government scheme"
which would "trench on individual liberty." This is a refinement of
their basic principle of the *right* of equal opportunity but distrust of
imposed total equality. They thought that "patriarchal planning in a
government" would lead to an "absolutism" which they felt was
appropriate only to societies still in a state of barbarism. France
represented to the Brownings the most advanced state of civilization;
so it was there that individual freedom should be greatest: "Liberty
and civilization when married together lawfully rather evolve individuality than tend to generalisation." When he advocates "generalisation" or equality imposed by government, "Louis Blanc knows
not what he says." Impractical utopian dreams hold a further danger
because such "mad theories promising the impossible may, in turn,
make the people mad" and lead to even greater social disorder.[89]

The Brownings watched the events in France with a greater seriousness than they viewed the political histrionics of Florence. To be sure, some of those on the scene in Paris thought the French, too, were being theatrical. Proudhon, alluding to the revolutions of 1792 and 1830, wrote privately the day after Louis-Philippe's abdication: "Drunk on historical novels, we have given a repeat performance of the 10th of August and the 29th of July. Without noticing it, we have all become characters in some farce."[90] The apparent confusion between literature and life also suggested itself to de Tocqueville, who confided to his journal: "Our French, especially in Paris, freely blend recollections of literature and the theatre with the most serious events."[91] This blending of literature and politics was perhaps natural and appropriate for a state of affairs in which Hugo, de Vigny, Karr, Sue and even Balzac stood for election to the assembly. The poet Lamartine became Foreign Minister in the provisional government; and George Sand, as Elizabeth would say later, was "writing 'banners' for the 'Reds'" and had become "Ledru-Rollin's *confidante* and councillor."[92] Elizabeth would eventually become disillusioned by Lamartine's indecisiveness; but in her April 15, 1848, letter to Miss Mitford, she thought Lamartine's actions had refuted Miss Mitford's habitual charge that poets were weak and impractical like Balzac's Lucien de Rubempré. "Lamartine," she says, "has surely acted down the fallacy of the impractical tendencies of imaginative men."[93]

The Brownings probably were not immediately aware that George Sand was the anonymous author of numerous pamphlets and essays defending the communist and socialist programmes. Many of these, like her April 15 call for a workers' insurrection should the elections favour the moderates, appeared first in the *Bulletin de la République*, the semi-official newspaper published by the Minister of the Interior, Ledru-Rollin. Sand's own definition of communism may help to focus the Brownings' attitude. Retreating a bit from her call of April 15 to people to mount the barricades, in *La Vraie République* Sand addressed her more moderate opponents in this manner:

> If by Communism you mean a plot to sieze dictatorship-by-force, as was said on April 16, then, assuredly, we were not Communists. . . . But if by Communism you mean the wish and determination to use every legitimate means which the public conscience has seen fit to place at our disposal in order to destroy here and

now the revolting inequality of extreme wealth and extreme poverty, and to establish the beginnings of a true equality, then we are
Communists indeed. . . ."[94]

Such statements as these, extracted or summarized in other papers
and apparently emanating from the Ministry of the Interior, would
lead the Brownings to fear for the Republic and believe that
"Ledru-Rollin is more a tyrant, (as far as he dares) than ever was
Louis-Philippe." During the first two months the provisional government ruled, trade and manufacturing had seriously declined and
the numbers of unemployed in Paris grew to nearly 300,000. Whip-
ped up by Blanc and Sand and promised by Ledru-Rollin "legislation, for the sake of one class," the workers had become a threat to
all public order. By late April, Elizabeth wrote to her sister Henrietta that if the new government "went on in their present way of
governing, there would be an end of – not only trade and peace, but
art and literature – and for my part, I would rather live on bread and
water than see such a state of things."[95]
On May 1 Elizabeth wrote to John Kenyon a careful, full, and
thoughtfully frank letter, which articulates many of the basic political beliefs of the Brownings; and it is the kind of letter Henry James
must have had in mind when he praised Elizabeth's letters for their
"nameless intellectual, if it be not rather a moral, grace – a vibration
never suggesting 'manner,' as often in her verse."[96] She begins by
chiding wittily both herself and his "anti-Chartist magistracy"
Kenyon for having allowed their correspondence to dwindle to "dry
little notes, as short as so many proclamations"; she then rounds off
her lengthy discussion of French politics by returning to the subject
of the Chartists. She cannot understand why Kenyon should sing a
"hymn of triumph" because the English Chartists have failed to
follow the rest of Europe into revolution: "Are we to blow the trumpet because we respect the ruts while everywhere else they are mend-
ing the roads?" she asks. "As to the Chartists, it is only a pity in my
mind that you have not more of them. That's their fault. Mine, you
will say, is being pert about politics. . . ." Something of the
"grace," to use James' word, of Elizabeth's style and thought, lies in
the emphasis in the short sentence – *"That's* their *fault."* The weakness of the Chartists lies in their diminished numbers, not in their
just demands. Then, by shifting the emphasis to the pronoun in the

next sentence – "*Mine*, you will say" – she gracefully withdraws from the impertinence of speaking so forcefully about politics.

She had begun the allusion to the Chartists by way of apology for the lapse in their correspondence, a lapse which has come about because "the world has turned over on its other side, in order, one must hope, to [have] some happy change in the dream." In this metaphor the world still sleeps but the revolutionary turmoil of the past two months at least holds hope of a happier "dream." She admits that she "was never much celebrated for acumen on political economy," but during the past few months she has been trying to "understand financial difficulties and social theories with the best will in the world." In answer to the question being asked in England whether "Robert and I are communists," she replies that they have not yet embraced that doctrine as "'a vérité sociale.'"

For we really are not communists, farther than to admit the wisdom of voluntary association in matters of material life among the poorer classes. And to legislate even on such points seems as objectionable as possible; all intermeddlings of government with domesticities, from Lacedaemon to Peru, were and must be objectionable; and the growth of absolutism, let us theorise as we please. I would have the government educate the people absolutely, and *then* give room for the individual to develop himself into life freely. Nothing can be more hateful to me than this communist idea of quenching individualities in the mass. As if the hope of the world did not always consist in the eliciting of the individual man from the background of the masses, in the evolvement of individual genius, virtue, magnanimity.[97]

Voluntary association, government limited to education, the individual free to develop himself: those are their principles. "This seems a very tame liberalism nowadays, does it not?" Robert would ask his new French friend, the critic Joseph Milsand, in 1853 while endorsing much the same set of political beliefs. "I cannot understand going a hair's-breadth beyond, however."[98] It was, nevertheless, a liberalism shared by a wide variety of those disillusioned by the Revolution of 1848. Robert made his comment in response to his reading of Proudhon's *Les Confessions d'un révolutionnaire* (1849). Among the *bêtises* (stupidities) to which Proudhon confesses in that work is that trust in the power of government to legislate social and economic progress; he advises voluntary association or "mutualism" because

> revolution from above is inevitably, . . . revolution which takes place through a prince's good pleasure, a minister's whim, the gropings of an assembly or the violence of a club. It is revolution by dictatorship and despotism . . . . Revolution [should be] based on the concerted action of the citizens, the experience of the workers, and the increase and spreading of enlightenment. It is a revolution based on liberty. . . .[99]

Even George Sand would adopt something like this "very tame liberalism." In her late novel, *Monsieur Sylvestre* (1865), the author's mouthpiece Pierre Sorrède lectures the disillusioned 1848 revolutionary Sylvestre on the foolishness of believing that human progress can be imposed by government action: "Virtue and faith decreed are no longer faith and virtue; they become detestable."[100] The political principals Elizabeth articulated in her May 1, 1848, letter to Kenyon are certainly moderate, but they are rather close to those that would eventually be espoused by at least two of the more prominent "Reds" of 1848. They are the same principles Robert still held in 1885 when asked why he was a liberal.

> . . . If fetters, not a few,
>   Of prejudice, convention, fall from me,
>   These shall I bid men – each in his degree
> Also God-guided – bear, and gayly too?
>
> But little do or can the best of us:
>   That little is achieved through Liberty.
> Who, then, dares, hold, emancipated thus,
>   His fellow shall continue bound? Not I,
> Who live, love, labour freely, nor discuss
>   A brother's right to freedom. That is "Why".

By the late spring of 1848 both Brownings had made the basis of their political faith a strong trust in individual liberty and an equally strong distrust of attempts to legislate abstract, impractical programmes. Such abstraction was the "absurdity of communism"; and, as Elizabeth told Miss Mitford on May 28, the French "had better kept Louis Philippe after all, if they are no more practical."[101] They associated many of these schemes with the Fourierists; and, as Elizabeth said in 1850, she hated the idea of "a Fourier machine, with my individuality sucked out of me by a social air-pump." Robert uses the same metaphor of machine and air-pump in his poem of 1850 – *Christmas Eve and Easter Day* – to scorn the rationalist "Higher Critic" who with "his cough, like a drouthy piston" subjects the Christian myth to analysis in the "exhausted air-bell of the Critic" and then "Pumps out with ruthless ingenuity/Atom by atom, and leaves you – vacuity." In the *Easter Day* section the speaker openly rejected "Fourier's scheme" when, in search of individual faith, he asked

> Fairly and frankly, what might be
> That History, that Faith, to me
> – Me there – not me in some domain
> Built up and peopled by my brain,
> Weighing its merits as one weighs
> Mere theories for blame on praise,
> – The kingcraft of the Lucumons,
> Or Fourier's scheme, its pros and cons,
> But my faith there, or none at all.

Elizabeth echoes the sentiment in a letter of the same year when she approves the "Christian Socialists" for retaining the "religious principle," but believes that

> upon merely human and earthly principles no such system can stand, I feel persuaded, and I thank God for it. If Fourierism could be realized, (which it surely cannot) out of a dream, the destinies of our race would shrivel up under the unnatural heat, and human nature would, in my mind, be desecrated and dishonoured . . . to elicit individuality has been the object of the best political institutions and governments. Now in these new theories, the individual is ground down into the multitude, and society must be 'moving all together if it moves at all' – restricting the very possibility of progress by the use of the lights of genius. Genius is *always individual*. [102]

In her *Aurora Leigh*, the hero Romney Leigh would pay for his Fourierist enthusiasm with destitution and blindness; and it is the vicious Lady Waldemar who "'read half Fourier through,/

Proudhon, Considérant, and Louis Blanc,/With various others of his socialists. . . .'" The Brownings' personal Christianity blended with their distrust of abstract systems and their trust of individual freedom; for that reason they rejected the more radical of the French revolutionaries. Once again, although they would not have known it at the time, the Brownings' responses to the events in Paris were quite close to that of George Sand, who, in late May, 1848, wrote privately to Théophile Thoré declaring her intention of breaking with the more radical leaders:

> As long as these men enroll themselves under our banner, I will abstain. They are pedants and theocrats. I don't want to see the individual crushed, and I will go into exile the day we make the mistake of bringing them to power. . . . They wanted to impose by surprise (and if they could have done so, by force) an idea which the people had not yet accepted. They would have established the reign of fraternity, not like the Christ but like Mahomet. Instead of a religion, we would have had fanaticism.[103]

June of 1848 brought events in Paris which would lead the Brownings to seriously disagree on the question of political leadership. The disagreement would last the rest of their lives and would be the cause of a number of "domestic 'émeutes'" between them. In that month the Parisian workers finally rose in revolt and, in being repressed by the Minister of War, Cavaignac, nearly five thousand were killed. When news reached Florence of the six days of bloody street fighting in late June, Elizabeth's faith in the provisional republican government was shaken; and, though Robert held onto a hope for the Republic, she began to place her hopes in a strong leader. "Poor France, poor France!" she wrote to Miss Mitford on July 4:

> News of the dreadful massacre at Paris just reaches us, and the letters and newspapers not arriving to-day, everybody fears a continuation of the crisis. How is it to end? Who "despairs of the republic?" Why, *I* do! I fear, that it cannot stand in France, and you seem not to have much more hope. My husband has a little, with melancholy intermediate prospects; but my own belief is that the people have had enough of democratic institutions and will be impatient for a kingship anew. Whom will they have? How did you feel when the cry was raised, "Vive l'Empereur"? Only Prince Napoleon is a Napoleon cut out of paper after all. The Prince de

Joinville is said to be very popular. It makes me giddy to think of the awful precipices which surround France – to think, too, that the great danger is on the question of *property*, which is perhaps divided there more justly than in any other country of Europe. Lamartine has comprehended nothing, that is clear. . . .[104]

When the elections came the following December, the vastly expanded French electorate obviously agreed with Elizabeth's estimate of Lamartine: of the nearly seven million votes cast for President of the Republic, he received but 17,910. Louis-Napoleon, whom Elizabeth thought only a "paper" Napoleon, received nearly five and a half million. Her trust in Louis-Napoleon would become, in the 1850's, a nearly neurotic obsession. In 1848–50, however, she was slow to accept him: she did not think him strong enough to lead. Two months before the election, while commenting sarcastically upon the "child's play" of Tuscan politics, she changes her tone to admit that in Italy "Brave men, good men, even sensible men there are of course in the land, but they are not strong enough for the times or for masterdom." Even a great people like the French, she goes on, have failed to bring forward the kind of Carlylean hero she now thinks the times demand:

> For France, it is a very great nation; but even in France they want a man, and Cavaignac is only a soldier. If Louis Napoleon had the muscle of his uncle's little finger in his soul, he would be president, and king; but he is flaccid altogether, you see, and Joinville stands nearer to the royal probability after all. 'Henri Cinq' is said to be too closely espoused to the Church, and his connections at Naples and Parma don't help his cause. Robert has more hope of the *republic* than I have; but call ye *this* a republic?[105]

That Robert continued to hope for the Republic indicates the widening differences of opinion between the Brownings about the form the government should take. Robert clearly distrusted the radical leaders, and he was "furious" over the Republic's continued imprisonment of Abd-el-Kader, the Algerian rebel leader whose heroism he had sung in "Through the Metidja to Abd-el-Kader" (1846). He would be equally furious when the French Republic, the following year, sent troops to crush the Roman Republic and restore Pius IX. But for all his distrust of the Republic, he clearly preferred it to

democratic caesarism. Elizabeth was beginning to put her hopes in a
strong leader, but it would be some time before she saw such a leader
in Louis-Napoleon. The news of the presidential elections reached
Florence quickly; and on December 3 she wrote to her old London
friend Mrs. James Martin that the Italians were, perhaps, no more
"childish than these French patriots and republicans, who crown
their great deeds by electing to the presidency such a man as Prince
Louis Napoleon, simply because 'C'est le neveu de son oncle.' A
curious precedent for a president, certainly. . . ." Although it is
"the *people* to whom and to whose cause my natural sympathies
yearn," she continues, the results of the election have taken the
savour from the word *liberty*. In liberty's name the Republic "turns
out a military dictatorship, a throttling of the press, a starving of
finances and an election of Louis Napoleon to be President."[106]

During the remainder of the winter of 1848–49, while Louis-
Napoleon was consolidating his power, Elizabeth wrote little of politics. She was in the last months of her only successful pregnancy. On
March 9 her son was born, and a few days later news came of the
death of Robert's mother. This "drawing together of life and death"
had been extremely painful, she wrote to Miss Mitford on April 30,
1849, before turning to the subject of Paris, the Republic and Balzac. She now found Louis-Napoleon "astonishing the world . . . by
his firmness and courage." She was uneasy over the sending of
French troops to Rome "to extinguish the republic there"; however,
if the Roman Republic is like the one tried in Florence – "imposed
by a few bawlers and brawlers on many mutes and cowards" – it is
just as well that the French put an end to it.[107] Louis-Napoleon's
attempt to gain French Catholic support by overthrowing the
Republicans in Rome and restoring Pius IX, militated against
Elizabeth's growing admiration for his firmness of leadership. Writing to Mrs. Martin on May 14, 1849, she is not yet sure what has
happened in Rome, but she warns that were Florence ever to have "a
republic *in earnest*" then "Louis Napoleon should not try to set his
foot on it." She admits that she was "vexed rather" at the French
election of Louis-Napoleon but has come to believe that it was "a
selection since justified by the firmness and apparent integrity of the
man."[108] By August she speculates that the President may soon "sit
on Napoleon's throne," for he has shown "prudence, integrity, and
conscientious patriotism" in a difficult situation. However, "the

Rome business has been miserably managed; this is the great blot on
the character of his government. But I, for my own part (my husband is not so minded), do consider that the French motive has been
good, the intention pure. . . . Robert is especially furious."[109]

After General Oudinot had crushed the Roman Republic in June
and restored a now even more reactionary Pius IX, Louis-Napoleon
hypocritically arranged for the publication of a "private" letter in
which he denounced the renewed oppressions of the Pope. We must
distrust, I think, Elizabeth's use of the first-person-plural pronoun
when she tells Miss Mitford in October that "The President's letter
about Rome has delighted us." The Brownings had read the letter in
the Italian papers before it was published in Paris. Perhaps Robert's
delight in the letter came not from a trust in Louis-Napoleon but
from the mistake in the translation which changed the "influence
hostile" of the reactionary Cardinals around Pius IX into "orribili
influenze." Both, however, were undoubtedly pleased to see Pius
denounced by French authority. They had had some admiration for
Pius when he initiated modest reforms after his election in 1846. Still
Elizabeth knew that the

> Pope is just a pope; and, since you give George Sand credit for
> having known it, I am more vexed that Blackwood (under "orri-
> bili influenze") did not publish the poem I wrote two years ago, in
> the full glare and burning of the Pope-enthusiasm, which Robert
> and I never caught for a moment. Then, *I* might have passed a
> little for a prophetess as well as George Sand! Only, to confess a
> truth, the same poem would have proved how fairly I was taken in
> by our Tuscan Grand Duke.[110]

The completed poem, *Casa Guidi Windows*, would reveal that she
was taken in by Louis-Napoleon as well. In Part I of *Casa Guidi
Windows* ("the poem I wrote two years ago") Pius IX is characterized
as a man reluctantly moved to minor reforms by the aspirations of
the people. In Part II she records her bitter disillusionment at the
collapse of the various European revolutions: "Annihilated Poland,
stifled Rome,/Dazed Naples, Hungary fainting underneath the
throng,/And Austria wearing a smooth olive-leaf/On her brute forehead. . . ." Pius IX is treated with particular scorn:

> . . . Peter's chair is shamed
> Like any vulgar throne the nations lop

86

To pieces for their firewood unreclaimed;
And, when it burns too, we shall see as well
In Italy as elsewhere. Let it burn. (Stanza XVII)

Louis-Napoleon, who ordered the stifling of the Roman Republic
to increase his political support among the French aristocracy and
bourgeoisie, escapes any mention in her scathing indictment of
European conservative reaction of 1849. In a letter written on the
first anniversary of Louis-Napoleon's election she says she has not
yet "made a demi-god of Louis Napoleon"; nevertheless, he has
"shown himself up to this point to be an upright man with noble
impulses, and [for] that I give him much of my sympathy and
respect in the difficult position held by him." She is watching to see
how he will "manage" the situation in Rome. The "Roman affair"
remains a "stain upon France" (though not its President) for the
casting of "Rome helpless and bound into the hand of the
priests. . . ."[111] Elizabeth claims that "I don't shut my eyes" to the
French action in Rome, but her eyes were beginning to droop. By
the following June she realizes that if Louis-Napoleon continues to
keep French troops in Rome to support Pius IX, both the French
Republic and its President will be dishonoured. On the other hand,
she sees no need to be alarmed about "the change in the electoral
law."[112] This recision of universal male suffrage limited the French
electorate to a fraction of what it had been in 1848; exploiting the
growing distrust of democratic government, Louis-Napoleon prepared for his *coup d'état* of December 2, 1851. Elizabeth would cheer
that action not from her window at Casa Guidi but from one
overlooking the Champs-Élysées.

4

Paris and Politics, 1851–52

i

EBB and RB Recognize the Advantages of Paris over Florence – Plans to Try Paris – They Arrive in Paris in July, 1851 – After Three Weeks in Paris They Visit London for Six Weeks – Family, Friends and the Great Exhibition of the Industry of All Nations – EBB Unwell and Feels Like "une âme perdue" in London.

ii

Carlyle Accompanies the Brownings on Their September Return to Paris – Apartment at 138 Champs Élysées – An Introduction to George Sand Promised – Louis-Napoleon's Coup d'État on December 2 and Street Fighting on December 4 – the Coup Causes "domestic émeutes" between RB and EBB – EBB's Defence of Louis-Napoleon and the Oppression Subsequent to the Coup.

iii

RB's Indictment of Louis-Napoleon – His Anger at Political Arrests, Press Censorship and Manipulated Elections – RB on Montalembert and Académie Française – His "Respectability" – RB's Analysis of Louis-Napoleon's Hypocrisy and Broken Promises – RB Retains his Scorn of Louis-Napoleon in Prince Hohenstiel-Schwangau.

i

The Brownings had not intended to remain so long in Italy, but, as Elizabeth wrote after a year in Florence, what with the "incredible cheapness, the climate so divine," they found it possible to "just

linger and linger" on in Italy, wishing that Florence were as near to
London as was Paris or that Paris were as cheap and as warm in the
winter as Florence.[1] By the spring of 1849 Elizabeth, anxious to see
her sisters and show them her child, wrote to Henrietta that "Robert
and I agree that it is melancholy work to live here." Still, a journey
to London would be too expensive: "I do wish that Florence were
nearer London – oh, I wish it! From Paris one might go [to London]
in fourteen hours for a guinea a-piece, instead of fifteen a-piece."[2]
Lacking the funds to go to Paris, they spent the summer of 1849 at
Bagni di Lucca. During the winter back in Florence Elizabeth
matured a plan which she had had in her "private head for some
time," a plan to finally satisfy

a great longing for making trial of Paris as a residence – because
Paris combines so much, and is so near England that we could all
meet in a few hours at any time, whereas here the distance
frightens me. Then Paris is delightful; and one lives there in the
midst of a brilliant civilization, as free a life as a mountaineer
in the mountains. We might carry our furniture up the Rhone.[3]

Elizabeth wrote an amusing account to Henrietta about how she
cleverly brought up the subject of moving to Paris. Robert was, of
course, exceptionally compliant with his wife's wishes so long as her
health was not endangered. In this little scene she played upon that
easy compliance indirectly and on Robert's prejudice against
America, in order "to watch his inclinations":

He is in antagonism, as you may suppose, with the very idea of
America under the narrow, hard money-prizing unartistical social
character. In the midst of a burst of his against this, about a
fortnight since, I said suddenly:
"Conceive, Robert! If I were to set my heart on going to live in
New York! What then?"
"Why then, you should go directly! Only *don't* set your heart on
it, Ba."

Threatened with living in New York, Robert apparently began to
think of alternatives to both Florence and the American city. "Of his
own accord," he brought the subject up one evening:

"I know you like Paris; and really after we have seen a little
more of Italy, and when your chest is a little stronger, I shouldn't

at all mind going to live there. Oh, I shouldn't dislike it indeed. We might try it in any case &c. &c."

So I was delighted, and we really have a prospect, you see. The winter is cold but short, and I am scarcely ever able to go out in the winter, from one cause or another, even here; and the climate is free from the fogs and uncertainties of England.[4]

In May, Henrietta married and was promptly and expectedly banished from the family by Mr. Barrett. She and her husband, Surtees Cook, went to live in Somerset. In her letter of congratulations and sympathy Elizabeth advised Henrietta to "be very *slow* about taking a house" and to consider living in Paris or Northern France, which was, she said, as accessible to London as was Somersetshire. Further, she thought that the "social exigencies" and the "positive taxes" made England the most expensive place in the world, "Except perhaps California." France would be much cheaper and more socially pleasant: "It would virtually double your income, and give you more freedom in every way. On the continent you escape a quantity of Mrs. Grundyism, and can live as you like, nobody making you afraid." Her other sister, Arabel, had thought of Pau, but Pau was after all "nearly as far as Florence."[5] By summer Henrietta and Surtees were apparently still uncertain about where to take up permanent residence. Elizabeth acknowledged that both Germany and Switzerland were "accessible" to London by railway. However, she and Robert had fixed upon Paris:

We shall have art and literature in Paris, and Robert being a member of the Historical Institute, and another literary society, (for which they sent him diplomas) we shall be able to know the best people we like to know. So that's our scheme! We shall avoid the English and live our own free lives. As to revolutions, I am never afraid of them – I have seem them too near. The nearness of England is an immense recommendation, and I like Paris of itself. I like that life, and mobility, and above all that continual beat of mind. Robert always prophesied that I should drag him to Paris one day, and now he sees the advantages as I do, and is not dragged but runs. Well, we are not gone yet.[6]

But by the next summer, 1851, they were gone, and they would not return to Florence for nearly two years. Most of that time they were in Paris enjoying "that life, and mobility, and above all that con-

tinual beat of mind." They did not, however, take their furniture up
the Rhône, as Elizabeth had earlier hoped. Instead, they rented their
furnished Casa Guidi apartment and left Florence on May 3 for
Venice, where they stayed several weeks. In Venice they visited the
museums, palaces, and churches and "swam" along the canals in
gondolas. And "every evening at half-past eight, Robert and I are
sitting under the moon in the great piazza of St. Mark, taking excellent coffee and reading the French papers."[7] From Venice they went
quickly through Padua, Milan, Lucerne and Strasbourg, where between the unfinished railroad and the diligence they "travelled from
Strasburg to Paris in four-and-twenty hours, night and day, never
stopping except for a quarter of an hour's breakfast and half an
hour's dinner." Despite this final hectic dash reminiscent of the one
in 1846 from Le Havre to Paris, Elizabeth "came into Paris as fresh
in spirit as if just alighted from the morning star, screaming out with
delight at the shops!" There follows in this letter to John Kenyon
one of those descriptive passages which Percy Lubbock felt so distinguished Elizabeth's epistolary style:

Well, now we are in Paris and have to forget the 'belle chiese';
we have beautiful shops instead, false teeth grinning at the corners
of the streets, and disreputable prints, and hats and caps, and
brilliant restaurants, and M. le Président in a cocked hat and with
a train of cavalry, passing like a rocket along the boulevards to an
occasional yell from the Red. Oh yes, and don't mistake me! for I
like it all extremely, it's a splendid city – a city in the country, as
Venice is a city in the sea. And I'm as much amused as Wiedeman,
who stands in the street before the print shops (to Wilson's great
discomfort) and roars at the lions. And I admire the bright green
trees and gardens everywhere in the heart of the town. Surely it is
a most beautiful city! And I like the restaurants more than is
reasonable; dining *à la carte*, a mixing up one's dinner with heaps
of newspapers, and the 'solution' by Émile de Girardin, who suggests that the next President should be a tailor. Moreover, we find
apartments very cheap in comparison to what we feared, and we
are in a comfortable quiet hotel, where it is possible, and not
ruinous, to wait and look about one.

As to England – oh England – how I dread to think of it![8]

While looking for more permanent accommodation the Brownings stayed at the Hôtel aux Armes de la Ville on the rue de la Michaudière just off the Boulevard des Italiens. To Mrs. David Ogilvy, who was living at Casa Guidi, Elizabeth wrote that they had intended to stay at the same hotel as on their wedding journey in 1846, but by "some strange mistake" found themselves at the Armes:

> Still, we are excellently off here, in a centrical situation & a quiet, comfortable, clean house, *au premier* . . . a salon (very good indeed) a small dining room & ante-chamber, a bedroom for Wilson & the babe, with two dressing rooms attached, and a bedroom for ourselves, . . . all for six francs the four & twenty hours. Nothing so cheap (observe) is to be had in Italy – not in an hotel, I mean – and the prices at the hotel must be a fair gauge of the expensiveness of the place.[9]

Neither Robert nor Elizabeth was especially eager to go on to London for even a brief visit. Elizabeth dreaded the English dampness and the still adamant refusal of her father and brothers to approve her marriage: "Airs and hearts are against me in England," she wrote to Kenyon.[10] Robert was unwell when they arrived in Paris and "fell into such a state of morbid nervousness" when he thought of "taking his wife & child to New Cross & putting them into the place of his mother" that Elizabeth tried to persuade him not to go to England at all. His father and sister had written that they could come to Paris; Henrietta, still living in Somerset, thought she could come to Paris during winter. Arabel, however, could not come over; so Robert, not wishing to disappoint Arabel, decided " 'he would go to a lodging in London near her, &, so visit his own home by himself & get it over with.' "[11] They all went to London on July 22, but first they remained for three weeks at the Paris hotel.

Apart from Elizabeth's account to Kenyon of the shops, boulevards, restaurants and newspapers, we hear little of these three weeks in Paris. The first day they went along to a restaurant they had known five years before and "were magnificently served upon gilt silver plate . . only we paid seven francs for our dinner which was *de trop*." Not only the price of the dinner – which was more than they were paying for their suite of rooms – but also the amount of food was apparently *de trop*. The next night they "went a step lower in the scale, & paid five francs," but it was still more than they could eat. They once again visited the Louvre; the excursion tired Elizabeth but she revived when, that evening, Tennyson and his wife came to the hotel for tea. The new laureate was on his way to Florence, having left "England to escape from the dirty hands of his worshippers."[12] London was especially crowded that summer with visitors to the Great Exhibition of the Industry of All Nations at the Crystal Palace. It was, perhaps, in reference to that great display of industrial might and ornate, eclectic design that Tennyson told them that evening in Paris that England was "the greatest nation in the world and the most vulgar."[13] Elizabeth had, upon first hearing of the Exhibition in Florence, expressed her enthusiasm for it; and, in *Casa Guidi Windows*, she had turned the event into an elaborate symbol of international unity:

> . . . Imperial England draws
> The flowing ends of the earth, from Fez, Canton,
> Delhi, Stockholm, Athens and Madrid,
> The Russias and the vast Americas,
> As if a queen drew her in robes amid
> Her golden cincture, – isles, peninsulas,
> Capes, continents, far inland countries hid
> By jaspar-sands and hills of chrysopras,
> All trailing in the splendours through the door
> Of the gorgeous Crystal Palace.

But her enthusiasm diminished by the time they had left Florence. From Venice she had written to Miss Mitford: "No, indeed and indeed, we are not going to England for the sake of the Exposition. How could you fancy such a thing, even once."[14] In late July, at dinner at Kenyon's in London, they would hear Carlyle growl about the Exhibition: " 'There was confusion enough in the universe, without building a chrystal [*sic*] palace to represent it.' "[15] They went with Anna Jameson to see the Exhibition, but they were predictably disappointed and also vexed that they had missed a visit from the English actress Fanny Kemble, who had called while they were out to leave tickets for her reading of *Hamlet*.

The two months the Brownings spent in London – July 22 to September 24 – were filled with dinners and visits to friends: the Carlyles, Forster, Proctor, Rogers, Horne, Kenyon, Anna Jameson. Though they missed Miss Kemble's visit, they did attend her reading of *Hamlet*. One evening the young American Bayard Taylor was asked by Elizabeth about the condition of the arts under the republican form of government in the United States; Elizabeth's allegiance to democratic caesarism had been growing, and she doubted that literature and the arts could flourish under a republic. Robert, with vigour and at some length, argued the other side of the question. They had carried back to London those political differences which had developed while they had watched the decay of the French Republic and the rise of Louis-Napoleon.

On arrival in London they had taken lodgings in Devonshire Street, near the Barrett home, and Arabel visited them frequently. Elizabeth also saw several of her brothers; George in particular became quite cordial. (This reconciliation is especially fortunate for it is in Robert's long letter to George from Paris that we have one of the few surviving accounts from Robert of his and Elizabeth's political arguments.) From the Devonshire Street lodgings Robert visited his father and sister at New Cross and was "himself again." The delight in family and friends was clouded, however. Robert got influenza; Elizabeth had started to cough the minute they landed in England. Their rooms were small and gloomy. When Elizabeth's indispensable and veteran maid Wilson left for a fortnight to visit her family, leaving Elizabeth with unaccustomed household responsibilities, she wrote to Mrs. Martin that she felt like *"une âme perdue"* and reiterated their hope "to take a house and settle in Paris."[16]

ii

Carlyle accompanied the Brownings when they left London to return to Paris on September 24. Travel always brought Carlyle "agitation, sleeplessness, horrors, and distress"; so it was only with the greatest reluctance that he brought himself to fulfil his promise to meet and spend a week with Lord and Lady Ashburton in Paris. Irritable and impatient after a water-cure at Great Malvern and with the confusion arising from passports, timetables, and the problem of getting *"visaed*,*"* Carlyle welcomed the news that the Brownings were going to Paris:

> At Chapman's shop, I learned that Robert Browning (poet) and his wife were just about setting out for Paris: I walked to their place – had, during that day and the following, consultations with

these fellow pilgrims; and decided to go with them, by Dieppe, on Thursday; Wednesday had been my original day, but I postponed it for the sake of company who knew the way. Such rumours, such surmises, guesses, cautions; each public office (Regent's Circus, Consul's House, or elsewhere) proclaimed its own plans, *denying*, much more, ignoring, that there was any other plan. For very multitude of guide-posts you could not find your way! The Brownings, and their experience and friendly qualities, were worth waiting for during one day.[17]

Carlyle was determined, as his cantankerous memoir *Excursion (Futile Enough) to Paris* makes clear, not to enjoy himself. His vivid account reveals the Brownings to be seasoned, efficient travellers at ease with things French and able to find comfort and delight in Paris; Carlyle is irascible and prejudiced, impatient with French bread, the "talkee-talkee" of salons, the "canine libertinage" of the Parisian stage. The Brownings had rather fully and thoughtfully pondered the French political scene for the past three years; in contrast, Carlyle announced that General Cavaignac, who had brutally suppressed the workers' rising in June of 1848, was the only Frenchman he "cared a straw to see."

Carlyle was delighted to find the Browning party (Robert, Elizabeth, Wilson, their son Pen and Flush) on time at London Bridge railway station on the morning of September 24; and further, his Scot's heart warmed when he learned that the price of a return ticket to Paris was cheaper – because of the crowds visiting the Crystal Palace – than he had expected. The journey down to Newhaven and the boarding of the ferry were uneventful. Robert "managed everything"; Carlyle smoked his pipe, watched the landscape and generalized upon national characteristics on the evidence of physiognomy. The French travellers were bustling and noisy while boarding the ferry, but once in the Channel everyone "sank into the general sordid torpor of sea-sickness, with *its* miserable noises, Hoahah – hotch! and hardly any other amid the rattling of the wind and sea." Elizabeth, Wilson and Pen were below deck and sick; Robert "was sick, lay in one of the bench-tents horizontal"; and Carlyle, habitually dyspeptic, lay quiet and had nothing but a single cigar during the eight-hour crossing. Also, a number of "once elegant Frenchmen lay wrapt in blankets, huddled into any corner with their heads hid. We had some sharp brief showers: darkness fell; nothing but the clank of the paddles, raving of the sea, and 'Hoah-oh-ho-ahh!'" They landed at Dieppe at 9 p.m.; all but Robert went directly to the Hôtel de l'Europe, where they got rooms, "some very bad cold tea, and colder coffee." It took Robert until past 10.30 to get their baggage through customs.[18]

The next morning after a breakfast of cold coffee but good butter and "bread eatable though of *crusty-sponge* contexture," Carlyle and Browning walked along the windy cliffs and talked with fishermen about a commemorative plaque given by Napoleon le Grand; they then went with the rest of the party to the railway terminal. There the French functionaries created a "Maximum of fuss" and an "infinite hub-hub" by weighing, haggling over, and measuring baggage. "I – ," Carlyle comments smugly, "had only to wait and be silent" while Robert "fought" for their baggage and places in the carriage. Towards four in the afternoon the palace at St. Cloud appeared, then the Arc de l'Étoile; moments later they stepped out of the carriage into a "crowding, jingling, vociferous tumult, in which the brave Browning fought for us, leaving me to sit beside the women." Even Robert "had at last grown heated" before Carlyle had his trunk, some French coins for tipping, his key and a cab directed to the Hôtel Meurice where the Ashburtons were staying.[19] The Brownings went to the Hôtel aux Armes de la Ville where they stayed for a fortnight before finding an apartment at 138 Avenue des Champs-Élysées.

The Brownings spent that first night back in Paris resting at their hotel. Carlyle, after dinner and a walk while smoking his cigar, went with the Ashburtons to the Théâtre Français, where Lord Normanby had furnished a box: "Very bad box, 'stage-box,' close to the actors; full of wind-draughts, where we all took *cold* more or less." The first play, *La Gageure Imprévue*, a comedy of jealousy in the provinces under the *ancien régime*, Carlyle judged as "worthless racket and cackle." The actors were good in the second play, *Maison de Saint-Cyr*, a comedy of courtship in a convent culminating in a forced marriage. Carlyle, however, dismissed this play even more harshly: "their wretched mockeries upon marriage, their canine libertinage and soulless grinning over all that is beautiful and pious in human relations were profoundly saddening to me; and I proposed emphatically an adjournment for tea; which was acceded to, and ended my concern with the French theatre for this bout. Pfaugh!" The face of General Changarnier, pointed out to him by Lady Ashburton, interested Carlyle more than did the plays. This old campaigner with Cavaignac in Algeria had recently been dismissed by Louis-Napoleon as commander of the regular forces and the National Guard in Paris. By scrutinizing Chagarnier's features, Carlyle found him a "man probably of considerable talent; rather a dangerous-looking man."[20] A few days later Lord Ashburton took Carlyle to call on General Cavaignac, who was not at home.[21]

The morning after the excursion to the Théâtre Français, Carlyle declined a museum tour with Ashburton and went instead to "call on the Brownings, whom I found all brisk and well rested in the Rue Michodière [*sic*]. . . ."[22] He envied them their "queer old quiet inn," and frequently in the evenings he escaped the "talkee-talkee" – by Thiers, Mérimée, Lamartine, La Borde – in the Ashburton's drawing-room and went to the Brownings': "Great welcome there: and tea in quiet; Browning gives me (being cunningly led to it) copious account of the late 'revolutions' at Florence, – such a fantastic piece of Drury-lane 'revolution' as I have seldom heard."[23] It was probably during one of these evenings that the Brownings asked Carlyle to get for them from Mazzini a letter of introduction to George Sand. Carlyle obliged them a week after his return to London: "Mazzini can at once afford you and Mrs. Browning, without any difficulty, the required introduction to Madame Dudevant; only he says this sublime Highpriestess of Anarchy is seldom now in Paris, only when there is some Play coming out or the like. . . ."[24]

By the second week in October the Brownings had moved to their apartment at 138 Avenue des Champs-Élysées. They had hoped to find a place nearer the Madeleine in order that they might be closer to the hotel John Kenyon stayed at while in Paris and closer to Elizabeth's Uncle Hedley's household, which had moved from Tours to their old apartment in the Faubourg Saint-Honoré. The apartment on the Champs-Élysées, however, met their needs for space, sunshine and price. It was, as Elizabeth wrote to Anna Jameson later in the month, "on the sunshiny side of the way, to a southern aspect, and pretty cheerful carpeted rooms – a drawing room, a dressing and writing room for Robert, a small dining room, two comfortable bedrooms and a third bedroom upstairs for the *femme de service*, kitchen, etc., for two hundred francs a month. Not too dear, we think."[25] They had paid more for the dark and cramped rooms in Devonshire Street during London's off-season. Elizabeth's preference for continental life was reinforced by this cheerful apartment. "Talk of English comforts!" she wrote to Miss Mitford, "It's a national delusion. The comfort of the Continental way of life has only to be tested to be recognized. . . ."[26] Beyond the windows was a terrace large enough to serve as a garden and, as Elizabeth wrote to Mrs. Ogilvy,

> all the brilliant life of Paris sweeping to & fro among the trees beyond. . . . Why, there's the balloon that fills & goes up within a stone's throw – and there are four Punches in the immediate neighbourhood! There's civilization for you! – To say nothing of dancing dogs, turn-about horses, and the President at the head of the troops, who with trumpet & drums passes & repasses our windows for the review outside the barrière.[27]

Louis-Napoleon's constitutional three-year term as President was drawing to an end. His attempts to alter the constitution to allow him to continue in power having failed, speculation about his next course of action was rife. "People say," Elizabeth wrote a few days after the President's unsuccessful attempt to rescind the edict of May which had limited the franchise, "that the troops which pass before our windows every few days through the 'Arc de l'Étoile' to be reviewed will bring the President back with them as 'emperor' some sunny morning not far off."[28] She concludes: "Vive Napoleon III!" By mid-November Robert " 'felt it in the air' " that a *coup* was near. Continuing the theatrical metaphor they had adopted for political ferment, Elizabeth commented: "What a fourth act of a play we are in just now! It is difficult to guess at the catastrophe."[29] By late November, reports in the English newspapers about the mounting crisis in Paris had alarmed Henrietta. On December 1 Elizabeth wrote to assure her sister that the reports were exaggerated: "Where is the danger, as long as one stays in the house? In these Champs Élysées, they could only hear the sound of the cannons at a distance, in the last revolution."[30]

That night Louis-Napoleon used no cannon. Instead his troops quietly seized the Bourbon Palace, newspaper offices, the Imprimerie Nationale, private printing shops and strategic points throughout Paris. Drums that might be used to rouse the citizenry were seized or broken and troops guarded the bell-towers of churches or muffled the bells. Posters were put up declaring a state of siege, dissolving the assembly, restoring universal suffrage, and promising new elections. "Not a carriage in the street," George Sand recalled of that night. "A deep silence, the dull glow of the gas lamps on the rough, shining cobble stones. It was one o'clock in the morning. Manceau and I came back [from the circus] via the Avenue Marbeuf and passed behind the garden of the Élysée. The same silence, the same obscurity, the same solitude. 'It's not for tomorrow,' I said to him with a laugh, and as I was tired, I slept soundly all night."[31] The next morning on the anniversary of Austerlitz, Louis-Napoleon rode at the head of his troops out of the Élysée Palace and along the Champs-Élysées. The Brownings watched from their windows. Elizabeth was delighted to be in Paris at such a time and to "have the great heart-beat of the world under [her] hand."[32] She would not have missed the spectacle, as she repeated to several correspondents, even for a sight of the Alps. The pomp and circumstance of the military parade, she told Henrietta, "might well move older children than our babe."[33] "Also," she wrote to Mrs. Ogilvy,

> the dramatic effect of the second of December cannot be exaggerated. The pouring in of the troops into Paris in a real sunshine of Austerlitz, & the immense shout of soldiers & people through which Louis Napoleon rode on horseback under our windows . . the long living shout, sweeping from the Carrousel to the Arc de L'Étoile, and triumphing, as a living thing should, over the triumph of the military music . . these things are indescribably like an electric shock, & thrilling to you much the same.[34]

The cannons began two days later on December 4.

Elizabeth began a long letter that day to her brother George. She wrote to assure him they were quite safe, to describe the parade of the 2nd, and to pass along some misleading news: that Thiers, who alone among the political leaders had anticipated the *coup d'état*, had escaped to Le Havre; that cards calling for the President's assassination and signed by Victor Hugo were being distributed in the streets. There had been some fighting as near to them as the rue de Richelieu; and Robert, who had walked down to the end of the Champs-Élysées, was turned back by their landlord, who claimed to have been just barely missed by a rifle ball. Wilson had taken Pen out but was turned back also. "The danger is," Elizabeth says rather calmly, "from the sudden sweep of the cannons, from which there would be no escape." That evening they heard trumpet calls from the Carrousel and the rumbling of gun-carriages along the Avenue des Champs-Élysées; soon they could hear the heavy cannonading from the Boulevard Poissonnière and the Porte St. Denis. Robert spent the evening writing, and Elizabeth sat up with him until one in the morning: "one shrank," she said, "from going quietly to sleep while human beings were dying in heaps perhaps, within earshot . . . the fighting was not over till three in the morning, and I fear that much blood was shed, particularly in the great barricade of the port St. Denis – . . . ." A bit farther on she comments rather chillingly: "They had a lovely soft air & glittering moon last night for cutting one another's throats – . . . ."[35] When Henrietta wrote, fearful of the "carnage" as *The Times* reported it, Elizabeth replied that to "talk about 'carnage' is quite absurd. The people never rose – it was nothing but a little popular scum, cleared off at once by the troops –. . . ."[36]

Two days later, on Saturday the 6th, Elizabeth went out with Robert in a carriage "to examine the field of battle on the boulevards & count the cannon-holes & windows dashed in."[37] She was struck by the extreme quietness although the "asphalte was black with crowds" and shops had re-opened. On Sunday the theatres were open and "our Champs-Élysées had quite its complement of promenaders."[38] Their carriage probably did not go along the Boulevards Montmartre and Poissonnière where troops had fired indiscriminately into crowds of innocent onlookers – over fifty killed in front of the Théâtre des Variétés – and into shops and cafes like Tortoni's and the Café Anglais. Victor Hugo was among the "popular scum" cleared off by the troops on the 4th, and he later memorialized that Thursday as "the day of the massacre of the boulevards." During the next few days – days which to Elizabeth's eyes saw Paris return to normality and gaiety – Hugo was one of the few to escape the arrests of thousands. From exile Hugo wrote angrily of Louis-Napoleon's "crime" that day: "There are certainly abominable massacres in history, but they have their reasons for being . . . one suppresses the enemy, destroys the foreigner: crimes with good motives. But the carnage of the Boulevard Montmartre is crime without knowable reason."[39]

Robert was "not as one" with Elizabeth in welcoming the *coup d'état*. Their opinions on democratic caesarism as opposed to republicanism had begun to diverge as early as the summer of 1848. Elizabeth gradually warmed towards Louis-Napoleon as an appropriately strong Caesar, while Robert's distrust of this particular Bonaparte increased. As late as her December 4 letter to George she still expressed some reserve towards this self-styled "saviour of society." "One can't quite trust a man in his position," she wrote, "& with the Napoleon blood in him. . . . My sympathy with his audacity & dexterity, is rather artistical sympathy than anything else – just as one cries 'Bravo' at a 'tour de force.'" She would, however, over the next few weeks develop an elaborate defence of both the man and his actions. She was forced to strengthen her arguments, as she told Mrs. Ogilvy, because of "Robert & I having had various domestic émeutes on the subject."[40] She was convinced from the beginning that the "people" supported Bonaparte. In this she was correct, as Hugo, Edgar Quinet and others, who tried on December 3 and 4 to organize resistance, discovered to their cost. Her sources of information were, of course, limited: "our own tradespeople & their retainers, wine-merchant, water-carrier, milk-bringer, poulterer, baker, & the rest, . . yes, our very cuisiniere & concierge were full of sympathy & exultation." She, who had earlier doubted that Napoleon le Petit had the strength to follow the example of Napoleon le Grand, now could hear her concierge say: "Ah Madame – c'est le vrai neveu de son oncle! il est admirable. (He's the true nephew of his uncle! he is wonderful.)"[41]

Since October the Brownings had come to know a number of Parisian journalists – Émile Lorquet of the *National*, Gavarni of *Charivari*, Émile de Girardin, Eugène Pelletan. At the salons of Lady Elgin or Madame Mohl or in her own drawing room, Elizabeth heard the "agonies of rage" and the "gnashing of teeth & wild-beast roaring" by writers who, their newspapers seized and the people not rising, could offer no other resistance. She listened with discerning amusement to these men, who had for so long supported the principle of universal suffrage and then seen Louis-Napoleon manipulate that principle to seal his own success, now speak of a franchise limited to "intelligent minority." "Their abuse of the 'masses,'" she wrote, "keeps pace, I assure you, with their abuse of the president." The peasants had become "'des animaux,'" the bourgeoisie "'des hommes sans conscience,'" the capitalists "'des hommes sans coeur.'" She notes the continued impracticality of the Republicans as evidenced in Émile de Girardin's plan to set up a government in exile in London; she deplores the bitterness of Lamennais who "exhales his private wrath by declaring that the 'whole people is putrified at heart.'" "I ventured to ask," she wrote with delicate sarcasm of one evening in her drawing room, "what could have been done, if there had been no iniquitious coup d'etat (for, observe, nobody defends the assembly, everybody of every party admitting that the assembly was out of sympathy with the people) – when a moderate suggested that Lamartine might have done something."[42] Robert was among those who refused to defend the assembly: it was, as he wrote to George Barrett in February, "stupid, selfish, & suicidal." And he must have shared something of his wife's attitude towards angry arguments of the frustrated Republicans. The more conservative opponents of Louis-Napoleon clearly had none of Robert's sympathy. "Robert and I have had some domestic *émeutes*," Elizabeth wrote to Mrs. Martin on December 11, "because he hates some imperial names; yet he confessed to me last night that the excessive and contradictory nonsense he had heard among Legitimists, Orleanists, and *English*, against the movement [the *coup*] inclined him almost to a revulsion of feeling."[43]

Throughout that winter Elizabeth evolved a quite complete and fairly consistent apologia for Louis-Napoleon's *coup d'état*. She repeatedly asserted that she was not a Bonapartist and that Louis-Napoleon's character was not the main issue: "I profess no faith in Louis Napoleon as a pure patriot & political moralist." She did, however, believe that he was earnest and honest in his promises to restore order, prosperity and freedom to France. Guizot, George Sand, the Brownings' new friend Joseph Milsand all testified to these qualities in the President. Elizabeth was happy to discover that Landor – so long a contentious anti-Bonapartist – also had expressed admiration for the President's "'wonderful genius.'"[44] Whatever Louis-Napoleon's character might be, Elizabeth believed he was fully justified in dissolving what had become an unrepresentative assembly and in abolishing an unworkable constitution. To have kept his oath to step down at the end of his term, she felt, would have thrown France in "mortal convulsions", and to decry the *coup* as illegal was to have a "strained reverence for formalism." She notes the irony

that those who acted illegally in 1830 and 1848 were called heroes "&
the world clapped its hands." Model constitutions and "American
forms of republicanism," she thought, were not congenial to the
French, especially in times of crisis. And, in the political crisis of the
past year, *"a Washington might have done"* what Louis-Napoleon did,
"under the circumstances, if he had the necessary intellect."[45] With
the social "adhesion" of the nation threatened, she found, the
"French people are very democratical in their tendencies, but they
must have a very visible type of hero-worship, and they find it in the
bearer of that name Napoleon."[46] The charge made in letters and
newspapers from England – that Louis-Napoleon maintained power
only by military force – particularly angered her. His *Appel au
peuple*, his restoration of universal suffrage, his overwhelming
approval in the December 20 plebiscite, all were evidence against
those charges:

> What has saved him with me from the beginning was his appeal to
> the people, and what makes his government respectable in my
> eyes is the answer of the people to that appeal. Being a democrat, I
> dare to be so *consequently*. There never was a more legitimate chief
> of State than Louis Napoleon is now – elected by seven millions
> and a half; and I do maintain that, ape or demi-god, to insult him
> where he is, is to insult the people who placed him there.[47]

Reports in the English press that the elections had been manipulated
and that there were "voters pricked forward by bayonets," she
thought stupid and absurd. She notes with amusement that the
English – including friends like *The Examiner*'s critic and reviewer
John Forster and Mrs. Tennyson – should be so outraged by Louis-
Napoleon but indifferent to other corrupt and brutal governments in
the world. "Caligula's horse or the people's 'Messiah,' as I heard him
called the other day – ," she told John Kenyon, "what then? You are
wonderfully intolerant, you in England, of equine consulships, you
who bear with quite sufficient equanimity a great rampancy of beasts
all over the world – Mr. Forster not blowing the trumpet of war, and
Mrs. Alfred Tennyson not loading the rifles."[48] She vigorously
defends the French people's right to choose even if they have chosen
wrongly:

> As to the worst of the President, let him have vulture's beak,

hyena's teeth, and the rattle of the great serpent, it's nothing to
the question. Let him be Caligula's horse raised to the consulship
– what then? I am not a Bonapartist; I am simply a 'democrat,' as
you say. I simply hold to the fact that, such as he is, the people
chose him, and to the opinion that they have right to choose whom
they please.[49]

Elizabeth did disapprove of many of the President's early actions,
although she never wavered in her belief that the *coup d'état* was
necessary, that it was justified, and that the plebiscite had made it
legitimate. She thought, for example, that the confiscation of the
Orleanist properties was wrong. She had opposed such confiscation
when it was first proposed by the Republicans in 1848; now, however, she recognized the act was part of Louis-Napoleon's political
astuteness and that "the decree is likely to prove to be popular with
the ouvrier class."[50] She regretted also the suppression of the press –
"I like compression of the journals no better than the journalists do"
– and the formalization of that censorship by the decree of February
17.[51] She found it "very melancholy" that the proposed new constitution offered "no prospect of even comparative liberty of the
Press."[52] Cabet and other radical Reds, she observed sardonically,
had long argued that suppression of all journals but the *right* one was
"a condition of a perfectly 'free state.' " Books, and hence literature,
she believed, would not suffer from censorship. And foreign journals
were freely admitted; even *Punch*, which Louis-Philippe had banned, was now available. Censorship and other "stringencies" like
mass arrests and reliance upon military force, she told John Kenyon,
must be thought of as temporary: "Let us wait until the dust from the
struggle clears away. . . . These new boots will be easier to the feet
after half an hour's walking." Universal suffrage, she hoped, was a
sufficient safety-valve against dictatorship. The French people, with
their democratic tendencies, their love of liberty and their "national
habits of insurrection" would remove Louis-Napoleon if he "dis-
appoints their expectation. . . ."[53] Yet two months after the new constitution was overwhelmingly approved by the elections in March,
she was forced to acknowledge that the repression continued: ". . .
the Press palpitates again – ah, but I wish it were a little freer of the
corset. This Government is not after my heart after all. I only tolerate what appear to me the necessities of an exceptional situation."[54]

There were, of course, moves by Louis-Napoleon which were

after her heart. An early one was the President's refusal to give in to
Montalembert and other ultramontanists on the issue of clerical control of education. "Montalembert," she wrote to Miss Mitford, "was
certainly in bed the other day with vexation, because 'nobody could
do anything with Louis Napoleon – he was obstinate'; 'nous nous en
lavons les mains,' and that fact gives me hope that not too much
indulgence is intended to the church."[55] Elizabeth was further
delighted when Louis-Napoleon began to act as she had hoped he
would when she first began to follow his career through the newspapers in Florence in 1848: she now welcomed his protests against
the "reactionary iniquities of the Tuscan Grand Duke," and she
applauded the reception at the Élysée Palace of Prince di Canino,
who had been President of the short-lived Roman Republic. "Pio
Nono's time," she wrote, "is but short, I fancy. . . ."[56] Though she
supported Louis-Napoleon largely because of his domestic policies,
she was thinking once again of the potential French role in Italy. For
the next decade she was more interested in Louis-Napoleon as
saviour of Italy than as saviour of French society. Her witnessing of
events in Paris, what she heard in the salons, her arguments with
Robert, all helped forge her belief that through democratic caesarism
"right, truth, justice, and the people" might prevail. Her stance,
though more comprehensive, remained much as it had been in Florence. "As it was in the beginning, from 'Casa Guidi Windows,'" she
wrote to Kenyon, "so it is now from the Avenue des Champs-
Élysées."[57] Most of her French and English friends and her family,
including Kenyon and her brother George, as well as Robert, seriously disagreed with her, but she held strongly to the rightness and
independence of her beliefs: "I am most humanly liable, of course,
to mistakes," she forcefully told Kenyon, "and am by temperament
perhaps over hopeful and sanguine. But I do see with my own eyes
and feel with my own spirit, and not with other people's eyes and
spirits, though they happen to be the dearest. . . ."[58]

iii

"I dare say you fancy us in the middle of noise & bustle, as indeed
we are," Robert wrote to his brother-in-law George in February,
"but our little nest hangs at the far-end of a twig in this wind-shaken
tree of Paris, and the chirpings inside are louder to our ears than the

bluster without."[59] In this manner Robert begins his only surviving letter that provides some sense of what positions he would take in those "domestic *émeutes*" so frequently referred to in Elizabeth's letters. Normally in Elizabeth's letters what the two disagreed about is quite vague. For example, after several pages detailing her own opinions on a wide variety of political events, she ends simply by saying: "Robert & I do not agree on this subject with our usual harmony. . . ."[60] Only occasionally is the source of conflict more specific: Robert "sympathizes with some of the fallen" more, apparently, than she; and "Robert says frankly that having a 'personal hatred' to the man (& the blood, he might add) he has not patience to analyze things very closely."[61] The notion that Robert recognized that his intense dislike of Louis-Napoleon was emotional and that hence he did not try to rationally appraise the man or his actions is repeated several times, as in this passage to Anna Jameson: "Robert, too, will tell you that he hates all Buonapartes, past, present, or to come, but then *he* says *that* in his self-willed, pettish way, as a manner of dismissing a subject he won't think about – and knowing very well that he doesn't think about it, not mistaking a feeling for a reason, not for a moment."[62] Robert's letter to George Barrett belies this charge.

The letter suggests that their discussions of Louis-Napoleon's assumption of power may have begun as "chirpings," to use his figure, but they must have progressed until they were "louder to our ears than the bluster without." When conversation turned into *émeute*, Robert chose to end the impasse by admitting his prejudice or by feigning ignorance. "And so our debate ends," he told George, "till the arrival of the next newspaper." The scarcity of reliable, factual news about what really was going on in France acerbated, in Robert's view, his arguments with Elizabeth. In her letters Elizabeth regularly denounced the lies and ignorance of the English press and maintained that only "we French" in Paris could properly judge the new regime. Robert took an opposite tack and noted not only the suppression of the Parisian press but an informal censorship within the conversation of the salons. "You are infinitely better able to see how affairs go, you in England, than we are here – " he tells George, "for all our information is reflected from your newspapers – every other voice is mute – & 'voice' means the speech of a man to his neighbour in the street, or of a lady to her guest in the drawing room." However much Elizabeth might be impressed by the "clash of speculative opinions" she heard in the occasional salon she visited, Robert thought opinions were being carefully guarded as the arrests of opponents of the regime mounted into the thousands. Indeed a Parisian journalist who often called upon the Brownings – Eugène Pelletan – apparently suffered for such conversational subversiveness. After his failure to appear one evening at their apartment as expected, they learned that he had been arrested, imprisoned at Saint-Germain, and threatened with deportation. "If he talked in many places as he talked in this room," Elizabeth wrote to Miss Mitford, "I can't be very much surprised, but I am really sorry. He is one of those amiable domestic men who delight in talking 'battle, murder, and sudden death.' "[63]

Far from being irrational or ignorant about such a state of affairs, Robert traced very subtly for George "the oblique line by which opinion must travel to be harmless" in Paris under Louis-Napoleon. He cited as example the induction of Montalembert into the Académie, a ceremony he planned to attend on the morrow. Montalembert had long been a leader of the clerical party and had in 1848 begun to support Louis-Napoleon in hope of church control of education. He had also opposed, in assembly debates of 1851, Victor Hugo's liberal proposals for constitutional reform, reforms which were designed to blunt Louis-Napoleon's drive for autocratic power. For this Montalembert was anathema to all liberal Republicans and the anti-clerical left. However, he finally broke with Louis-Napoleon over the disposition of the Orleanist properties, which he thought should go to the church and which Louis-Napoleon planned to use for grants to mutual aid societies and housing for workers. Montalembert's induction into the Académie coincided with his break with Louis-Napoleon. If liberals cheered Montalembert at the ceremony, was it to be taken as safe but "oblique" criticism of the government or was it hypocrisy? Here is how Browning saw it:

those who, as liberals, hate him most (for his ultra-montane bigotry, 'legitimate' opinions & so forth) will see it their duty to applaud him to the echo, on the ground of his having broken with the government on its promulgation of the spoliation measures – just as if he had not done his utmost to help that government when it most needed help – and now that, in consequence, it can act as it

107

pleases, Montalembert cries out on it & expects sympathy! None of mine shall he have when I hear him tomorrow, as I hope to do.

Robert would distil his disgust at such distortion of free opinion in his poem, "Respectability," in which he ironically contrasts society's disapproval of the "unrespectable" love of a woman like George Sand to society's approval of Montalembert's hypocritical reception into the Académie. The woman speaks bitterly to her lover while embracing him on a dark street just before they must assume a more respectable pose as they walk out onto the lighted boulevard:

> I know! – the world proscribes not love;
> Allows my fingers to caress
> Your lip's contour and downiness,
> Provided it supply a glove.
> The world's good word! – the Institute!
> Guizot receives Montalembert!
> Eh? Down the court three lampions flare:
> Put forward your best foot!

In this poem, as in so many of Browning's, the "world's good word" is both deceitful and self-deceiving. He must have sensed something similar in the conversations with Elizabeth about the events of the real world of Paris in the winter of 1851–52.

"Is it not strange that Ba cannot take your view," he asked George, "not to say mine & most people's, of the President's proceedings? I cannot understand it – we differ in our appreciation of facts, too – things that admit of proof." He then tried to explain how the "split" in their attitudes habitually came about. They would begin by agreeing that the assembly under the Marrast constitution of 1849 had become "stupid, selfish & suicidal" and that the government under it had become unworkable. It had become, metaphorically, a knot which various proposed reforms – by Victor Hugo and others – had tried to untangle during 1851. Their failure made the *coup d'état* possible. Robert opposed that extreme remedy: "when Louis Napoleon is found to cut the knot instead of untying it – Ba approves – I demur." He may not have chosen his words so carefully in his letters as he did in his poems, but in the figure of the *cutting* of the knot there is implied both violence and destruction of continuity. Robert was, it seems, more sensitive and alert to the violence Louis-Napoleon (even to his own regret) found necessary to establish his regime. Elizabeth's comment that Robert "sympathizes with some of the fallen" jars with her own angry assertion that there was no "carnage" during the December 4 fighting but only a "little popular scum, cleared off at once by the troops." Her description of the carriage ride to "survey the field of battle" and to count the cannon-holes also conveys a tone of callousness. Robert, who went out more frequently and talked to more people than she, doubtless heard some tales of the savage and indiscriminate firing on, clubbing, and bayonetting of innocent onlookers around the Porte St. Denis and along the rue Poissonnière. Added to that violence were the mass arrests of potential opponents; arrests, imprisonments and deportations to Cayenne and Algeria would, by the time Robert wrote to George in February, have numbered between twenty and thirty thousand. Enclosed along with Robert's letter was one from Elizabeth which defended the arrests and deportations. "No revolution," she assured George, "ever took place in France without six or seven times more bloodshed than we have had this time. The expulsion from France of distinguished men implicated in various parties, was probably the mildest way found possible, of maintaining the peace of the country."[64] These facts of violence, obviously, were points of disagreement. So too was the violent destruction by the *coup d'état* of the continuity of republican governmental forms. Ever since the June uprising of 1848, Elizabeth had looked to a strong leader and despaired of the republican government's ability; Robert had continued to hold out hope for constitutional representative government. He had to demur when Louis-Napoleon cut that knot.

"Still, one must not be pedantic and overexacting," Robert says rather reasonably to George, "and if the end justifies the beginning, the illegality of the step may be forgotten in prompt restoration of the law – the man may stop the clock to set it right." Like one of his monologuists, Robert has switched his metaphor for the French government from a knotted rope to a defective timepiece. The remainder of his assessment of Louis-Napoleon is expressed in an elaborate extension of the metaphor of the clock. Admitting rather charitably that Louis-Napoleon may be justified in stopping the mechanism of government if he intends to repair it correctly, Robert continues:

But his next procedure is to put all the wheelwork in his pocket, and promise to cry the hour instead – which won't do at all. Ba says, good arrangement or bad, the parishioners, seven millions strong, empowered him to get into the steeple & act as he pleased – which I don't allow that they were in a condition to judge of the case, at liberty to speak their judgment, or (in the instance of the very few who may have been able to form & free to speak it) of any authority whatever on the previous part of the business – for I or you might join with the rest as to the after-expediency of keeping a bad servant rather than going altogether without one – we might say, "Now that you have stolen our clock, *do* stay & cry according to your promise – for certainly nobody else will." But he does *not* keep his promise. . . .

Because this extended metaphor, condensed though it is, contains one of the few surviving expressions of Robert's political views, it is worth glossing the metaphor with reference to political events in Paris during the winter of 1851–52.

The metaphor which makes the French government and by extension all of France into an inaccurate or stopped clock, and which makes Louis-Napoleon Bonaparte into an unreliable and finally larcenous repairer of timepieces, is an exceptionally mild one. Although it may be appropriate to the context of a letter concerned about facts and news, the figure trivializes the French political crisis and the violent creation of a military dictatorship. It is not, that is, an effective vehicle to express what Elizabeth called Robert's "'personal hatred'" of the President. Further, the metaphor is extended by a series of concessions and demurs. The initial concession is that the government, and more specifically the assembly, is defective and unworkable and perhaps should have been dissolved as it was on December 2. The stealing of the clock was announced the same day, but the process of assuming autocratic rule – the suppression of the press, the subduing of armed opponents and arrests of others, the appointment of loyal prefects and judges – took longer. And the consolidation of power proceeded simultaneously with reiterated promises of free elections and of return to constitutional government once the state of siege was no longer necessary. In the meantime two elections had taken place. One, the plebiscite of December 20, saw the electorate – expanded by the restoration of universal suffrage – cast over seven million votes to give Louis-Napoleon dictatorial powers or, in the terms of the metaphor, "get into the steeple & act as he pleased." Robert, the English press, and French opponents of the regime thought that the elections were not free, that they were manipulated by propaganda in the absence of an opposition press, by Bonapartist agents and newly appointed prefects, and by the presence if not the overt force of the military.

Whether or not the plebiscite was the free expression of the people's will was one of the major points of contention between the Brownings. Some French leaders who had been in opposition did soon accept the new regime as a *fait accompli* – Guizot, Lamartine, even to a degree, Proudhon and George Sand. Once again Robert was willing to concede, as an "after-expediency," that such acceptance of Louis-Napoleon might be better than the political chaos that would come from having no one at all in the steeple to call out the time. Robert's condition was, however, that the promise of return to constitutional government be kept. When he was writing in early February, the new constitution was being discussed. It was an instrument designed not to restore constitutional government and liberties but to make legitimate the continued dictatorship. The press was muffled by provisions making it necessary for any journal to have government permission before speaking on political or social issues; the number of crimes journals and journalists could be tried for – and without jury – was enlarged. Legislation was to be initiated not within the elected assembly but from the office of the presidency; and the President was to retain the power to nominate not only ministers and administrative officers down to the sub-prefect level, but also judges and officers of the *Sénat*. Watching these developments and no doubt hearing rumours of how the Bonapartist agents and prefects were preparing for yet another "free" election in March, Robert ends his assessment of Louis-Napoleon with these words: "he does *not* keep his promise, as you see by the decrees from first to last; on that point Ba agrees with us again – but she will have it that 'they chose him' – and you return to my answer above, that denies the facts."

Twenty-five years later, after the surrender at Sedan, the siege of Paris, and the convulsions and crushing of the Commune, Robert gave Louis-Napoleon a long dramatic monologue. There, under the guise of Prince Hohenstiel-Schwangau, Napoleon III utters an extended apologia detailing what, as Robert said, "the man might, if he pleased, say for himself."[65] The poem rightly belongs to Robert's later career, after he had watched Louis-Napoleon for nearly a quarter of a century. The passages in which Louis-Napoleon defends his actions of the winter of 1851–52, however, are apposite to Browning's letter to George Barrett. Robert had, as he told Isa Blagden shortly after the publication of *Prince Hohenstiel-Schwangau* in 1871, "thought badly of [Louis-Napoleon] at the beginning of his career, *et pour cause*."[66] Among the causes were Louis-Napoleon's failure to abide by his promises of a free press and free elections and his excessive defences of economic freedom. These principles he supported before his assumption of power, when he was but a "voice." As he looks back, he hears his own voice and then the voice of his critics, his "censors," who raise the old charges against him:

"Unfettered commerce! Power to speak and hear!
And print and read? The universal vote!
Its rights for labour!" This, with much beside,
I spoke when I was voice and nothing more,
But altogether such an one as you
My censors. "Voice, and nothing more, indeed!"
Re-echoes round me: "that's the censure, there's
Involved in the ruin of you soon or late!
Voice, – when its promise beat the empty air. . . ."

The ghostly critics, reviewing Louis-Napoleon's career, find the promises but mere words while the President, Judas-like, is posted as a sentry at the doors of the assembly. They remember, too, the fate of and the effect on those who spoke in opposition:

"The power to speak, hear, print and read is ours?
Ay, we learn where and how, when clapped inside
A convict-transport bound for cool Cayenne!
The universal vote we have: its urn,
We also have where votes drop, fingered-o'er
By the universal Prefect."

During the first few months following the *coup d'état*, Louis-Napoleon had managed to revive trade and commerce – a success Elizabeth frequently drew to the attention of his critics – and he had moved, by grants to mutual aid societies and by building housing for the workers, to gain the support of the labouring classes. But the "voices" reject these accomplishments for their cost in essential freedoms:

> . . . "Say, Trade's free
> And Toil turned master out o' the slave it was:
> What then? These feed men's stomach, but his soul
> Craves finer fare, nor lives by bread alone,
> As somebody says somewhere."

Elizabeth had heard, she told Kenyon, Louis-Napoleon called the "Messiah." He is audacious enough in Robert's monologue to accept that role when, in defence of his tampering with the elections, he claims that had he not so manipulated the voters they would have chosen Barabbas. Barabbas represents, apparently, those socialists who threatened social chaos by adherence to impractical theories like those of "Fourier, Comte, and all that ends in smoke!" In his early propaganda Louis-Napoleon played upon the fear the French peasants and bourgeoisie had of socialist programmes. It was a fear that even Elizabeth thought exaggerated. Later, in *Aurora Leigh*, utopian socialism is foolish but not especially dangerous.

In February of 1852 Robert had compared the French state to a defective timepiece and Louis-Napoleon to someone chosen to repair it. This metaphor, as I have suggested, minimizes, even trivializes and dehumanizes, the violence necessary to the establishment of the regime. In his monologue Louis-Napoleon uses an expanded mechanical figure to justify his dictatorship. Here French society is not a clock but a machine which only a single person can effectively regulate:

> I rule and regulate the course, excite,
> Restrain: because the whole machine should march
> Impelled by those diversely-moving parts,
> Each blind to aught beside its little bent.
> Out of the turnings round and round inside,
> Comes that straight-forward world-advance, I want. . . .

In his letter to George, Robert clearly distrusted Louis-Napoleon and was angrily impatient with his slowness in meeting promises to restore constitutional liberties. But the letter reveals no irrational hatred of the man. And when Robert came to give Louis-Napoleon his "say" in the poem of 1871, he allowed him to plead a very good case for himself. At any rate, the apologia spoken by the "saviour of society" was sufficiently complex that one reviewer thought it constituted an "eulogium on the Second Empire," while another objected that it was a "scandalous attack on the old constant friend of England."[67]

5

Paris and Literature, 1851–52

i

RB's Father and Sister Visit, Then Move to Paris – RB and EBB Attend Various Salons – They Seek Out and Discover George Sand – Spiritualism a Salon Topic – Meetings with Lamartine, Paul de Musset, Thierry, Ary Scheffer – Louis Jadin Provides Gossip about Dumas père *– They Attend Dumas* fils' La Dame aux Camélias.

ii

Milsand's Essay on RB in the Revue des Deux Mondes *– Philarète de Chasles Lectures on EBB at Collège de France – Essay on EBB in* Revue des Deux Mondes *– Various Writers for the* Revue: *Gautier, Nerval, Renan, Baudelaire – RB's General Similarities to Younger French Writers.*

iii

RB Writes Essay on Shelley, *November–December, 1851 – The* Essay *Reflects Milsand's Appreciation of RB's Poetry – RB's Stress on Objective Poetry Attuned to Parisian Literary Scene – Leconte de Lisle, Renan, Balzac, Baudelaire.*

iv

RB's Poems Associated with this sojourn in Paris – "Memorabilia," "Popularity," "Transcendentalism," "How It Strikes a Contemporary" as Extensions of Shelley Essay — Other Poems Written in Paris or Inspired by the Visit: "Respectability," "Women and Roses," Childe Roland, *"Love Among the Ruins" — The Brownings Watch Louis-Napoleon Return to Paris in October, 1851, as Napoleon III.*

i

The Brownings had not come to Paris to watch Louis-Napoleon transform the Second Republic into the Second Empire. The phenomenon was perhaps predictable, but it came as a bonus. They came to make a trial of Paris as a permanent residence, to see their families either there or in London, to "have art and literature" and to be a part of "above all that continual beat of mind."[1] The hope that the climate in Paris would be warm enough for Elizabeth faded only gradually during the winter. After a month both she and Robert had been persuaded that one could live cheaply in Paris "if one knows how to set about it"; but, she adds, she wishes she "were as sure about the climate."[2] An early November cold spell made her "a prisoner as usual." Long-time English residents assured her, however, that the cold was "exceptional"; it was some comfort to learn that it was below zero in London and "that Scotland stands eight feet deep in snow."[3] She would, she said a bit later, rather face Louis-Napoleon's cannons than January in London.

When Robert's father and sister Sarianna came to visit them in early November, Elizabeth and Robert discussed plans "to establish them in Paris if we can stay, and if no other obstacle should arise before the spring. . . ."[4] An obstacle did arise, but it made it necessary that the elder Browning and Sarianna make Paris their permanent home: a Mrs. Von Muller, an attractive, middle-aged widow whom Mr. Browning had courted, brought a successful breach-of-promise suit against Robert's father. In early July of 1852, while Robert and Elizabeth were still in Paris, a London court found against Mr. Browning and ordered payment of £800 in damages. Robert hastily removed his father and sister to Paris, where in the rue de Grenelle they lived until Mr. Browning's death in 1866. By the time Mr. Browning had made Paris his home, Robert and Elizabeth had already decided to spend the following winter in Italy. Elizabeth had had only intermittent relief from her coughs and colds during the winter, and Robert suffered a bout of "la grippe." Towards the end of the winter Pen, too, had been quite ill; when Elizabeth reported on his health to her sister on April 1, it is apparent that the decision had been made: "We shall spend next winter in Italy if we live, and bathe him in his native air. It will do us all good."[5] With reluctance they finally left Paris in early November of

1852: "We have done our business in Paris, but we linger . . . ," she wrote to Kenyon, "it's rather dangerous to let the charm of Paris work – the honey will be clogging our feet very soon, and make it difficult to get away."[6]

An important part of the "business" the Brownings had done during their year in Paris was to make a rather wide-ranging acquaintance with Parisian artistic, literary and intellectual life. The salons of Lady Elgin and of Madame Mohl initially provided them with an introduction to this life. And Robert went to Madame Buloz' salon. Elizabeth's health limited her going out often in the evenings during the winter, but she conducted her own more informal and less regular salon on Tuesdays or Saturdays; and she urged, indeed insisted, that Robert go out more often: "we might as well be in Florence if he shuts himself up here. . . ." So, she told Henrietta, "I leave him no peace till he gets into acquaintance with all the delightful scamps of feuilletonistes and artists in Paris."[7] Her letters are sprinkled with names of people met, nearly met, that they expected to meet, or about whom they heard gossip: Lamartine, Thierry, Michelet, Musset, Gavarni, Béranger, Delphine Gay, her husband Émile de Girardin, François Buloz, Ary Scheffer, Philarète Chasles, Alexis de Tocqueville, Madame Viardot, Louis Jadin, Dumas *père* and *fils*, Sue, Hugo and, of course, George Sand.

"I won't die, if I can help it," Elizabeth promised, "without seeing George Sand."[8] With Balzac dead, Sand was for Elizabeth the premier literary attraction of Paris. She suspected that Sand would be wary of "lion-hunters and book-making people," but the campaign was planned early. By mid-October of 1851, when Carlyle sent promise of a letter of introduction from Mazzini, Robert had already gathered some intelligence about Sand's recent life and movements. The letter from Mazzini would be most welcome, Robert wrote to Carlyle,

> and I shall no doubt be able to find out, from people here, the best way of bringing it to bear with effect on the great person. We heard quantities about her the other night – from what may possibly be an authentic source – how she had grown visibly aged of a sudden (like Mephistopheles at the Brocken when he says he finds people ripe for the last day), and is getting more resigned to it than she had expected, seeing that with youth go "a Hell of Passions" –

(which is all she knows about it). Meanwhile, the next best thing to youth, and the Hell and so on, is found to be strenuous play-writing. She writes in the country and her friends rehearse, test effects, prophesy of hits or misses of the Paris auditory; whereat she takes heart and writes again, points this, blunts that. . . .[9]

As Robert's tone makes clear and as Elizabeth's subsequent letters complain, Robert pursued this particular lion with something less than enthusiasm. His amusement at her premature ageing and dis-illusionment with youthful passion reflect anecdotes told by other witnesses. Alexis de Tocqueville notes that, at a dinner party given by Monckton Milnes, Prosper Mérimée had even failed to recognize his former bedmate across a dinner table.[10] Sand herself often com-plained in letters that, disillusioned with the course of the Republic, saddened by the death of close friends (Chopin, Marie Dorval, Char-lotte Marliani), and worn out by squabbling with her daughter Solange, she often felt eighty years old. Since 1849 she had lived increasingly at Nohant, where, with her son Maurice as stage-manager and various friends and servants as players, she wrote and staged private showings of her plays.

Sand was in Nohant working on *Le Mariage de Victorine* when the Brownings settled in at the Champs-Élysées apartment in October. She came up to Paris with her new lover Alexandre Manceau in November for rehearsals and the opening of the play at the Gym-nase. Elizabeth, armed now with Mazzini's letter, heard of the impending arrival and informed an interested Miss Mitford that she and Robert "must make a rush and present it, for her stay here is not likely to be long. . . ."[11] Sand was in Paris until December 4, two days after the *coup*, when she returned quickly to Nohant. In her Christmas letter to Miss Mitford, Elizabeth described her vexation at missing Sand. A certain M. François had promised to deliver Maz-zini's letter, but when he proposed that the letter be left for Sand at the Gymnase, Robert objected that it would get "mixed up with love letters of the actresses" or be read aloud in the green room for the amusement of the cast. "Robert was a little proud and M. François very stupid," Elizabeth wrote, "and I, between the two, in a furious state of dissent from either." She did learn that when Sand came to Paris she stayed at her son Maurice's apartment – "a mere 'chambre de garçon' " – and received selected friends at a café.[12]

Sand returned to Paris on January 25 to begin months of arduous but highly successful meetings with government officials to plead on behalf of persons arrested and imprisoned or sentenced to deportation. On January 30 she met with and made her plea to Louis-Napoleon. Elizabeth was pleased at this meeting between two people whom she so admired:

> When George Sand had audience with the President, he was very kind; did I tell you that? At last he said: "Vous verrez, vous serez contente de moi." To which she answered, "Et vous, vous serez content de moi." It was repeated to me as to the great dishonour of Madame Sand, and as a proof that she could not resist the influence of power and was a bad republican. I, on the contrary, thought the story quite honourable to both parties. It was for the sake of her *rouge* friends that she approached the President at all, and she used the hand he stretched out to her only on behalf of persons in prison and distress. The same, being delivered, call her gratefully a recreant.[13]

In early February they finally sent Mazzini's letter to Sand. Robert had remained reluctant but, as Elizabeth told Miss Mitford, "At last I pricked Robert up to the leap": she wrote a note to go with the letter, they both signed it, and it was given "to a friend who was to give it to a friend, who was to place it in her hands, her abode being a mystery and the name she used unknown." The next day Elizabeth received a brief but gracious note from Madame Sand asking them to call upon her on Sunday, February 15. "Kindly accept a thousand heartfelt thanks to you," Sand ended the note, "as well as Mr. Browning, whom I hope to see with you, for the sympathy you have accorded me."[14]

"So we went," Elizabeth announced to Kenyon the day after the visit to Madame Sand. "Robert let me at last, though I had to struggle for even that. . . ." Robert worried about the sharpness of the cold air; so, in addition to the precautions of shawls, furs, and a closed carriage, Elizabeth also wore her gauze respirator. This device, when she took it from her muff and showed it to George Sand, elicited from Sand a look of disdain and the comment that she thought life not worth such precaution. Sand was, otherwise, quite gracious:

> She received us very kindly, with hand stretched out, which I,

119

with a natural emotion (I assure you my heart beat), stooped and kissed, when she said quickly, 'Mais non, je ne veux pas,' and kissed my lips. She is somewhat large for her height – not tall – and was dressed with great nicety in a sort of grey serge gown and jacket, made after the ruling fashion just now, and fastened up to the throat, plain linen collarette and sleeves. Her hair was uncovered, divided on the forehead in black, glossy bandeaux, and twisted up behind. The eyes and brow are noble, and the nose is a somewhat Jewish character; the chin a little recedes, and the mouth is not good, though mobile, flashing out a sudden smile with its white projecting teeth. There is no sweetness in the face, but great moral as well as intellectual capacities – only it never could have been a beautiful face, which a good deal surprised me. The chief difference in it since it was younger is probably that the cheeks are considerably fuller than they used to be, but this of course does not alter the type. Her complexion is of a deep olive. I observed that her hands were small and well-shaped. We sat with her perhaps three-quarters of an hour or more – in which time she gave advice and various directions to two or three young men who were there, showing her confidence in us by the freest use of names and allusion to facts. She seemed to be, in fact, the man in that company, and the profound respect with which she was listened to a good deal impressed me. . . . What is peculiar in her manners and conversation is the absolute simplicity of both. Her voice is low and rapid, without emphasis or variety of modulation. Except one brilliant smile, she was grave – indeed, she was speaking of grave matters, and many of her friends are in adversity. But you could not help seeing (both Robert and I saw it) that in all she said, even in her kindness and pity, there was an under-current of scorn. A scorn of pleasing she evidently had; there never could have been a colour of coquetry in that woman. Her very freedom from affectation and consciousness had a touch of disdain. But I liked her. I did not love her, but I felt the burning soul through all that quietness, and was not disappointed in George Sand. When we rose to go I could not help saying, 'C'est pour la dernière fois, (It is for the last time)' and then she asked us to repeat our visit next Sunday, and excused herself from coming to see us on the ground of a great press of engagements.[15]

The Brownings did call again the following Sunday and were

invited to call each Sunday. In early March Sand sent Elizabeth tickets for the opening performance of her *Les Vacances de Pandolphe* along with a note apologizing that the tickets were not for loge seats, "but those are given to the journalists."[16] Elizabeth wrote back saying she gratefully intended to make this her first visit to a Parisian theatre. The weather, however, turned cold; so Robert went without her. During February and March Robert saw Sand some six times; once Robert strolled with her in the Tuileries gardens. Elizabeth saw her only on those two Sundays in the rue Racine. In a letter to Miss Mitford in early April, after Sand had left Paris for Nohant, Elizabeth seems satisfied with those two visits and only regrets they did not occasion a greater intimacy:

I could only go with Robert three times to her house, and once she was out. He was really good and kind to let me go at all, after he found the sort of society rampant around her. He didn't like it extremely, but, being the prince of husbands, he was lenient to my desires and yielded the point. She seems to live in the abomination of desolation, as far as regards society – crowds of ill-bred men who adore her *à genoux bas*, betwixt a puff of smoke and an ejection of saliva. Society of the ragged Red diluted with the lower theatrical. She herself so different, so apart, as alone in her melancholy disdain! I was deeply interested in that poor woman, I felt a profound compassion for her. I did not mind much the Greek in Greek costume who tutoyéd her, and kissed her, I believe, so Robert said; or the other vulgar man of the theatre who went down on his knees and called her "sublime." "Caprice d'amitié," said she, with her quiet, gentle scorn. A noble woman under the mud, be certain. I would kneel down to her, too, if she would leave it all, throw it off, and be herself as God made her. But she would not care for my kneeling; she does not care for me. Perhaps she doesn't care for anybody by this time – who knows? She wrote one, or two, or three kind notes to me, and promised to "venir m'embrasser" before she left Paris; but she did not come. We both tried hard to please her, and she told a friend of ours that she "liked us"; only we always felt that we couldn't penetrate – couldn't really touch her – it was all vain.[17]

Elizabeth ends this passage by noting that Sand's play has failed and by expressing the wish that she return to writing novels.

121

While in Florence, Elizabeth had thought of contemporary French novels and French newspapers as a means by which she could "look through a loophole at the world." In Paris, the salons that she – and more frequently Robert – visited became what she called "the shop windows of the world."[18] Soon after they settled into their apartment in October, Robert and Elizabeth began to attend the Monday evening soirées of Lady Elgin, and on Fridays they went to Madame Mohl's. Lady Elgin was, Elizabeth assured George, "the widow of the marble man – 'fixed statue on the pedestal of shame' as Lord Byron called him without reason. . . ."[19] Now white-haired and a long-time resident of the Faubourg St. Germain, Lady Elgin presided over one of the "'best houses' in Paris," a salon in which, as Elizabeth told Henrietta, "we are likely to meet various of the french 'celebrities' . . . which is just our reason for going."[20] The Brownings and Lady Elgin became quite close friends that year, and when the Brownings were again in Paris in 1855–56, Robert went once a week to read poetry to her. She had by that time become confined to a wheelchair; Robert read, appropriately, not Byron but Keats. Madame Mohl, too, was English, but she had lived in France since childhood and had been a protégée of Madame Récamier, whose brilliant salon under the First Empire and the Restoration remained the model. Madame Mohl's husband Julius was the first of four scholars of oriental languages at the Institut de France with whom Robert would eventually become acquainted. The others were Jean-Jacques Ampère, Ernest Renan, whom Robert would meet in the 1860's, and James Darmsteter, who translated Robert's *Hervé Riel* in 1882 and whose wife Mary, a mutual friend of Robert and Renan, was Renan's first biographer and the author of the long essay introducing *Poèmes de Robert Browning* (1922).

At her first evening at Lady Elgin's, Elizabeth had "expected to see Balzac's duchesses and *hommes de lettres* on all sides." She didn't, but she found the conversation and the unexpected informality quite agreeable.[21] From then until the colder weather came later in November, she and Robert went often to Lady Elgin's and Madame Mohl's. Throughout the winter Robert went alone and enjoyed himself. "Robert is charmed with Paris," she wrote in December, "& I don't very much wonder, – particularly as he is popular & receives all sorts of kindness & attention."[22] Lady Elgin and Madame Mohl also began to come to the Brownings' apartment in late November. During the first call they had a "great long talk about Shelley and poets generally."[23] Robert, who was finishing his essay on Shelley, must have joined in the conversation. When Lady Elgin called in January, however, the conversation centred on a subject about which he would become less enthusiastic: Lady Elgin told them about "all sorts of supernaturalisms"; and she had brought along the English abolitionist George Thompson, who "knew all about the 'Rappists,' had heard many spirits 'rap,' knew how a spirit gave a kiss to one lady, and an autograph to another –. . . ."[24] During the next few years Elizabeth's interest in spiritualism would grow to an obsession rivalling her defence of Napoleon III; this new mania would lead Robert to other than political *émeutes* with her. The potential for angry contention over the subject was revealed one evening when both the commonsensical Anna Jameson and Lady Elgin were at the Brownings':

> We had Lady Elgin here last Saturday evening again, and the evening did not go off half as well as usual –, because of a decided dyspathy between her & Mrs. Jameson – Lady Elgin is a great spiritualist with a leaning to Irvingism & a belief in every sort of incredible thing. While she talked of a communion of souls, Mrs. Jameson began talking of private madhouses – in a way which made my blood run cold – I really thought there would be an explosion between the two women, & that Robert & I, who agree so admirably with Lady Elgin, (for whom I bear quite an affection) would never carry the evening to an end safely. Lady Elgin *did* say – "Perhaps you think me mad."[25]

Robert would soon take the view of Anna Jameson or, indeed, that of Henri Dabot, who recalled the Paris of about this time: "Everyone is turning tables, or trying to do so. It's the favourite occupation of the moment. It's people's heads which are turning, not the tables."[26]

Lady Elgin told the Brownings that Lamartine was "particularly interested about both of us, and desirous of seeing us."[27] On March 14, after many delays, Lady Elgin took Robert to spend an evening with Lamartine; she also promised to bring the great man to see Elizabeth. When Lady Elgin fell ill, the task of bringing Lamartine to the Brownings' apartment fell to Eugène Pelletan. Pelletan assured Elizabeth that Lamartine was "extremely anxious to come,

both on account of our poetry, which he thinks highly of, and the
agreeable impression which Robert made on him during the evening
they were together. 'He was struck,' M. Pelletan told me, by
Robert's 'elevation of thought.' "[28] M. Pelletan's arrest and
threatened deportation interfered, and so Elizabeth did not meet
Lamartine. Both also missed meeting the old popular poet Béranger,
who lived near them and whom Robert had seen "in his white hat
wandering along the asphalte." At seventy-two, the poet of ribald
chansons and political satire had for more than twenty years since his
brief imprisonment lived in retirement. He "lives quietly and keeps
out of scrapes poetical and political," Elizabeth told Miss Mitford,
"But we can't make up our minds to go to his door and introduce
ourselves as vagrant minstrels, when he may probably not know our
names."[29] Musset, too, was missed. Robert went to François Buloz'
home "on purpose to meet him," but Musset did not appear, though
Robert met Musset's brother Paul instead. Paul de Musset's *Lui et
Elle* (1859), a sarcastic novel written in retaliation against Sand's
novel about herself and Musset, *Elle et Lui*, had not yet made Paul a
lion. As if to account for Alfred de Musset's failure to appear,
Elizabeth relays some gossip to Miss Mitford about Musset's recent
liaison with the actress Rachel: "He is said to be at the feet of Rachel
just now, and a man may nearly as well be with a tigress in a cage. He
began with the Princess Belgiojoso – followed by George Sand –
Rachel finishes, is likely to 'finish' in every sense. In the intervals he
plays chess."[30] Another disappointment was that Eugène Sue was
not invited, upon a decision by the hostess that he was too "scamp-
ish," to a Christmas party attended by little Pen. "Now I should like
to see Eugène Sue with my innocent little child in his arms,"
Elizabeth told Miss Mitford; "the combination pleases me somewhat."[31]

There were several disappointments in their efforts to meet the
"best people," but there were also successes. Augustin Thierry,
perhaps because of Robert's membership of the Historical Institute,
invited them to call, and they went. At the painter Ary Scheffer's
home Elizabeth talked with Pauline Viardot, the original of Sand's
Consuelo. Another associate of Sand, a man who had helped her
revise some of the socialist manifestos of 1848, the historian Henri
Martin, asked Elizabeth at Scheffer's whether she did not find Paris
melancholy since the *coup d'état*. Elizabeth, in her obvious delight

with Paris, could not agree:

> Not even the rain (much less the president) has prevented the
> nightly dances at the château des Fleurs – & although I remember
> a tragic situation in Ford (which has been much admired) of a
> woman who dances on, dances on, while one misery after another
> is announced to her, & then suddenly drops and dies, . . I don't
> quite expect a like catastrophe from the Parisian population in the
> middle of the Cancans dance.[32]

Particularly as the spring weather came, Paris enchanted Elizabeth.
"What a beautiful Paris it is!" she announced to a number of correspondents. Here one could hear delightful anecdotes about Balzac's
house at Passy and the walnut tree there "about which he delighted
himself in making various financial calculations after the manner of
César Birotteau." The anecdotes revealed, Elizabeth thought, something of Balzac's genius for realism: "the *idée fixe* of the man was to
be rich one day, and he threw his subtle imagination and vital poetry
into pounds, shillings, and pence with such force that he worked the
base element into spiritual splendours! Oh! to think of our having
missed seeing that man."[33] Two other great persons – Hugo and
Dumas – were out of Paris. Both were in Brussels, where Hugo was
safe from Louis-Napoleon's police and Dumas from his creditors.
When Hugo's extended invective *Napoléon le petit* appeared,
Elizabeth dismissed it as "an inarticulate cry of a bird of prey, wild
and strong – irrational, and not a book at all."[34] We hear nothing
more of Hugo until the late 1850's.

Two aspects of Dumas' current career most interested Elizabeth at
the moment. One was his improvidence and consequent indebtedness. Another was the literary debt he owed to his principal col-
laborator, Auguste Maquet, for the endless stream of historical
romances appearing under Dumas' name. For years Elizabeth had
admired not only Dumas' exciting narratives but also the copious
regularity with which he produced them. She was, then, pleased to
announce to Miss Mitford:

> Now listen. Alexandre Dumas *does* write his own books, that's a
> fact. You know I always maintained it, through the odour of
> Dumas in the books, but people swore the contrary with great
> foolish oaths worth nothing. Maquet prepares historical materials,

gathers together notes, and so on, but Dumas writes every word of his books with his own hand, and with a facility amounting to inspiration, said my informant.

Her informant was Louis Jadin, a painter and friend of Dumas with whom he had travelled in Italy and with whom he had worked on *Speronare*. The Brownings apparently came to know Jadin fairly well. He called several times at their apartment; and Robert, while at Jadin's home, was favoured with a showing of his collection of historical curios, including Louis-Philippe's umbrella and the coffee cup from which Napoleon I drank just before signing the papers of abdication. Jadin assured Elizabeth that Dumas was nearly as prodigal as he was prolific. If Dumas, Jadin said, "has twenty sous and wants bread, he buys a pretty cane instead. For the rest, 'bon enfant,' kind and amiable. An inspired negro child! In debt at this moment, after all the sums he has made. . . ."[35] Elizabeth looked to Jadin for a chance to meet Dumas. During an interval in London before returning to Paris, she read more Dumas: "He never flags," she told Miss Mitford. "I *must* see Dumas when I go again to Paris, and it will be easy, as we know his friend Jadin."[36] Robert did not quite share Elizabeth's enthusiasm for Dumas' romances, but that he was interested in Dumas the man is suggested when we learn that after Brownings' return to Florence Robert read, apparently, the twenty-one volumes of Dumas' *Mes mémoires*.

Dumas *fils* also enlivened the Parisian spring for the Brownings. His dramatized version of *La Dame aux camélias* was enjoying a striking success that season at the Vaudeville. The play's mixture of realism and romance, of scenes from the demi-monde blended with the redemption through pure love of the courtesan Marguerite, of sordidness and luxury and lovers' reconciliation come too late for happiness, all worked to make the play shocking, sensational, and successful at the box-office. Robert and Elizabeth went in early April to the fiftieth performance. It was with a tone of mock-bravado that Elizabeth informed George of this, her first excursion to a Parisian theatre:

> Now ask Arabel to skip this paragraph. Guess what enormity I have committed lately George! We went to see "La Dame aux Camelias," which you moral English are crying out against, & which we immoral French dont admit "Les demoiselles" going to

see at all. I wont allow (I being neither French nor English but a mere citizeness of the world) I wont allow that it is immoral, or is in the least calculated to do harm by its influences – . . . .[37]

The charges of immorality were aimed at the theme of the virtuous prostitute. It was a theme Balzac, for one, had fully explored in the character of Esther, La Torpille, lover of Lucien de Rubempré in *Splendeurs et misères des courtisanes*. Dumas' play, while retaining realistic scenes, heightened the suspense and pathos of the courtesan's progress towards saintliness and death. It was the kind of plot which Robert's Bishop Blougram has in mind when he tells his journalist visitor that contemporary society has an extraordinary fascination with such apparently incongruous characters:

Our interest's on the dangerous edge of things.
The honest thief, the tender murderer,
The superstitious atheist, demirep
That loves and saves her soul in new French books –
We watch while these in equilibrium keep
The giddy line. . . .

La Dame aux camélias, performed with "exquisite acting," certainly held the Brownings' interest: "it really almost killed me out of my propriety," Elizabeth told George, "– I sobbed so, I could scarcely keep my place – & had a splitting headache for four & twenty hours afterwards. . . ." She had been too strongly affected to go a second time when asked by Anna Jameson: " 'Take Robert if you like –,' " she replied, " 'but for my part I have had too much of it already.' "[38] Robert probably didn't go a second time, but he was strongly moved also; as if in self-defence, Elizabeth reported: "Even Robert, who gives himself out for *blasé* on dramatic matters, couldn't keep the tears from rolling down his cheeks."[39] The affective pathos of the play had already become a subject for journalists, and Elizabeth was amused by "a caricature representing the whole pit with umbrellas up to defend themselves from the tears raining out of the boxes."[40]

Although Elizabeth saw the humour of the excessive pathos of the play, she also made a more serious criticism of Dumas' blending of social realism and sentimentality: "The exquisite acting, the too liberal truth to nature everywhere, was *exasperating* – there was something profane in such familiar handling of life and death. Art

127

has no business with real graveclothes when she wants tragic drapery
– has she? It was too much altogether like a bull fight."[41] Elizabeth
would soon strive for a similar blending of social realism and pathos
in *Aurora Leigh*, and she had never been impatient with such a
mixture in the novels of Sand, Soulié, Sue, or even Balzac. But she
found Dumas' theatrical realism excessive: "When people want their
hearts broken, they have only to go & see. . . . It is too affecting – it
passes the bounds of art – and that's the worst of it to my mind."[42]
Her criticism reminds one of the objections a reviewer had recently
made to Robert's *Christmas Eve and Easter Day*: he complained of
Robert's too realistic treatment of the sacred subject of Christian
faith and so warned that "Realism in Art has Truth as an aim,
Ugliness as a pitfall."[43]

ii

A long appreciative essay on Robert's poetry appeared in the *Revue
des Deux Mondes* two months before the Brownings moved into their
apartment in the Champs-Élysées in October of 1851. The essay was
the second in a series of three studies on *La Poésie anglaise depuis
Byron* which Joseph Milsand was writing for Buloz' journal. The
first essay, on Tennyson, had appeared in the July 15, 1851, issue;
the second on Robert, on August 15; a third, on John Reade, Henry
Taylor and Elizabeth, came out on January 15, 1852. The major
contention of Milsand's series is that the contemporary English poets
had evolved essentially new forms and modes of thought and expression which set them apart from but made them equal to the great
English romantic poets, especially Byron, whom the French continued to consider the last great English poet. Milsand praised Tennyson for his fresh lyricism combined with an intensity and variety
of moral thought. The recently published *In Memoriam* could
become "one's Bible", Milsand thought: "I say this deliberately that
I do not know a book which leaves one with a more tremendous idea
of human nature. The conceptions of certain thinkers give us a
glimpse of the infinity in the capacities of the mind. Tennyson's
book gives us a glimpse of infinity in the moral faculties."[44] Tennyson's inability to sustain his brief lyrics worries Milsand: such brev-
ity may not augur well for his future development. In his next essay
Milsand found Browning sufficiently copious. He ends the essay –
given over largely to close analyses of the two longest poems avail-

able to him, *Paracelsus* and *Christmas Eve and Easter Day* – with this comparison of lyric poets like Tennyson to Browning: "To each his own role: some bring together all human emotions, others bring together all our ideas. For some, lyricism; for Mr. Browning, epic poetry." He goes on to say that although Browning does not imitate either the manner or the matter of the older epic poets, "of the poets I know, he is the most capable of summing up the ideas of religion, morality, and theoretical science of our epoch, while giving them a poetic form."[45]

Throughout, Milsand stresses the essential newness and modernity of Browning's thought and expression. This quality, he apologizes at the beginning, makes "non-sens" of any attempt to apply traditional critical principles and vocabulary to Browning's poems: "for all of his adventures have been set in countries which are not drawn on the map. . . . In order to understand his work, a very special nomenclature must be created" (661–62). Milsand's opening remarks remind one of Browning's angry letter to his publisher when, in Paris in 1856, he read the harsh reviews of *Men and Women*: "they cry out for new things and when you furnish them with what they cried for, 'it's so *new*,' they grunt."[46] Milsand's lengthy commentary on *Paracelsus* is concerned mainly with the explanation of ideas expressed by Paracelsus himself, but he also praises Browning's success in condensing "abstractions into poetic and living forms" (662). In so doing, Browning begins "at the opposite of other poets" who begin with grand theories whose "prétentions colossales" mask a very thin slice of experience. "Mr. Browning, on the other hand, appears at once as a man who has known the world" (663). Though Milsand recognizes and praises what might be called Browning's nascent realism in *Paracelsus*, he also recognizes that in that early poem it is his interest in ideas and power of generalization that dominate: in *Paracelsus* Browning "sought to paint general laws, moral laws, without painting them by actions and effects which, in this world, are their sole way of being shown" (680).

Milsand was a careful and systematic reader. When he turned to the plays and dramatic lyrics and romances of Browning's *Bells and Pomegranates*, he was "struck by a complete alteration in manner" (680). Now, in this more recent work, Browning, while remaining "le penseur," had become "un observateur myope." He built up scenes and characters by careful attention to external detail. Browning has, Milsand observes, recognized the dangers of not clothing ideas in sights and sounds, as Browning would tell Milsand himself two years later. "Thinker that he has been," Milsand says, "he preserves the advantages while avoiding the disadvantages of thoughtful natures, who too often have the air of knowing the powers which manifest themselves in things without knowing the things of which they are manifestations" (680). The change of manner Milsand discovers and approves is that now Browning generalizes only after minute observation. His achievement is comparable to that of the Flemish realist painters: "That doubtless explains why his generalizations," argues Milsand, "instead of being idealizations, are thousands of realities in a single definition" (680). Milsand notes that Browning in his latest poem, *Christmas Eve*, has continued in the "Flemish mode of which I spoke." He is, however, more interested in that poem and *Easter Day* in relation to the question of religious faith in the contemporary world. He ends with the assertion that he knows of no other poet so capable of embodying in poetic form the religious, moral and scientific questions "de notre époque" (689).

Both Robert and Elizabeth were, of course, pleased to find in a leading Parisian journal such full, thoughtful, and generous criticism, whereas in England Robert's work had, by and large, been either ignored or often harshly criticized for the past decade. Elizabeth was especially pleased that Milsand had recognized the accomplishments in new English poetry. "And do you ever catch sight of the 'Revue des Deux Mondes?'" she asked Miss Mitford in November:

> In the August number is an excellent and most pleasant article on my husband, elaborately written and so highly appreciatory as well nigh to satisfy *me*. "Set you down this" that there has sprung up in France lately an ardent admiration of the present English schools of poetry, or rather of the poetry produced by the present English schools, which they consider *an advance upon the poetry of the ages*. Think of *this*, you English readers who are still wearing broad hems and bombazeens for the Byron and Scott glorious days![47]

Wider Parisian interest in Elizabeth's poetry and an indiscretion by Miss Mitford would soon reveal to the Brownings that Joseph Milsand was as thoughtful and generous as a man as he was as a critic. Milsand had by early December sought out the Brownings either by letter or by a call. He was expected to call the night of December 4, but that was the night of the heaviest street fighting, so he was unable to come. "I hope he wasn't shot on the road," Elizabeth told George the next day.[48]

On January 3, the *Athenaeum* reviewer quoted a long selection from Miss Mitford's recently published *Recollections of a Literary Life*. The selection recounted the deep sorrow Elizabeth felt at the drowning of brother Edward in 1838. Elizabeth was greatly distressed by this indiscreet revelation of her private life. The Brownings heard about the review and book in a roundabout way. Apparently her Uncle Hedley had been attending the Collège de France when Philarète Chasles, while announcing a series of lectures on English writers, referred to the review and the book. Milsand, whose essay on Elizabeth was to appear in the January 15 issue of the *Revue des Deux Mondes*, was also asked by Buloz to make use of the information. Milsand, however, realizing that such use of Miss Mitford's revelations would be painful to Elizabeth, called and asked Robert what he should do. "Do observe," Elizabeth wrote to Mrs. Martin, "the delicacy and sensibility of this man – a man, a foreigner, a Frenchman! I shall be grateful to him as long as I live."[49] Chasles, however, went ahead with two lectures about Elizabeth in early March. Uncle Hedley attended both and Robert one. By this time Elizabeth had recovered from the original shock and could report light-heartedly to Mrs. Ogilvy about Chasles' extravagant additions to her life story:

> M. Chasles, not finding the Mitford story sufficiently romantic for his ends, embroidered deeply with gold & silk, & produced a tragedy about a fiancé, which would have done honour, Robert says, to Dumas himself. Not one word of truth from beginning to end, but the most picturesque details (en revanche) including the "waving of handkerchiefs", the consolations received "in farm-houses", & and final residences in "magnificent palaces of the Medici", called Casa Guidi.

Robert, too, was brought into M. Chasles' lecture. Robert was described, Elizabeth reported, as "ce poète obscur, mystique . . . du reste celebre. (this obscure, mystical poet . . . yet famous.)"

Elizabeth's poem *The Poet's Vow*, Chasles asserted, was written to reclaim Robert from his "deeply dyed" pantheism.[50] At a soirée some weeks later, Elizabeth was pleased to inform a Polish princess, who "was full of M. Philarète Chasles' lectures," that the lectures contained little truth about her. She was similarly pleased to learn that Alexis de Tocqueville had made a kind of apology for Chasles: de Tocqueville "& friends who were with him, were offended by the indelicacy of the whole exhibition." Such public discussion of private affairs, de Tocqueville said, was "'not commonly done in France, & could only be considered ungentlemanly.'"[51]

In the meantime, Milsand's essay had appeared; and, although he had at Buloz' urging made some reference to Elizabeth's life, he had "cut out the 'sting' of Miss M's remarks. . . ."[52] The part of the essay devoted to Elizabeth was a critique of her two-volume *Poems* (1844–50) and *Casa Guidi Windows* (1851). As in the essays on Tennyson and Robert, Milsand focused on the longer, more ambitious poems and looked for a sense of development within the poet's career. He praised the long *A Drama of Exile*, but he objected to the recent long poem *Casa Guidi Windows* because he thought contemporary politics not a proper subject of great poetry. Elizabeth urged George to find a copy of the *Revue des Deux Mondes* and read the essay "because it pleased me (with some drawbacks) & because I have really a regard for the writer. . . ."[53] Milsand became a regular caller at the Brownings' that winter and spring. His knowledge and love of English literature, his serious and thoughtful interest in contemporary political theory, his early experience as an art student in Italy, his conversion from Catholicism to Protestantism, all must have contributed to the friendship which grew up among them. It is probably Milsand whom Elizabeth describes but appropriately does not name to Miss Mitford in a letter in February: "A very philosophically minded man (French) . . . one of the most thoughtful, liberal men I ever knew of any country, and high and pure in his moral views – also (let me add) more *anglomane* in general than I am."[54] Further, Milsand delighted in the intellectual toughness of Robert's work and was not impatient with what other critics found obscure in Robert's style. Milsand himself wrote "'in a language which defied superficial attention.'" Later in a letter from Florence, Robert assured Milsand that he did not find Milsand's style obscure: "'In what is it obscure? – Strong, condensed, and direct it is, and no doubt the common readers of easy writing feel oppressed by twenty pages of such masculine stuff, as the habitual sippers of *eau sucrée* would at the proffer of a real *consommé*. . . .' "[55] It is fitting that when Robert reprinted *Sordello* he dedicated that difficult poem to Milsand; nor is it surprising that Milsand would supply a number of proof-corrections for the equally difficult *Fifine at the Fair*.

Milsand's connection with the *Revue des Deux Mondes* raises an interesting if necessarily speculative question about Browning's relationship to the younger generation of French writers. The question is interesting because Robert shares a number of interests with Théophile Gautier, Gérard de Nerval, and Ernest Renan, all of whom were in one way or another then associated with Buloz' journal; the question is speculative because none of the Browning correspondence mentions these writers. The Brownings had begun reading the *Revue* certainly as early as the August, 1851, issue that contained Milsand's essay on Robert, and they remained sporadic readers thereafter; further, Robert attended the Buloz salon and may have heard there some talk of such writers, among whom there was a sense of an important difference between themselves and the older generation. Baudelaire, sixteen of whose *Fleurs du mal* were to be published in the *Revue* in June, 1855, also felt that difference as did writers not associated with the journal, the young Gustave Flaubert and Leconte de Lisle, whose manifesto calling for a new kind of poetry appeared as the preface to *Poèmes antiques* while the Brownings were in Paris.

The Brownings quite naturally thought of the Parisian literary world largely in terms of the older generation and of the novelists. By 1851–52, however, Stendhal, Balzac, Soulié, and Bernard were dead; Sue had become a propagandist, Sand a writer of plays. Hugo had not published any imaginative work for nearly a decade; nor, with the exception of the *Nouvelle Raphaël* (1849) and *Le Tailleur de pierres de Saint-Point* (1851), had Lamartine. Béranger, too, was silent. Dumas *père*, in exile, remained prolific; but it was the new note of social realism by Dumas *fils* that was causing the sensation in Paris. Musset, whom Robert hoped to meet at Buloz' but did not, published *Premières Poésies, Poésies nouvelles* in 1852. The newer poems aimed at greater restraint and impersonality in contrast to the intensely personal lyrics of his early career. Musset had announced this deliberate shift in his poetry as early as *Les Lettres de Dupuis et*

Cotonet in the *Revue* in 1836–38. Impersonality, "impassibilité," detachment, the critical spirit, attention to external detail, the use of irony, all were valued by the younger generation as literary strategies by which they could avoid or supplant the exaggerations of personal feelings, the introspection, even the visionary hopefulness of the older generation of poets. This was the generation Thibaudet would call a "génération critique" and Saulnier a "génération objectiviste." They brought into poetry, as Henri Lemaître suggests, something of the realism which had been developed in the novels of Balzac and Stendhal.[56]

Ernest Renan's work, especially his eloquent advocacy of the application of the critical, scientific spirit to our understanding of the historical origins of Christianity, would directly influence Robert's work in the 1860's. Renan had begun writing in 1848 articles for the liberal republican and anti-clerical journal *La Liberté de Penser*. Baudelaire, Sue, Quinet, Michelet, too, were contributors. Among the essays Renan published there was one attacking the kind of clerical liberalism Montalembert represented; Renan, strongly anti-clerical already, thought those who believed the Church could be anything but absolutist and dogmatic were deceiving themselves. Another article, printed in March and April of 1849, discussed the "Higher Criticism" of the Bible growing up in Germany; although approving the general soundness of such work, Renan deplores in these essays and in a later one in September, 1850, the German tendency to be "hard, crabbed, negative, mocking" and the failure of writers like Strauss and Feuerbach to see any of the beauty of Christianity.[57] Renan's distrust of an absolutist church, his support of the republican cause, and his distaste for the crabbed ugliness of German biblical criticism, all would have appealed to a Robert Browning who at the time was both republican and anti-clerical and who, in the spring of 1850, published in *Christmas Eve* his portrait of "The hawk-nosed high-cheek-boned Professor" from Göttingen, who, coughing through piston-like lungs and peering with spectacled eyes "like lamps," pumps all the vitality out of the life of Jesus until "the pearl of price, at reason's test, / Lay dust and ashes levigable / On the Professor's lecture-table."

La Liberté de Penser was, of course, suppressed after the *coup d'état*. In the December 15, 1851, issue Renan, introduced to Buloz by Thierry, published his first article for the *Revue des Deux Mondes*.

Later, Renan would recall how difficult it was at the time to publish anything not either frivolous or assumed to be so by the censors. On the grounds that no one was stupid enough to believe in such a religion, Buloz rejected Renan's essay on Buddhism and accepted instead "Mahomet et les origines de l'Islamisme," one of Renan's *Études d'histoire religieuse*. Renan managed to criticize obliquely the new regime by concluding his essay with a declaration of the individual's right to freedom of conscience.[58] That the Brownings saw this issue of the *Revue* is likely. By then Milsand was a Tuesday night visitor and was preparing for the next issue of the *Revue* his essay on Elizabeth.

Another of Buloz' writers was Gérard de Nerval. Nerval was often in the Maison Dubois for treatment for mental instability during the winter of 1851–52, but in the spring he was well enough for Buloz to commission him to write an article on the May Festivals in Holland, an article printed in the June issue. Nerval also published that year his volume of erudite essays on esoteric, obscure historical figures, *Les Illuminés*; one of them, "Les Confidences de Nicolos" (an exposition of Nicolos' pursuit of ideal love in real women), appeared in the *Revue* in August and September 1850; another, "Quintus Aucler," came out in the *Revue de Paris* in November of 1851. His *Sylvie* was in the *Revue* in August 1853. The poems that went to make up Nerval's *Les Chimères* did not begin to appear in periodicals until 1853, when for example "El Desdichado" was printed in *Le Mousquetaire*, the newspaper Dumas kept going largely by instalments of his own *Mémoires*. Robert could not have read before 1853 the Nerval poem which is so close in mood and image to his own *Childe Roland to the Dark Tower Came* (1852):

I am the gloomy – the widowed – the disconsolate,
The Prince of Aquitaine in the ruined tower;
My only star is dead – and my star-studded lute
Bears the black sun of Melancholy.

More interesting, perhaps, is the coincidence of mood and manner in such essentially diverse poets as Browning and Nerval. Browning wrote his poem at the Champs-Élysées apartment in early January, 1852. Nerval's account of his travels in the Levant and Egypt, *Voyage en Orient* (1851), would certainly, had he seen it, have interested Robert. There Nerval describes his fascination with the dervishes in

135

Cairo and the Druses in Syria. He also describes his own dream of marrying a Druse, a description mixed with the retelling of the Druse God Hakeem's hopeless love for his sister. Browning's play about Hakeem and Anael, *The Return of the Druses*, had been published in 1843, the year Nerval made his journey. (By coincidence Elizabeth begins to use the image of Egypt and desert sands – as refuge from her chagrin at Miss Mitford's revelations of her private life – in letters that winter; it was not until 1858 that the Brownings made serious plans for travel to Egypt and the Levant.)[59] In retrospect, Nerval the melancholy creator of intense dreamlike poems seems far removed from the cheerful Browning, whose more characteristic mode was the extended and carefully detailed dramatic monologue. But in Paris in 1851–52 the two shared interests and acquaintances and at least once – for *Childe Roland's* "surnaturalisme" is highly unusual in the Browning canon – they shared a remarkably similar poetic impulse.

Théophile Gautier, Nerval's friend since the days of *Hernani*, also seems, in retrospect, a very different kind of poet. Gautier's famed advocacy of "l'art pour l'art" may obscure the fact that his doctrine was a protest against the personal effusiveness and the emotional subjectivism of poets like Hugo and Lamartine and the early Musset. Gautier worked for a more impersonal poetry attentive to external details of place or time or individual personalities: "the manner, gesture, bearing, breath, colour, sound, aroma, everything that is life. . . ."[60] To some extent his carefully constructed objective poems in *Émaux et Camées* (1852) brought into French poetry something of the realism that was primarily associated with the novels of Stendhal and Balzac. He had early revealed a satiric and ironic bent in *Albertus* (1832); and he ridiculed romantic excess in *Les Jeunes-France* (1833); his interest developed in more objective and dramatic modes in stories of local colour; and he had published in the *Revue des Deux Mondes* (March 1, 1846) his satire of romantic pastoralism, *La Fausse Conversion*. Gautier did not write again for the *Revue*; indeed, in 1851–52 Buloz was still pressing him with a lawsuit for failure to deliver work for which he had received a sizeable advance. But the finely crafted poems Gautier published in 1852 as *Émaux et Camées* had that quality of detachment and care for external detail that was increasingly valued. In the *nouvelle* published later, *Spirite*, his hero Guy de Malivert describes this more impersonal kind of writing while making a distinction between "un auteur subjectif" and "un auteur objectif":

> the first expresses his sentiments . . . and judges society and the universe in pursuance of an ideal; the second presents objects as nature supplies them; he proceeds by image, by description; he brings the things under the eye of the reader; he draws, clothes, and colours his characters exactly and puts into their mouths the words they must have spoken and withholds his opinion.[61]

Had Browning noticed *Émaux et Camées* when it came out, he would have discovered such an objective poet exercising his skill on a number of Italian scenes and in a style replete with difficult rhyme and ingenious metaphor, a style so compressed that relative pronouns and conjunctions often are left out – all stylistic mannerisms Browning himself was often criticized for.

Baudelaire, who dedicated his *Les Fleurs du mal* to Gautier, thought Ernest Renan had a poetical counterpart in Leconte de Lisle.[62] Leconte de Lisle would only begin his long association with the *Revue des Deux Mondes* in 1855. In 1852, however, he published his *Poèmes antiques* prefaced by his forceful manifesto calling for a poetry free of "émotions personnelles," a poetry which would be an impersonal and scholarly study of moments in history, especially those moments of the past marked by strong religious belief. This idea Leconte de Lisle offers in the preface to his carefully documented poems about ancient Greece and the Orient so as to explain what he calls "l'impersonalité et la neutralité des ces études."[63] Browning, who was soon to extend his *Saul* and to recreate in dramatic form the religious ideas of Cleon and Karshish, would doubtless have had some sympathy from both Renan and Leconte de Lisle despite their disbelief in the resurrected Christ which Browning's poems affirm. A strong current of opinion among the younger French writers sought a more impersonal, dramatic, often ironic and frequently erudite poetry. The visionary, intuitive, prophetic didacticism of Hugo in *Les Voix intérieures* (1837) or *Les Rayons et les ombres* (1840) could not be the model for a more critical and less illusioned generation. By 1852 Hugo was to men like Gautier and Leconte de Lisle what Shelley was to Browning: the younger men continued to admire the power and force of the older poets, but, to use Browning's phrase from the *Essay on Shelley*, there was now "the imperative call for the appearance of another sort of poet."[64]

iii

Browning began his essay on Shelley soon after he and Elizabeth moved into the Champs-Élysées apartment in October of 1851; he completed it the night of December 4, the night they stayed up until early morning listening to the cannonading in the boulevards. Browning had by then read and been greatly pleased by Milsand's essay, and Milsand was expected to visit the night he finished his essay on Shelley. In his essay on Browning Milsand had emphasized the essential newness of Browning's poetry, praised his critical and intellectual force; Milsand noted and approved Browning's decided shift towards the dramatic mode in which scenes and characters are built up by realistic detail as though by "un observateur myope." The result was a poetry not dependent upon generalizations without reference to the external world, but rather a poetry whose intellectual generalizations arose out of "milliers de réalités," not "idéalités." Philip Drew is right when he argues that "the ideas underlying the *Essay* [on Shelley] had been with Browning for some years"; however, Drew exaggerates when he asserts that "Milsand's article bears almost no relation to the *Essay* and cannot have been a source for it."[65]

The similarities in the two essays range from the common emphasis upon the need for a new kind of poet to express new ideas and experiences, to the common assertion that such a poet will evolve his work out of careful attention to the external world, to the open assertion by Browning and the clear implication by Milsand that the biography of what Browning calls an objective poet is not of special interest: "I know nothing of the personal history of Mr. Browning," Milsand says after quoting from Jules' letter in *Pippa Passes* and then pointing out that what matters is that ideas similar to those of the dramatic character are also found in *Paracelsus*. Milsand's reluctance to use biographical material in his essay on Elizabeth, even at Buloz' insistence, is known. That his essay could have been a "source" for Browning's essay is clear: as Browning wrote his essay he had Milsand's before him, had read it with delight and had asked its author to his home. But Drew is, most important,

138

certainly correct in his observation that Browning's ideas were his own and had long been with him; and correct, too, is Drew's appreciation of the originality and soundness of Milsand's essay. Milsand, almost alone among reviewers by 1851, was a "real authority on the matter" of Browning's work, as Browning rather testily informed his publisher, who had used a rather meaningless quote from an English reviewer to advertise *Christmas Eve and Easter Day*.[66]

Browning might have written this essay, had the occasion arisen, at any time since he had worked out many of its ideas in *Sordello*. That it was composed in Paris at a time when a writer for the *Revue des Deux Mondes* had recognized Browning's startling modernity and realism, and at a time when younger French writers were making a similar break with their immediate romantic predecessors, gives the essay an added interest. English writers and artists were less given than their French comrades to forming schools and issuing manifestos. Still, the *Essay on Shelley* is in some ways Browning's equivalent to, say, Leconte de Lisle's preface to *Poèmes antiques*. Browning, however, unlike Leconte de Lisle, did not adopt the strategy of condemning his great and greatly admired predecessor. As an introduction to recently discovered letters of Shelley, the purpose of the essay is to assess and acknowledge Shelley's greatness and to make a special case for the importance of the letters because they offer new information about Shelley's life. The biography of a subjective poet like Shelley is essential, Browning says, if we are to judge and more completely understand the poetry. The rhetorical strategy Browning adopts to make these claims for the importance of Shelley and the letters accommodates, indeed enhances, the purposes of what I have called Browning's manifesto. The first third of the essay is given over almost entirely to a description and defence of the objective poet; that is, the kind of poet Shelley definitely *is not* but Browning himself presumably, and according to Milsand, *is*. Browning does not make the case for "the subjective poet of modern classification" until he has fully made a superior case for the "objective poet, as the phrase now goes." He assumes that the distinction between the two kinds of poets is commonplace, and is indeed a bit contemptuous of the new jargon. Then, in a long paragraph, Browning describes the distinguishing qualities of the objective poet in terms nearly as commonplace as the original distinction: the qualities he enumerates are, at any rate, often invoked in the many prefaces, discursive asides, speeches by characters or personal letters of Balzac, Stendhal, Gautier, Leconte de Lisle, to name, as my purpose is, only some recent or contemporary French writers. The objective poet, Browning says, is

> one whose endeavour has been to reproduce things external (whether the phenomena of the scenic universe, or the manifested action of the human heart and brain) with an immediate reference, in every case, to the common eye and apprehension of his fellow men, assumed capable of receiving and profiting by this reproduction. It has been obtained through the poet's double faculty of seeing external objects more clearly, widely, and deeply than is possible to the average mind, at the same time that he is so acquainted and in sympathy with its narrower comprehension as to be careful to supply it with no other materials than it can combine into an intelligible whole.[67]

Browning's emphasis upon the relationship between the reader and the poem takes an expected realist bias. The objective poet enhances the significance of external phenomena and so directs the reader's attention from the poem back to "the reality it was made from." Such reference back to a reality accessible to both writer and reader allows the reader to either "corroborate" his previous impressions of the external world and hence to measure the poet's fidelity and insight, or to broaden his knowledge of the "inexhaustible variety of existence." To the extent that Browning insists that a poet and reader share a common reality, his claims resemble Balzac's claim that he was secretary to his time; Stendhal takes a similar position with his figure of the novelist as a man carrying a mirror along the road of life. Both novelists used the argument in part to defend themselves against charges that they wrongly portrayed what was unflattering, ugly, or sordid in human nature. Browning had been similarly charged by reviewers and had recently been warned that "Realism in art has . . . Ugliness as a pitfall." Milsand, too, had noted that Browning's penchant for accurate detail carried with it the danger of slipping into the grotesque. Browning is not, of course, overtly defending his own practice in the *Essay*; he simply makes use of an argument which served at times as the realist defence against charges of vulgarity, coarseness, and ugliness. His Fra Lippo Lippi would make a fuller argument in 1855, the same year Courbet would angrily defend the coarseness of his figures in *Funeral at Ornans* (which had also been shown in the Salon of 1851) by asserting that his subjects "were not beautiful, so I cannot make them beautiful."[68] The most startling declaration that readers could, if only they would (in Browning's phrase) "corroborate their impressions of things known already," appeared in the June 1, 1855, issue of the *Revue des Deux Mondes*: "You, reader, know this discerning monster, – Hypocrite reader – my fellow-man – my brother!" – the closing lines of Baudelaire's "Au Lecteur."

The separation of the poet's life from his work – his impersonality and objectivity – had been a preoccupation of Browning's at least since the publication of *Pauline*. More than any other British writer of his generation, Browning strove in his art to develop techniques whereby such distance could be achieved and made apparent to the reader. Thomas J. Collins rightly emphasizes that in the *Essay* Browning puts special weight upon the craft of poetry, and for him "the essential difference between the two poets [objective and subjective] is not so much in their methods of perception as in the adaptability of the materials they employ."[69] By renaming the objective poet "the fashioner," Browning effectively shifts his emphasis away from the quality of insight to stress the craft of presentation of diverse materials; at the same time he opens up the desired distance between the writer and his work: "the thing fashioned, his poetry, will of necessity be substantive, projected from himself and distinct." We may, he says, be interested in the biography of the "fashioner" but such knowledge is not essential to the understanding of the work. The poem has become an object in its own right: "The man passes, the work remains. The work speaks for itself, as we say." This is not quite *l'art pour l'art*, but it is an attitude shared by a number of French writers – Renan, Leconte de Lisle, Baudelaire, Gautier, Flaubert – who distrusted the personal mode of Lamartine, Hugo, Musset, and valued instead conscious craftsmanship which provided detachment and play for the critical mind.

Renan's statement in the preface to *Feuilles détachées* catches well this attitude: "Many times I have criticized the minds of our times for being too subjective, for being too occupied with themselves, for not being sufficiently involved with and absorbed in the object, that is to say, with what is before us, the world, nature, history."[70]

Renan's testimony admittedly comes late in his life, but he claims that he learned this lesson while still in seminary in the 1840's. Younger French writers with whom Browning shared a common sensibility reinforced attitudes espoused by older writers whom Browning admired. Balzac was, of course, among the latter. As early as his original preface to *La Peau de chagrin* (1831) Balzac had alerted his readers that they should be careful not to confuse an artist's work with his personal life: "Doubtless there are many writers whose personalities are vividly reproduced by the nature of their writing, and for them the work and the man are the same thing; but there are other writers whose mind and manner strongly contrast with the form and depth of their works. . . ."[71] In 1852 Gautier achieved that impersonality through careful craftsmanship in *Émaux et Camées*; Leconte de Lisle called for such objectivity in his preface to *Poèmes antiques* and advised greater intellectual toughness in the service of historical scholarship. In the spring of 1852 Baudelaire published his essay *Edgar Allan Poe, sa Vie et ses ouvrages* in the *Revue de Paris* and noted with approval Poe's emphasis on craft rather than feeling to affect the reader. Poe had first condemned those writers who "prefer having it understood that they compose by a species of fine frenzy – an ecstatic intuition."[72]

Browning, clearly, did not condemn Shelley for such "fine frenzy" and for basing his poetry "in his own soul as the nearest reflux of that absolute Mind, according to the intuitions of which he desires to perceive and speak." Still, after lengthy initial description of the objective mode, Browning goes on to assert that the "fashioner" is at least of equal value to the "seer," that the external world must be "the starting point and basis" for all true poetry, and that at this moment in history there was a definite need for the objective poet or perhaps some combination of the objective and subjective. Further, the powerful vision of an authentic, subjective "seer" is inherited by a "tribe of successors" who rarefy and dilute the original vision, "till, at unawares, the world is found to be subsisting wholly on the shadow of a reality, on sentiments diluted from passions, on the tradition of a fact, the convention of a moral, the straw of last year's harvest."[73] A listing of charges against unnamed imitators who attenuate a previously valid mode is frequently used rhetorical strategy in artistic manifestos. In Browning's "Popularity," written at this time, Keats' pallid imitators are simply Hobbs,

Nobbs, Stokes and Nokes. Leconte de Lisle, in his preface to *Poèmes antiques*, disdainfully dismisses the anonymous imitators of, one assumes, Hugo and Lamartine, as "Oh Poets, teachers of souls, strangers to the basic rudiments of real life no less than of the ideal life . . . careless writers who humour you with a fundamental ignorance of man and the world." Such poets, he says, are responsible for the age turning away from poetry: "the age no longer listens to you because you have pestered it with your sterile complains."[74] Positing a similar crisis in poetry caused by pallid imitation of great predecessors, Browning announces in the Shelley essay the age's need for a poet who will be "prodigal of objects for men's outer not inner sight." At such a time there is, he asserts eloquently, "the imperative call for the appearance of another sort of poet, who shall at once replace this intellectual rumination of food swallowed long ago, by a supply of the fresh and living swathe."[75]

Browning was, as we have seen, greatly pleased to find in Milsand's essay such intelligent and appreciative commentary on his work. Milsand's essay certainly confirmed for Browning that his attempts to manifest in poetry his theoretical ideas were recognized and valued. Milsand was highly appreciative of the more objective mode of the *Bells and Pomegranates* series, especially *Dramatic Lyrics* and *Dramatic Romances*. If nothing else, Milsand must have given Browning greater confidence by which to plead strongly the case of the "fashioner" as against the "seer" and hence write a kind of manifesto disguised as a preface. Paris was a congenial place to do this. In London, reviewers were hostile to his realism and impatient with his obscurity, erudition, and intellectuality. Some too, like Charles Kingsley, regretted that Browning so often drew his subjects from continental rather than English life and so urged him to cast "all his rugged genial force into the questions and struggles of [his] mother-country. . . ."[76] Nationalism, social and political reform, utopian hopes were enthusiasms more distrusted in the literary temper of Paris. Leconte de Lisle, whose hopes for the Revolution of 1848 had been so high, was the most disillusioned and was now violently opposed to the intrusion of contemporary politics into poetry. Baudelaire, who briefly carried a rifle in February of 1848 and who wrote, along with Renan, for *La Liberté de Penser*, claimed that "Le 2 DÉCEMBRE m'a physiquement dépolitiqué."[77]

Dislike of Louis-Napoleon and critical detachment from political

action were further traits Browning held in common with the
Parisian generation of 1848. But most important was the common
valuing of critical detachment and impersonality in literature, of
imagistic detail instead of personal statement, of poems as objects
rather than as vehicles for a poet's intuitions, passions or ideas. That
is the kind of poetry Browning told Milsand in 1853 he was writing:
poems "with more music and painting than before, so as to get
people to hear and see." In the same letter he comments on his
English contemporaries:

> The vice I hate most in what little English literature I see now,
> is the inveterate avoidance of simplicity and straightforwardness.
> If a man has a specific thing to say, little or great, he will not say it,
> he says something else in altogether an alien tone to the real matter
> at hand, such as it is, and though, thanks to the triviality and
> obviousness of the matter, you understand it readily enough *by
> rebound*, as it were. . . . The reader at present, while the mode is
> not stale, goes on translating easily and almost without notice; but
> one day the trick will grow wearisome, and then good-by to the
> books that have used it![78]

In *How to Read* (1929), Ezra Pound called his readers' attention to
the objective, imagist mode of any number of mid-century French
writers. He added: "England can offer only Robert Browning."[79]

iv

Four Browning poems probably written while he was in Paris in
1851–52 address directly the nature of poetry and literary genera-
tions: "Memorabilia," "Popularity," "Transcendentalism," and
"How It Strikes a Contemporary." The first of these begins with the
anecdote of Browning being strongly moved by meeting a man who
had once seen "Shelley plain." Browning's startled response had
provoked laughter from the man. In the third stanza, Browning
shifts to a metaphoric equivalent of the experience: the sudden discovery of an eagle feather (associated with Shelley) upon a sunlit
moor:

> I crossed a moor, with a name of its own
>   And a certain use in the world no doubt,
> Yet a hand's-breadth of it shines alone
>   'Mid the blank miles round about;

IV

For there I picked up on the heather
And there I put inside my breast
A moulted feather, an eagle-feather!
Well, I forget the rest.

The metaphor seems a rhetorical, romantic inflation of the original interesting but not especially significant encounter. The metaphor, that is, builds towards sentimental posturing. Browning quickly deflates the metaphor and mood with the quick, wry dismissal of the metaphor in the short final line: "Well, I forget the rest." The effect of this final line, turning as it does on both the poem and the reader, is to give to the memory of Shelley balance and common sense. "Memorabilia" provides some counterpoise to the memory of a famous and powerful predecessor. "Popularity" celebrates the as yet unrecognized poet whose present endeavours are to distil something of great value for the future. The extended analogy of this poet to a Tyrian fisherman contains a description of the poetic process rather similar to the mode described as "objective" in the *Essay*. The diverse objects of the fisherman's net seem unpromising, indeed even ugly, sources of beauty:

Live whelks, each lip's beard dripping fresh,
    As if they still the water's lisp heard
Through foam the rock-weeds thresh.

Bystanders "criticize and quote tradition," content with, in terms of the *Essay*, "last year's harvest." But the fisherman has harvested what is fresh and living; then, by craft, the beauty is extracted and distilled. Once the new poet's work is completed, the cycle begins again as the "tribe of successors" grows up to imitate and reap undeserved reward:

Hobbs hints blue, – straight he turtle eats:
    Nobbs prints blue, – claret crowns his cup:
Nokes outdares Stokes in azure feats, –
    Both gorge. Who fished the murex up?
What porridge had John Keats?

The discursive, meditative, didactic element of the older romantics is forcefully rejected in "Transcendentalism." Wordsworth's recently published *The Prelude* may provide an immediate reference for Browning's poem; so, too, may Browning's own earlier tendency towards philosophical generalization which gave way to his more recent shift towards more dramatic and imagistic modes. It was this shift in his work which had so struck (*frappé*) Milsand. In France the discursive, didactic mode of Hugo was being rejected. This was the Hugo who, as Browning said later, "can't let truth be truth, or a number of remarkable poetical pieces speak for themselves, without assuring you that he meant to join Man to God, with the like pleasant practicabilities."[80] Against such pretension (*"prétentions colossales"* Milsand called them), Browning opposes a poetry of aural and visual imagery that will "repair our loss" of delight in "Objects [which] throng our youth." Ranging himself in alliance with the mage John of Halberstadt instead of the drily didactic Jacob Boehme, Browning addresses and instructs the older poet:

> Stop playing, poet! May a brother speak?
> 'T is you speak, that's your error. Song's our art:
> Whereas you please to speak these naked thoughts
> Instead of draping them in sights and sounds.
> – True thoughts, good thoughts, thoughts fit to treasure up!
> But why such long prolusion and display,
> Such turning and adjustment of the harp,
> And taking it upon your breast, at length,
> Only to speak dry words across its strings?
> Stark-naked thought is in request enough:
> Speak prose and hollo it till Europe hears!
> The six-foot Swiss tube, braced about with bark,
> Which helps the hunter's voice from Alp to Alp –
> Exchange our harp for that, – who hinders you?

In "How it Strikes a Contemporary" the poet is a man inordinately curious about and observant of the external details, objects and human acts within his town. Walking the streets and tapping the pavement with his cane, this man was "scenting the world, looking it full in the face." He could sometimes be seen poking with his stick to test

> . . . the mortar's temper 'tween the chinks
> Of some new shop a-building, French and fine.
> He stood and watched the cobbler at his trade,
> The man who slices lemons into drink,

The coffee-roaster's brazier, and the boys
That volunteer to help him turn its winch.
He glanced o'er books on stalls with half an eye,
And fly-leaf ballads on the vendor's string,
And broad-edge bold-print posters by the wall.
He took such cognizance of men and things,
If any beat a horse, you felt he saw;
If any cursed a woman, he took note. . . .

At night the man's observations are put into writing which conveys the "touch" and "tang" of the city's life. The accumulation of such seemingly unimportant details effectively makes the man "not so much a spy, / As a recording chief-inquisitor, / The town's true master if the town but knew!" He is true poet, not the "personage" who in plumed hat and lacquered breeches "blew a trumpet and proclaimed the news. . . ." The self-effacing man had become the unacknowledged general-in-chief of his town by obscurely

Doing the King's work all the dim day long,
In his old coat and up to knees in mud,
Smoked like a herring, dining on a crust –

Because the man sends his reports to "Our Lord the King," who then apparently intercedes in the lives and fates of the townspeople, commentary on this poem has often focused upon the allegorical elements: that is, the King is God, the poet his servant.[81] Certainly the hints towards allegory are strong, especially in the passage where the King exhorts the poet, "Beseech me not!", and in the poet's ceremonial death. Too strong an insistence upon the allegory can, however, be misleading. It can, for example, place Browning in the position of believing that a poet should speak not to men but to God. Indeed, Browning's angry letter of frustration to Ruskin in 1855 is often cited as a gloss for this poem: "A poet's affair is with God, to whom he is accountable, and of whom is his reward. . . ." That letter was written in bitterness at the failure of even people of intelligence and goodwill to understand what he had achieved in *Men and Women*. In the *Essay on Shelley* Browning had clearly endorsed a poetry whose "auditory" was men who shared a common reality with the poet; in his 1853 letter to Milsand he expressed his determination to write as "to get people to see and hear"; to his Fra Lippo he gave an extensive argument that the artist who grows up observ-

147

ant in the streets "Watching folk's faces" is able to paint the realities of men's lives and thereby enhance other men's understanding and appreciation of

> . . . things we have passed
> Perhaps a hundred times nor cared to see;
> So they are better, painted – better to us,
> Which is the same thing. Art was given for that;
> God uses us to help each other so,
> Lending our minds out.

Too much stress on the allegorical element in "How It Strikes a Contemporary" would distort further, I think, Browning's notion of God's nature. This King "has an itch to know things" and so reads the poet's reports "in his bedroom of a night"; on the basis of such reports the King executes ("A.'s surprising fate?"), exiles ("Old B. disappeared"), and doles out a mistress to "young C." The spy for such a king seems akin to Balzac's Peyrade, who in his old clothes and outmoded hat pokes about the streets of Paris gathering information reported late at night to the Minister of Police for Charles X. The spy Peyrade's former excessive love of fleshly pleasure has cooled by the time Balzac presents him in *Splendeurs et misères des courtisanes* as still carrying on his spying operations while enjoying the domestic haven he shares with Lydia. The rumour proves false that Browning's spy loved to dine in a blaze of light with "twenty naked girls to change the plate"; instead, he now sits in the evening with his dog, plays cribbage with his maid, and goes to bed at ten o'clock. A fitter analogue than Peyrade would be Balzac himself as portrayed in the *Avant-propos* to *La Comédie humaine* (1842) as the recording secretary to French society. The portrait Browning gives of himself poking around the stalls in a Florentine flea-market in *The Ring and the Book* is a later and equally fit analogue. That scene was a "pointless photograph of still life, such as I remember in Balzac," or so Gerard Manley Hopkins complained. That the narrator of "How It Strikes a Contemporary" is a worldly boulevardier who has known but one poet adds complexity to the poem. Yet surely the poet is approvingly associated with the objective, realistic mode rather than the visionary, subjective one.

During his early married years in Italy, Browning had written little: the brief "The Guardian Angel" and the long but rapidly composed *Christmas Eve and Easter Day*. His sojourn in Paris was relatively more productive. In addition to the Shelley essay and the four poems about poetry, six other poems are generally ascribed to this period. "A Heretic's Tragedy" grotesquely memorializes the burning at the stake of Jacques du Bourg-Molay in Paris in 1314; the poem also satirizes the Catholic Church, now making a bid for renewed influence under Louis-Napoleon. "Respectability" was occasioned by Browning's attendance at the Académie Française when Montalembert was admitted in February of 1852; here Browning expresses his implicit approval of the true if illicit love of a woman like George Sand and vents his overt scorn of the hypocrisy of Guizot and the ultramontane bigotry of Montalembert. "A Light Woman" is a cynical self-defence by a man who has seduced his friend's mistress because the mistress's promiscuity might harm his friend. The seduction was easy but leads to revulsion:

> And she, – she lies in my hand as tame
>   As a pear late basking over a wall;
> Just a touch to try and off it came;
>   'T is mine, – can I let it fall?
>   X
> With no mind to eat it, that's the worst!
>   Were it thrown in the road, would the case assist?
> 'T was quenching a dozen blue-flies' thirst
>   When I gave the stalk a twist.

More extensive and more overt sexual imagery of insects sucking at nectar invests the poet's search for perfect love in "Women and Roses," a poem Browning remembered having written on January 1, 1852.[82] "Women and Roses" also bears an incidental similarity to Nerval's "Les Confidences de Nicolas," an essay that had appeared in the *Revue des Deux Mondes* in 1850. In Nerval's essay, too, there is the figure of circling and searching for perfect love in a succession of real women. "Women and Roses," Browning said, was written early in 1852 along with *Childe Roland* and "Love Among the Ruins" as a kind of New Year's resolution to write a poem a day. *Childe Roland* came upon him "as a kind of dream." The pervasive anxiety, weariness, and sense of failure in the poem (similar, as I have said elsewhere, in mood and image to Nerval's "El Desdichado") have been variously attributed: to Browning's sense of failure as a poet, to his apostasy from Shelley, to the shock of learning of his father's relations with Mrs. Von Muller, to his own domestic *émeutes* with Elizabeth about Louis-Napoleon. With its lurid clarity of a nightmare landscape through which Roland enigmatically journeys, the poem is among Browning's richest and certainly the greatest of what might be called his Paris poems. Paradoxically, it is also a poem far removed from the objective, realistic mode he had been more consciously endorsing in his recent writing.

"Love Among the Ruins," the last of the triad thought to be written in early January, is less explicitly anxious in tone and has indeed often been cited as Browning's affirmation of the closing line "Love is best," – that love between man and woman can be self-sufficient, that is, is superior to all other human achievement as well as a secure refuge from the decay of great civilizations. Isobel Armstrong recently has shifted the interpretation of the poem to emphasize the disintegrating society portrayed alternately with the affirmations of love: "the energy of the dead, historical past makes itself felt in the cross-cutting rhythms of vigour which alternate with the muted languor of the present."[83] Leconte de Lisle's forceful call for a return of poetic attention to the vigour of the antique world, away from the enervating present, issues from a common sensibility similar to that discerned by Isobel Armstrong. "Love Among the Ruins" is surely a Browning poem Henri Peyre has in mind when he comments that "Baudelaire and Browning probably never heard of each other; and yet their pursuit of analysis in love, their blending of the past with the present and a note of tenderness makes them, in spite of their differences, closer than were Baudelaire and the other English poet who celebrated him in 'Ave atque vale.' "[84] As the author of *Ave atque vale*, Swinburne would have disagreed with M. Peyre: Swinburne thought Browning's poetry offered a "model of intense and punctilious realism . . . so triumphant a thing that on its own ground it can be matched by no poet; to match it we must look back to Balzac."[85]

A final poem, "In Three Days," was written while Robert was in Paris and Elizabeth in London. They had given up their apartment on the Champs-Élysées in early June and arrived in London on July 5. The breach-of-promise suit against Mr. Browning had just concluded with an order of £800 damages to be paid to Mrs. Von Muller. To avoid payment, Robert and his father made arrangements for

Mr. Browning and Sarianna to move permanently to Paris. In mid-July the three went to Paris, where Robert's father and sister settled at 151 rue de Grenelle. Robert was back in London by July 20, and for the next two and a half months the Brownings enjoyed visits from or to the Carlyles, Mazzini, the James Russell Lowells, the Milnes, the Ruskins, the Tennysons, Rogers, Kingsley. They delayed their return to France for a few days in early October so that Robert could attend the christening of Hallam Tennyson. Elizabeth was unable to attend because of damp weather, but she relayed Robert's account of the occasion to Miss Mitford: "the Laureate," she ends, "talks vehemently against the French President and the French; but for the rest he is genial and good, and has been quite affectionate to us. . . ."[86] On October 12 they returned to Paris via Folkestone and Boulogne and took rooms at the Hôtel de la Ville-l'Évêque. They remained in Paris less than two weeks before starting for Florence: long enough for another look at Louis-Napoleon and spiritualism.

The scene for both Louis-Napoleon's final triumph and a minor tiff over spiritualism between Robert and Elizabeth was not their hotel but the fifth-floor apartment of Fraser Corkran, the Parisian correspondent for the *Morning Chronicle* and a friend of Joseph Milsand. Henrietta Corkran, then a child, later recreated this visit by the Brownings to her parents' apartment. Elizabeth was fondling Pen's golden curls and Robert was eating great slices of buttered bread and plum cake, when Mrs. Corkran said something favourable to spiritualism: "'What!' boomed out Mr. Browning in astonishment. 'A clever woman like you to be taken in by such humbugs and charlatans!' Then Mrs. Browning in her thin, little voice, said something about her interest in the subject, and then everyone spoke at once. Flush barked and Pen yawned."[87]

From the Corkrans' balcony on October 16 the Brownings and the American actress Charlotte Cushman watched Louis-Napoleon's entry back into Paris after his tour of France. The tour had consolidated support for his policies and for his move to be proclaimed Emperor. Elizabeth told Kenyon that the change from Republic to Empire had unanimous support throughout France and that a "very intelligent Frenchman" had told her that the "opinion everywhere was curiously the same, not a dissenting matter. . . ." She advised him to "smooth down the lion's mane" of the London *Examiner* and to hint to John Forster that "roaring over a desert is a vain thing."

Victor Hugo's tirade of charges in *Napoleon le petit*, published in Brussels in July, was to her "an inarticulate cry of a bird of prey. . . ." With no opposition at home and only irrational criticism from abroad, Louis-Napoleon, with his "usual tact and courage," entered Paris on horseback riding at a dramatic distance from his escorts. The weather conspired, Elizabeth noted, to complete the triumph:

> The day was brilliant, and the sweep of sunshine over the streaming multitude, and all the military and civil pomp, made it difficult to distinguish between light and life. The sunshine seemed literally to push back the houses to make room for the crowd, and the wide boulevards looked wider than ever. . . . For the drama of history we must look to France, for startling situations, for the "points" which thrill you to the bone. . . .

Elizabeth admits that were they going anywhere but to Florence, and were her cough better she would "gladly stay and see in the Empire with M. Proudhon in the tail of it, and sit as a watcher over whatever things shall be this year and next spring at Paris."[88] Two days later on October 23, the Brownings went to the railway terminus in the Boulevard Mazas, near the Pont d'Austerlitz, to board the train for Chalon. From Chalon they went by steamer to Lyon, then by diligence and private carriage to Chambéry, over Mont Cenis to Turin and Genoa. They were back in their Casa Guidi apartment by the second week of November. On the 14th Elizabeth wrote to Sarianna in Paris:

> Robert has been perfectly demoralised by Paris, and thinks it [Florence] all as dull as possible after the boulevards: "no life, no variety." Oh, of course it *is* very dead in comparison! but it's a beautiful death, and what with the lovely climate, and the lovely associations, and the sense of repose, I could turn myself on my pillow and sleep on here to the end of my life; only be sure that I *shall do no such thing*. We are going back to Paris. . . .[89]

6

Back to Paris after an Italian Interlude, 1853–55

i

The Brownings had planned to spend only one more year in Italy:
time to visit Rome and the South, especially Naples, before removing to Paris as their permanent residence. For a number of reasons,

however, the return to Paris was delayed until 1855, time enough for them to think of Italy more than France as "home." On their return from Paris in November of 1852, they had thought to go on to Rome and the South after a few weeks' rest at Florence, while arranging for someone to rent their Casa Guidi apartment. "If we don't let it," Elizabeth wrote to Kenyon soon after the return to Florence, "we shall continue to occupy it, and put off Rome till spring, but the probability is that we shall have an offer before the end of December, which will be quite time enough for a Roman winter." After "the palpitating life of the Parisian boulevards," Robert found Florence "dead, and dull, and flat."[1] They lingered on in Florence through the spring of 1853, "living the old life just as if we had never known Paris. Paris is cast into a parenthesis," Elizabeth told Mrs. Ogilvy, "and the sentence goes on. I can scarcely realize to my fancy the great whirl & thunder of Paris & London, in this silence and stillness."[2] The Roman trip was then delayed until the following winter, so they had to "lie *perdus* in Italy meantime."[3]

In July of 1853, shortly before they took a villa for three months at Bagni di Lucca, Elizabeth reiterated her sense that Florence, where she had been well and happy and where her son had been born, had taken on all the associations of home: "Yet we shall not live in Florence – we are steady to our Paris plan."[4] After returning from Lucca they stayed a few weeks in Florence, then went on to Rome for the winter of 1853–54. Had not financial difficulties developed – the trading vessel in which Elizabeth held shares paid no dividends for 1854 – they would have been back in Paris by early summer of 1854. As it was, they remained yet another year at Casa Guidi, and were not back in Paris until July of 1855. As during their earlier sojourn in Italy, the Brownings during these thirty months followed the progress of French politics, literature, and even Parisian spiritualism in journals and books found at the various lending libraries and in letters from Paris.

French political life was less dramatic now than it had been during those years when the Brownings watched the swift succession of events from February of 1848 to Louis-Napoleon's establishment of the Empire in late 1852. Tuscany, too, "so trodden flat in the dust of the vineyards by these mules of Austria and these asses of the Papacy," was politically quiet.[5] The Brownings read in French reassessments of the recent political turmoil: Lamartine's *Les Confi-*

dences (1849), *Nouvelles Confidences* (1851), *Histoire de la Révolution en 1848*; Louis Blanc's serial version of *Histoire de la Révolution en 1848* (published as a book in 1870); Proudhon's *Les Confessions d'un révolutionnaire* (1849). Elizabeth thought Lamartine and Blanc, with their analyses of the impractical nature of many of the more radical programmes and their accounts of the ineffectiveness of the legislative assemblies, had in effect written "the best apologies for Louis Napoleon."[6] Robert was particularly interested in Proudhon's rather penitent personal analysis of mistaken hopes and theoretical errors.

Milsand's essay on Proudhon had appeared in the *Revue des Deux Mondes* in December of 1852, just after the Brownings left Paris. Milsand, a thoughtful convert to Protestantism, attacked Proudhon's critical atheism and his reliance upon materialism – economic, social, political, educational – to explain human inequality and to advocate reform. Though in more contorted prose, Milsand sounds a bit like Dr. Benassis in *Le Médecin de campagne* or the Abbé Brossette in *Les Paysans*, when those Balzacian mouthpieces descant upon natural inequality and the importance of industry, thrift, and religion or the danger of abstract political theory. Browning read Milsand's essay and Proudhon's *Confessions*; he wrote to Milsand in February that he too had "remarked many of the inherent faults of his [Proudhon's] original views of human nature. . . ." Although he makes *inequality* sound more like *infinite variety* in human personality, Browning told Milsand he agreed entirely with Milsand's "representation of human nature, with its inevitable inequalities of all sorts. . . ." Browning, however, was more interested in the particular human nature of Proudhon himself as revealed in his *Confessions*. He appreciated Proudhon's intellectual freedom but detected a blend of repentant confession and dangerous casuistry in his book:

Do you know Proudhon? He could not in the least be offended at your criticism. There, now, is a man absolutely *free*, as far as intellect is concerned; he gives it full wing and free course; then, according to his own doctrine, it never errs; yet it is not infrequently that he tells you: "I was *bête* enough to think this, *lâche* enough to believe the other"; how had it been, then, with a freedom of power commensurate to that intelligence and will? What but *bêtise* and *lâcheté* in action, and vehement action enough! And with a nation of emancipated Proudhons, whether combining or opposing each other's *bêtise* and *lâcheté*, were the result so desirable?[7]

Browning sounds a little like his own Bishop Blougram lecturing that lesser freethinker Gigadibs on the dangers of everyone following his own free will: some will be Napoleons pursuing an idea others cannot see, but

> . . . we do see
> The blown-up millions – spatter of their brains
> And writhing of their bowels and so forth,
> In that bewildering entanglement
> Of horrible eventualities
> Past calculation to the end of time! (lines 458–62)

Browning would compose Blougram's monologue within the next year or so (1853–55): in doing so he made his urbane churchman alert to the social dangers of what, in the letter to Milsand, Browning called "a nation of emancipated Proudhons." Blougram often taunts Gigadibs to

> Put natural religion to the test
> You've just demolished the revealed with – quick,
> Down to the root of all that checks your will,
> All prohibition to lie, kill, and thieve,
> Or even be an atheistic priest!

The personal and social danger of individual will wedded to action is made clear: it is the chaos and anarchy which a later Browning churchman, Pope Innocent XII, foresees and condemns in the unrestrained wilfulness of men as diverse as Abate Paul, Guido, or even Caponsacchi.

The war in the Crimea provides Blougram with an illustration – as do zealous idealism and *l'art pour l'art* – of specious or impractical ambition. The Brownings had come to hear rumours of war by early summer of 1853; much of their interest in French policy centred on the progress of that conflict. From the beginning, Elizabeth distrusted the English attempts under Aberdeen to negotiate between Turkey and Russia; Louis-Napoleon, of course, "acted excellently" and with "integrity and boldness."[8] She was amused to watch British distrust of France as reflected in, for example, Forster's *Examiner*, give way to a policy of cooperation. Once that cooperation was formalized by treaty in March, 1854, Elizabeth began to relay in her letters stories that the French people would welcome eventual political union with Britain. The mismanagement and suffering of the various military campaigns were lamentable, but, as she told Mrs. Ogilvy, she was "considerably comforted by the fact of the Anglo-French alliance which is good for each nation, and for the general civilisation of the world."[9] The inept leadership, the breakdown of supply systems, the waste of life in the various campaigns led Robert angrily to denounce the English system of class privilege in the government and military. A few days before Lord Raglan's unsuccessful (and for him, fatal) storming of Sevastopol, Elizabeth wrote to Robert's sister in Paris:

> Robert has been frantic about the Crimea, and 'being disgraced in the face of Europe,' etc. etc. When he is mild he wishes the ministry [of Aberdeen] to be torn to pieces in the streets, limb from limb. . . . if they [the English] *do tear up the system*, then shall we all have reason to rejoice at these disasters, apart from our sympathy with individual sufferings. More good will have been done by this one great shock to the heart of England than by fifty years' more patching, pottering, and knocking impotent heads together.[10]

The notion that it would be well were the war to bring revolutionary reform to England is repeated in Elizabeth's letters. By the early summer of 1855, Robert shared such thoughts. In the letter to Sarianna in which she explains why Robert is "frantic" about the Crimea and is calling for the "system" to be torn up in the streets, Elizabeth alludes to the English tendency to attribute superior French military success to the training the French had received in their long Algerian war. But the English military has had plenty of experience in "our Indian wars, Chinese wars, Caffre wars."[11] The fault lies not in want of experience but in the social system that, as she says elsewhere, is "oligarch in all things," not only in the military and parliament but in education which keeps the literacy rate far below that of France and in the selfish individualism that makes London the "largest and ugliest city in Europe."[12] The British military, she goes on, needs properly trained officers rather than "Lord Nincompoop's youngest sons." The disaster in the

Crimea had clearly revealed the "plague" of the system:

> As it is in the army, so it is in the State. Places given away, here and there, to incompetent heads; nobody being responsible, no unity of idea and purpose anywhere – the individual interest always in the way of the general good. There is a noble heart in our people, strong enough if once roused, to work out into light and progression, and correct all these evils. Robert is a good deal struck by the generous tone of the observations of the French press. . . .[13]

The war ended in September of 1855 when French troops under MacMahon successfully stormed Sevastopol. By then the Brownings, having spent a few weeks in Paris, were in London before returning to Paris for the winter. In late September, in London from his home on the Isle of Wight, Tennyson on two successive nights read at their apartment his new poem, *Maud*. Tennyson's distraught narrator rails at English social justice and economic civil war, but he ends by welcoming the battle along the Black Sea where in the "deathful-grinning mouths of the fortress, flames / The blood-red blossom of war": the violence has reconciled the speaker in *Maud* to his native land. But the war had estranged the Brownings from England and increased their distrust of it, while their admiration for France grew.

Censorship by the "blue pencil regime" of Napoleon III continued to interest them, dependent as they were while in Italy upon foreign newspapers. Elizabeth regretted this particular repression which she had earlier believed only temporarily necessary. Censorship, she felt, was especially unfortunate in France with its tradition of lively public discussion and its high literacy rate. Only a handful of upper-class readers would be deprived were *The Times* to be suppressed, she wrote to Mrs. Jameson in April of 1853: "But everybody reads in France. Every fiacre driver who waits for you at a shop door, beguiles the time with a newspaper. It is on that account that the influence of the press is so dangerous, you will say. Precisely so; but also, on that account too, it is necessary."[14] Milsand, now a regular correspondent with the Brownings and a professional essayist on religion and politics, topics especially proscribed by the censors, must have been particularly sensitive to this issue. He must

also, as did Anna Jameson and others, have seen in the press censorship a threat to literature in general. Writing to the Brownings in
July of 1854 Milsand complained of "stagnation in imaginative literature" in Paris. But Elizabeth did not admit the danger; rumours of
"the sudden death of French literature" were to her exaggerated.
"Newspapers breathe heavily just now, that's undeniable," she told
Anna Jameson, "but for book literature the government *never has*
touched it with a finger. I ascertained *that* as a fact when I was in
Paris."[15]

Perhaps she was right about books; however, had she had greater
interest in theatrical literature while in Paris in 1851–52 she might
have ascertained that a revival at the Gymnase of Balzac's satire on
financial speculation, *Mercadet*, had been altered to fit the censorial
demands; or that Musset's *André del Sarto*, revived at the Odéon the
same year, was changed so that Lucrezia's lover is killed in order
that the play should not end with elopement and consummation of
adultery. Musset's play about tyrannicide, *Lorenzaccio*, was refused
altogether a licence for revival while the Brownings were in Paris in
1852. In 1853, while Elizabeth denied a link between newspaper
censorship and restrictions on "book literature," the Brothers Goncourt were prosecuted for a light-hearted article in *Le Paris*, a journal to which Robert's acquaintance Gavarni also contributed. For a
woman who had read so much of her French "book literature" first
as *romans-feuilletons*, Elizabeth seems wilfully blind on this issue.
Maxime Du Camp believed that the government's prosecution of the
Revue de Paris, when it began to serialize *Madame Bovary*, was an
attack not on Flaubert's novel but on the too-liberal newspaper.
Indeed, the *Revue de Paris* survived only a few months beyond the
government's unsuccessful prosecution. Years later, Du Camp analysed the effects of the decree of February 17, 1852, against which
Robert had reacted so strongly: "The decree of 17 February," Du
Camp wrote, "was not simply directed against political journalism,
but incidentally struck at and ruined those writers who depended on
newspapers for their livelihood, either as dramatic critics, art critics,
novelists or scientific popularizers."[16] Elizabeth's line of reasoning
could not have accounted for the fact that her favourite French
periodical, the *Revue des Deux Mondes*, was ignored by the censors
when it published most of *Les Fleurs du mal* in June, 1855; when
Baudelaire published the poems as a *book* two years later he was

159

tried, fined 200 francs, and the edition was suppressed until objectionable poems were excised.

Whether or not censorship had helped stagnate imaginative French literature, it is true that the Brownings refer less frequently to French novels during their 1852–55 stay in Italy than they had during their earlier Italian stay. There are, of course, those twenty-two volumes of Dumas' *Mémoires* ("*un peu hasardé*") and Dumas' "'last,'" probably *Ange Pitou*. "Dumas is astonishing," Elizabeth told Isa Blagden, "he never *will* write himself out; there's no dust on his shoes after all this running; his last books are better than his first." Dumas *fils*, she thought, was an unusual example of "intellectual heirship," clever and promising. Robert read his tale "Diane de Lys" in March of 1853 and commented: "'You must read that, Ba – it is clever – only outrageous as to the morals.'"[17] But apart from the two Dumas and a few general references to Balzac and "the French novel," we hear nothing more of French fiction. This relative paucity of reference makes all the more exciting – and saddening – Frederic Kenyon's pre-dating by five years (1853 for 1858) a letter in which Elizabeth writes excitedly to Robert's friend since Camberwell days, Fanny Haworth, about Feydeau's *Fanny* and Flaubert's *Madame Bovary*.

Elizabeth was reading more French poetry than usual; however, the "truth is," she wrote to Miss Mitford soon after the return to Florence, "I don't know as much French modern poetry as I ought to do in the way of *métier*." Miss Mitford had asked about the poetry of a Madame Valmore, but Elizabeth could only reply that she knew the lady to be esteemed in Paris "for a certain *naïveté*, and happy surprises in thought and feeling, *des mots charmants*."[18] But she had read recently Musset, probably his *Poésies complètes* (1840) rather than the just-published *Premières Poésies, Poésies nouvelles* (1852), for she refers to poems in a single volume. She found Musset at his best in the short lyric, "when he says things in a single breath." His more elaborate attempts, possibly the oriental verse tale *Namouna* or the long diatribe against Voltarian rationalism in *Rolla*, she found to be "defective." His Spanish ballads, intimate in tone but suffused with local colour, were "perfect, really." A similar fusion of personal tone and local colour was also an attractive feature of *Primel et Nola* (1852) by a poet whose name neither Robert nor Elizabeth could at the moment recall; so Miss Mitford was directed to the *Revue des*

Deux Mondes to "hunt out" this Breton poet. He was Auguste Brizeux, who published regularly in the *Revue* from 1832 until his death in 1858 and who was a particularly active contributor during the years 1851–55. Miss Mitford was also urged to "get St. Beuve's poems." As it would be nearly impossible for her to get the privately printed love lyrics, *Le Livre d'amour*, addressed to Madame Victor Hugo, the reference must be to Sainte-Beuve's early collections, *Vie, poésies et pensées de Joseph Delorme* (1829) or *Les Consolations* (1830). The Brownings no doubt knew Sainte-Beuve for his *Causeries du lundi* essays and his careful portraits of men and women variously collected from 1832 onwards. Robert later – in a letter written from Pornic in 1863 – would cite with approval Sainte-Beuve's portrait of Lamennais.[19] Had Robert been a regular reader of Sainte-Beuve's *Causeries*, he would have found there, as Gamaliel Bradford long ago recognized,

> many detached psychological observations as subtle as they are perfectly expressed. But it is not the detached observations; it is the complete portraits of human beings that count. As in Browning, so here, we find all sorts and classes. . . . literary men and artists, studied, like Browning's, not as artists, but as men. . . . quiet people, living thoughtful lives apart, utterly unknown to the general reader, yet furnishing sometimes the most interesting portraits of all."[20]

Edgar Quinet's writings about Italian revolutions and religious history and his anti-clericalism would have appealed to both Brownings, though his voluntary exile after the *coup d'état* might have appealed only to Robert. Quinet is singled out by Elizabeth as a poet of "grand, extravagant conceptions" and of "positive genius."[21] Her taste generally favoured the personal lyric, but Quinet was a poet whose epic ambition was embodied in historical and philosophical allegory: *Napoléon* (1836), *Prométhée* (1838), and the verse drama about Spartacus, *Les Esclaves*, published in 1853. Elizabeth mentions only *Ahasuérus*, which takes as its theme the various historical incarnations of the Wandering Jew. Her naming of Quinet's *Ahasuérus* follows a pattern of hers to think of "French modern poetry" largely as that written by the generation of 1830; *Ahasuérus*, Quinet's earliest epic attempt, came out in 1833. Further, the work is in prose dialogue. She was more attracted to French prose than to verse because she believed that the "French essential poetry seems to me to flow out into prose works, into their school of romances, and to be least poetical when dyked up into rhythm."[22] This opinion was expressed, of course, at a time when she herself was engaged upon her *roman*-poem *Aurora Leigh* and when Robert was writing so many of those poems in which his men and women speak in conversational rhythms "dyked" only by flexible iambic pentameter. Yet it was a long-held notion. Her comment of the same year, 1853, to a new correspondent, Mr. Westwood, suggests so: "Balzac convinced me that the French language was malleable into poetry." This she wrote before admitting ruefully that in Italy it is difficult to keep up on current French literature: "We are behindhand here in books, and elderly ones seem young to us."[23]

ii

Robert particularly regretted the loss of " 'that blaze of life in Paris,' " and though Elizabeth told Anna Jameson that she and Robert did not "absolutely moulder" in their intellectual life while in Italy, she often refers to Florence and Tuscany as a "wilderness," an "extinct civilization," or a kind of delightful prison where one can be just "within the limits of civilization yet out of the crush of it."[24] Rome they thought might combine something of the urban excitement of Paris with milder winters. A winter in Rome (1853–54) was a disappointment, and its fevers brought threat to Pen and death to the son of their close friend, W. W. Story. Added to its miasmal atmosphere, they found it "a palimpsest Rome – a watering-place written over the antique."[25] From Rome Robert wrote to Sarianna in Paris of their plans to attend Christmas midnight mass when "all the city will be illuminated with gas for the first time, – I don't care a straw about such things. The Thackeray girls find everything delightful – 'better than Paris.' My own indifference will go off no doubt. . . ."[26] Later, to Forster, Robert wrote: "We left Rome last week, after no very prosperous sojourn – the good we found being just what we had least expected, in an influx of friends old and new."[27]

Among the old friends was Robert's early French friend, Amédée de Ripert-Monclar; among the new, Matilda Hayes and Jean-Jacques Ampère. Miss Hayes is best remembered as the translator of

George Sand's *Mauprat* and *Fadette*. Ampère, with whom the Brownings picnicked in the campagna, was a classical and oriental scholar at the French Institute and another prolific contributor to the *Revue des Deux Mondes* of essays ranging from the history of Buddhism, Chinese theatre, Lao-tseu, and the *Bhagavata-Purana* to articles he published early in 1855 on the influence of Greek sculpture on the monuments of republican Rome. Ampère, some twenty years earlier, had Stendhal as his guide through the campagna. Despite the pleasure of new and old friendships, Elizabeth wrote bluntly to Sarianna: "I don't like Rome, I never shall. . . . I quite agree with you that there's no situation like the Champs Élysées – really, there is scarcely anything like it in Europe. . . ."[28] Rome as a substitute for Paris had failed its first test with the Brownings. Although subsequent stays in Rome brought greater pleasure, by the time he was back in Florence in June of 1854 Robert declared to Forster that Rome "is ill-starred, under a curse seemingly, and I would not live there for the Vatican with the Pope out of it."[29]

Robert was pleased that his father's and sister's removal to Paris had, as he said to Kenyon, "gone on without a hitch." His father now "reads at the Library and draws at the Louvre, having got leave for both, goes book-hunting as of old" in the Parisian shops and stalls along the Seine. Milsand had become a frequent visitor to the Browning household in the rue de Grenelle. And Sarianna wrote "cheerfully enough" about her new life in the French capital.[30] Among the surviving fragments of Sarianna's letters is one in which, though nearly as sceptical as Robert, she attended a seance in Paris given by a Miss Kemp. "'Once, when the table answered wrongly [Miss Kemp] gave it a slap and cried "Que tu es bête" – *It twisted itself up and down like a child in a passion.*'"[31] The epidemic of spiritualist manifestations was most virulent among the Brownings' American friends in Florence; still, Elizabeth was pleased to know that the "'tables' are speaking alphabetically and intelligently in Paris."[32] However much the commonsensical Michael Faraday might in the *Athenaeum* try to debunk the strange phenomena, Elizabeth countered that one could always "*Ask Lamartine*," that Frenchman of genius who was reported to be in ecstasies because the spirit of Henry Clay had spoken and said "'j'aime Lamartine.'" In France spiritualism was given, it might be said, imperial approval by the new Empress Eugénie and by "Louis Napoleon who gets oracles from the 'raps.' "[33] In "A Lovers' Quarrel," written about this time, Robert registered his amused contempt for both the Imperial couple and table-rapping:

> What's in the "Times?" – a scold
> At the emperor deep and cold;
>   He has taken a bride
>   To his gruesome side,
> That's as fair as himself is bold:
>   There they sit ermine-stoled,
> And she powders her hair with gold.

After this attack on the Imperial couple's materialism and an atrocious pun on the manner of their succession to the ermine, Browning continues:

> Try, will our table turn?
> Lay your hands there light, and yearn
>   Till the yearning slips
>   Thro' the finger tips
> In a fire which a few discern,
>   And a very few feel burn,
> And the rest, they may live and learn!

"Instans Tyrannus," written about the same time, is a more oblique but harsher comment, as Paul Turner suggests, on the brutality with which Louis-Napoleon had established his Empire.[34]

The quiet interludes at Casa Guidi were particularly fertile ones for both Robert's and Elizabeth's poetry. They had promised each other to be "industrious *a faire frémir*"; each hoped to have some seven or eight thousand lines completed before returning to Paris. Elizabeth was writing, Robert told Forster, "a long one, a novel in verse."[35] "It is intensely modern," she wrote Anna Jameson, "crammed from the times (not the 'Times' newspaper)."[36] She did not finish *Aurora Leigh* until she was back in Paris in 1856, and when it was published later that year, the poet and painter William Bell Scott told the Rossettis that it was "only a novel à la Jane Eyre, a little tainted by Sand."[37] Robert's work progressed more rapidly and was more varied. He was now writing, he said, "poems of all sorts and sizes and styles." He extended "Saul," and he perhaps revised the ten or so poems written earlier in Paris. He also wrote during 1853–54 the forty or so additional poems which went to make up

Men and Women. These poems were, he believed, "a beginning of an
expressing the spirit of all the fruits of the years since I last turned
the winch of the wine press" to compose *Christmas Eve and Easter
Day* (1850). The "manner will be newer than the matter" in the new
collection, he told Forster.[38] Certainly in the great dramatic monologues – "Fra Lippo Lippi," "Andrea del Sarto," "An Epistle,"
"Cleon," and "Bishop Blougram's Apology" – his earlier realist
manner is intensified and its resources are more fully and subtly
exploited. Conversational rhythms and diction, historical detail,
accumulated facets of setting, gesture, bodily attributes, all go to
produce convincing illusions of particular times and places and
people. These poems also blend a critical spirit and irony with sympathy for characters caught up in unique conditions so that they
reveal their strengths, weaknesses, ambivalence, frustration, hypocrisy or casuistry.

All this blending created a psychological realism as successful in
its compression as the more extended and detailed realism of the
novelists. In the simpler, more lyrical poems – "A Woman's Last
Word," "Any Wife to Any Husband," "Two in the Campagna,"
"One Way of Love," "Another Way of Love" – there is sufficient
irony, ambiguity of tone or ambivalence of intention within the
characters to establish Browning's break with both the personal and
the visionary mode of the romantics, whether they be Shelley or
Hugo, Byron or Musset, or, for that matter, Arnold or Tennyson.
Men and Women reveals a Browning distrustful of certainty, fond of
objective, critical, ironic detachment, sharing *la peur d'être dupé* of
Gautier, Leconte de Lisle, Baudelaire and Flaubert. Only two of
these poems refer directly to contemporary French life: "Respectability," with its satiric comment upon Guizot and Montalembert; "A
Lovers' Quarrel," in which Napoleon III and his new Empress are
but one cause of contention between husband and wife. Bishop
Blougram, of course, has been reading new French novels about the
"demirep / That loves and saves her soul," and he yearns to own the
recently advertised Houssiaux edition of Balzac's *Oeuvres complètes*.
This worldly Bishop somehow "smells of the continent," as reviewers would complain of Browning himself. Blougram was clearly
modelled upon Bishop Wiseman, whose mother the Brownings met
at Fano in 1848: she was "a very intelligent and vivacious person,
and having been used to the best French society, bears but ill this
exile [in Italy] from the common civilities of life." Elizabeth hoped

that her bishop son would ask this civilized woman to "minister to the domestic rites of his bishop's palace in Westminster."[39] The Bishop's mother would not have been shocked by his taste for Balzac or by his reading "a French book" which speculates on why it is modern men and women now prosecute their sexual pleasures in private rather than public places, a book variously identified as Stendhal's *De l'amour*, Diderot's *Supplément au voyage de Bougainville* or Balzac's *Physiologie du mariage*.[40]

Among Robert's new poems only "Andrea del Sarto" shows a quite possibly direct influence from a contemporary French work, Musset's *André*. Louis Étienne, when he reviewed *The Ring and the Book* for the *Revue des Deux Mondes* in 1870, implied no influence by Musset's *André* upon Browning's poem, but he did believe that "the historical veracity is on the side of the English author" in the literary treatment of Andrea.[41] As Barbara Melchiori has argued well, there are many significant similarities between Musset's and Browning's versions; the most significant perhaps is their common departure from Vasari's *Life* in supplying Lucrezia with a cousin as a lover.[42] When the play was revived at the Odéon during Browning's stay in Paris, however, the censors had forced Musset to kill off the lover. Further, as Rose M. Bachem had argued some years before Melchiori's essay, a comparison of the two works on Andrea shows "how a common subject, taken from one literary source, can nevertheless vary according to romantic or realistic treatment." Against the violent, turbulent, romantic melodrama of Musset's *André*, Bachem finds that Browning's "Andrea" is the deeper psychological study of the two, because it shows under the guise of stagnation a modern analysis of a mind in perpetual conflict."[43] In "Andrea" as in so many of the poems of *Men and Women*, human aspiration towards love, towards artistic endeavour, towards religious belief, is conditioned and shaped by domestic, social, economic, and cultural forces at play at that particular place and time. "It is customary," Geoffrey Tillotson said some time ago, "to think of Browning's 'dramatic monologues' as offshoots of drama, but it would be truer to say that the form we see lying behind them is the novel form."[44]

Browning's condensation into meter and sometimes into rhyme of the novelistic elements of character analysis set within a realistic context resulted in much of the obscurity of which the British reviewers complained. But they also complained of the prosaic and ugly elements, of his mixture of the tragic and the comic, of his "scrutinising glance into the byeways, alleys, and noisome dens" of the world. Though most recognized the originality of these poems, *Men and Women* did not fit contemporary British notions of either drama or poetry. One, searching for English parallels, thought that an appropriate comparison might be either the "random style of address of Dickens' Mrs. Nickleby" or the "love of exquisite detail" in Pre-Raphaelite painting."[45] In the *Westminster Review* George Eliot, though uneasy over the "disagreeable puzzling effect of a charade" produced by the poems, claimed she "would rather have 'Fra Lippo Lippi' than an essay on Realism in Art."[46] But most reviewers found this metrical realism discomfiting and objectionable. Most, like Brimley in *Fraser's Magazine*, wanted a poetry which distilled a lyric beauty or ideal from life. Brimley and other British reviewers were not ready for the methods of Louis-Jacques-Mandé Daguerre to be applied to English verse: "art's realism is surely not to be confounded with literalness, the artist's business is not to make people speak and look exactly as they would speak and look, with all the accidents of human weakness about them. It is a large subject to discuss, but surely art is not daguerreotyping, even if the literal truth for which we value the sun-picture were attainable by the artist."[47]

Browning read these various "zoological utterances" at Galignani's back in Paris in 1855–56. He had hoped *Men and Women* might be a popular success. Disappointed, bitter, angry and frustrated, he took on, at least momentarily, yet another attitude he would share with the younger French writers: disdain for the common reader. Replying to a particularly tortured but obtuse letter from Ruskin, Browning wrote: "I shall never change my point of sight, or feel other than disconcerted and apprehensive when the public, critics and all, begin to understand and approve me."[48] To Carlyle, who praised the poems but admitted to Browning that they were "dreadfully difficult to understand," Browning said he had not intended his poems to be a substitute for an after-dinner cigar or a game of dominoes to an idle man.

iii

With his poems nearly finished, Robert wrote to Forster in June of 1854 that he would have to "be in London, or Paris at farthest" to publish them.[49] But while they delayed their return to France, the

Brownings' original plans to make Paris a permanent residence gradually faded. Despite Florence's intellectual dullness, its climate, comfort and economy became increasingly attractive. There was no place "as cheap as Florence"; and they had heard that rents were rising rapidly in Paris because of "the abolition for the nonce of so many streets," as Napoleon III began, under the supervision of Haussmann, to modernise Paris.[50] By the early autumn of 1854 the question seems to have been settled; and, metaphorically, Elizabeth had reached a verdict on Paris before the trial: "I hold Florence to be the most desirable place of residence in Europe," she wrote to Mrs. Ogilvy, "and it seems to me very probable that the result of giving another trial to Paris will be our return here to make an ultimate settlement. Oh – we shall try Paris fairly. But . . . even Robert says he loves Florence since he has been at Rome."[51]

Elizabeth's severe illness that winter led Robert to consider not going as far north as Paris again. But as spring warmed and the decision was made to spend only a year in Paris, Elizabeth's enthusiasm revived. The newly opened railway from Marseille to Paris would make travel across France much easier and faster; and the opening of the Exposition Universelle in Paris seemed a promising attraction. Writing to Madam Émile Braun, an old London friend now sadly "nailed down at Rome," Elizabeth exulted in the coming journey: "Railroads open from Marseilles; the Exhibition open at Paris!" Even England seemed attractive now that the "American 'medium' Home is turning the world upside down in London with this spiritual influx."[52] On June 20, 1855, they took a steamer from Leghorn to Marseille. Murray's new guide warned that all the hotels in Marseille remained "inferior, dirty, and noisy"[53] but the Brownings found rooms at one of them. And, to their surprise, they found in the room next to theirs Elizabeth's brother Alfred. Still in Marseille perhaps on War Office business, Alfred welcomed them and bought them champagne; but he told them nothing of his plans to marry in Paris in August. By June 24 they were in Paris, where they spent a fortnight in rooms below Robert's father's apartment in the rue de Grenelle before going on to London.

That fortnight in Paris was a busy one and was complicated by their search for a French priest liberal enough to marry their pregnant protestant servant Wilson to their Catholic servant Ferdinando. Still, they had time to meet, however briefly, a number of old friends – Milsand, Thackeray and his daughters, and the Corkrans – and a number of new celebrities. They visited Rosa Bonheur, whose *Hay Harvest in Auvergne* was hanging in the Exposition Universelle and had received a first-class medal; another of Mlle. Bonheur's more famous paintings, *Horse Fair*, was creating a sensation at the French Exhibition in London. She was but thirty-three, but already famous for the animal paintings she had been exhibiting at the Salon since 1840. A number of older celebrities were gathered at Madame Mohl's one evening. Among them was the liberal historian François Mignet, whose most recent work had been *Marie Stuart* (1851). Stendhal's cynical old travelling companion, Prosper Mérimée, was also there. Mérimée was only three years Elizabeth's senior, but his creative work had been over for a decade, although he had recently published a one-act play, *Les Deux Héritages* in the *Revue des Deux Mondes* (1853). After his long tenure as inspector of monuments, Mérimée was now in the *Sénat* and an intimate of the court – the court jester, by his own admission – of the Empress Eugénie. Another guest was Victor Cousin. Elizabeth had spoken approvingly of Cousin in earlier letters; it is likely that both she and Robert associated Cousin with the organization of the French educational system which they admired. During her earlier sojourn in Paris, she referred approvingly to Cousin's criticism of the insularity of English thought. Robert might well have admired Cousin for his resignation from the Sorbonne after the *coup d'état* and his criticism of the ultramontanists' attempts to gain clerical control of the educational system he had helped to organize. Adelaide Ristori, the Italian challenger in classical drama to Rachel, must have added some youth to the gathering, but Robert continued to prefer to Ristori the more established Rachel, whom he had seen play Phèdre a decade before in London.

The Brownings saw more of their English friends during this stay in Paris than they had during their previous Parisian stay. Apart from the English residents of Paris such as the Corkrans and Lady Elgin, Dickens, Thackeray, Macready and Milnes also met the Brownings in Paris during the winter and spring of 1855–56. Rossetti came over for ten days in mid-November of 1855.[54] He came to Paris to see the Brownings and Elizabeth Siddal, who was there before going on to the South of France in quest of a warm winter which might restore her health. Neither Elizabeth Siddal nor

Elizabeth Barrett ventured out on the cold November evenings, but Rossetti and Robert apparently saw one another frequently. They toured the Louvre together, and Rossetti found Rober's "knowledge of early Italian Art beyond that of anyone I ever met, – *encyclopaedically* beyond that of Ruskin himself".

One evening at the Brownings' apartment at 102 rue de Grenelle, Rossetti "met a miraculous French critic named Milsand" who knew Robert's "works to the very dregs – and had even been years in search of *Pauline* . . . ,"[55] the poem Rossetti had recognized as Browning's when he had copied it out in the British Museum a decade before. Milsand was then translating some of *Men and Women* for the *Revue des Deux Mondes*, translations Rossetti thought "must be curiosities." He also met Robert's sister and father. Rossetti, who had subjected the early Pre-Raphaelite Brotherhood to readings of *Sordello*, was delighted to learn that Sarianna had "performed the singular female feat" of making the first fair copy of that poem and still remembered "it all – even *Squarcialupe*, *Zin the Horrid*, and the *sad dishevelled ghost*." The elder Mr. Browning he found "a complete oddity – with a real genius for drawing."[56] It seemed paradoxical to Rossetti that the father of Robert Browning preferred the realistic "Dutch boors" – Bouwer, Ostade, and Teniers – to all other painters. When Rossetti finally gave one day to a visit to the Salon at the Exposition Universelle, his own taste squared with that of the official judges: the best were Delacroix and Ingres. Delacroix in the privacy of his *Journal* returned the compliment, in a sense, by praising paintings in the Salon by Rossetti's Pre-Raphaelite friends Millais and Hunt.[57] The rebellious banner – *Le Réalisme: G. Courbet* – hanging on that painter's separate stand, apparently escaped Rossetti's notice.

The apartment at 102 rue de Grenelle had been taken for the Brownings by the Corkrans, who were attracted to the sofas covered in yellow satin. Such poetic furnishing did not make up for the lack of room and the eastern, draughty exposure which soon revived the cold Elizabeth had caught in London. The apartment was a "pit" in which they "fell upon evil days and satin sofas"; so, for six weeks, with Pen sleeping on the floor and their trunks unpacked, they were "lying *perdus* in our hole" while Robert sought another apartment. The unexpectedly cold, damp weather of early November set Robert to thinking seriously of spending the winter in Pau or Nice. But by mid-December he had found a larger and warmer apartment at 3 rue du Colisée right off the Champs-Élysées. "Clean, carpeted; no glitter, nothing very pretty – not even the clocks – but with sofas and chairs suited to lollers . . . ," Elizabeth told Mrs. Jameson; "an 'apartment' on the Continent is twenty times more really 'comfortable' than any of your small houses in England."[58] To make the move to the new apartment, they hired a *fiacre* to which Robert carried a heavily bundled and swathed Elizabeth and into which he shoved her upside down, all the while explaining to the concierge: " 'Elle se porte très bien! elle se porte extrêmen bien. Ce n'est rien que les poumons.' (She's very healthy! She's extremely healthy. It's only the lungs.)" Later, they continued to laugh when they thought of the concierge's wonderment at " 'cet original d'anglais' " and his odd manner of treating his wife.[59] While still in the rue de Grenelle, Elizabeth began to apply to Paris metaphors she usually reserved for Florence – "the wilderness," "the desert." Even George Sand, whose memoirs they began reading, seemed to be "dull on purpose." Soon after the move to the rue du Colisée, a warm rain broke the frost, more evening visitors came, Robert began to go out more, and Sand's eighteenth volume of memoirs – "the volume which concludes with the views upon the *sexes* – [was] magnificent." With that volume, Robert joined Elizabeth "at last" in her enthusiasm for Madame Sand: "He is intensely interested, and full of admiration."[60]

Free of the "abominable quarters" in the rue de Grenelle, Robert went out more often. He searched the records at the Library of the Chamber of Peers to clear up for Carlyle some genealogical information about the "Marquise of Voltaire," the Marquis de Breteuil, and Talleyrand.[61] He went weekly to read poetry to Lady Elgin, who was now confined to a wheelchair. He saw Dickens in early January; and in early April, at Dickens' hotel, Dickens and Macready depreciated Ristori's performance of Legouvé's *Médée*, while Browning gave "his verdict on Ristori midway between the contending parties."[62] Ristori had, if not imagination, at least admirable sensibility. Browning could not, however, agree with others whose admiration for the Italian actress amounted to madness: he would not "join in the cry about miraculous genius and Rachel out-Racheled." With the spring weather Richard Monckton Milnes, too, came to Paris "for a pleasant fortnight," and extended his already considerable circle of literary acquaintances by giving a dinner attended by Browning along with the historian Mignet, Cavour, George Sand and "an empty chair in which Lamartine was expected to sit," but did not.[63] Robert, unable to "rest from serious work in light literature," went frequently to the Louvre to sketch.

Beginning in December, he also went out frequently to read British reviews of *Men and Women* and found "heaps of critiques at Galignani's, mostly stupid and spiteful, self-contradicting and contradictory of each other," he wrote bitterly to Chapman.[64] He pretended to be largely indifferent to the hostile and uncomprehending reviewers, but his anger and disappointment at the "zoological utterances" he read at Galignani's is clear: " 'Whoo-oo-oo' mouths the big monkey – 'Whee-ee-ee' squeaks the little monkey and such a dig with the end of my umbrella as I should give the brutes if I couldn't keep my temper, and consider how they miss their nut[s] and gingerbread!"[65] Browning's hopes that he might gain some popularity with his "newer" manner were not realized. As he read the various notices throughout the spring in Paris, the reviewers had, in his mind, descended from monkey-like imitation to swinish grunting; and his close and influential friends had done nothing to help:

> As to my own Poems [he wrote from Paris in April] – they must be left to Providence and that fine sense of discrimination which I never cease to meditate upon and admire in the public: they cry out for new things and when you furnish them with what they cried for, 'it's *so* new,' they grunt. The half-dozen people who know and could impose their opinions on the whole sty of grunters say nothing to *them* (I don't wonder) and speak so low in my own ear that it's lost to all intents and purposes.[66]

Ruskin, Carlyle, Tennyson, Dickens, Thackeray, Rossetti, all remained publicly silent. Ruskin, after a night's instruction by Rossetti on the magnificence of *Men and Women*, wrote Browning a bulky letter full of obtuse questions and ambivalent praise. Browning responded with a justifiably testy letter stating that Ruskin spent too much time poking around in the poems with his alpenstock fearfully examining what Ruskin thought to be impassable crevices. Carlyle found an "opulence of intellect" and the keenest pair of eyes "inspecting human life" as he had met "this long while." But the poems were "dreadfully difficult to understand"; more than one, indeed, "was a very enigma." So Carlyle advised Browning to take up *"one* great subject" alone with a vow to be clear and intelligible to the common reader.[67] Rossetti was the most discerning and enthusiastic of Browning's readers; and he knew a good bit of damaging Fleet Street gossip about some of the more hostile of Browning's critics. He regretted that Tennyson's *Maud* was creating so much excitement in London while *Men and Women,* his "Elixir of Life," was being met with general "torpor" and "stagnation." Still, Rossetti felt he must "hold his peace" and not make any public statement because "it isn't fair to Browning, (besides, indeed, being too much trouble,) to bicker and flicker about it."[68]

Hurt and disappointed by the British reviews and by the silence of his influential English friends, Browning looked forward to a critique being written by his "proper critic," Joseph Milsand. Before *Men and Women* had been published on November 17, 1855, Milsand had already begun translating several of the poems in preparation for the review which Robert expected to be in the January 1 issue of the *Revue Des Deux Mondes.* There was no doubt that the review would be highly favourable: in early November Milsand had told Elizabeth "that he considered the poems 'superhuman' – Mark that! only superhuman."[69] An illness, however, delayed Milsand's completion of the review, and it was never published in the *Revue des Deux Mondes.* Rather, it came out in the less influential *Revue contemporaine et athenaeum français* on September 15, 1856.

Much like Carlyle, who admired the "opulence of intellect" and the keen observation of *Men and Women,* Milsand praises the poems for being "more intellectual while at the same time more objective" than is the poetry of Browning's great romantic predecessors.[70] Unlike Carlyle, who of course was writing a private letter, Milsand develops a careful formal argument with generous citations of the texts to show that Browning has brought to English poetry "nearly the opposite of Wordsworth and his school" (516). Browning had, in effect, met his own call "for a new kind of poet" in the *Essay on Shelley,* a work Milsand cites with approval. Milsand especially emphasizes Browning's realism, although he is careful to use the words "réaliste" and "réalisme" only in the sense that Shakespeare or Scott were realists who could maintain an idealism. Factual detail, sensuous imagery, conversational tone, rhythm and diction blend in

Browning's poems to give a physicality to human hopes, feelings, thoughts. As in his review of 1851, Milsand points to Browning's success in allowing the general to be implied only through the particular. Browning's focusing on a single, perhaps ostensibly even insignificant, event in a character's life allows "great truths . . . to reveal themselves in miniature episodes" (538). The robustness and variety of Browning's portraiture provided the reader, "en un mot," with a poetry revealing the "vital principles which are at work in this world" (540). In an important demur about Browning's manner, Milsand echoes a warning made by many of Browning's English critics: too intense a striving for honest, accurate, realistic expression can lead to ugliness. Milsand called this quality "le grotesque" (543). Browning and Milsand would live to see the descent of realism into increasingly ugly and sordid subjects. And in his old age, at least in letters to his daughter, Milsand was given to memorable "bursts of indignation against the so-called *Naturalistes* in France."[71] Already alert to Browning's tendency towards the ugly and the sordid, Milsand nevertheless thoroughly admired his realism.

7

The Brownings and *le Réalisme*, 1856–61

i

Réalisme *in the Paris of the 1850's: Courbet and Champfleury –
George Eliot on the Realism of RB's* Men and Women *– Publication
and Prosecution of Flaubert's* Madame Bovary *– EBB Completes
and Publishes Her* Aurora Leigh.

ii

Montégut's Criticism of Aurora Leigh *in the* Revue des Deux
Mondes *and of Feydeau's* Fanny *– EBB's Debt to French Fiction:
Sand, Sue, Balzac – French and Parisian Scenes in* Aurora Leigh *–
RB's "Apparent Failure" Evokes Paris of 1856 – Similarity to
Baudelaire – "Mr. Sludge" and Daniel Home in Paris.*

iii

*Through the South of France to Italy – Thoughts of Living at Nice or
Pau – Reading Hugo's New Poems – RB's Comment on* La Légende
des siècles *– Paris and Le Havre in the Summer of 1858 — RB's
"Dîs Aliter Visum; or, le Byron des nos Jours."*

iv

Visit to Rousseau's Chambéry – Discovering Feydeau's Fanny *and
Flaubert's* Madame Bovary *– French Troops in Florence, 1859 –
EBB's* The Dance, *"An August Voice," and* Poems Before
Congress *– RB's Renewed Distrust of Napoleon III – EBB's Death
and RB's Return to Paris.*

---

i

In 1850 Browning had been admonished by an English reviewer for the "realism" of *Christmas Eve and Easter Day*; in 1856 George Eliot had praised the "realism" of *Men and Women*. In the Paris of 1856, however, Joseph Milsand would have done his friend no favour by openly recommending *Men and Women* as a work of "réalisme." For by then the term carried political and moral as well as aesthetic associations that Milsand would not have wished to evoke while praising Browning's poetry. Use of the word without Milsand's long opening qualification of it might well have intensified the charges against Browning of vulgarity, coarseness, and ugliness. *Réalisme* was then closely associated with Courbet. From 1848 onward Courbet had found defenders in such men as Proudhon and Champfleury. Gautier, remembering Courbet's *Après-Dîné à Ornans* in the 1849 Salon, found in that painting the virility and robustness of "les réalistes"; to Gautier the term was apparently descriptive and rather neutral.[1] The anonymous critic for the *Revue des Deux Mondes*, however, thought the painting's "exactness produces nothing but a trivial truthfulness' compounded with an objectionable emotional and moral neutrality.[2] The same journal labelled as socialist Courbet's offerings at the Salon of 1850–51; the even more conservative *Journal des Débats* objected both to the perceived politics and to Courbet's "worship of ugliness" in paintings like *Les Paysans de Flagey revenant d'une foire*, *Les Casseurs de pierre*, and *Enterrement à Ornans*.[3] The last painting was vigorously defended by the young Champfleury, who used the term *réalisme* in his essay in the journal *L'Ordre* on September 21, 1850. The following year Champfleury drew a favourable comparison between Balzac's fiction and Courbet's painting.[4]

By 1853 there was sufficient hostility to literary realism for Champfleury to adopt an interesting strategy when he published his novel, *Les Aventures de Mlle Mariette*. In his preface Champfleury mockingly poses as a reviewer antagonistic to the realistic mode: "Is there anything easier than copying the individuals who walk before us, listening to them chat, reproducing their conversations as if by stenography? No more is needed than mentally sketching their daguerreotype-portrait."[5] Brimley's censure of *Men and Women* in

Fraser's Magazine three years later is remarkably close in tone, diction, and hostility: "Art's realism is surely not to be confounded with literalness, the artist's business is not to make people speak and look exactly as they would speak and look, with all the accidents of human weakness about them. It is a large subject to discuss, but surely art is not daguerreotyping. . . ."[6] In September of 1855, in an open letter to George Sand in *L'Artiste*, Champfleury once again defended Courbet, who had refused to show at the Exposition Universelle, had set up his own *pavillon de réalisme*, and had issued a manifesto in his catalogue. But by now Champfleury complained that the terms *réalisme* and *réaliste* were so widely used and abused as to become meaningless. He in his fiction, as Courbet in his painting, were, Champfleury argued, really only interested in portraying honestly and objectively individual human beings.[7]

That the word had taken on amorphous connotations is clear in Elizabeth's use of the word *realist* at this time. It appears in a letter she wrote to Ruskin the day before the Brownings left London for Paris on October 17, 1855. The Brownings had just gone through the traumatic and embarrassing encounters with the American medium, Daniel Home. Admitting playfully that she is a "wicked spiritualist," Elizabeth thus defines herself as "a *realist* in an out-of-the-world sense – accepting matter as a means (no matter for it otherwise!)."[8] Her witty inversion of the term – she was fairly certain a *spirit* had *materialized* that evening at Ealing – indicates some familiarity with the word. Her use of *realist* implies not a literary mode, of course, but a general philosophical attitude towards the material universe. Such widening use of the term had exasperated Champfleury, who complained that soon "we shall have realism in medicine, in chemistry, in industry, in the historical sciences."[9] Elizabeth's amused inversion of the general meaning of *realism* also, I think, disparages the term. A similar disparagement of and impatience with the growing debate over realism is evident in George Eliot's review of *Men and Women*, published anonymously in the *Westminster Review* in January of 1856. Hers was one of the most favourable reviews. She found, when she turned "from the ordinary literature of the day" to Browning, that there was "nothing sickly or dreamy in him." Eliot attributed Browning's "obscurity" not to the poet but to the "drowsy passivity" of readers who were used to

177

conventional melodious verse. His power and originality, she argued, comes from

> a clear eye, a vigorous grasp, and courage to utter what he sees and handles. His robust energy is informed by a subtle, penetrating spirit, and this blending of opposite qualities gives his mind a rough piquancy that reminds one of a russet apple. His keen glance pierces into all the secrets of human character, but, being as thoroughly alive to the outward as to the inward, he reveals those secrets, not by a process of dissection, but by dramatic painting.

Eliot's admiration of Browning's ability to reveal the inward by "painting" the outward leads to her assertion that she "would rather have 'Fra Lippo Lippi' than an essay on Realism in Art."[10] Eliot's own appeal to the realistic tradition in Dutch painting would become overt in Chapter XVII of her *Adam Bede* (1859). In "Fra Lippo Lippi" Eliot apparently found not only the portrait of a realistic painter who fluently defends realism in art but also a realistic rendering of both the painter and his argument. She preferred the poem to any abstract discussion of realism.

The aggressive tone and iconoclastic stance of the journal *Réalisme*, which began its short life in the autumn of 1856, added further controversy and confusion to the word as a literary term. Under the leadership of Edmond Duranty, *Réalisme* advocated many of Champfleury's and Courbet's ideas: the use of common subjects, the need to carefully study or research a subject, the need to treat it prosaically. Duranty could disdain equally Hugo's *Les Contemplations* (1856) and Banville's *Odes funambulesques* (1857). Banville had already got in first with the poem "Réalisme," a clever satiric attack on the realist artists who gorged and discoursed at Andler's brasserie in the rue Hauteville. Baudelaire, whose *Fleurs du mal* had appeared a year earlier in the *Revue des Deux Mondes*, was still jokingly dismissed as an imitator of Poe; nevertheless, the following year the judge in the censorship action against *Les Fleurs du mal* in passing sentence admonished Baudelaire for his "réalisme grossier et offensant."[11] Although the realist Duranty oddly preferred *Uncle Tom's Cabin* to *Madame Bovary*, he and other writers for *Réalisme* distrusted didacticism in literature. The careful avoidance of didacticism is a marked feature of Browning's *Men and Women*;

178

there is, as George Eliot had said, "no didactic laying-out of a subject" in these poems. To have called this quality a realist trait in the mid-1850's would have neither enlightened nor mollified those hostile readers who found discomfiting the absence of a clear meaning in poem after poem.

An allied characteristic is Browning's ability to create convincing and even sympathetic portraits of characters whose ideas and attitudes might be almost antithetical to the poet's assumed audience: a perhaps sceptical Catholic bishop, a licentious monk, a failed painter who weakly accepts his wife's love affair, a Parisian mistress scornful of public respectability, an infidel naturalist probing like a medical student the strange "case of mania – subinduced / By epilepsy" when he finds in Bethany a man named Lazarus who claims to have been cured by a "learned leech from Nazareth," or a Greek artist-philosopher proudly scorning the doctrine of "a mere barbarian Jew, / As Paulus proves to be, one circumcised. . . ." By careful irony and subtle revelation of character, Browning, it is true, does control the reader's moral judgment of these characters. But it is also true, as George Eliot remarked, that the mode "requires the reader to trace by his own mental activity the underground stream of thought" which will reveal that judgment. Georg Lukács thought the premier identifying mark of Balzac's realism was the "inexorable veracity with which he depicts reality even if that reality ran counter to his own personal opinions, hopes and wishes."[12] Clearly Browning shared that realistic trait with the novelist he and the younger French writers so admired. In his subtler psychological rendering of character, however, Browning resembles more closely another realistic novelist he soon would come to admire greatly: Gustave Flaubert. With Flaubert, Browning shared that more modern realistic mode, which Barbara Smalley, in her fine book *George Eliot and Flaubert*, defines as the process of "putting all the significant action inside the minds of the characters."[13]

On their 1851–52 visit to Paris, the Brownings had been fortunate to witness the *coup d'état*, the decree of February 17 imposing more stringent rules of censorship, the tempestuous performance of *La Dame aux camélias*, and the triumphant return in the autumn of 1852 of Louis-Napoleon. In 1856 they just missed what in retrospect was the first interesting battle between book-literature and the government of Napoleon III: the publication and prosecution of *Madame*

Bovary. Only after another visit to Paris in 1858 does the novel enter the Browning correspondence, when Elizabeth links it to that other *succès de scandale*, Feydeau's *Fanny*. Not until January of 1859 is Flaubert's novel referred to as Robert's "'favourite book.'" Two years after Elizabeth's death, Robert wrote from Pornic of his "old, and still continuing passion for 'Ma^de Bovary.'" And in 1868 in a contorted allusion he associated the novel with the 1855 seance by Home at Ealing and compared himself to Charles Bovary who, upon reading the love letters of Emma after her death, felt no hatred for his wife's seducer.[14]

In Paris in 1856, however, the Brownings were understandably unaware of Gustave Flaubert, who had not yet published any fiction and who was thought even by his close circle of friends to be something of a hermit at Croisset. He finished *Madame Bovary* to his satisfaction in April of that year and brought the manuscript to Paris, where in late May he sent it to *La Revue de Paris*. The Brownings left Paris for London in late June of 1856; they stayed there until late October overseeing the final revisions and printing of *Aurora Leigh*. The editors of *La Revue de Paris* – Du Camp, Louis Ulbach, and Laurent Pichat – agonized over Flaubert's manuscript throughout the summer. They wanted corrections and deletions, in particular a shortening of the now infamous cab-ride episode, because, as Ulbach said later, "We were spied upon, watched and endlessly menaced. They [the government] would have delighted to catch us red-handed in a charge of immorality."[15] But Flaubert held out against changes, and finally on October 1 the *Revue* published uncut the first instalment. Not until November did Du Camp become seriously alarmed about rumours of possible prosecution, and not until December did Flaubert angrily demand that the *Revue* either continue publication without change or return the manuscript to him.[16] By that time the Brownings were back in Florence, quite absorbed in the immediate success of *Aurora Leigh* (published November 15, 1856).

The public success of *Aurora Leigh* and the public prosecution of *Madame Bovary* are phenomena which must be left to the historian of official and popular taste of the Second Empire and Victorian England. No poem in English had derived so much of its inspiration from French fiction as had *Aurora Leigh*; no novel had yet so masterfully extended the realistic tradition in French fiction as had

180

Madame Bovary. Fear that others might be encouraged to further imitate or extend such realistic depiction of contemporary life was explicit in the main arguments made by the Public Prosecutor Pinard for the suppression of Flaubert's novel. Failure to prosecute would be viewed as approval of "the kind of literature that Monsieur Flaubert cultivates and which he exploits with none of the restraints of art but with all the resources of art: that is, the descriptive kind, realistic painting." Concluding his unsuccessful plea to the court, Pinard warned: "Morality stigmatizes realistic literature, not because it depicts the passions: hatred, vengeance and love; the world lives on these things; and art must depict them; but when it does depict them without restraint, without measure. Art without rules is no longer art; it is like a woman who removes her clothes."[17]

ii

Aurora Leigh was Elizabeth's attempt to depict realistically the passions of love, hatred and vengeance in contemporary life while, at the same time, keeping art's clothes on. Her strategy was to blend devices of poetry (the restraining measure of iambic pentameter, elaborate literary allusion and imagery, settings of pastoral calm suited to lyric reverie and meditation) with elements of contemporary fiction (Romney's Fourieristic scheme, debates about the utopianism of Cabet and Considérant, scenes of low life in London and Paris, a symbolic marriage of the rich and poor frustrated by cynical intrigue and the rape of the poor, orphaned Marian Erle, Aurora's own steadfast pursuit of a woman's right to make her way independently in the literary world). Although the poem was praised extravagantly by some reviewers and sold rapidly, most of the British and American reviewers were uneasy with and hostile towards the uglier episodes, scenes and such images as this one in which Aurora declaims her steadfast intention of writing boldly about the contemporary world so as to bring to birth a new literature for the next age:

. . . Never flinch,
But still, unscrupulously epic, catch
Upon the burning lava of a song
That full-veined, heaving, double-breasted Age:

That, when the next shall come, the men of that
May touch the impress with reverent hand, and say
"Behold, – behold the paps we all have sucked!"

Elizabeth's unstable mixture of novelistic elements and lyric expression was probed most acutely by a French critic, Émile Montégut, in the *Revue des Deux Mondes*. "The novel is our epic," Montégut argued near the beginning of his long and careful analysis, "the epic of an age without heroism, without an ideal, and a very complex age. Only the novel reproduces for us the features of our lives; only it is capable of expressing the vulgarity and decadence of our time."[18] He argued that poetry must necessarily remain *subjectif*, personal and lyric. If in more recent English poetry (and he used Robert Browning as an example) we seem to get "a strong impression of reality" we are, in a sense, mistaken because "this is an imagistic reality resulting from the force of interior vision; it is not the reality of external facts and of common life" (334). *Aurora Leigh* he thought an interesting but finally unsuccessful attempt to infuse into the prosaic present some heroism and idealism. To accomplish this "mêlée" of the vulgar and the ideal, "Mrs. Browning, wishing to present an image resembling modern life as much as possible, has naturally been led to unite two opposing literary forms, the novel and the poem" (336). Though clearly unhappy that novelists had not been successful in "their attempts to poeticize contemporary life" (327) and clearly grateful for Mrs Browning's experiment, Montégut felt it pointless for her to build up *mise en scène*, incidents and episodes which clashed too strongly with the lyric passages. The final effect is that

> The plot of *Aurora Leigh* is little more than the libretto for an opera, little more than the scenario for a ballet; the effusions, the transports, the meditations of the subtle and profound Aurora are the true poem. Thus, the attempt by Mrs. Browning to wed harmoniously the poem and the novel ends, in spite of the author, with the destruction of the novel, that is to say the impersonal part of the work, and in the triumph of lyricism, that is to say the personal poetry. (337)

Montégut's review is a fair, acute and serious analysis of *Aurora Leigh* and in the same mode as those by Milsand of Robert's poetry.

The Brownings may have been acquainted with Montégut: Carlyle wrote to Robert in Paris in 1852 that he had just "given a Card of introduction to a certain M. Montegut of the *Revue des Deux Mondes*; which document I left him free to present or suppress."[19] The Brownings would also have been interested in Montégut's angry explanation in the *Revue* in 1858 of the sensational popularity of Feydeau's *Fanny*. Feydeau had, he said, condensed in a single work all the more sordid elements of the realistic fiction of the past decade: "It has everything: the affectation of a moral purpose, lascivious crudeness, sexually stimulating descriptive passages, the idolatry of matter."[20]

Elizabeth noted with amused contempt that the Dublin *Tablet* had branded her poem as "a romance in the manner of Frédéric Soulié – in reference, of course, to its gross indecency."[21] But *Aurora Leigh* does, perhaps unconsciously, reflect situations, characters, episodes, and attitudes which Elizabeth's commentators have found in scores of novels. George Sand (née Aurore Dupin) both in her life and in her heroines blends with Elizabeth's own autobiography to form the narrator-heroine, Aurora. The strong-willed, independent poetess Corinne of Madame de Staël is a common ancestor to both Elizabeth's heroine and many of Sand's. Elizabeth's attention to physiognomy and to the details of streets, architecture, and interior furnishings as indices to character clearly owes something to Balzac; so too, perhaps, does the poem's overt scorn of impractical and abstract utopian socialism. Gardner Taplin points to Eugène Sue's mysterious philanthropic aristocrat, M. Rudolphe, as a model for Romney and to the slum-bred but innocent and refined Fleur-de-Marie as a model for Marian Erle. *Les Mystères de Paris*, Taplin further suggests, provides an antecedent for the rape of Marian in the drugging and violation of Louise Morel by Jacques Ferrand.[22] Althea Hayter remarks flatly: "Marian Erle in *Aurora Leigh* would never have been imprisoned in a brothel, drugged and raped if Mrs. Browning had never read Soulié or Sue."[23] Possibly; but Elizabeth also read Balzac's *Les Splendeurs et misères des courtisanes*, in which Peyrade's daughter Lydia is kidnapped, drugged, raped and set to wander alone, a deed designed by Lucien de Rubempré's protector, Vautrin. That rape is rather soon followed by a typically Balzacian digression on the social and economic nature of prostitution (another theme of Elizabeth's poem), a diatribe against the ignorance of utopian socialists, and, for good measure, a brief essay on Parisian slang. But then Aurora by her own testimony learned "classic French / (Kept pure of Balzac and neologism)" (I, 399–400). One important difference between the rape episodes in both Sue and Balzac and that in *Aurora Leigh* is worth mention. Like Gaetano, in *The Ring and the Book* born of Guido's rape of his child-wife Pompilia, Marian's child becomes a vessel of innocence and the symbol not of her shame but of her progress towards saintliness. The child born to Louise in Sue's novel dies of exposure; Balzac's Lydia, though the great physicians Desplein and Bianchon hope an awakening of the maternal instinct may restore her sanity, is carted off to the asylum at Charenton.

Elizabeth's narrative technique to describe the rape of Marian is a complicated one; it was, however, effective. Even reviewers hostile towards the coarseness and ugliness of some images and diction or impatient with the strident feminism or the eulogies to Napoleon III, were moved by this episode. The largely unsympathetic writer for the *Westminster Review* found nothing in the book "so grand as the revelation to Aurora of her [Marian's] dreadful secret." The critic read the lines "with a sort of breathless fear and wonder."[24] The writer for *Blackwood's*, though he wished Elizabeth to "refine and purify as to purge out the grosser matter" of much of the poem, thought this episode a greater triumph even than her *Cry of the Children* – "one of the most pathetic and tear-stirring poems in the English language."[25] Elizabeth's narrative strategy is primarily that of delaying the revelation. Although Marian mysteriously fails to appear for her wedding to Romney in the middle of Book IV, it is not until two years and two books later (at the end of Book VI) that Aurora and hence the reader learn the reason for Marian's disappearance. What had happened in the chronology of the plot was this: Lady Waldemar, perhaps in conspiracy with Sir Blaise Delorme and certainly in concert with her waiting-maid-turned-procuress, lured Marian aboard a ship on the promise of a better life in Australia. At the first French port-of-call, Marian was taken off the ship into a brothel, drugged, raped, and turned loose to wander the roads of rural France until she finally arrived at Paris. There she is briefly employed as a servant to a fashionable young matron too preoccupied with her lovers to notice immediately Marian's preganncy; when she does discover Marian's "filthy secret," she lectures her on the virtues of chastity and turns her out. Marian, predictably, thinks she might as well sleep under the waters of the Seine, but instead finds work and bears her child.

Meanwhile, Aurora, leaving England to return to her childhood home in Florence, stops over in Paris. She meditates upon the comparative insularity of English thought, regrets the French tendency towards impractical idealism, but is comforted that the French have Napoleon III as a "Caesar [who] represents, not reigns, / And is no despot, though twice absolute: / This Head has all the people for a heart; / This purple's lined with the democracy . . ." (VI, 70–73). So musing, Aurora strolls the splendid boulevards until she suddenly catches sight of Marian's face in the crowd. She pursues Marian through the crowd, but Aurora collides with a gentleman walking bemusedly along the pavement. The gentleman is probably, Aurora thinks, some member of the Institut de France musing distractedly over a rumour that Dumas may be admitted to the Académie. While the gentleman apologizes, Marian disappears. Weeks later, at the flower market, Aurora meets her again; the two walk together to Marian's lodgings. The walk is one of the more Balzacian passages of the poem: the crowded streets of central Paris give way to the poorer sections of jerry-built houses, then vegetable gardens and livestock begin to mix with the "half-built habitations" and cellars of the poor on this raw edge of Paris. It is a "waste" which is neither city nor country though the pastoral hills and vineyards can be seen in the distance. Then comes the immediate neighbourhood where Marian lives, the house itself, the stairs, the landing, and finally "a room / Scarce larger than a grave, and near as bare; / Two stools, a pallet-bed" and a curtainless window with a "torturing eye" (VI, 500 ff.). And the child.

From this point it takes Marian over seven hundred lines to finally acknowledge and describe the rape so that the uncomprehending Aurora can understand. Marian's progress towards the revelation is impeded, much as is Pompilia's acknowledgment that Guido's rape has fathered her child, by Marian's sense that she is already dead. Like Pompilia, Marian phrases her story in imaginary of flowers trampled by wild beasts or a lamb torn by wolves. But whereas Pompilia's utterance is impeded by her almost amnesiacal repression of the violence done her, Marian is more hindered by her sense of social inferiority and personal shame. Aurora's misunderstanding and her

185

constant interruption with pious remonstrances further delay the revelation. Frustrated and with understandable indignation, Marian finally blurts out the story:

> . . . "You feel?
> You understand? – no, do not look at me,
> But understand. The blank, blind, weary way,
> Which led, where'er it lead, away at least;
> The shifted ship, to Sydney or to France,
> Still bound, wherever else, to another land;
> The swooning sickness on the dismal sea,
> The foreign shore, the shameful house, the night,
> The feeble blood, the heavy-headed grief, . . .
> No need to bring their damnable drugged cup,
> And yet they brought it. Hell's so prodigal
> Of devil's gifts, hunts liberally in packs,
> Will kill no small creature of the wilds
> But fifty red wide throats must smoke at it,
> As HIS at me . . . when waking up his last . . .
> I told you that I waked up in the grave."

The ellipses are Marian's; they indicate she has reached the limits of language in this description of her rape. She then continues with lines that not only indicate dramatically her continued sense of social estrangement from the high-born Aurora, but further suggest that Elizabeth knew very well what she was doing by presenting her most sordid scene with such extreme circumlocution:

> "Enough so! – it is plain enough so. True,
> We wretches cannot tell out all our wrong
> Without offence to decent happy folk.
> I know that we must scrupulously hint
> With half-words, delicate reserves, the thing
> Which no one scrupled we should feel in full." (VI, 1219 ff.)

Much of what the public prosecutor found offensive in *Madame Bovary* was Flaubert's refusal to clothe the passions with "art," to "scrupulously hint / With half words, delicate reserves" while representing contemporary life. Flaubert was scornful of the attempt by the editors of *La Revue de Paris* to soften *Madame Bovary* by judicious deletions here and there: "You attack details," Flaubert wrote angrily to Pichat, "it is the whole that must be blamed. The brutal element is deep down and not on the surface."[26] From the moment he began the novel, Flaubert was aware of the difficulty of inextricably fusing manner and matter, style and subject, but he held steadily to his purpose. The day after he began to write *Madame Bovary* in September, 1851, he wrote to Louis Colet: "I began my novel yesterday evening. I now foresee stylistic difficulties which terrify me. Being simple is no small matter. I am afraid of falling into the manner of Paul de Kock or of creating chateaubriandized Balzac."[27] Metaphoric allusiveness and narrative evasion soften what is sordid, brutal, and ugly in the contemporary life depicted by *Aurora Leigh*. Once Marian, after extreme circumlocution, describes her rape, she and Aurora take the new railway – to Marseille via Dijon – and soon find a pastoral retreat in the Tuscan hills. There, what is selfish, brutal, or just foolish in the modern world is overcome by renunciation of pride, by forgiveness, and by Christian charity and love. "Chateaubriandized Balzac" might as aptly describe *Aurora Leigh* as does William Bell Scott's phrase – "Jane Eyre à la Sand."[28]

Robert Browning wrote no new poems while in Paris in 1855–56. He sketched and worked a bit at revising *Sordello*. Not until a decade later did he gather eighteen recently completed poems into *Dramatis Personae* (1864). This was the volume which the offended Walter Bagehot thought revealed Browning "the most of a realist, and the least of an idealist of any poet" he had read. Swinburne, however, praised especially "Mr. Sludge" and "Caliban" as "just a little below" Stendhal.[29] Two of these poems evoke memories of the 1855–56 sojourn in Paris: "Apparent Failure" directly; "Mr. Sludge, 'The Medium'" more obliquely. "Apparent Failure" was probably written at Pornic while Browning was there on holiday in 1863. He had read in a Parisian newspaper that the "Doric little Morgue" along the Seine was about to be demolished during the renovation of central Paris, and he jocularly resolves to save the building by immortalizing it in verse:

> . . . I'll save it! Seven years since,
>   I passed through Paris, stopped a day
> To see the baptism of your Prince;
>   Saw, made my bow, and went my way:
> Walking the heat and headache off,

I took the Seine-side, you surmise,
   Thought of the Congress, Gortschakoff,
   Cavour's appeal and Buol's replies,
So sauntered till – what met my eyes?

Only the Doric little Morgue!
   The dead-house where you show your drowned:
Petrarch's Vaucluse makes proud the Sorgue,
   Your Morgue has made the Seine renowned.

The birth of the Prince Imperial, the convening of the European powers to resolve the Crimean conflict, the hopes that the victorious allies might chastise Austria and recognize Cavour's Piedmont government, all set the time and place. Browning is unable to resist the rhyme of "Sorgue" and "Morgue," and with grim humour contrasts Petrarch's pastoral retreat with the "dead-house" used to display urban suicides. Inside, behind a "screen of glass' shielding the gazers from the stench, are the bodies of three men who killed themselves the night before; their coats still drip the water of the Seine. The poet imagines the men to have been among the wretched of Paris *inconnus* who sleep huddled under bridges or on "the plain asphalt." Now, at least, each has his own bed, "his copper couch." Their individual identities destroyed by death, the men become representative Parisian types in the poet's imagination:

How did it happen, my poor boy?
   You wanted to be Buonaparte
And have the Tuileries for a toy,
   And could not, so it broke your heart?
You, old one by his side, I judge,
   Were, red as blood, a socialist,
A leveller! Does the Empire grudge
   You've gained what no Republic missed?
Be quiet, and unclench your fist!

The third man was red not in his politics but in his passion for women, and so turned to cards and dice to get money to serve that passion. In death he has turned blue; the poet comments coldly,

. . . one clear nice
Cool squirt of water o'er your bust,
The right thing to extinguish lust!

The poet then reads these *misérables* a sardonic bourgeois sermon to the effect that "It's wiser being good than bad; / It's safter being meek than fierce: / It's fitter being sane than mad." The sardonic tone continues, I think, into the concluding couplet with its pious hope that "what began best, can't end worst, / Nor what God blessed once, prove accurst." Nowhere in the poem, or for that matter in Browning's biography, is there evidence that he considered aspiring Bonapartism, red socialism, or the lust of the boulevardier to be blessed of God.

"Apparent Failure" is one of the more Baudelairian of Browning's poems. The metropolitan setting, the boredom with the great public events, the turn for relief to contemplation of the wretched, the stench of decomposed bodies, the brief evocation of a better earlier world, the ironic sermon, the cumulative implication that the city is "accurst," all are elements in Browning's poem which Baudelaire exploits more obsessively and subtly. Of course, Browning's persona is more bumptiously English: "No Briton's to be balked!" he loudly proclaims as he strides into the morgue; but he enters that cool half-light of the dead-house to escape the oppressive heat of the summer sun, and there discovers the broken dreams of the *demimonde*. Baudelaire's persona characteristically inhabits the "Teeming city, city fraught with dreams, / Where in plain day the spectre grasps the passer-by!" If Baudelaire is to discover such mysteries as those which come to him in "Les Sept Vieillards," however, he must go – "steeling my nerves like a hero" – into the yellow fog and foul half-light along the "quays by a swollen river." Baudelaire's persona exhibits more consistently "a bizarre and captivating taste" as he studies "the teeming tableau" of Paris (*Les Petites vieilles*); yet, like Browning's poet there in the morgue, Baudelaire must imagine "the dying in the depths of asylums / Heaving out in hiccups their death-rattles. / The debauchees return home, worn out by their work." ("Le Crépuscule du matin"). Browning's poet retains, however, an almost gentlemanly detachment necessary to the poem's irony as he questions his corpses. Browning does not, in this poem, give expression to anything like the Baudelairian disgust of "Un Voyage à Cythère":

Ridiculous dangling corpse, your sorrows are mine!
Looking at your floating limbs, I felt
Rise up against my teeth, like a vomiting,
The long bitter river of old sorrows. . . .[30]

There are passages in *Sordello*, in Guido's second monologue, or even in Mr. Sludge's apology, when he "somehow vomits truth today," that are as uncompromisingly brutal as Baudelaire; not, however, in "Apparent Failure." That poem is closer, finally, in tone, to Baudelaire's "Le Cygne," a poem also provoked by the demolition of the old buildings of Paris by Haussmann's workmen, and which ends with a meditation upon "the captured, the defeated . . . and of so many more!"

Although Browning is closer to Baudelaire, as Henri Peyre has said, than is Baudelaire's more famous English publicist and admirer Swinburne, it is also probably true that Browning and Baudelaire never heard of each other. The opportunity for Browning to take at least passing notice of *Les Fleurs du mal* came with the publication of those poems in the Parisian journal Browning most frequently read, the *Revue des Deux Mondes*. The poems, however, came out in the June 1, 1855, issue – just at the time the Brownings were busy preparing for their journey from Florence to Paris. While they were in Paris in 1856 Baudelaire's translation of Poe, *Histoires extraordinaires*, was published, at a time when Baudelaire was still generally thought of as an art critic and a translator and commentator on Poe. The Brownings had evinced no interest in Poe since the days of their courtship when Elizabeth wrote to Robert of her puzzlement that the young American wrote reviews of her work containing the "two extremes of laudation & reprehension" and of her amusement at Poe's dedication to her of *The Raven and other Poems*. Baudelaire's scholarly curiosity may have been pricked by this dedication, but there is no record that he ever tried to find out anything about the woman whom Poe called "the Noblest of her Sex."[31] The only new author currently publishing whom Elizabeth mentions during the stay in Paris was Octave Feuillet, whose *La Petite Comtesse* was then running in the *Revue des Deux Mondes*.[32]

In May of 1856 Elizabeth reported to Anna Jameson that Robert was beginning to soften in his opposition to Napoleon III: "At last he is sick of the Opposition, he admits." She then goes on rather testily: "In respect to literature, nothing can be more mendacious than to say there are restraints upon literature. Books of freer opinion are printed now than would ever have been permitted under Louis Philippe . . . books of free opinion, even licentious opinion, on religion and philosophy. *There is* restraint in the newspapers only."[33]

190

When in 1857 Baudelaire was prosecuted for the book publication of *Les Fleurs du mal*, the Brownings were back in Italy. They knew the two novels that had recently been prosecuted, *Madame Bovary* and *Fanny*. Even had they not been interested in the poetry, they doubtless would have been interested in its suppression by the government. But that the edition was suppressed and that even reviews of it were suppressed increases the probability that Baudelaire would have escaped the Brownings' notice until, perhaps, Robert became acquainted with Swinburne in the 1860's.

The relationship of "Mr. Sludge, 'The Medium'" to the Brownings' residence in Paris in 1855–56 is much more tangential than is that of "Apparent Failure." The model for Sludge, Daniel Dunglas Home, was, along with the new Marseille-Paris railway and the Exposition Universelle, one of the primary attractions to which Elizabeth looked forward when they left Florence for Paris and London in June of 1855. Within a fortnight of their arrival in London from Paris, the Brownings attended the famous seance conducted by Home at the Rymers' in Ealing. Elizabeth was deeply moved when a spirit-hand placed a wreath of clematis on her brow. Robert was repelled and disgusted. Two days later at the Rymers' Browning confronted Home, and according to Home "Browning's face was pallid with rage, and his movements, as he swayed backwards and forwards in his chair, were like those of a maniac."[34] Such spiritualist charlatanry, Robert told a certain Miss de Gaudrion a month later, could lead even the best people to an "abnegation of the regular tests of truth, rationality [and even] voluntary prostration of the whole intelligence."[35] The following June the peripatetic Mr. Home was in Paris. "Think of my horror at Robert's having heard to-day that Home the medium is in Paris," Elizabeth wrote to Henrietta. "I thought he was in Rome. I looked so scared that Robert promised me he would be 'meek as maid' for my sake, and that if he met the man in the street he would pass without pretending to see." They had just received a heavy letter (postage was three-and-a-half francs) from W. W. Story in Rome reporting the progress of Home and of spirits in that city. "Robert and I read the letter together on the sofa, like the lion and the lamb," Elizabeth continues, "– but Home personally is still a bone in the lion's throat."[36] Elizabeth closes the letter with an account of Napoleon III's popularity and his compassion and heroism during the spring floods along the Seine.

191

The Brownings left Paris for London shortly after the letter was written and returned for only a few days later in October. Home stayed in Paris and found his way into the imperial circle at Prince Napoleon's and at the Tuileries. Madame Jules Baroche reported on April 2, 1857, that "People have seen tables leave the floor at his [Home's] command, and rise up, without any strings attached; bells have moved around in circles, an accordion moved across people's legs, playing tunes. A little bell, which the Empress was holding very firmly, went and put itself in the Emperor's hand, in spite of all her efforts to keep it."[37] Elizabeth soon learned of these seances conducted by Home for the Bonapartes, and she was pleased that he was "under the shadow of the Emperor's wing."[38] That Browning associated Home with the imperial family is slightly suggested when he has his Mr. Sludge refer to Jerome Napoleon. In "A Lovers' Quarrel" (1855) news of the Emperor's marriage and table-rapping alternate as domestic distractions. Browning did not publish his portrait of Home until after Elizabeth's death. When he did, he charitably allowed the spiritualist charlatan to place the blame for his chicanery not upon himself but upon a society eager to fool itself, desperate to prove immortality by table-rapping, willing to see Providence in signs and omens, bored with its flat, routine life and impatient for a Sludge to slap colour and mystery back into the world with his "harlequin's pasteboard sceptre."

With a sharp eye for bourgeois gullibility and a vicious instinct for survival, Sludge preys upon the pretension and foolishness of a society that always threatens him. He argues that however base and sordid his life he is but the creature of society. Born into the servant class, he early determined not to fall further in the social scale and land among the "ragged sons o' the gutter . . . in the thick of the filth." The world for him is a breeding ground for the "swarm of busy buzzing flies" upon which he can feed. As he "vomit[s] truth," his mind runs habitually to images of competing and voracious animals or to lower forms – toadstools, vermin, stomach-cysts. From this fecund world Sludge plucks and artfully shapes his spiritualist deceptions. In doing so he is like – and no worse than – a kind of proto-naturalist novelist: a "picker-out of pearl / From dung-heaps, – ay, your literary man. . . . He's the man for muck; / Shovel it forth, full-splash, he'll smooth your brown / Into artistic richness, never fear!" In this poem of 1864 Browning has taken a subject from

contemporary life, and embedded it in sordid, ugly, brutal particulars; he then allows his speaker to articulate an elaborate if specious
philosophy of environmental determinism. "Mr. Sludge, 'The
Medium'" provides an interesting balance between imitation and
ridicule of evolving literary naturalism.

iii

The Brownings left Paris by rail in late October of 1856. With only a
brief stop at Dijon, where Milsand met them at the station, they
went directly to Marseille. The late autumn weather was warm and
clear the entire way; "the scenery of the southern half of France,"
Elizabeth told George, had never been properly appreciated. At
Marseille they dropped into "absolute summer," warm enough so
that Elizabeth could walk and sit along the boulevards after sunset,
sleep soundly with the hotel windows open, and recover quickly
from the cough she had developed in London. She hoped this time
not to sail to Italy but to travel the coast road through Toulon,
"Hyères, Cannes, Nice & the rest."[39] As a child Elizabeth and
Arabel had taken the roles of "the empresses of Hyères" when the
Barrett children assumed royal titles, held mock-battles, stormed
fortresses and took prisoners. Later, on a cold March day in her
room in Wimpole Street, she dreamed of being "imparadised at
Hyères."[40] With a note of premonition, Elizabeth wrote to George
that if she does not now get "actual sight" of those romantic villages
along the coast, they will have to remain "visions," for she shall not
have another chance. Murray's description of Hyères would have
tempered the romantic vision. A three-miles-broad marsh gave the
village little view of the sea, there was "want of good accommodation
and pure water to drink," and there was "little beauty in its situation." Although "the mildness of its climate causes Hyères to be
chosen as a winter residence for invalids, and renders it perhaps one
of the best resorts for invalids, during that season," Murray
cautioned, "it is not satisfactory during the summer months."[41]
Robert was grudgingly willing to take the coast route until he discovered that the fare only as far as Genoa was £20, twice that of steamer
fares to Leghorn. They left for Leghorn on a new French steamer on
October 28. Within days they were back in Florence, where
Elizabeth enjoyed "the repose, the quiet."[42] They found Florence,

as usual, "duller and quieter than Paris and London, and we seem to ourselves to have dropped suddenly down a wall [*sic*] out of the world."[43] Never again while Elizabeth was alive did the Brownings consider spending the winter as far north as Paris. They did, however, during this eighteen-month stay in Italy begin to think, encouraged by Milsand, of living in Paris during the warmer months and in "the South of France during the winters." Not only the cold and damp of the French capital but its bustling social life had become unattractive to Elizabeth. "People tear at us, Robert and me," she wrote in reply to Henrietta's question about when they would return to London and Paris; "For such things – for London and Paris, this year – I am not in a condition. I couldn't bear it – it would drive me mad, I think." She was sure, however, Robert might agree to six or seven months in Pau or Nice.[44]

Back in Florence, Robert soon hunted out many of the reviews of *Aurora Leigh*. He saw in the various reviewers' charges of Elizabeth's coarseness, indecency, and unintelligibility echoes of those reviews of *Men and Women* he had so recently read in Paris. Such critics, he wrote to Chapman, were "like those night-men who are always emptying their cart at my door, and welcome when I remember that after all they don't touch our bread with their beastly hands, as they used to do." He was clearly angry that hostile reviewing of his own work had kept his own royalties to almost nothing; yet he was pleased that despite the critics *Aurora Leigh* was selling very well. He took over the task of urging Chapman to more effective promotion of the book and of correcting proofs for new editions by "looking after commas and dots to i's."[45] He also drilled Pen in French verbs; he sketched and began modelling in clay. No doubt to aid these new pastimes, he ordered drawing instruction books from Chapman and even bought and hung up in Casa Guidi an articulated human skeleton. When in December of 1857 John Kenyon's generous bequest of £11,000 was made to them, Robert watched over their investments and indulged himself by the purchase of a horse which he rode frequently. They spent the late summer and early autumn of 1857 at Bagni di Lucca again. "We are having a delightful time of it here," he wrote, "– everything is green and cool. My wife is regaining strength."[46]

But back in Florence Elizabeth's health turned worse, and Robert began to talk of spending the winter in Rome and Naples, perhaps Egypt and the Holy Land.[47] During the recent stay in Paris he had been invited to join an expedition to Egypt and the Holy Land, but he had declined on the grounds that he could not leave Elizabeth alone for several months. They didn't go to Egypt or Rome or anywhere else in the winter of 1857–58. Elizabeth, who was reading German romances with difficulty because she had no dictionary, was still deeply depressed by the deaths in the past year of Kenyon and of her father. She describes herself at this time as "brooding, brooding, brooding, and reading German, German, German."[48] Robert rode, went often to Isa Blagden's, undertook a course of homeopathic treatments and, at Carnival, rented a box for the masked ball at the opera house, had his tailor make him a "black silk domino," and at the last minute persuaded Elizabeth to rent a similar domino and mask and attend the festivities with him.[49]

While struggling through German romances – "heaps of Madame Hahn-Hahn," – Elizabeth also read unspecified "French" romances. Pen was reading, in Italian translation, something by Madame Guizot. Pen's progress in languages is fully, phonetically and wittily described by Elizabeth in her letters from the moment her son began to utter sounds. He spoke a polyglot of English, Tuscan and French. Now his father started him on the more systematic drills in French verbs. Noting with approval that Edward Lytton (who would become much later the British ambassador in Paris) was planning to live with an Italian family near Lake Como the better to perfect his Italian, Elizabeth read a rather schoolmarmish, sisterly lecture to Henrietta, who she worried might neglect her son's education in modern languages: "We must make our boys familiar with living languages, Henrietta, for the character of the times makes them indispensable to success in life. In fact, the world is *thrown open* now; and an intelligent man mustn't be simply an Englishman or a Frenchman but a citizen of all countries."[50] Pen had not started on Latin yet, but when in a good mood he could translate "a page of Grimm's German . . . quite fluently." By the following year the lessons became yet more systematic: "German, French & English, & Italian daily, & writ[ing] English and Italian *dictations*."[51] Pen's Latin instruction lagged until after Elizabeth's death when Robert moved back to London. It was a move made, in part, because Robert wanted to make "something definite," that is, an Englishman, out of his son. Intensive instruction by his father and tutors eventually got Pen, briefly, into Oxford.

Victor Hugo's *Les Contemplations* (1856) is the only new French work specifically referred to by Elizabeth at this time. These poems, in contrast to the harsh invectives against Louis-Naopleon in *Les Châtiments* (1853), evoke lyric memories of childhood, the tragic drowning of Hugo's daughter and her husband, or his more visionary ponderings of the oneness shared by Hugo, God and Nature. Hugo himself in a letter of February 21, 1856, to his friend Paul Meurice described the shift in manner in this way: "I believe it would be a good time to publish a volume of calm verse. *Les Contemplations* after *Les Châtiments*; after the red effect, the blue."[52] "Have you read Victor Hugo's 'Contemplations'?" Elizabeth asked Anna Jameson in April, 1857. "We are doing so at last. As for *me*, my eyes and my heart melted over them – some of the personal poems are overcoming in their pathos; and nothing more exquisite in poetry can express deeper pain."[53] Elizabeth was moved enough by Hugo's poems to draft, but not send, a letter beseeching Napoleon III to forgive Hugo and allow his return to France. She hoped, she told the Emperor, that when future historians "count gratefully the men of commerce, arms, and science secured by you to France, no voice shall murmur, 'But where is our poet?' "[54] Elizabeth's underlining of the word *me* in the letter to Anna Jameson suggests that Robert was not as one with his wife in appreciation of Hugo's latest but rather dated poetic mode. Two years later, when *Madame Bovary* was his " 'favourite book,' " in a letter thanking Isa Blagden for a copy of Hugo's *La Légende des siècles* (1859), Robert complained of Hugo's poetry in general that "he can't let truth be truth, or a number of remarkable poetical pieces speak for themselves, without assuring you that he meant them to join Man to God, with like pleasant practicabilities."[55] Browning's distrust of such effusive transcendental egotism is akin to Renan's complaint about similar poems, e.g., *Dieu des Bonnes Gens*, by Béranger. Such poems, Renan complained, present God as a person "whom one can slap on the shoulder and treat as a comrade." Renan found such "usurpation of noble title" by poets extremely irritating.[56] It must have been with delicious and complex irony that Robert, in *Prince Hohenstiel-Schwangau*, allowed Napoleon III himself to refute Hugo by clever parody of the visionary posturing of the Bard of Jersey, who had labelled Louis-Napoleon "le petit":

"O littleness of man!" deplores the bard;

And then, for fear the Powers should punish him,
"O grandeur of the visible universe
Our human littleness contrasts withal!
O sun, O moon, ye mountains and thou sea,
Thou emblem of immensity, thou this,
That, and the other . . ." (lines 517 ff.).

Robert resolved "to try the Atlantic breezes on the French coast" for the summer of 1858. Apparently under the counsel of Dr. Harding, the Brownings had decided to no longer risk Elizabeth's health by a return to England; instead, they planned to go briefly to Paris and then, as Elizabeth told Henrietta earlier, to summer at "one of the many pleasant French summer-places, at Fontainebleau or elsewhere. . . ."[57] They left Florence on July 1 and took a French steamer from Leghorn. The night voyage to Genoa was calm but hot and the vessel so crowded that they slept on the deck without mattresses: "fancy Ba, the luxurious chair-lover," Robert wrote Isa Blagden, " 'pricking for a soft plank,' as the sailors call it." From Genoa to Marseille the steamer was nearly empty, but the water nearly as rough as a channel-crossing, so they went without food for twenty-four hours. They spent the evening of July 3 in the Hôtel du Louvre in Marseille before going on, in Robert's phrase, "gently to Paris."[58] By "gently" he meant they would travel by express in three easy stages, staying overnight in Lyon at the Hôtel Colet, and at the Hôtel du Parc ("comfortable but dear," says Murray) in Dijon. Kenyon's bequest and additional royalties from Elizabeth's work had nearly tripled the Brownings' income. So this time they went to Paris in "unbridled extravagance"; in contrast to earlier exhausting diligence rides or twenty-four-hour train rides, "Travelling has really become a luxury." Even the customs official at Marseille had been exceptionally polite and courteous, opening but a single piece of luggage and then accepting Robert's declaration with " 'Je vous crois, monsieur.' " Passports were simply glanced at, and in the first-class express coaches there were few other passengers, so there was room to stretch and quiet to read the French newspapers or Marguerite Ancelot's memories of salon life with the likes of Stendhal and Mérimée in her newly published *Salons de Paris; foyers éteints* (1858). Elizabeth describes this novel type of travel with a word she normally reserved for the comfort of Casa Guidi – *repose*. No chance of visitors, no writing or anticipation of letters: "There you are, shut in, in a carriage! Quite out of reach of the telegraph even, which you mock at as you run alongside the wires." Robert was, during the journey, "in a heavenly state of mind." They both appreciated more than ever "the French people – public manners, private customs, general bearing, hostelry, and cooking. . . ."[59]

Rested by the journey and revived in spirits, the Brownings took comfortable rooms near the Tuileries in the Hôtel Hyacinthe, rue St. Honoré. Elizabeth found that "Paris looks more beautiful than ever," partly because of the expanded boulevards and the "development of architectural splendour everywhere."[60] They took carriages for drives along the boulevards and in the Bois de Boulogne. Despite unseasonably cool weather – "Siberian and subversive" – Elizabeth went out to the shops, Robert to the Louvre, and the evenings were spent "dining round and round" at the restaurants. "Paris is so full of life," Elizabeth wrote Fanny Haworth who was thinking of leaving England for Italy, "– murmurs so of the fountain of intellectual youth for ever and ever – that rolling up the rue de Rivoli (much more the Boulevards) suggests a quicker beat of the fancy's heart; and I like it – I like it." Robert, too, found "everything, from cutlets to costumes" admirable in Paris. He was deeply pleased to find his father looking, on his seventy-sixth birthday, ten years younger; and he himself kept "boasting of his influx of energies."[61] The last time he had come to Paris he brought with him the manuscript for *Men and Women*, and it was there that he read bitterly the hostile reviews of it. This time he brought no poems. He had written nothing for nearly four years, yet he seems to have given little outward evidence that he was either discouraged or disappointed. Browning's admiring fellow-poet, William Allingham, records in his diary a telling anecdote about Browning in Paris at this time. Allingham, after calling on the Brownings, stopped to see Thackeray, who was ill and bedridden:

> "Browning was here this morning," Thackeray said, "what spirits he has – almost too much for me in my weak state. He almost blew me out of bed!"
> "A wonderful fellow, indeed!"
> "Yes, and he doesn't drink wine."
> "He's already screwed up to a concert pitch."
> "Far above it. But I can't manage his poetry. What do you say?" (I spoke highly of it.)

"Well, you see, I want poetry to be musical, to run sweetly."

"So do I –"

"Then that *does for* your friend B.!"

I spoke of Browning's other qualities as so splendid as to make him, as it were, a law in himself. But Thackeray only smiled and declined further discussion.

"He has a good belief, in himself, at all events. I suppose he doesn't care whether people praise him or not."

"I think he does, very much."

"O does he? Then I'll say something about him in a number."[62]

Browning apparently hoped to begin writing again once they had settled in some small coastal village. They ended up in Le Havre where, Robert wrote in perhaps a mockingly morose tone, he "began pretty zealously – but it's no use now: nor will the world very greatly care."[63] The only poem even possibly associated with this period is the rather cynical "Dîs aliter visum; or, le Byron de nos Jours."

Étretat was the coastal village the Brownings chose from lists they had made of possible places to spend the summer. The village was not, as Browning would later say of the Norman village of St. Aubin, a "hitherto un-Murrayed bathing-place," but Murray had dismissed it within three sentences: "About 10 m. S.W. of Fecamp, on the coast, is the fishing village of *Etretat*, situated amidst rocks which have been excavated by the sea into arches, aiguilles, and other fantastic shapes. It is resorted to by French artists, and there is a tolerable and cheap little inn (Au Rendezvous des Artistes). The road thither is bad."[64] Robert immediately took rather spacious if barely furnished lodgings for 200 francs a month. Elizabeth thought the countryside "very pretty, and the coast picturesque with fantastic rocks," but she had some objections. She thought the rent exorbitant for such poorly appointed rooms with a view of only a potato patch. Further, the small beach area was " 'commanded' by all the windows of the primitive hotel." Were she to bathe there according to doctor's order, she would feel like "a fly in a microscope, feeling my legs and arms counted on all sides, and receiving no comfort from the scientific results."[65] With the loss of only ten francs to the concierge, they moved on down to Le Havre, where, in a town they had previously thought of as only "commercial," they found at the Maison Versigny, 2 rue de Perry, access to a quiet beach if not a view. Writing to Isa Blagden, Robert anticipates her surprise that they are summering in Le Havre; but his account of Étretat, if more earthy, is close to Elizabeth's:

> Etretat has good cliffs, and a fresh open country to my taste – but the hole of a town is vile and you jostle with everybody else – for you are all poured forth funnel-wise on to the narrow bit of sea and must get it with the manners of hogs at a trough: here [Le Havre], the ugliness of everything in immediate view is surprising – but you have it all to yourself, and the sea-faringness of the place is good & interesting.[66]

Robert's father and sister had rooms at the same house, and his father was in good health and spirits and enjoyed the local library. Robert himself was less impressed with the subscription reading-room: at the cost of a napoleon, he wrote, one is entitled

> to study one "Constitutionnelle" three days stale, several numbers of the 'Guide Dentaire' (full of information about curious teeth), – all the back livraisons of a certain Journal of useful inventions containing models of improved cheese-toasters, novel implements of use in drill-husbandry & the like, – the remaining three-quarters of the table being cleverly littered over with tradesmen's prospectuses, cards for a dancing-master's Ball and so on.[67]

But Elizabeth's health was improving with daily bathing; and Pen was "minnowizing away among the Tritons," or, changing the metaphor when he wrote to Chapman, his "boy bathes like a duck."[68] Later in August, Milsand came for a ten-day stay; George and Arabel Barrett also came over for a visit. "I go mechanically out & in and get a day through – whereof not ten minutes have been my own," Robert wrote to Isa in early September. But he was happy to hear that Isa had become friendly with Félicie de Fauveau, so long self-exiled in Florence after her support of the royalist uprising in the Vendée in 1830. And he was amused by Isa's report of a young lady medium in Florence through whom "French Spirits" were able to speak while "the Flemish spirits stick in her throat." He was happy to be away from that sort of thing and "at this living and veracious Havre."[69] He was content with Le Havre, though he rather wished they had tried Nouville (Neuville?). If this sojourn on the French coast was not entirely satisfactory, it at least initiated a pattern Robert would adopt after Elizabeth's death: that of stopping a few days in Paris, then retiring for two or three months to some remote and relatively unfrequented bathing place: St. Énogat, Audierne, Sainte Marie près Pornic, St. Aubin, or later to mountain villages above the Rhône.

"Dîs aliter visum; or, le Byron de nos Jours," if not written at Le Havre, may take its inspiration from this seaside holiday. It was one of a number of poems in *Dramatis Personae* which dramatize the frustrations and failures of love and marriage. Others are, of course, "James Lee's Wife," "Too Late," "Youth and Art," "The Worst of It." In the poem, the surf, sand, gulls, the sea-caves, "the cliff-road edged with heath," combine with the bath-houses, the graveyard, and "the grey, sad church" to provide appropriate imagery and topography for the internalized dialogue of a young woman who has met again, after ten years and at the same seaside resort, an older man who had failed to propose marriage. Now, as they stroll the beach and the cliffs, the woman imagines what must have been the thoughts of this elderly Parisian man-of-letters, one sure of eventual election to the Académie, as they strolled the coast ten years before:

> Did you determine, as we stepped
>   O'er the lone stone fence, "Let me get
> Her for myself, and what's the earth
>   With all its art, verse, music, worth –
> Compared with love, found, gained, and kept?
>
> Schumann's our music-maker now;
>   Has his march-movement youth and mouth?
> Ingres's the modern man that paints;
>   Which will lean on me, of his saints?
> Heine for songs; for kisses, how?"

The chiding sarcasm of the woman is underscored by these references to Schumann, Ingres and Heine – all three were old and old-fashioned at the presumed time of the poem. This ageing Parisian Byron was too cautious; he did not grasp the love offered him. The woman married another; the man has taken as mistress or wife a dancer named Stephanie. Two lives might, the woman charges, have been fulfilled; instead, now four people live bored and empty lives. The sad, passionate, remorseful reverie gives way at the close to curt dismissal:

201

. . . Stephanie sprained last night her wrist,
   Ankle or something. "Pooh," cry you?
At any rate she danced, all say,
   Viley; her vogue has had its day.
Here comes my husband from his whist.

iv

The Browning party returned to Paris in late September, and a
fortnight later (October 13) Robert, Elizabeth and Pen left by train
for Lyon. At Lyon they took the diligence to Chambéry, where they
spent a day "for the sake of Les Charmettes and Rousseau." During
the excursion to the little farmhouse where Madame de Warens had
sheltered Rousseau for so many years and which Rousseau had
rendered idyllically in his *Confessions*, Robert played one of Rousseau's songs "on the old harpsichord, the keys of which rattled in a
ghastly way, as if it were the bones of him who once so 'dreamed.'"[70]
Elizabeth further noted that the watch of the old watchmaker's son
hung there on the wall "without a tick in it." Troubles with the
diligence forced them to spend the night at Lans le Bourg before
crossing the Mt. Cenis pass to Turin. They rested a month at Casa
Guidi, then went on through Arrezzo, Camuscia, Perugia, Spoleto,
Terni, Civita Castellana to Rome. Robert took an apartment at 43
Bocca di Leone for four months, intending after that to go on to
Naples. It was from this apartment that Elizabeth wrote the letter to
Miss Haworth which Kenyon has misdated as December 27, 1853.
Fanny Haworth had apparently been "struck" by Ernest Feydeau's
sensational novel of Fanny's boredom with her older husband and of
her adulterous affair with the young Roger. Capitalizing on
Flaubert's *succès de scandale*, Feydeau had given a hackneyed theme
a new rendition by having Fanny return to her husband's bed in the
final scene. Young Roger watches through the window while his
young mistress and her old husband make love. Roger was disillusioned, but the reading public was titillated and shocked by such
"realistic" voyeurism. To a chatty letter to Fanny Haworth about
whom they've seen in Rome and about Christmas Day at St. Peter's,
Elizabeth adds as a postscript: "Robert's love, and Penini's. If
'Fanny' strikes you, 'Madame Bovary' will thunder-strike you."[71]
Pen was working his way through an Italian translation of *Le Comte*

de Monte-Cristo. At breakfast in early January, 1859, he announced
to his parents: "'I mean to read *novels*. I shall read all Dumas's, to
begin. And then I shall like to read papa's favourite book, "Madame
Bovary."'"[72] Both parents laughed at the evidence in their nine-
year-old son of "such hereditary tendencies" – presumably his
mother's taste for Dumas, his father's for Flaubert.

War between Piedmont and Austria finally broke out in April,
1859. Napoleon III's troops came in support of Cavour, and when
the Brownings arrived back at Casa Guidi that month they found a
large French force garrisoned in Florence. In *The Dance*, as the
"Florence Beauties" and the "gallant sons of France" tread the
measure on the meadows of the Cascine, Elizabeth celebrated the
hopes that the marriage between Piedmont and France would lead to
the liberation of Tuscany and all Italy. Robert clearly shared
Elizabeth's desire to see Northern Italy freed of Austrian domina-
tion; and, if he did not share her view of the greatness of Napoleon
III, he did share her anger at the Derby government's refusal to have
England side against Austria. The French victories at Magenta (June
4) and Solferino (June 24) gave promise that liberation would be
carried clear to the Adriatic. But the meeting of Napoleon III and
Franz Josef at Villafranca on July 8 brought a convenient, premature
end to the war. Only Lombardy had been liberated and placed under
Piedmont. Napoleon III supported the return to Florence of the
Austrian puppet, the Grand Duke. Elizabeth's monologue spoken
by Napoleon III, "An August Voice," records with heavy sarcasm
her disgust and disillusionment. Recovering at Siena from the heat
of Florence and a nervous collapse brought on by the war, Elizabeth
could only offer feeble resistance to Walter Savage Landor's "savage
invectives" against the Emperor. The raging old Landor was also
writing "Latin alcaics against his wife and Louis Napoleon"; the
leonine, rancorous Landor laughed "carnivorously" when Elizabeth
suggested playfully that he write "an ode in honour of the Emperor"
if only to please her.[73] She recovered her strength sufficiently at
Siena to write a score of lengthy letters defending Napoleon III,
damning Austria, and analysing the conspiracy of England and Prussia against France. After a few weeks back in Florence, the Brownings returned to Rome for the winter of 1859–60.

Shortly before the treaty of Villafranca in July, 1859, Robert and
Elizabeth began to write together on "the Italian question"; and

Robert suggested that they publish their work jointly. What Robert began was apparently a poem attacking the Derby government: when Elizabeth showed him her *Napoleon III in Italy*, Robert commented that she "was gentle to England in comparison to what he had been."[74] Once the more liberal Palmerston government came in, Robert destroyed his poem. Elizabeth condensed and versified the ideas and sentiments so fully poured forth in her letters: exaltation of the French Emperor set against sound scourging of England and Austria. In Rome she prepared seven of these poems for publication; to this "thin slice of a wicked book," as she called it, she added an eighth poem invoking a terrible curse on a sinful nation.[75] So strident was her anger at England throughout the first seven poems that she and Robert should not have been so shocked when their long-time friend Chorley mistook the nation being cursed for England rather than the American slave states. These *Poems Before Congress* were published in March, 1860. In her preface dated "Rome, *February, 1860*," she anticipated charges from the English reviewers that the poems were unpatriotic. Both the Derby and Palmerston governments had followed and counselled a policy of non-intervention in the Italian struggle for freedom. This policy she strongly attacked:

> . . . non-intervention in the affairs of a neighbouring state is a high political virtue; but non-intervention does not mean, passing by on the other side when your neighbour falls among thieves. . . . Freedom itself is virtue, as well as privilege; but freedom of the seas does not mean piracy, nor freedom of land brigandage; nor freedom of the senate, freedom to cudgel a dissident member, nor freedom of the press, freedom to calumniate and lie.[76]

The thieves, pirates, and brigands are, of course, Austria; the lying newspaper is *The Times*; the cudgelled senator was the anti-slavery leader from Massachusetts, Charles Sumner. Sumner delivered in the Senate his "Crime Against Kansas" speech, a powerful philippic against the pro-slavery forces which had in 1854 invaded Lawrence, Kansas, smashed the presses and burned abolitionist newspaper offices as well as the Free State Hotel. For this, Sumner was brutally beaten on the floor of the Senate by Congressman Brooks of South Carolina. The Brownings had met Sumner in Paris in 1858, where he was undergoing medical treatment: a "burning torture at the hands of French surgeons," Elizabeth called it. She compared this treatment to the torture of the Jesuit priest in Sue's *Le Juif errant*. She then added: "Isn't it a true martyrdom? I ask. What is apprehended is paralysis, or at best nervous infirmity for life, for the effect of the blows (on the spine) of that savage."[77] Elizabeth thought of *Poems Before Congress* as a plea for intervention on behalf of human freedom anywhere in the world.

In Rome Robert also began in a short prose sketch an apologia for Napoleon III. It would not be shaped into a poem – *Prince Hohenstiel-Schwangau* – until after Robert had watched the Emperor's career end with the surrender at Sedan. There are many voices conflicting and advising during the "ghostly dialogue" Napoleon carries on in this complex exercise in self-justification. Sometimes a voice will sound much like Elizabeth's. While lamenting the French nation's historic penchant for wars of conquest, Napoleon admits that at times war is necessary:

> . . . I foresee and I announce
> Necessity of warfare in one case,
> For one cause: one way, I bid broach the blood
> O' the world. For truth and right, and only right
> And truth, – right, truth on the absolute scale of God. . . .
> Come with me and deliver Italy!
> Smite hip and thigh until the oppressor leave
> Free from the Adriatic to the Alps
> The oppressed one! (lines 1862–83)

Elizabeth's poems were published in March of 1860; in April, Napoleon III sent French troops into Savoy and Nice to ensure that the plebiscite there would favour the integration of those provinces into the French Empire. For the rest of her life, Elizabeth would defend this annexation – often on the old grounds that the people had democratically chosen to join France. But to Forster she admitted that "Savoy has given me pain; and I would for the world's sake that a great action [the liberation of Italy] had remained out of the reach of the hypothetical whispers of depreciators. I would rather not hear Robert say, for instance: 'It was a great action; but he [Napoleon] has taken eighteen pence for it, which is a pity.' "[78] In *Prince Hohenstiel-Schwangau* the whispering voice is called Sagacity, and it taunts Napoleon III for taking payment for his great action of delivering Italy:

> . . . 'All for nought –
> Not even, say, some patch of province, splice
> O' the frontier? – some snug honorarium-fee
> Shut into glove and pocketed apace?"
> (Questions Sagacity) "in deference
> To the natural susceptibility
> Of folks at home, unwitting of that pitch
> You soar to, misdoubting of Truth, Right
> And the other augustnesses repay
> Expenditure in coin o' the realm, – but prompt
> To recognize the cession of Savoy
> And Nice as marketable value!"

But Napoleon III denies he fought Austria for either love of war or for territorial conquest. His troops had fought in Italy a "war for the hate of war." (lines 1891 ff.)

The Brownings returned to Florence in June of 1860. They again spent the late summer and early autumn in Siena before returning to Rome in November. Elizabeth's letters dwell obsessively with Italian politics and the French role in the drive towards unification. She saw growing up about her a "religion to hate France, and to set up a 'Boney' as a 'raw head and bloody bones' sort of scarecrow."[79] Still, she kept her sense of humour and could be amused by an English reviewer, hostile to her *Poems Before Congress*, gravely fusing her known interest in spiritualism with her defence of Louis-Napoleon. The reviewer claimed, Elizabeth wrote to Mrs. Martin, that she had been lately " 'biologised by infernal spirits' in order to the production of certain bad works in the service of 'Moloch,' meaning, of course, L.N."[80] For all her love of France, Elizabeth began to sense that she would never again be able to return there. In Rome in January of 1861, Robert began to plan to spend the summer in France. He especially wanted to see his now seventy-eight-year-old father. Arabel wrote to ask if she could meet them in France; Elizabeth thought it might be best for Robert and Pen to go alone to Paris, but perhaps her strength would revive by spring. By the end of March she had formed vague plans of a visit to Paris in the summer. She rather shrank from the "noise of Paris," she wrote to Sarianna, and because "the sea is so far" she asked Sarianna to give up, this once, a bathing holiday. Instead, she suggested that they "summer out at Fontainebleau in the picturesque part of the forest."[81] By May 11 she has had reports of recent snows in Paris; she worries that Fontainebleau may be damp. Perhaps if the new railway has been completed to Trouville? – "if the railroad is there, it would not prolong the journey (in relation to Fontainebleau) more than two or three hours, if so much would it?" she asks Sarianna. "We shall cut Florence quite short," she adds.[82]

The Brownings arrived back in Florence from Rome on June 5, and the following day they learned of the death of Cavour. Elizabeth was deeply distraught by the news, and Robert immediately wrote to Sarianna that the journey to Paris must be cancelled. On the 20th Elizabeth was stricken with lung congestion; she died on the 29th. Robert stayed in Florence through July, closing up Casa Guidi and arranging for the crating of their books and household effects. With Pen and Isa Blagden, he left for Paris on August 1. After a few days there, he left with his father, sister, and son for the Breton coastal village of St. Énogat.

8

Breton Holidays, 1861–68

i

Return to France and Sojourn at St. Énogat – By Rail from Paris to Boulogne – RB Sees Tennyson – Social Life in London Becomes Crowded – A Holiday at Sainte Marie près Pornic – "James Lee's Wife".

ii

Paris in the Spring of 1863 – Return to the Quiet and Rusticity of Sainte Marie – Féval's Annette Laïs *and Maurice de Guérin's* Reliquiae *– RB Disappointed by Flaubert's* Salammbô *– "Gold Hair: A Story of Pornic" – Renan's* Vie de Jésus *and RB's "Epilogue" to* Dramatis Personae *and "A Death in the Desert".*

iii

A Sojourn in the Pyrenees and at Biarritz – Plans for The Ring and the Book *– Another Holiday at Sainte Marie près Pornic – Fifine at the Fair –* Le Croisic *and* Hervé Riel *– The Two Poets of Croisic – A Pardon Near Audierne – A Parisian Review of* The Ring and the Book.

i

The journey back from Florence to Paris was both slow and painful for Browning. Though he, Pen, and Isa took "the straight road" from Marseille to Paris, they had to take local trains to accommodate Pen's pony. Browning had intended to go almost immediately on to London, "but the process of going over the old ground, stopping at the old Inns &c was too much" for him. Paris, too, with its associations of Elizabeth's delight in the city, was also "unbearable," as he wrote to the Storys from St. Énogat, "and I only breathe freelier since we arrived at this primitive & lonely place – by St. Malo – with a solitary sea, bays, sands & rocks, & green, pleasant country."[1] The solitude of the unfamiliar Breton coast was restorative. After a fortnight he wrote to Isa, who had returned to England: "I don't feel the miserable contrast between then & now, as when first coming on the old Paris nights, peculiarities, nothings that only grew to be somethings from their first association."[2] The quiet and unexpected wildness of the Breton coast delighted the entire family. Sarianna, also deeply grieved by Elizabeth's death, grew better and found the "loneliness & roughness of the place to her taste."[3] Pen rode his pony, swam daily, and sketched with his grandfather, now seventy-nine but robust enough to take three long walks each day. The weather was good: the mornings and evenings "*fresh* not to say chilly" and the days sunny and warm. Browning hiked along the coast and nearby fields to tire himself so he could sleep. He was grateful for "the solitude of the bays – any one of many – the sands & rocky inlets – & the quiet, pastoral character of the inland with its few inhabitants. . . ."[4] By the end of August, Browning's letters turn away from his private grief towards light conversation about various friends, to his anger at rumours that the American North might seek peace after early defeats in Virginia and Missouri, to his maturing plans to settle in London, and, most importantly, his plans to remedy the defects in his son's education.

The Brownings stayed on at St. Énogat longer than they had planned. Milsand, who had just returned from a Norman seaside holiday, reported of Paris "that the heat was still oppressive there" and urged them to remain awhile in Brittany, where the weather remained "warm & favourable" despite "autumnal signs."[5] When the fine weather finally "broke up suddenly" in mid-September, they returned to Paris, again by slow trains because of the pony, and arrived there on September 22. Browning and Pen left Paris after a day or two and after a few hours' delay at the railway station, where Browning threatened to "prosecute" unless a horse-car for the pony were attached to the express train to Boulogne. "I was upwards of two hours in this weary work of battling with them," Browning told the Storys, " 'it *could not* be'! – but at the last moment, literally, it *was* – they pushed me into the train, put the horse-box on, which there was no time to even pay for, & so I got off, reached Boulogne in time to get the pony thro' the custom house, & consequently not miss the boat. . . ." With self-satisfaction Browning further reported to the Storys that the train which the railway functionaries wanted him to take had crashed at Amiens and injured twenty-two persons with " '10 or 12 killed.' " It was also at Amiens that Browning saw Tennyson board the train; at Boulogne he "kept out of sight" of Tennyson until he had seen to the luggage and pony. Then, with his hat pulled over his face, Browning went with Pen down to the quay. There he pointed out to Pen the Poet Laureate with his wife and two children boarding the boat to Folkestone. Two hours after midnight, Browning and Pen boarded the direct boat to London.[6]

Browning's sojourn in Brittany set a pattern he would follow for the next twenty years: two or three months of nearly every year would be spent in France. Until his father died in Paris in 1866, he normally came to Paris for a week or two in the early spring; then he returned in late July for a few days before removing for ten weeks or so to some remote seaside or mountain village. In the 1860's he went to the Breton villages of St. Énogat, Sainte Marie près Pornic, Le Croisic and Audierne. In 1864 he made one rather unsuccessful attempt to try the more fashionable Biarritz, but was forced to seek accommodation in the Basque mountain village of Cambo. In the early 1870's he went regularly to less remote but still little frequented villages along the Calvados coast; in the late 1870's and early 1880's mountain villages above the Rhône – Collonge, Lans, St. Pierre-de-Chartreuse – attracted him. During the last five years of his life, his travel in France was largely limited to brief stop-overs in Paris while coming and going from London to Venice.

French scenes and subjects continued in his poetry. Six of the eighteen poems in *Dramatis Personae* (1864) were inspired by his life in France or by his interest in the work of Ernest Renan. His plans for *The Ring and the Book* (1868–69) matured while he was at Cambo and final revisions were made at Audierne. In 1867 he wrote *Hervé Riel* to celebrate the nearly forgotten naval hero from Le Croisic – the village in which Browning was then staying. The Franco-Prussian War and the Siege of Paris urged him to close analysis of the career of Napoleon III in *Prince Hohenstiel-Schwangau* (1871); the attractions of a gypsy girl at the fair at Pornic led a Breton Don Juan into metaphysical reveries about adultery in *Fifine at the Fair* (1872); an examination of a Parisian's life and suicide in Normandy figured in *Red Cotton Night-Cap Country* (1873). The mountains around Collonge – with views of the Jura, of Savoy and of Geneva with its memories of Voltaire and Rousseau – become the scene for Browning's own meditations on the immortality of the soul in *La Saisiaz* (1878). In a companion poem *The Two Poets of Croisic*, Browning treats rather gaily the poetic "immortality" of forgotten Breton poets. During these years he continued to read Balzac, Sand, Flaubert, even Alphonse Karr; his friendship with Milsand deepened, and he made acquaintance with French artists like Doré, Gérôme, and Rodin. He came to know at least slightly Renan and Taine as well as lesser intellectuals such as James Darmsteter and his wife Mary, friend, travelling companion and first biographer of Renan. Browning did not, however, seek in France – as he and Elizabeth had earlier – the bright and stimulating centre of contemporary intellectual and literary life. He sought at the coastal villages "salt and solitude" and bracing air and peace in the mountains. France became for him a place of restoration and recuperation after the year's intense life of writing and going out in London.

For four months after his return to London in 1861, Browning remained rather secluded, seeing only Arabel Barrett and a few close friends, arranging his household and Pen's lessons, checking the proofs of Elizabeth's *Last Poems* (1862), seeing to it that the *Daily News* published W. W. Story's articles defending to a British public the war policy of the American North, and reading with satisfaction "the news from Italy – & Paris" announcing the withdrawal of French troops from Rome. In early February of 1862 Browning announced rather emphatically that his period of semi-seclusion was at an end: "I go, as you know, at the end of next fortnight, to Paris & return in March," he told Miss Blagden. "The days lengthen (what wonderfully mild days!) and my time increases . . . *I shall go out now in earnest, & not in promise!*"[7] There was little going out during the week he and Pen were in Paris; he made only "a call or two" and spent the rest of his time with his father, sister and Milsand. Once back from Paris, however, Browning began to go out into society in earnest. A letter to the Storys soon after his return in early March testifies to his immersion into London social and literary life so characteristic of him from this time onwards:

I saw Miss Weston lately: that Miss Dempster wrote & appointed a day to be seen at Reeves – speaking delightedly of a letter from you: I met her sister too. . . . I dined two days ago at Mrs. Marshall's father's, Ld Monteagle . . . Aubrey de Vere is in Athens or thereabout . . . tonight I dine with Emerson Tennett – but I can't go on with the week's work: enough is said to show you that I try and see old friends – when my true *treat* would be an evening over the [pile] of unread books. . . . Well, – Rossetti has had a miserable loss of his wife, a month ago. . . . He is in trouble indeed, poor, kind fellow. I met Dickens at dinner the other day – looking very well & young. Thackeray has just resigned the Editorship of the Cornhill. . . . The Editorship has, under the circumstances &c &c been offered to – *me*! I really take it as a compliment because I am, by your indulgence, a bit of a poet, if you like – but a man of the world and able editor, hardly! They count on my attracting writers, – I who could never muster *English* readers enough to pay for salt & bread![8]

Browning's June letter to Isa Blagden suggests that as spring turned to summer his life was becoming even more crowded:

Let's see: I dined two days ago with Mrs. Fitz-Patrick: I sat by my old friend Mrs Cust – who confirmed what I heard six months before of Gertrude having refused Mr. Beaumont and 80,000 a-year. At the same place I found Ma^{de} B. de Bury, of whom I have a fear, besides an unanswered letter praying me to go & see her. . . . Kinglake sat next her – sucking in authentic news about cessions of territory & so on. Yesterday I met the Storys at dinner, & afterward went with them to the Athenaeum, where I saw nothing worth the trouble of going but the Parsee girls, – prettier to my corrupt & rotten cheese loving taste than any of the English fineness & loveliness (aquiline nose between two pudding cheeks with lightish hair & eyes, & "fine" complexion – give me these coal black little bitter-almonds!) Today I dine at the Martin's – as I did last week – charming people they are, – Thackeray & his girls to be there. I was at a House four days ago, where an English young bride of a year's standing began the dinner by getting hold of her husband's hands, with other significancies before us all. . . . Thackeray was there too, and I mean to ask him what he thought of it. . . . I saw Rossetti on Monday, – mean to go & see him soon, and meet his sister & mother. Hatty and Gibson arrive in a week.[9]

In July, Browning determined upon a day on which nothing would induce him to leave his house: "I received *eight* invitations!" he told Isa in mock complaint. His life in London was turning metaphorically into a "campaign" from which he had decided to retire to France for a while: "I hope to get there early in August – not to escape the heat, however – but for quiet & change of scene. I shall stay two months & then return for another campaign, – improving by the experience of the present – which, on the whole, has been satisfactory." A week later he complained: "My engagements are just as wearisome as ever – but in a fortnight at farthest I shall escape from it all." Then, on August 1: "I go to-morrow to Paris, & thence to whatever place my sister & father may decide upon. My address will be *always 151, Rue de Grenelle, Faubourg St. Germain*."[10]

Browning left London "precipitately . . . engagements to the very last," and he vowed – once he and his family had taken pleasant, bare, clean rooms in the tiny hamlet of Sainte Marie près Pornic – that when he returned to London he would "go *nowhere*." Sainte Marie was much like St. Énogat though smaller and more remote. His sister and Pen swam; his father walked and sketched; Browning was content to "sit in [his] room all day & walk in the evening." With a dozen houses facing miles of low, rocky shore and open country behind, Sainte Marie was "perfectly lonely" though but a half-hour's walk away was Pornic, "full & gay enough." The country was solitary and bare and "the sea," he wrote to the Storys, "is everywhere and the land harmonises entirely with it."[11] The land and seascape also harmonized with Browning's feelings; the place was, as he told Isa, much to his mind, and he had needed the change. Two long letters to Isa are crowded with rather wistful memories of Florence and with more practical problems about the commemorative monument planned for Elizabeth's grave in Florence. He felt strongly but resisted a longing to return in the autumn to Florence. He distracted himself by reading the newspapers and relaying news of the resurgent clericalism of France as instanced by the case of a French priest named de Laurière being illegally denied a civil marriage. There was also Napoleon III's appointment of more conservative ministers to Italy and the impending resignation of the anti-clerical Édouard Thouvenel as Foreign Minister.

Browning had brought along some books, "odd things in Latin and antique French." In one, a "crazy old Latin joke book," he was amused to find a Latin version of "Piper of Hamelin," the piper turned into a bagpipe-playing devil. Pen, pushed so hard by his father at his lessons during the winter, did not open a book the entire two months. Browning declared flatly, "I don't at all care."[12] He read, wrote, walked in the evening and sat for long periods of time at his window overlooking the sea. "If I could," he wrote, "I would stay just as I am for many a day. I feel out of the very earth sometimes; as I sit here at the window – with the little church, a field, a few houses, and the sea; on a week day there is *nobody* in the village: plenty of haystacks, cows and fowls – all our butter, eggs, milk are produced in the farm-house. Such a soft sea & such a mournful wind!" The scene is flecked with the sights, sounds and tastes of the village life; but into the sense of lonely peace Browning infuses a poet's sense of bleak isolation. He ends the scene with: "I wrote a poem yesterday of 120 lines – & mean to keep writing, whether I like it or no."[13]

Looking sadly from the window of her small house on "this bitter coast of France," the young woman of "James Lee's Wife" finds in the decline of summer harbingers of the death of love and the estrangement of her husband:

Ah, Love, but a day
  And the world has changed!
The sun's away,
  And the bird estranged;
The wind has dropped,
  And the sky's deranged:
Summer has stopped.

Musing before a fire of wood tossed up from wrecks along the rocky coast, she imagines that sailors – "mute, / Drenched and stark" – fighting the dangerous surf may look at her window and envy the warmth and security of the couple's home. The sailors would be mistaken by the deceptive appearance of domestic happiness. Within the seemingly safely anchored house a process worse than the sea's tempest has been at work:

For some ships, safe in port indeed,
  Rot and rust,

Run to dust,
All through worms i' the wood, which crept,
Gnawed our hearts out while we slept:
   That is worse.

Outside the doorway are the red, rough fields, desolate of all but a
few blades of grass; it is an emptiness where a single bird would be
an event. The leaves of the salt-tortured fig tree furl like hands
opening towards the vanished sun of summer. The little vineyard
mimics the wife's painful anguish: "How the vines writhe in rows,
each impaled on its stake! / My heart shrivels up and my spirit
shrinks curled." Walking along the beach – probably alone but carrying on an internal dialogue with her husband – she tries to analyse
their estrangement; but it is in the turf and rock along the cliff that
she finds the metaphor for their failed marriage. The grass is "Dead
to the roots" and the anvil-flat rock is "Baked dry; of a weed, of a
shell, no trace: / Sunshine outside, but ice at the core, / Death's altar
by the lone shore." A poem she reads under the cliff asks if the
mournful wind may assuage grief, but the wind turns into a grotesque image of the death moans of a tall, spent nun, "'Her shrunk lids
open, her lean fingers shut / Close, close, their sharp and livid nails
indent / The clammy palm; then all is mute. . . .'" Rather than
bringing solace, the wind finally turns into a whining, hand-licking
dog lost upon the sand. Some consolation comes from the young
wife's recognition that in the wasting trials of love given but not
returned she herself has grown in moral strength. This "doctrine,
simple, ancient, true" she also reads into the rocks:

Oh, good gigantic smile o' the brown old earth,
   This autumn morning! How he sets his bones
To bask i' the sun, and thrusts out knees and feet
   For the ripple to run over in its mirth;
   Listening the while, where on the heap of stones
The white breast of the sea-lark twitters sweet.

As she sketches the hand of a peasant girl, a hand coarsened by
labour, she discovers a more profound beauty than the superficial
physical beauty so prized by her shallow and perhaps unfaithful
husband. Strengthened by the lessons she has learned, it is she who
ends the painful marriage and takes ship away from the "bitter coast
of France."

"James Lee's Wife" does not contain the topographical accuracy Browning would – in *Fifine at the Fair* – give to the coast stretching westward from Pornic along the Baie de Bourgneuf, the Île de Noirmoutier looming in the distance. In this earlier poem Browning appropriately portrays a generalized Breton coast and invests it with metaphorical meanings which mark the stages of the young wife's growth towards understanding and acceptance of lost love. The mood and tone of the poem resemble closely Browning's own sense of being "out of the very earth sometimes" as he sat at the window in Sainte Marie. He sometimes found himself walking in memory "among the hills, or turnings by the villas, certain doorways, old walls, points of sight" in Florence. These memories came to him with a painful sense that he "could not bear a repetition of them"; he felt they "would fairly choke" him. At such times he feared thoughts of a return to Florence, but his moods shifted abruptly so that a strong desire came to go at once to Florence. With an unusual display of personal emotion, he wrote to Isa Blagden of that desire to return in a letter which reflects the imagery of swallows and the encroaching chill of autumn of "James Lee's Wife": "I have such yearnings to be there! Just now, at the approach of Autumn, I feel exactly like a swallow in a cage, – as if I *must* go there, have no business anywhere else, with the year drawing in." But, like the young woman at the end of the poem, he rejects the temptation to return to the past and turns instead to a new life. "How thankful I am," he continued, "that all these foolish fancies never displace for a moment the solid fact that I can't go but have plain duty to do in London, – if there could be a doubt about that, I should drift like a feather. . . ."[14]

The mood of grey lassitude mixed with anguish and regret in "James Lee's Wife" is new to Browning's poetry. There may be a literary source for the poem in *Modern Love*, which Meredith had published in June, when he sent a copy to Browning. Browning's poem, however, avoids the cutting, cynical wit of Meredith; further, "James Lee's Wife" is a series of nearly private reveries quite different from the socially constricted language of *Modern Love*. Indeed, Browning's own attempt to explain the poem emphasized the young married couple's freedom from the pressures of social convention, pressures so important to Meredith's poem. Julia Wedgwood read the poem soon after its publication in 1864 and found that it was an

"artistic fault" to place the young couple in "such a proletarian, to
use the horrid new slang, background. Those are not the feelings of
people who are earning their bread," Miss Wedgwood went on, "I
suppose you meant to escape the vulgarity of chateaux, but it gives
one a feeling of masquerading to read the complication of those
reflections with the slight touches of background."[15] Browning
accepted the criticism graciously and apologized: he had, he said,
misled Miss Wedgwood into thinking the couple were " 'pro-
letaire' ". He had "meant them for just the opposite – people
newly-married, trying to realize a dream of being sufficient to each
other, in a foreign land (where you can try such an experiment) and
finding it break up, – the man being *tired* first, – and tired precisely
of the love. . . ."[16] The husband's *tiredness* of the marital experiment
is little emphasized in the poem itself, but it is a word which might
well describe Browning's own uncharacteristic lassitude during the
sojourn at Sainte Marie. And into the young wife's reveries he suffused a strong sense of *ennui*. The following year, 1863, Browning
was again at Sainte Marie and wrote of his "old and still continuing
passion for 'Ma^{de} Bovary,' " that masterful study of how ennui gnaws
away at love. A year later, to Miss Wedgwood, Browning pointed to
the tiring of love as the central theme of "James Lee's Wife." There
is less of Meredithian social tragi-comedy than there is Flaubertian
ennui: Flaubert asked: "Do you know that modern ennui which
gnaws at a man's entrails and turns an intelligent person into a
walking shadow, a thinking phantom?"[17]

ii

In early October Browning left Sainte Marie for a week in Paris
before returning to London, which he found "all much as [he] left it
& very black & blank. . . ." By mid-winter he once again felt
"plagued with work & calls," and he "suffered from bile & cold".[18]
He planned to go to Paris in late February but then Pen caught a
severe cold, so Browning was in London to observe the events
attending the marriage of the Crown Prince. Dickens had, for five
pounds, hired a huge van in which he and Browning and a dozen
other people planned to follow the route of festive illuminations from
London Bridge to Regent Street. The cumbersome van, however,
became entangled in traffic under a railway bridge in Southwark.

Browning used the incident to contrast unfavourably, in a manner reminiscent of Elizabeth, London with Paris. From Paris a week later he described the failed expedition to Isa:

> the illuminations I went to see with Dickens – we left Waterloo Bridge in a Van at 7 o'clock – were to go by a by-way to Southwark Bridge in order to do the thing superiorly: spent *five* miserably cold & black hours in trying vainly to do so, got out again in despair, & walked back – by which means I saw a little – far more, however, than was worth seeing: the English can't manage anything of the kind – I notice every night that the illuminations here of the Place de la Concorde & all round are so strangely superior that I can't understand how people with love of fireworks & lights in their large souls don't go to Paris & return – at less expense than Dickens' Van which cost £5![19]

Paris was superior in other ways: "the clear, bracing, exciting character of the air has a great effect on me," he wrote, "& I have got rid of a sort of cough which plagued me for weeks." He found his father and sister well and happy; he talked with Milsand, who earlier in the year had told Browning he would consult with Renan about a "Sanskrit Professor" sought by Isa Blagden. Browning went to see a production of *Macbeth* at the Odéon. He did not, apparently, take any notice of what in retrospect was to be one of the most significant artistic events in Paris in the spring of 1863. For the Salon of 1863, over half of the five thousand canvases submitted had been rejected by the conservative jury of the Académie. Serious and widespread criticism of the selection process began in early 1863. In February and March, Louis Martinet had challenged the jury's standards by exhibiting in his gallery on the Boulevard des Italiens fourteen paintings by Manet. Throughout March criticism of the jury mounted sufficiently to cause a politic Napoleon III to issue his edict in April that a *Salon des Refusés* be established: Manet, Pissaro, Whistler, Cézanne and scores of much lesser artists had received semi-official recognition. Browning's love of painting did not extend to the newer currents in French art. He knew the illustrators Gavarni and later Doré, and in Paris in 1855 he and Elizabeth had met Rosa Bonheur. In October of that year he had impressed Rosetti with his knowledge of early Italian painting at the Louvre, and he perhaps had gone with Rossetti to the Exhibition where Rossetti judged Delacroix and Ingres the best of that Year's Salon, passing by unnoticed Courbet's *pavillon de réalisme*. In "Dîs Aliter Visum" (1864), Ingres is called, perhaps ironically, "the modern man that paints": Gérôme and Doré seem to fill that role in *Fifine at the Fair* (1872); he allows one of his characters in *Red Cotton Night-Cap Country* (1873) to be openly contemptuous of newer French painting, though the character herself is compared to a Meissonier. In the early 1870's Pen began his career as a painter of large, academic, historical and mythological canvases. With those paintings, he would win some medals at exhibitions in Paris. By then Browning's taste in contemporary painting seems to have been limited to the tradition in which Pen worked.

Browning returned to Paris in early August of 1863. After the coolness of London he found himself "really broiled" in Paris where he read "on a Fahrenheit thermometer in the Place Royale, one day at 2 oclock 96!". After a week he left, with his father, Sarianna, Pen, and old English friend Mrs.Mary Bracken and her son Willy, for Sainte Marie près Pornic via Tours and Nantes. There the heat had passed leaving the grass "brown as rusty iron." The Browning family picked up the previous year's routine of walking, sketching, eating simple meatless meals, reading and bathing. Browning himself now began to swim daily, an activity he delighted in for years afterwards while on holiday along the French coast. He reported proudly to Isa that Pen had displayed courage and good sense in saving another swimmer; and Pen had further displayed a self-confident impatience at the foolish advice of a bystander whom he bade " 'Allez au diable!' "[20] Gone was the longing to return to Florence, which Browning had felt so strongly the year before while sitting for hours before the window in the house of M. Laraison at Sainte Marie. That Italy and France would be linked by rail when the Mt. Cenis tunnel was completed in five years, as he read in a French paper, did not interest him and drew from him only the dry comment: "What is it all to me, however? Something perhaps in my old age."[21] Nor was he anxious to return to London. He had been, as he told the Storys, "very tired with work and play, as it is counted" in London, and so had looked forward to the "extreme quiet and rusticity" of Sainte Marie. He liked the little Breton village even better than he had the previous year, and "the barrenness of the country is not a bad thing –," he assured his American friends in

Rome, "the silence, and surrounding sea, all one could wish."[22] The quiet and solitude and simple routine brought on forgetfulness and lassitude which made Browning reluctant to return to London. "I . . . feel tired," he told Isa in late September, "and think of going to London with 'ribrezzo' [nausea] – I could live here, as far as myself am concerned, for many a year to come."[23]

His reading that summer was varied: a little Virgil, some "sea-songs" he thought stupid and sentimental, an instalment of Paul Féval's new *roman-feuilleton*, Maurice de Guérin's *Reliquiae*, Flaubert's *Salammbô*, and, as he reported to Isa, "some novels that I mean to read, besides books of my own, – so I shall get through some six weeks more." Féval's *Annette Laïs*, then running in *L'Opinion nationale*, Browning found "delicious." He apparently knew something of Féval's earlier sensational fiction, perhaps *Les Mystères de Londres* (1844) or *Les Amours de Paris* (1845). Féval's new work surprised him: "I did not think anything so delicate and witty had been in the man."[24] The literary "remains" of Maurice de Guérin collected in the two-volume *Reliquiae* (1861) disappointed Browning for a number of reasons. De Guérin's lyric evocations of nature seemed limited and lacked the psychological penetration Browning valued: "it's one thing to say pretty things about swallows, roses, autumn &c and another to look an inch into men's hearts." The style he dismissed as "limpid & deep as water in a teaspoon." De Guérin's work might be "pretty, & true in its little way," but he did not find it sufficiently important to draw such praise as that "deep thinker" Sainte-Beuve had given in his preface to *Reliquiae*. Browning had admired Sainte-Beuve's study of Lamennais, and he admired Lamennais, "who died detesting their [Catholic] doctrine." After being closely associated with Lamennais and influenced by him, de Guérin had reconciled himself to the Church. Hence, Browning thought it amusing that Sainte-Beuve now took de Guérin rather than Lamennais "for a model Catholic."[25] Flaubert, too, displeased Browning when he read *Salammbô*, which Mrs. Bracken had brought along. He asked Isa if she remembered his "old, and still continuing passion for 'Ma^{de} Bovary?'" Flaubert's reconstruction of the violent pageantry of the destruction of ancient Carthage was quite another thing than the careful and penetrating psychological realism which had made *Madame Bovary* Browning's favourite book. "If you have read *this*," he continued to Isa, "– as you probably have, my immense disappointment will be easily understood."[26]

Since *Sordello*, Browning had taken great care to be authentic when he incorporated historical materials into his poetry. He was or would soon be at work on a poem reconstructing the death of Saint John; and he had for the past two years intermittently considered how he might give literary form to the documents he found in Florence bound up in the Old Yellow Book and thus resuscitate that seventeenth-century Roman murder case. His keen interest in the problems of the literary reconstruction of historical material is further evidenced by his frequent references that summer to George Eliot's novel *Romola* set in Savonarola's Florence. Though he was unable to get a copy of *Romola* until he was back in London in November, again he was disappointed, for Eliot in her third and final volume had turned too much attention to the uninteresting hero "while the great interests, Savonarola and the Republic, which I expected would absorb attention and pay for previous minutenesses, dwindled strangely."[27] He had also by then finished Renan's historical reconstruction of the life of Jesus. Given his curiosity about the problems of writing historical fictions, Browning was not necessarily disappointed that Flaubert had turned from a study of contemporary provincial manners to the problem of bringing to life a grand historical event. What he criticized in *Salammbô* – and here his criticism was in concert with that of Sainte-Beuve and others – was Flaubert's failure to create a documentary verisimilitude: "I take nine-tenths of the 'learning' – the historical touches &c to be pure humbug," he wrote and then added, "'all made out of the carver's brain.'"[28] Browning was wrong to think Flaubert's learning was "pure humbug." Flaubert had successfully refuted such a charge when he patiently responded to criticisms Sainte-Beuve had made in his three-part review of December, 1862. Flaubert fought Sainte-Beuve point by point ("Je vous combats pied à pied"), citing authorities ancient and modern or his own observations at the site or at least the historical probability of such things as the existence of an aqueduct at Carthage, the slaughter of the mercenaries, the immolations of infants, leprosy cured by "le lait de chienne," carbuncles formed by "l'urine des lynx." For the exquisitely gorgeous costumes and chambers of Salammbô, which Sainte-Beuve had dismissed as "chinoiserie," Flaubert claimed biblical authority. Angry that Sainte-Beuve had classed *Salammbô* with Chauteaubriand's romantic epic *Les Martyrs*, Flaubert insisted that he had tried to fuse historical and realistic fiction: "I have wanted to stabilize a mirage by applying

221

to antiquity the methods of the modern novel." But the extravagance of the actions and settings, often presented with sadistic delight, left little room for Flaubert to create a convincing psychological dimension in his characters. Salammbô could not be Emma Bovary, as Flaubert admitted: "Salammbô, in contrast, remains nailed down by a fixed idea."[29] Flaubert's recognition of this weakness is more explicit when he commented later that "what mocks me is the psychological side of my story."[30]

In his reading during the summer of 1863 in Brittany, Browning had been critical of Maurice de Guérin for not looking "an inch into men's hearts." Even those "sea-songs" he read seemed false to him because they did not reflect the feelings of real "sailors [who] drive their trade and get their bread by means of the sea. . . ."[31] Flaubert's slight attention to the inner lives of Salammbô, Matho, Hamilcar, and Narr'Havas must have added to the disappointment Browning felt reading the new novel by the author of *Madame Bovary*. In *The Ring and the Book* Browning would find a way to resuscitate an historical milieu while maintaining special emphasis upon the psychology of his characters. In 1869, while Browning was enjoying the great critical acclaim *The Ring and the Book* brought him, Flaubert published his great realist masterpiece, *L'Éducation sentimentale*. But Browning, after his disappointment with *Salammbô* in the summer of 1863, apparently read no more Flaubert.

Browning did some writing during the summer of 1863. Poems associated with Sainte Marie or Pornic are "Apparent Failure," his sardonic commemoration of a visit he had made to the Paris morgue in 1856; "Dîs Aliter Visum; or le Byron de nos Jours," which evokes more closely than Sainte Marie the 1858 sojourn of Browning at Le Havre. This latter poem, like a number of others he would publish the following year – "Youth and Art," "The Worst of It," "Confessions," "Too Late," "A Likeness" – is a brief study in frustrated and failed love set within contemporary cosmopolitan society. Characters in these poems remember dances at Vichy, anticipate election to the Académie or to the Royal Academy, play at whist or triumph at a *bal paré*, muse upon the "spoils of youth":

. . . masks, gloves and foils,
And pipe-sticks, rose, cherry-tree, jasmine,
And the long whip, the tandem lasher,

And the cast from a fist ("not, alas! mine,
　But my master's, the Tipton Slasher"),
And the cards where pistol-balls mark ace,
And a satin shoe used for cigar-case,
And the chamois-horns ("shot in the Chablais")
　And prints – Rarey drumming the Cruiser,
　And Sayers, our champion, the bruiser,
　And the little edition of Rabelais. . . . ("A Likeness")

These characters, with their worldly ambitions and conventional successes mixed with memories of youthful passions, inhabit a world not dissimilar to that of Rastignac, Lucien de Rubempré or even Frédéric Moreau. The society they move in is only briefly sketched, but it is marked by materialism and rather frivolous idleness and boredom. Browning detailed and satirized such a society more fully in the longest poem of this period, "Mr. Sludge, 'The Medium.'"

Materialism is also the theme of "Gold Hair: A Story of Pornic," one of two poems specifically related to his residence at Sainte Marie. Here Browning versified the tale he had found in Carou's *Histoire de Pornic* of the golden-haired Breton girl thought to be too pure and innocent for this world, "meant for heaven, not earth." Shortly before her death and her burial in l'Église St. Gilles, she asked only that her golden hair be left undisturbed in the grave. Years later workmen repairing the pavement above her grave discovered a double louis-d'or. Spurred on by an avaricious priest, the workmen dug deeper:

And lo, when they came to the coffin-lid,
　Or rotten planks which composed it once,
Why, there lay the girl's skull wedged amid
　A mint of money, it served for the nonce
To hold in its hair-heaps hid!

In grotesque images the poet asks rhetorical questions:

　. . . Could the girl be wont
　(She the stainless soul) to treasure up
Money, earth's trash and heaven's affront?
　Had a spider found out the communion-cup,
Was a toad in the christening-font?

223

He then answers without compromise:

> Truth is truth: too true it was.
>> Gold! She hoarded and hugged it first,
>> Longed for it, leaned o'er it, loved it. . . .

The saintly girl's unexpected avarice is compounded by that of the priest, who upon observing the parents' shame impounds the thirty gold coins to pay for a new altar. The story, the poet asserts, affirms the truth of the doctrine of original sin. Rather obliquely he also asserts that the poem tells against the threats to the Christian faith most recently posed by the controversial studies of scriptural history in *Essays and Reviews* (1860) and Bishop Colenso's *Critical Examination of the Pentateuch*.

Ernest Renan, his lectures at the Collège de France suppressed, had published his *Vie de Jésus* in June of 1863. Successive printings of this critical biography of the historical Jesus were rapidly exhausted during the ensuing weeks. Renan, away from the controversy his book had created in Paris, wrote in late August from Brittany with surprised pleasure that "the sale, far from slowing up, goes even faster."[32] By the time Browning read the book, in November, eleven French editions had appeared along with Dutch, German and Italian translations. The English translation appeared in December with this rather guarded preface:

> The great problem of the present age is to preserve the religious spirit, whilst getting rid of the superstitions and absurdities that deform it, and which are alike opposed to science and common sense. The works of Mr. F. W. Newman and of Bishop Colenso, and the "Essays and Reviews," are rendering great service in this direction. The work of M. Renan will contribute to this object; and, if its utility may be measured by the storm which it has created amongst the *obscurantists* in France, and the heartiness with which they have condemned it, its merits in this respect must be very great. It needs only be added, that whilst warmly sympathizing with the earnest spirit which pervades the book, the translator by no means wishes to be identified with all the opinions therein expressed.[33]

Browning probably got his copy in Paris when he stopped there briefly on his journey back from Brittany to London. He had been aware of Renan's prominence among French biblical scholars, and he was also aware of the controversy surrounding the suppression of Renan's lectures. In the winter of 1863 Isa Blagden had asked Browning for information about a certain Sanskrit professor who was apparently connected with the Collège de France. Browning asked Milsand to make enquiries, "but it all ended in nothing – nobody will tell," he informed Isa, "– the other professors have some sort of dread of committing themselves: M[ilsand] is to see Renan & ask *him* – & if I get anything worth transmitting, expect it."[34] When Browning first became acquainted with Renan's work or reputation is not clear. In all likelihood he had seen the issue of the *Revue des Deux Mondes* in which Renan's first essay had appeared in December of 1851. From that time forward, while Renan's reputation was rising, he and Browning shared a number of common acquaintances: Milsand was one, of course, but also the French orientalists Julius Mohl, Jean-Jacques Ampère, and later James Darmsteter as well as Buloz, Thierry, and Ary Scheffer, whose niece, Cornelia, Renan married in 1856. Browning had long been interested in the historical origins of Christianity. That had already been the subject of a number of his poems; and, by the time he came to read *Vie de Jésus*, Browning had in partial draft his long poem about the death of St. John. The general thrust of Renan's biography of Jesus, therefore, was neither novel nor surprising to him.

The scholarly weakness of Renan's book, however, did surprise Browning, who apparently came to it with a good deal of respect for the French scholar and with a fairly keen sense of what scholarly issues would be involved. Since the late 1840's Browning had followed the work of some of the German school of biblical criticism, a group he called "the Strauss school." Browning had to his own satisfaction apparently identified certain writers or reviewers as of this school, and he was puzzled by the Straussians' "complacency" with Renan's study of Jesus: "he admits many points they have thought it essential to dispute – and substitutes his explanation, which I think impossible," Browning told Isa soon after he finished Renan's *Vie* in November of 1863.[35] In earlier poems – *Christmas Eve*, "An Epistle," "Cleon," "Bishop Blougram's Apology" – Browning had variously responded to "the Strauss school". And, in poems he was now preparing for publication, he was investigating other religious phenomena: the primitive anthropomorphism and

natural theology of Caliban and the tawdry spiritualist chicanery of
Mr. Sludge. (His scorn of contemporary spiritualism was shared by
Renan, whose *Vie de Jésus* is sprinkled with assertions that the naïve
faith in miracles in Jesus' "world [is] analogous to that of the
'spiritualists' of our times."[36]) In his recently written "Gold Hair,"
Browning noted the recent British contribution to biblical criticism,
and he asserted – not insincerely, I think – that "Colenso's words
have weight." After nearly two years of public debate over the suppression of Renan's lectures, the Frenchman's words were expected
to have great weight also. As of course they did, especially with a
wide popular audience. But Renan's book was less forceful than
Browning had anticipated. "I have just read Renan's book," he
wrote to Isa in November, "and find it weaker and less honest than I
was led to expect: if he thinks he can prove what he says, he has
fewer doubts on the subject than I. . . ."[37]

What had raised Browning's expectations – beyond Renan's general reputation and the exceptional sales of the book – may have been
the quite laudatory reviews which appeared in prominent French
journals while Browning was in France during the summer and
autumn. Among them were Ernest Havet's article in the August 1
issue of the *Revue des Deux Mondes*, one by Edmond Schérer in *Le
Temps*, and another by Sainte-Beuve in his *Lundi* in the *Constitution-
nelle* for September 7. A more critical review, by Albert Réville, in
Revue germanique et française contains striking parallels to Browning's criticism. Réville objected especially to Renan's too easy acceptance of the authenticity of the Gospel according to John, his too
easy dismissal of Matthew's Gospel, and his unconvincing treatment
of the Lazarus story.[38] These are the specific objections Browning,
too, raises in his brief comment to Isa Blagden:

[Renan's] admissions & criticisms of St John are curious. . . . His
argument against the genuineness of Matthew – from the reference to what Papias says of the λογια [oracles] – is altogether too
gross a blunder to be believed in a Scholar – and yet is repeated
half a dozen times throughout the book. . . . What do you think of
the figure *he* cuts who makes his hero participate in the wretched
affair with Lazarus, and then calls him all the pretty names that
follow? Take away every claim to man's respect from Christ and
then give him a wreathe of gum-roses and calico-lilies. . . .[39]

William Irvine and Park Honan tell us that the wreathe of roses and lilies Browning attributes to Renan "clearly refers to the atmosphere of pastoral operetta, after the fashion of Rousseau's *Le Devin du Village*, that pervades the whole account of Jesus' youth."[40] While primarily interested in the scholarly issues, Browning was also alert to the literary qualities of Renan's book. He conceives of Renan as the kind of novelist who manipulates "his hero," that is, Jesus in the Lazarus affair; further, he complains that a reader "could no more deduce the character of his [Renan's] text from the substance of his notes, than rewrite a novel from simply reading the mottoes at the head of each chapter. . . ." More subtle, suggestive and peculiarly Browningian is his conception of Renan as a self-deceiving casuist or special-pleader not unlike so many Browning monologuists. Into his harsh judgment of Renan for manipulating textual evidence, Browning blends a sympathetic understanding: "I make no doubt he imagines *himself* stating a fact, with the inevitable licence," Browning comments before adding, "– so must John have done."[41]

Two poems – "A Death in the Desert" and "Epilogue" to *Dramatis Personae* – reflect Browning's response to Renan. In the former, an imagined St. John states the facts as he believed them to be; in the latter, Renan becomes a monologuist into whose utterance Browning weaves that peculiar blend of sympathy and judgment. Renan enters the "Epilogue" as a speaker after David has ritualistically celebrated the special revelation of God in the Temple when "the presence of the Lord, / In the glory of His cloud, / Had filled the House of the Lord." Here Browning makes Renan speak for modern men who, because of scientific scepticism, can no longer believe in such special revelation. As Renan puts it in his final chapter of *Vie*: "The kingdom of God, as we conceive it, differs notably from the supernatural apparition which the first Christians hoped to see appear in the clouds."[42] Although the general thesis of Renan's final chapter is that modern man has through reason advanced beyond the untenable superstition of Jesus' time, there is an undertone of elegiac regret at the loss of originality and spontaneity. The uniformity and conventionality of modern society, regulated as Renan says "par une police minutieuse," has sadly limited man's capacity to comprehend that earlier enthusiasm. Renan gives eloquent expression to his ambivalence midway through the final chapter:

Freed of our polite conventions, exempt from the uniform education which refines us, but which so strongly diminishes our individuality, these wholesome spirits brought an astonishing energy
into action. They seem to us like giants of an heroic age who could
not have been real. Profound error! These men were our brothers;
they had our form; they felt and thought like us. But the breath of
God was free among them; among us, it is chained by the iron
bonds of a petty society doomed to irreparable mediocrity.[43]

Rather than portray Renan as a surprisingly unscholarly but
nevertheless dangerous critic of Christian truth, Browning chose to
emphasize the poignant sense of loss Renan had expressed. Renan's
monologue becomes a sorrowful lament for man's diminished capacity to perceive divinity in the face of Christ:

> Gone now! All gone across the dark so far,
>   Sharpening fast, shuddering ever, shutting still,
> Dwindling into the distance, dies that star
>   Which came, stood, opened once! We gazed our fill
> With upturned faces on as real a Face
>   That, stooping from grave music and mild fire,
> Took in our homage, made a visible place
>   Through many a depth of glory, gyre on gyre,
> For the dim human tribute. Was this true?

At the close of the monologue Renan is forced to the sad conclusion
that what he has hailed as scientific advance has but led to a "Ghastly
dethronement." In the third and final section of the poem, Browning speaks *in propria persona* and initially rebukes Renan for being
"Witless alike of will and way divine." In the remainder of this
section, he does not debate or argue with the words Renan has been
forced to utter in the preceding section. Rather, he undertakes
primarily to refute those assertions Renan had made in the closing
chapter of *Vie de Jésus*, assertions that modern man has lost his
originality and individuality. Browning affirms the opposite: that
even "the least man of all mankind," such as himself, "differs from
his fellows utterly." In an extended simile, the poet then demonstrates how divine will works upon the individual as do arctic currents
upon some central rock. Hence, the divinity in the face of Christ
does not vanish for Browning as it had for Renan; rather, it "decom-

poses but to recompose" and form itself once more into the individual's "universe that feels and knows."

"A Death in the Desert" had, in all likelihood, been substantially completed by Browning before he read Renan's *Vie de Jésus*. St. John's monologue, which forms the heart of the poem, anticipates modern sceptics who have "reduced to plain historic fact" what had been visionary truth for John. Such sceptics may even doubt that John himself ever lived, a doubt more appropriate to "the Strauss school" than to Renan. One of the "admissions" by Renan that Browning found "curious" was, perhaps, that Renan does not doubt the historicity of John himself. He does, however, devote a good deal of time to a discussion of the authorship of the Gospel attributed to John in his introductory chapter "in which the sources of this history are principally treated." There Renan examines evidences of authorship, emendations, glosses and the transmission of the text of John's Gospel. If Browning added anything to "A Death in the Desert" after he read Renan's book in November of 1863 and before he published *Dramatis Personae* in May of 1864, the likely addition would be the scholarly, textual apparatus which frames the monologue of John and the "glossa of Theotypas" with which the anonymous compiler of the entire "document" interrupts John's monologue. Browning had, in "An Epistle" and "Cleon," already adopted the strategy of creating fictitious mock-documents purporting to date from early Christian times. In "A Death in the Desert," however, the poetic "imitation" of such textual history as Renan had supplied is much more elaborate than anything in the earlier Browning poems. This poem is prefaced with a précis of the preservation and transmission of the text:

(Supposed of Pamphylax the Antiochene:
It is a parchment, of my rolls the fifth,
Hath three skins glued together, is all Greek,
And goeth from *Epsilon* down to *Mu*:
Lies second in the surnamed Chosen Chest,
Stained and conserved with juice of terebinth,
Covered with cloth of hair, and *Xi*,
From Xanthus, my wife's uncle now at peace:
Mu and *Epsilon* stand for my own name.
I may not write it, but make a cross
To show I await his coming, with the rest,
And leave off here: beginneth Pamphylax.)

Then follows Pamphylax's narrative account of how he and others cared for the dying John and listened to his final testimony. That testimony is suddenly interrupted by the "glossa of Theotypas"; the words of John continue, then are broken off as Pamphylax announces John's death, describes his burial, and explains how and why he came to dictate this testimony by John to a certain Phoebas. The closing section of the poem presents an early sceptic of the Renanian mold, Cerinthus, whose belief that Christ was "mere man" is heatedly refuted by yet another anonymous writer of glosses. "A Death in the Desert" is an oddly structured, even disjointed poem: the textual history, the glosses, the narrative of Pamphylax, even the rather obscure and rambling monologue of John who, Pamphylax complains, "darkly spoke" and may be misunderstood – all are strangely mixed within the poem. It appears, in some ways, to be an overly ingenious parody of the kind of "documentary evidence" upon which Renan and other biblical critics built their cases.

iii

Browning's summer sojourn in France in 1864 took him to the Basque mountain village of Cambo, where he found a landscape "just like the Tuscan ranges, with plenty of oak & chestnut woods, and everywhere the greenest of meadows. . . ."[44] It was here that his plans for *The Ring and the Book* matured. The winter and spring had been characteristically busy ones, and he kept up his active social life "gallantly to the last in London, dining out in a way that looks absurd enough," as he told Isa. After a "last memorable dinner" with Edward Trelawny, Browning left in early August for Paris.[45] After a week there, he, his father, sister and Pen journeyed for two days to Arcachon opposite Cap Ferret south-west of Bordeaux. Browning had expected to find an isolated bathing village, a "mere sandhill and pine-forest along the sea. . . ."[46] But a rail line had been built out from Bordeaux to nearby La Teste a decade before; and, instead of a quiet seaside village like Sainte Marie près Pornic, he found "a toy-town with boulevards traced through the sand-hills, *tirs-au-pistolet*, a Casino and other French institutions, and the whole full to the edge of strangers. . . ."[47] No accommodation was available, but Browning did observe an incident which he would think of as an "omen" for his "next poem." A fisherman had caught and was

exhibiting on the beach "two mighty dolphins," one of them eight
feet long with "respectable teeth." The fisherman told Browning
that " 'had *le poltron* chosen to break my nets . . . he might have
done it like a cobweb, but he thought they were strong – I know the
nature of the beast and he let me get under his fin with my
knife. . . !' " Recounting the incident to Julia Wedgwood a week
later, Browning associated the net, the fisherman and the knife with
his critics and their familiar charge of unintelligibility. He intended
to answer that charge forcefully in the new poem he was contemplating about the Roman murder case of Guido Franceschini: "No," he
told Miss Wedgwood, "I shall charge the nets, for my part, and
mind nobody's voice. . . ."[48] Unable to find accommodation at
either Arcachon or La Teste, the Brownings went on to Bayonne and
St. Jean-de-Luz, "an exquisite little place, with a delicious sea, and
great mountains in the background. . . ." But the town was
crowded, especially with Spanish tourists, and every house was
taken; so the party "braved the awful Biarritz. . . ." Biarritz had
become the favourite resort of the Empress Eugénie and the seat of
the summer court. Not only did Browning find the place crowded
and noisy but "the prices, moreover, were calculated for Diplomat-
ists, ambitious senators, and so on. . . ." After two weeks of travel,
Browning had not found a place to settle for his annual holiday. He
had been, as he complained, "pushed up at the very end of France";
so he decided to retreat inland to the village of Cambo for a month to
await the departure of the crowds from St. Jean-de-Luz.[49]

Cambo was put "in unpleasant relief" by Browning's memories of
previous years at "that dear rough old St Marie, – stark naked as she
was of all comfort, to the British mind. . . ."[50] He thought the little
watering-place of Cambo "smug"; he himself felt dull, sleepy and
bilious. He had "made little or no provision for being not impossibly
bored" and had brought too few books: a volume of George Sand's
plays, some Virgil with which to "plague" Pen, and Euripides for his
own "solace."[51] Despite the greenness of the picturesque hills and
meadows, the weather was extremely hot, "the wind being so many
puffs from a blast-furnace."[52] He regretted being so far from the sea.
On August 20, however, he took an interesting excursion up to "le
pas de Roland," the mountain pass above St. Jean-pied-de-port
where, by tradition, Roland "opened a way through a rock that
effectually blocks it up, by one kick of his boot, and so let Char-

lemagne's army pass. . . ."[53] The little river and mountain walls reminded him of Tuscany. More important, Browning had been pondering for some time how he might shape into a poem the material he found bound in the Old Yellow Book he had purchased in a Florentine flea-market several years before. A week before at Arcachon he had associated the netted dolphin with some forceful or audacious creative act for his new poem. Then, before his excursion to the Pas de Roland, he had written at length to Miss Wedgwood about his concern that he "be quite intelligible, next poem. . . ."[54] Now he associated the mighty "kick" of Roland with his decision to shape in epic terms the story of Pompilia, Guido and Caponsacchi. It was there at the Pas de Roland, he told William Michael Rossetti later, that he "laid out the full plan of his twelve cantos. . . ."[55]

The plan for the complex and revolutionary structure of *The Ring and the Book* probably did not come with the sudden inspiration Rossetti's anecdote implies. Nevertheless, "Roland's feat," as Park Honan has said, "seems to have loosened some obstacles in his mind. . . ."[56] At any rate, Browning's sense of dull sleepiness passed after the excursion to the Pas de Roland, and he found Cambo "even prettier than I thought."[57] The sense of boredom also passed as he "got on by having a great read at Euripides . . . besides attending to my own matters, my new poem that is about to be; and of which the whole is pretty well in my head – the Roman murder story you know."[58] Anxious for the sea and swimming, the Brownings tried St. Jean-de-Luz again, but it was "still filled with Spaniards glad to use the new railway."[59] They went on to Biarritz where they took a house on the Plage des Basques, close to the sea and away from the noisier parts of the town. "The sea, sands, and view of the Spanish coast and mountains are superb," Browning wrote to Isa.[60] They made a day's rail excursion across the Spanish border to Fontarabia, Irun, and San Sabastian in late September. After a longer stay in Biarritz than they had planned "in order to get more of the wonderful weather and warm wide sea," they left via Bordeaux and Tours for Paris and were back in London by mid-October.[61]

With the design for *The Ring and the Book* well worked out, Browning wrote steadily at the new poem throughout the winter and spring of 1865. In his March letter to Isa he reported: "I am about a long poem to be something remarkable – work hard at it."[62] In late April he interrupted his work for a brief visit to his father and sister in Paris. He found Paris "brimful of English for the Easter Holidays"; and, although he intended to avoid the English, he did meet Fanny Haworth and Matthew Arnold. Arnold was in Paris to begin his inspection of French schools, and Browning took this opportunity to introduce him to Joseph Milsand, whom Arnold had "long wanted to know."[63] Once back in London, Browning began to think of his annual late summer holiday in France. The previous year's holiday in the Pyrenees and on the south-west coast he spoke of as a "return to the South" because it had evoked memories of Tuscany. He had found it attractive, but the heat "slackened" rather than "braced" him as had earlier holidays in Brittany.[64] So by May of 1865 he had determined to "try some new part of Bretagne: the Pyranées are very lonely but too hot for the good of a change. . . ."[65] By early July Browning had completed some 8,400 lines of his new poem, and so brought to an end what he called his year's "working season."[66]

He made arrangements to take the same house he had stayed at before in Sainte Marie près Pornic, where the Browning party arrived in early August. "Nothing is changed," he wrote, "– Pornic itself, two miles off, is full of company, but our little village is its dirty, unimproved self – a trifle wilder than before, if possible." The weather began rainy and cold – "a contrast to the wonderful Biarritz & Cambo blaze of last year" – but it soon warmed, and Browning swam regularly; by his own proud count, he had bathed sixty times by the end of the holiday. The sea and swimming had become "inordinately" important to Browning. More than physical recreation, sea-bathing was now for him "a great resource" and the sea was "the *obbligato* accompaniment to [his] last home but one."[67] The waters of the Baie de Bourgneuf off Sainte Marie become the setting and symbol of that zone between this world and the world of the spirit in "Amphibian," the prologue to Browning's long poem about Pornic, *Fifine at the Fair* (1872):

The fancy I had to-day,
   Fancy which turned fear!
I swam far out in the bay,
   Since waves laughed warm and clear.

. . . sometimes when the weather
   Is blue, and warm waves tempt

233

To free one's self of tether,
    And try a life exempt

From worldly noise and dust,
    In the sphere which overbrims
With passion and thought, – why, just
    Unable to fly, one swims!

[the] sea, to all intent,
    Gives flesh such noon-disport
As a finer element
    Affords the spirit-sort.

Such pleasurable freedom from "worldly noise" is seductive but temporary. The swimmer is, after all, an amphibian; if he tires or fears the surge of the tide, the land is nearby:

Land the solid and safe –
    To welcome again (confess!)
When, high and dry, we chafe
    The body, and don the dress.

During the summer of 1865 Browning held rather closely to the land: while Pen and his friend Willy Bracken might swim a mile and a half in the bay, Browning chose to watch them from under an umbrella and time them with his watch. He swam in a "little retired creek" close by. Perhaps that is why in the opening line of his poem Browning describes the swim far out into the bay as but a "fancy."

On land there were interesting signs of human vitality, stupidity and vulgarity. There was, for example, "the buxom servant girl, aged some 20," whom Browning asked Isa to imagine "washing clothes before my window (on the pianterreno, dressed in a blue gown & nothing else, I can see, just covering the naked legs below the knees – and so kilted, turning her back to me and burying herself with linen she has to stoop for on the ground! Primitive manners!"[68] This was the same girl who, because of the landlord's "piggishness," was made to sleep in the same room with the landlord and his son and three daughters. Browning seemed to be both attracted and repelled by people of Sainte Marie and Pornic. They were, he said, "good, stupid and dirty, without a touch of the sense of picturesqueness in their clodpoles."[69] Their stupidity and blindness to the picturesque had led the people of Pornic to raze the church of St. Gilles, which Browning had memorialized in "Gold Hair." And at the church at Sainte Marie across from the Brownings' house, workmen had "taken away old pillar-ornaments, column-heads with quaint figures, made all smooth and white-washed where they were, – and flung them where they now lie, on a heap of stones by the road-side – where my father goes to draw them in his sketch-book – groaningly."[70] Despite his testy disapproval of the people, Browning reiterated his earlier desire to live out his days in such a place, "in retirement, and near the sea"; and he found it reassuring "that here *is* such a good thing still in the world. . . ."[71]

Only in memory and imagination did Browning return to Sainte Marie and Pornic after 1865. Those villages and their environs become the setting of one of his "most metaphysical and boldest" poems, *Fifine at the Fair* (1872).[72] The "abstruser themes" of the poem, as the speaker himself calls them, are grounded in or anchored by the local topography. And the local churches, the graveyard, the beach and bay, cliffs and rivulets, dolmens and menhirs provide a rich source of example, illustration, simile and metaphor. The speaker of the poem is a modern and rather bourgeois Don Juan. He is, to adapt the title of another Browning poem, *Le Don Juan de nos jours*. Though chafing under the narrow code of respectability, he can near the end of the monologue resignedly describe himself this way: "In Pornic, say, / The Mayor shall catalogue me duly domiciled, / Contributable, good-companion of the guild / And Mystery of marriage." *Fifine* is conceived as the kind of response such a Don Juan might make to the taunting sarcasm of Molière's Elvire when that lady charged her Don Juan with an unexpectedly weak defence for his latest infidelity. Browning's Elvira and Don Juan stroll during the late afternoon of a sunny autumn day from their house in Pornic. They go first to the village fair, then pass St. Gilles church; they cross "the bridge, / Hard by the little port," walk along the beach, and watch while the "sun sets mild on Sainte Marie" while opposite them is "the streak of Île Noirmoutier." They observe a rill "race o'er yonder ledge / O' the fissured cliff," and watch dolphin fins rise and fall in the Baie de Bourgneuf. Don Juan prolongs the walk to lead his wife to the site of a menhir and dolmen. Finally, in the gathering dusk, they complete their "tramp of near a league" and trudge the "Last little mile" to their house. There, Don

Juan leaves Elvira to return to the fair to see the gypsy girl Fifine.

Don Juan's perambulatory monologue is both an apologia for and an enquiry into his desire for sexual variety and freedom. Like the pennon blowing atop the tent at the fair, he too is "Frenetic to be free." At the fair – among the *bateleurs* and *baladines*, the strong man and the six-headed sheep – he discovers Fifine, whose spangled hips flash in the sun. Alert to his wife's jealous disapproval, Don Juan spins out a contrast between the sexual and fleshly attractions of Fifine and the spiritual purity of Elvira's soul. A saint atop St. Gilles church provides him with a figure for Elvira in contrast to the sensual beauty of Fifine, whom he has just associated with Cleopatra. This saint, whose name he cannot recall, is "Cold-pinnacled aloft o' the spire, prays calm the seas / From Pornic Church, and oft at midnight (peasants say) / Goes walking out to save from shipwreck. . . ." Whatever the saint's moral beauty, she is associated in Don Juan's mind with the cold winter snow which "Covers each knee," then builds to cover all but her "smile benign." Another figure for Elvira is a Raphael painting Don Juan had long desired and had finally acquired after importunate Americans had bid the price up five-fold. The pure beauty of the Raphael makes it a valuable possession, but Don Juan cannot constantly admire it. Sometimes he must look away from the Raphael, as he had looked away from Elvira to Fifine, to peruse "With relish, leaf by leaf Doré's last picture-book." He admits that, compared to the Raphael, the Dorés are but *pochades* and of but fleeting attractiveness. When he and Elvira arrive on the sands of the beach, Don Juan himself sketches *pochades* in the sands with the broken stem of a sailor's pipe. The absurd exaggeration of the types of female beauty he draws – one figure's nose is a yard long – provokes his wife's laughter. Were he but Gérôme, he might soften and perfect the figure, but Don Juan still values what he calls the "wild grotesque," a quality he associates with the vitality and vulgarity of the fair at Pornic. As the couple pass beyond the precincts of Pornic and watch the setting sun light up the spire of the church at Sainte Marie, Don Juan's thoughts turn to death, imaged by the little iron crosses on the graves hidden beyond a hill. Leading Elvira to a breach in the sea-cliffs, from which they can see the bay, Don Juan develops an elaborate metaphor of sea, air and land to bolster his argument that the body, though needing air or spirit, cannot be sustained by it. A swimmer, to indulge in the "play o' the body," must remain immersed in the water however much he may strive to raise himself into the air. If such play finally tires him, he may retreat to "Pornic's placid shore" or his domestic life with Elvira.

Of all the metaphors Don Juan has drawn from the immediate environs the most significant is that of the dolmen and menhir to which he cunningly has led his wife. Throughout his monologue, Don Juan has argued for the claims of the flesh, and he has tried to shape in words his sense of a primal sexual urge that underlies the façades and artificial codes of society. As they stroll through the solitary waste, Don Juan tells Elvira that Fifine and the little fair in Pornic had made him think of Carnival and that the evening before he had played Schumann's *Carnival*. While playing, he was rapt into a vision of Venice at Carnival time. In some mysterious way he was possessed of the power to see beyond the grotesque masks of the revellers and perceive their individual souls. His vision evolved to include the entire world: all that mankind has created – in science, philosophy, religion, art – were like the buildings of Venice, which, though of stone, shifted and changed, became insubstantial and dissolved. He was left searching for some common form behind all the flux and diversity, some unity into which opposites and contraries could fuse. His vision ended with a question: "What common shape was that wherein they mutely merged / Likes and dislikes of form, so plain before?" To answer that question, Don Juan has prolonged his stroll and led Elvira, as he says,

> To where we stand at last, in order that your eyes
> Might see the very thing, and save my tongue describe
> The Druid monument which fronts you.
> . . . . . .
> How does it strike you, this construction gaunt and grey –
> Sole object, these piled stones, that gleam unground-away
> By twilight's hungry jaw, which champs fine all beside
> I' the solitary waste we grope through? Oh, no guide
> Need we to grope our way and reach the monstrous door
> Of granite! Take my word, the deeper you explore
> That caverned passage, filled with fancies to the brim,
> The less will you approve the adventure!

Like Childe Roland's dark tower, the Druid monument has been

237

the destination all along. But unlike Roland's enigmatic tower, the womb-like dolmen and phallic menhir have explicit significance. Don Juan had visited the site before, and he had read the work of scholars who in the 1860's were studying the symbols and pondering where such huge stones might have been quarried and how they were transported. He rather jauntily dismissed the "prosy wherefore" of the scholars, and instead asked peasant lads and lasses for explanations. One such lad had told him that the earliest of peoples had built these structures to remind themselves the earth has a creator who is beyond change, that "while / We come and go, outside there's Somebody that stays; / A circumstance which ought to make us mind our ways. . . ." The local curé had told the people that the "huge stone pillar" was the stone upon which Jacob had pillowed his head while he dreamt of the ladder ascending to heaven. When Jacob awoke, he set the stone upright and annointed its tip with oil. But the curé "tasked his lungs" in vain, for the village and country folk still clung to the "prime authoritative speech," the "arch-word" of the stones themselves. So, "when the earth began its life afresh in May," when fruit-trees bloomed and bird and beast sought mates, the people too turned from the insipid and refined doctrine of the curé and embraced the "Strong, savage and sincere" doctrine of the stones. In the lad's grandmother's time, the women danced around the erect stone until finally the curé "bade the parish in a band / Lay flat the obstrusive thing that cumbered so the land!" The menhir now lies, partly obscured by bushes, near the entrance to the dolmen and "'bides / Its time to rise again!'" A "pert" Parisian had told the peasant lad that the stone had already risen again, at least symbolically, in the erect spire of the village church. Here, then, in the huge, permanent female dolmen and male menhir is the form that embodies the primal truth.[73] Don Juan has mounted a mighty argument to justify to his wife the rendezvous he intends to keep with Fifine that evening.

The sea-air and bathing at Sainte Marie had, as usual, been restorative for Browning: "it seems," he told Isa, "to wipe out all my ailments and set the brain to-right, I come back aged sixteen. . . ." During the "blackness" of the London winter, he worked hard on his poem about the Roman murder; by spring the poem had grown to over fifteen thousand lines. Yet he found time for soirées, dinners and concerts. By March, weariness again set in: "I am just now getting very tired of the early season, all but at end now," he wrote, "and long to go to Paris, as I hope to do next Saturday week or thereabout. . . ."[74] In Paris Browning found his eighty-four-year-old father unwell and visibly failing. He hoped that, once the spring Parisian wind – "a razor wrapped in the flannel of sunshine" – abated, his father would be able to go into the French countryside for recuperation. Mr. Browning, now unable to haunt the bookstalls or sketch Parisian street scenes, turned his still considerable energies to gathering for his son information about a medieval pope. After Browning had returned to London, his father sent him "a regular book of researches, and a narrative of his own, exhausting the subject."[75] But Mr. Browning's health deteriorated rapidly. Dr. Vigla, "the head-surgeon of the Hôtel-Dieu," was consulted; on June 12 a telegram summoned Browning to his father's home in the rue de Grenelle. He left London for Paris immediately, "mentally blessing" Napoleon III for having finally abolished the cumbersome system of *visé* passports.[76] He arrived early the next day, and his father died the following day. On Saturday the 16th, Mr. Browning was buried in Père la Chaise; on Sunday a funeral sermon was preached at Chapelle Marboeuf. Browning stayed on a few days at 151 rue de Grenelle to help his sister Sarianna prepare to close the house so she, too, could return to live in London after fifteen years in Paris.

His father's death and the closing of the house in Paris altered the pattern of Browning's visits to France. That summer, instead of going first to Paris and then to a seaside village, he chose to sail to Brittany via the Channel Islands. At first he thought of going to Guernsey, and in preparation he solicited from Lord Houghton a letter of introduction to Victor Hugo.[77] Houghton supplied the letter, but Browning sailed not to Guernsey but to Jersey where he visited his old friend from Florence, Frederick Tennyson, whom he found "just as of old, pleasant and genial to the last degree . . . [but] wholly addicted to spirit-rapping and writing. . . ."[78] The Browning party – Robert, Sarianna, Pen and his friend Willy Bracken – sailed on to St. Malo, from which they made excursions down the coast to Mont-St.-Michel and up the Rance Valley to Dinan. Then, apparently by rail and diligence, they journeyed down to the little village of Le Croisic, lying across the Loire estuary to the north of Pornic. Le Croisic, usually "fashionable & full" in August, was nearly deserted because of reports of cholera, so Browning was able to find comfortable and spacious accommodation. He was soon bathing in the sea and walking in the surrounding countryside, "wild and primitive, even a trifle beyond Pornic perhaps. . . ."[79] He made plans for excursions to see some of "the great sights of the region," especially Carnac. "The whole district," he reported to Seymour Kirkup, "is wild, strange and romantic, with a fine fierce sea, and driving sands."[80]

Two aspects of this part of Brittany especially interested Browning. One was the imposing and pervasive presence of megalithic monuments and their associated legends. The other was the town of Guérande, across the Grand Trait and the *marais salants* from Le Croisic. It was a place, as he told Kirkup, "glorified to me long ago by the Beatrix of Balzac, which I used to devour as it came out in feuilletons in the 'Siècle' of those days."[81] Browning's memory of his reading of *Béatrix* is, after nearly thirty years, only a little misleading. He did not "devour" the whole of the novel; for, once Balzac got into the narrative, Browning was sadly disappointed. But he did find the long opening descriptive chapters "so delightful" in 1838 that he broke his practice of sending his copies of *Siècle* onto a friend after he had "skimmed" an issue.[82] It is Balzac's opening descriptions of the quaint old town and its environs that Browning follows closely in this letter to Kirkup:

Close by [Le Croisic] is the strange, solitary Bourg de Batz – a Saxon colony of stalwart men who retain exactly the dress of their forefathers, three hundred years ago – white tunic, baggy breeches, stockings, even shoes, all white, but a great black flap-hat with red fringes. These are the *paludiers* who collect salt from the salines, which forms the staple produce of the place. Still farther on, is the delicious old city of Guerande, intact with its moat, wall, towers and gates: it is the old seat of all the genuine Bretagne noblesse, who live on in the old way and with old ideas.[83]

A dozen years later Browning pressed this scene into an early stanza of *The Two Poets of Croisic*:

Croisic, the spit of sandy rock which juts
   Spitefully northward, bears nor tree nor shrub
To tempt the ocean, show what Guérande shuts
   Behind her, past wild Batz whose Saxons grub

The ground for crystals grown where ocean gluts
   Their promontory's breadth with salt: all stub
Of rock and stretch of sand, the land's last strife
To rescue a poor remnant for dear life. (Stanza XI)

Out of the window of "the most delicious & peculiar house," the
Maison du Bochet, he had rented in Le Croisic, Browning could
look across the salt marshes to Guérande. Once he and Sarianna
walked the nine-mile circuit to Guérande and back in two hours.
They went often to dine at an inn there, Les Guérandaises, where
they were served by "two pretty sisters." They would return to Le
Croisic early in the evening, "generally catching a wedding-dance at
some one of the intermediate villages – Saillié or Batz."[84]

Browning's delight in Le Croisic was increased by his fascination
with the megalithic monuments in the region. He had no doubt seen
dolmens and menhirs near Sainte Marie près Pornic in previous
years; the great megalithic *allées couvertes* of Noeveillard lay just off
the road from Sainte Marie to Pornic. This is the site to which Don
Juan in *Fifine* leads his wife during their evening stroll while he
develops his apologia for adultery. This is the only megalithic site in
the Pornic area to be mentioned in such books as *Guides-Joanne* as
late as 1888.[85] But megalithic remains are more numerous north of
the Loire, and Browning's desire to make an excursion to Carnac
suggests an increased fascination with those stones. His visit to the
Alignements du Menec and the Tumulus St.-Michel at Carnac was
delayed until he journeyed northward from Vannes through Auray
and Carnac on his way to Audierne in 1868. But when he wrote
Fifine in 1871, he seems to have imposed upon the topography of
Pornic the more pervasive sense of Breton paganism he discovered
first at Le Croisic. In his letter to Kirkup, Browning already
announces the central theme and symbol of the climactic moment in
Fifine: "Croisic," he told the old necromancer and connoisseur of
paganism, "is the old head-seat of Druidism in France, probably
mentioned in Strabo: the people were still Pagan a couple of hundred
years ago, despite the priests' teaching and preaching, and the
women used to dance round a phallic stone still upright there with
obscene circumstances enough, – till the general civilization got too
strong for this."[86] This is the same tale the peasant lad in *Fifine* tells
Don Juan, who then presents the dolmens and menhirs as evidence
of the primacy of sexual desire. Browning would return to this theme

in early stanzas of *The Two Poets of Croisic*:

> And still so much remains of that grey cult,
>   That even now, of nights, do women steal
> To the sole Menhir standing, and insult
>   The antagonistic church-spire by appeal
> To power discrowned in vain, since each adult
>   Believes the gruesome thing she clasps may heal
> Whatever plague no priestly help can cure:
> Kiss but the cold stone, the event is sure!
>
> Nay more: on May-morns, that primeval rite
>   Of temple-building, with its punishment
> For rash precipitation, lingers, spite
>   Of all remonstrance; vainly are they shent,
> Those girls who form a ring and, dressed in white,
>   Dance round it, till some sister's strength be spent:
> Touch but the Menhir, straight the rest turn roughs
> From gentles, fall on her with fisticuffs. (Stanzas XIV and XV)

Browning may have heard some such tale while walking the countryside around Le Croisic. Such walks were numerous in August and September. Towards the end of September, however, the weather turned cold and rainy, and walking as well as bathing was curtailed. In early October the Brownings left Le Croisic for three days in Paris. It was apparently there that Browning picked up copies of Sand's new novel *Le Dernier Amour*, which he admired for "its cleverness and return to the Indiana style of thing," and her *Tamaris* (1862), which he did not "believe in or care about." Back in London by mid-October, he recommended the new Sand novel to Isa, and he spoke well also of Dumas *fils'* newly published instalment of his autobiographical novel, *L'Affaire Clemenceau*.[87] These may have been – but probably were not – the novels Browning had in mind when the following spring he wrote a long, critical analysis of Isa's new novel *Nora and Archibald*, and then advised her to "make your incidents as simple as you can, put out your strength in the analysis of *character*, keeping in mind the immeasurable superiority (to my mind) of French models than English: oh, I know what the clever English find useful to say! – and I say, – Bosh!"[88]

Browning returned to Le Croisic in early August of 1867, after stopping a few days in Paris to see the Great Exhibition Napoleon III staged to celebrate the improvements in his capital and the progress of his Empire. He was able to secure the same house as the previous year, and with fine weather throughout the two months, the routine of bathing and walking continued. Browning's surviving letters say little about this sojourn at Le Croisic. The two written to Isa are filled with London gossip: the separation of Thomas Trollope from his wife, the paternity of her recent child being unknown; the rumour that Queen Victoria had married John Brown; confusion over just which wife or whose wife Edward Trelawney was now living with. Browning was happy that at his urging Matthew Arnold had reprinted *Empedocles on Etna*; he enjoyed Emerson's new volume of poems in which he found "very fine & true things, – but not in any new key, – the old voice & tone."[89] Only one incident in the two months is described at any length by Browning – a visit to the headlands, cliffs and sea-caves at Piriac. Not the natural landscape, but an abandoned tin and silver mine caught his attention and confirmed for him the wisdom of Balzac:

> an English company built houses, sank wells, brought machinery, spent "trois millions," then abandoned everything: there lie the boilers, pumps &c. exposed like rocks and sand. An old fellow, who had been to England, and was always in the employment of the head man . . . said all the money had been wasted in unnecessary expense, – house-building &c – and that when the mines began to be worked, and give good metal, – in rushed the sea, – their funds were at an end, – and there was no more to be done but go and leave all this ruin, "these fourteen years now"! Depend on it, the imaginative men are not exclusively the poets and painters, as Balzac knew well enough.[90]

Though Browning made little mention of Le Croisic in his letters that summer, he did compose a memorial to one of the village's forgotten heroes, "a simple Breton sailor pressed by Tourville for the fleet, / A poor coasting-pilot, Hervé Riel the Croisickese." Browning had read in a local guidebook – *Notes sur le Croisic, par Caillo jeune* – the story of Riel safely piloting the embattled French fleet to safety at St. Malo in 1692. After defeat by the English fleet off Cap de la Hogue, as Browning tells the story, Damfreville's fleet "helter-skelter through the blue, / Like a crowd of frightened porpoises a shoal of sharks pursue, / Came crowding ship in ship to

Saint-Malo on the Rance, / With the English fleet in view." Warned
by the local pilots that the large craft could not avoid rocks at ebb-
tide, Damfreville decided to beach and burn the fleet. Then the
sailor from Le Croisic, scornful of the cowardly "Malouins," guided
the fleet into harbour. He asked as his only reward shore-leave to
visit his wife at Le Croisic. Or so Browning thought, until fourteen
years later, in 1881, Dr. Furnivall of the Browning Society checked
the story with French naval authorities at St. Malo and discovered
that Riel had asked as reward "un congé absolu," a full discharge
from the king's service.[91] Browning acknowledged his error, but did
not alter the poem which he intended as a testament to Riel's loyalty
to home and country. In the concluding stanza, Browning is rather
testy in his disappointment that such a man has gone unhonoured
both in his native village and in Paris:

> Name and deed alike are lost:
> Not a pillar nor a post
>   In his Croisic keeps alive the feat as it befell;
> Not a head in white and black
> On a single fishing-smack,
>   In memory of the man but for whom had gone to wrack
>   All that France saved from the fight whence England bore the
>   bell.
> Go to Paris: rank on rank
>   Search the heroes flung pell-mell
> On the Louvre, face and flank!
>   You shall look long enough ere you come to Hervé Riel.
> So, for better or for worse,
> Hervé Riel, accept my verse!
> In my verse, Hervé Riel, do thou once more
> Save the squadron, honour France, love thy wife the Belle Aurore!

Perhaps Browning's admonition – translated into French by James
Darmsteter for the journal *Le Parlement* in 1882 – influenced the
Croisickese to raise in 1913 a statue to Hervé Riel at the foot of
Mont-Lénigo overlooking the port. Now Michelin directs the visitor
to the statue of the man who "after the disaster of La Hogue – a
naval engagement off Trouville (1692) against the English and
Dutch fleets – saved twenty French ships during their passage
through, at night, the dangerous Raz Blanchard."[92] In addition to

restoring the sailor's local fame, *Hervé Riel* also served the people of
Paris: in the autumn of 1870 Browning sold the poem to *Cornhill* for
£105, which he donated to the relief fund for those Parisians starving
under the Prussian siege.

A decade after this final visit to Le Croisic, Browning returned in
imagination, "In fancy to that land-strip waters wash," to write *The
Two Poets of Croisic*. The last time he had raked the apparently dead
ashes of Le Croisic's past, as he comments, the lively story of Hervé
Riel had blazed up. Le Croisic was not particularly rich in poetic
material, but for a poet like Browning, interested in human truths,
"Anywhere serves: for point me out the place / Wherever man has
made himself a home, / And there I find the story of our race / In
little, just at Croisic as at Rome." Now he had found a story of the
fleetingness of poetic fame as exemplified in the careers of the
Croisickese poets René Gentilhomme and Paul Desforges-Maillard.
Gentilhomme spent his early years at Le Croisic writing "songs and
sonnets, madrigals, and much / Rhyming thought poetry and
praised as such. /Rubbish unutterable (bear in mind!)." But Gentilhomme's art was sufficiently admired for him to become attached
to the household of the Prince of Condé, the assumed successor to
the sonless Louis XIII. One day in 1637 while he was polishing the
fourteenth line of a courtly love sonnet, he saw lightning strike and
smash to atoms the sculptured ducal crown of Condé. Seized by the
spirit of prophecy, Gentilhomme dashed off a poem announcing that
it was God's will that Condé should not be king and predicting the
birth of a dauphin, Louis XIV. When a son was born to Louis and
Anne the following year, Gentilhomme's fame spread and he became
"Royal Poet" to Louis XIII. "Moreover he got painted by Du Pré, /
Engraved by Daret also, and prefixed / The portrait to his book."
But Gentilhomme's fame soon faded, and the last known copy of his
book was destroyed when the house of a man named De Chevaye
burned at Nantes. Not only was Gentilhomme's book burned, but
memory of him too, Browning says, was "extinguished, – nay, I
fear, / Portrait is gone too: nowhere I discerned / A trace of it at
Croisic."

Memory of Paul Desforges-Maillard had not faded quite so completely as had Gentilhomme's. Desforges had by thirty written a
sonnet "to every belle / In Croisic's bounds," and his fame had
spread as far as Batz and Guérande. But he longed for the esteem of

Paris itself and so offered an epic on "The Art of Navigation" for the annual competition of the Académie. When another poem won, he sent the epic to the Paris *Mercure*, whose editor, La Roque, at first gently then savagely rejected it. Insulted and vengeful, Desforges thought to enter those eighteenth-century Parisian literary wars by writing a trenchant satire against La Roque and the Académie. But his spritely, cherry-cheeked sister proposed another stratagem: she copied in her fair hand the worst of Paul's verses, appended a demure and plaintive note, signed herself Demoiselle Malcrais de la Vigne, and sent Paul's poem to La Roque. La Roque published the poem immediately, wrote effusive praise to the lady, pleaded for more verses from this "Breton Muse," declared the Demoiselle a fit successor to Madame Deshoulières, and finally sent epistles declaring his love. Soon the French literary world was loud with praise for this "treasure . . . Unearthed in Brittany." The arrogant Jean-Baptiste Rousseau was a fervent admirer; so, too, was Rousseau's enemy Voltaire. The latter wrote to the young woman, in a gift copy of his *Histoire de Charles XII*, what Browning calls "A stomach-moving tribute." Browning savours the irony that the writer with the keenest of eyes for sham and deceit was here deceived. He lectures Voltaire:

> Ay, sharpest shrewdest steel that ever stabbed
> To death Imposture through the armour-joints!
> How did it happen that gross Humbug grabbed
> Thy weapons, gouged thine eyes out? Fate appoints
> That pride shall have a fall, or I had blabbed
> Hardly that Humbug, whom thy soul aroints
> Could thus cross-buttock thee caught unawares, –
> And dismalest of tumbles proved – Voltaire's.

Browning attributes Voltaire's "tragic fall" to personal vanity, a weakness he dramatizes in a comic scene in which Voltaire is undeceived. When Desforges vengefully revealed the true identity of the "Breton Muse" to La Roque, the good-natured La Roque laughed at himself; and then, because he had a score to settle, he stage-managed the confrontation of Voltaire and Desforges. At Voltaire's house La Roque tells Voltaire's page to announce Demoiselle Malcrais. The amorous Voltaire fusses over his toilet, choosing just the right trousers and coat, wig, pomatum, rouge and scents. Then, "high in

246

colour, proud in port," the great iconoclast and "Rod of iron for imposture" is ushered into the presence of the smirking and grinning Desforges and La Roque:

A moment's horror; then quick turn-about
  On high-heeled shoe, – flurry of ruffles, flounce
Of wig-ties and of coat-tails, – and so out
  Of door banged wrathfully behind, goes – bounce –
Voltaire in tragic exit!

Voltaire was to suffer further ridicule when Alexis Piron dramatized the affair in *La Métromanie* (1738) in which, as Browning comments, Desforges' sister appears as "Demoiselle No-end-of-names-behind! / As for Voltaire, he's Damis." Desforges, the pretentious poet and vengeful deceiver, is treated with sympathy by Browning. At the close of the poem, Desforges knows that powerful critics and famous writers can be humbugs; he chooses the obscurity of Brittany.

Browning's final visit to Brittany was made the following year, 1868. He had returned from Le Croisic to London in October of 1867 in good spirits and health. Soon, however, his by now habitual distaste for London came upon him. He would rather, he wrote in January, be anywhere but London: " 'Anywhere, anywhere out of this black rainy beastly-streeted London world.' "[93] The difficulties of changing publishers – from Chapman to Smith and Elder – were troublesome, as was the importunate son of Baron Tauchnitz, who wished to bring out cheap editions of Elizabeth's and his poems. And social engagements impinged upon the time he needed to put into final form *The Ring and the Book*: "I get quite sick of dining-out," he complained to Isa, "– refuse whatever invitations I possibly can. I want my life for myself, what remains enough: do you know I get up, – have got up all winter at 5? and even so, I can't get thro' my work."[94] With Pen spending the summer in Scotland, Browning and his sister were free to leave for France earlier than usual. So by late July they were in Paris at 151 rue St. Dominique, the home of Madame Louis, who had been so helpful during Mr. Browning's final illness two years before. After a few days, Browning and Sarianna left Paris for Rennes and Vannes. They stayed a few days at Auray, from which they made excursions to the pilgrimage church at Sainte Anne d'Auray, to Locmariaquer, and to Carnac. Their destination was the north-coast port of Roscoff, to which they journeyed via Brest and Morlaix. Roscoff was crowded and otherwise inconvenient; and so, as Browning wrote, they "had nothing for it but to 'rebrousser chemin' and get to the southwest again."[95]

At Quimper he was advised that the village of Audierne, near Pointe du Raz, was what he was looking for. Audierne, niched in "the most westerly point of Bretagne – and of the Mainland of Europe" suited Browning well. There he could swim, though "somewhat ingloriously in a smooth creek of mill pond quietude," or walk up the Goyen valley to see the church of Notre Dame de Confort or the one at Pont-Croix set "amid the cluster of clean bright Breton houses."[96] In late August the Brownings went several leagues by pony cart to a promontory above the sea to witness a Pardon for Sainte Anne. With childlike enthusiasm Browning described the scene for the young Lily Benzon, the niece of his good friend, the painter Rudolf Lehman:

> There was a procession, – no end to strange figures of men, with long hair down their backs, just as long, and sometimes more curly even, than yours – but in other respects very different: some of the faces were more like an animal's than a human creature. Then the women who took a principal part in the show were perfectly wonderful in their rich attire, flowered satin embroidered with gold, I am afraid to say how much the cost was, if people told me truly. Then came a crowd of pilgrims of all sorts, who had been encamped all night round the place, – for lodging, indeed house, there was none. The moment all this was over, they began to carouse, and on our way home we had to pick our path (that is, the horses' path) through the poor, reeling, rolling people. . . .[97]

Browning had to break off his letter to Miss Benzon because Audierne, too, was beginning its Pardon and the people had started to dance to Breton bagpipes under his hotel window. Even amid the gaiety and remoteness of Audierne, however, "black news – these rumours of wars, and prognostications in the 'Times'" disturbed Browning. He felt both "disappointed in & sorry for" Napoleon III, whose movement towards a more liberal regime had come too late. He was "struck by the unpopularity" of the Emperor among the Bretons, and to him it seemed "strange people should hate so deeply & yet bear so much."[98]

Browning returned to London from Paris in early October with corrected proofs of the first instalment of *The Ring and the Book*, to be published on November 15. During the winter he watched with both anxiety and pleasure as the four monthly instalments of his masterpiece were published and received unprecedented critical acclaim from the British reviewers. By April, however, he and Sarianna, both wanting "a change of air and scene," went to Paris for a month. Milsand met them at the station and took them to the Hôtel du Nord, rue de Bourgogne. Browning spent the month, as he said, "lazily enough": he visited Fanny Haworth in her new apartment at Fontainebleau, and he called upon Gustave Doré. Browning thought Doré's oil paintings failed to fulfil the "promise his sketches abound in," but he found Doré "a very pleasant clever fellow." Otherwise, Browning "saw very few interesting people," he reported to Isa, "– Renan, Doré, Gérôme, being the exceptions. . . ."[99] British praise of *The Ring and the Book* was soon echoed in Paris by Louis Étienne in a thirty-page essay in the February 1, 1870, issue of the *Revue des Deux Mondes*.[100] Étienne takes as his primary theme in "Une Nouvelle Forme de Poésie Dramatique" an idea emphasized by Milsand in his 1851 essay on Browning in the *Revue*, that is, the contrast between Browning's objective realism and the personal subjectivity of most poetry of the century. The opening sentence clearly indicates Étienne's preference for Browning's mode over that of the subjective poets: "The excess of personality into which many of the poets of our century have fallen has been so widely recognized that one must expect a reaction against this indiscrete habit of always talking about oneself" (704). Étienne then announces to his readers that finally the public has been offered a "poésie plus objective, c'est-à-dire, plus réelle . . ." (704).

In the manner of the *Revue*'s essays, Étienne surveys the whole of Browning's career before turning to *The Ring and the Book*, and he makes occasional comparisons between Browning and Musset, Mérimée, François Coppée, Swinburne and Tennyson. He prefers Browning's version of the Pied Piper to that of Mérimée; he notes the similarity between Browning's authorial intrusions in *Sordello* and the practice of Musset; he regrets he does not have the space for an extended comparison of Musset's and Browning's treatment of Andrea del Sarto, but does assert that "the historical reality is on the side of the English author" (723). But what Étienne most admires in

Browning is his objective realism, a realism that extends beyond factuality to psychological realism: "he has a very objective creative ability; that is to say, he places the object of his curiosity outside himself; he does not stop, however, at the events of history and human life – he seeks the roots of them in the minds of his characters" (709). In *The Ring and the Book*, Browning has brought this "genre" to "le point extrême"; and, Étienne believes, he has therefore captured not so much the historic past but "l'esprit contemporain" (715). Essential to that spirit, Étienne contends, is democracy. And, in Browning's treatment of both character and detail in *The Ring and the Book*, "Le spectacle est absolument démocratique" (723). Browning's novel method of presenting his narrative through numerous and contending points of view is, for Étienne, further proof of the democratic spirit; "Does not the choice of such a method," he asked rhetorically, "already give to the poem an entirely modern and truly contemporary character?" (724). Étienne may, in the manner of a French essayist labouring under the censorship of Napoleon III, so insist on Browning's democratic spirit as a means of criticizing his own government. If he could not openly criticize French autocracy, he could at least praise English democracy. At any rate, he thought that *The Ring and the Book* was "the most singular conception yet produced by democratic, practical England, the most valiant nation of our time" (728). Whatever Étienne's motive, his idea is an interesting one; and it seemed a sensible interpretation of *The Ring and the Book* when Chesterton repeated the idea over thirty years later.

Étienne had failed to appreciate the full richness of *The Ring and the Book*, or so Georges Connes would complain when introducing his (the first) translation of Browning's poem into French nearly a century later.[101] The failure is forgivable in a reviewer faced with placing this complex, intricate, extended masterwork both within Browning's career and within the context of nineteenth-century French and British poetry. Étienne's objections were relatively minor: the sheer bulk and the crowded detail made *The Ring and the Book* into a kind of "interminable dossier"; Browning had unnecessarily usurped the role of the historian in his scrupulous attempt to recover and reveal historical truth "in the ashes of the past." Étienne did praise qualities of this "nouvelle forme de poésie" which, by 1870, had become criteria for realistic art: Browning's resolute turning away from subjectivity towards events taken from documented history and "de la vie humaine" had infused the poem with a spirit "moderne et vraiment contemporaine"; that spirit was essentially democratic and, in contrast to Browning's French and English poetic contemporaries, "plus objective . . . plus réelle." Étienne's British counterparts now shared some of those criteria for realistic art. By the late 1860's, British reviewers, as Isobel Armstrong has shown with such care, were willing "to accept and explore a wider range of experience, subtlety and complexity in poetry" than they had in the 1850's when, it seemed to Browning, only Milsand in his essays in the *Revue des Deux Mondes* and *Revue contemporaine* had properly appreciated his art.[102]

This wider critical tolerance now allowed the *Fortnightly Review*'s fine critic, John Morley, to defend the vulgarity and "sordidity" of *The Ring and the Book* on the grounds that such elements enlarged the reader's understanding and sympathy for "many types of character and many changeful issues of conduct and fortune."[103] In *Macmillan's Magazine* John Addington Symonds could now praise Browning's "minute analysis of facts and motives" and advise readers that as "in a novel of Balzac's, their patience will be rewarded by the final effect of the accumulated details grouped together by the artist. . . ." Such detail allowed Browning the power "of photographing subtle and obscure phases of mental activity and emotion in condensed and artistic pictures. . . ."[104] In a long essay for the *North British Review* Richard Simpson found in this "minute realism" an attractive coarseness "something like that of Gustave Doré"; Simpson regretted that the French artist had chosen to illustrate *Idylls of the King* rather than the poetry of Browning. Simpson, like Étienne, found the spirit of democracy at work in *The Ring and the Book*. He found that spirit especially in Browning's creation of characters representative of popular opinion, "Collective humanity," which in Half-Rome, Other Half-Rome and Tertium Quid "individualizes itself in the average man, and in him manifests its way of looking at things." In phrasing that would have pleased Courbet, the Brothers Goncourt or Zola, Simpson argues that it is time that the average man take his rightful place in poetry for "The people is in its way a poet." The day was past when the exceptional character could dominate a literary work while the people were introduced only as "chaff and bran, porridge after meat." Already, he says, readers are turning away from the romantic novel of exceptional, often aristocratic heroes, to "matter-of-fact reporters and correspondents and journalists, and find it more interesting." And herein lay much of the originality and significance of *The Ring and the Book*, a poem Simpson calls "cousin-german to a series of newspaper articles" in which those social classes hitherto neglected in literature are allowed to "simply record their sentiments through the mouth of an average member."[105]

These early reviewers, then, recognized and welcomed the realistic elements of *The Ring and the Book*. And, although comparisons to older epic poets and to Shakespeare, Chaucer and Goethe were more frequent, the contemporary novel seemed an appropriate analogue to the world of intrigue, violence, petty hatred, domestic tragedy, and chicanery Browning found in the Old Yellow Book. That world was, as the poet says with a pun in Book I, "A novel country." In the opening book he tells how he made that world his own and transformed it into *The Ring and the Book*. In the process, Browning reveals attitudes towards art he shared with contemporary realistic novelists: what is the material of art? where can it be found? what is the relation between the word and the world, language and objective, factual truth? what role does the artist's imagination play in the transformation of observed phenomena into art? what is the purpose, finally, of the fiction and what does it provide for the reader? Addressing the British public which so far has liked him not, the poet shifts his tone back and forth: eagerness to engage the reader's attention; casual searching; excitement at discovery; ironic levity; indignation at those who think he deals only "in poetry, make-believe" or at those who are too slow-witted to catch his drift; earnest assertion of the significance of what he has discovered and what he has made of it; hope that he may be blessed with careful readers so that he will no longer be both writer and sole reader of his work. Like the Brothers Goncourt in their preface to *Germinie Lacerteux* four years earlier, Browning is sardonically apologetic for bringing this sordid murder story to the attention of a public which prefers, in the Goncourts' phrase, "false novels . . . the memoirs of prostitutes, alcove confessions." Rejecting such books as "the fond tale / O' the Frail One of the Flower, by young Dumas" and "The Life, Death, Miracles of Saint Somebody, / Saint Somebody Else, his Miracles, Death and Life," Browning seizes upon an old quarto packed with "pure crude fact." And just as the Goncourts justify their novel of "human suffering, here and now and alive" because it teaches charity and *"humanité,"* Browning will allow "this old woe" of the Franceschini murder case to "step on the stage again" within his poem where "It lives, / If precious be the soul of man to man."

Browning jokingly suggests that he was predestined by Providence to discover the subject of his most ambitious work, but he emphasizes the casualness of his poking about " 'Mongst odds and ends of ravage" of the Florentine flea-market. The material for his art is there among the cast-off clothes and furniture, the broken bric-à-brac, the noise of the "thick-ankled girls" and marketmen, forged Leonardos, "Skeleton bedsteads, wardrobe drawers agape," frayed tapestries. The vital human tale of Pompilia, Guido, and Caponsacchi, "Secreted from man's life when hearts beat hard, / And brains, high-blooded, ticked two centuries since," has shrunk into the single, neglected old volume, "part print part manuscript." Although Browning with high spirits calls attention to the book's restorative, medicinal, even magical qualities, he has clearly allied himself with that part of the realist's credo that insists that the subject for art can be found anywhere, that there are no "appropriate" subjects. He shares with Flaubert the belief that "in literature there are no fine artistic subjects, that therefore Yvetot is worth just as much as Constantinople; and that consequently one subject is as good as another." "If we have souls, know how to see and use," Browning would say, "One place performs, like any other place." An obscure Norman village is worth as much as the great capitals to the poet of *Red Cotton Night-Cap Country*. In that letter to Louise Colet, Flaubert continues: *"It is up to the artist to raise everything*; he is like a pump, he has a big tube in him which goes down to the vitals of things to the deepest layers."[106] Literary imagination as a long-tubed pump is a singularly unromantic metaphor. Browning's initial metaphor for how the artist retrieves the vitality of his material and then shapes it is taken from metal-smithing; he later resorts to analogies of an archaeologist calculating from a fragment the lost proportions of a pillar, of resuscitation of corpses and what he calls, "mimic creation, galvanism for life." Throughout his description of how he delved to the deepest levels submerged within the "pure crude fact" of his material, Browning allies himself yet further with attitudes towards art held by those then interested in the realistic French novel.

Browning was more sceptical than most of his contemporaries

about the correspondence between the word and the world. The one lesson he asks the reader to find in his work, he says at the end of Book XII, is "that our human speech is nought, / Our human testimony false, our fame / And human estimation words and wind." Still, the observing, recording, transcribing poet of Book I is quite close to the court stenographer Stendhal recommended as the model for novelists. Browning insists that the language of the Old Yellow Book holds the "pure crude fact" of the murder case, and he is careful to reproduce "the voices we call evidence." He is not so naïve as to believe that language can be a nearly transparent medium to re-present the real world. The "live fact" of the events in Arrezzo and Rome in the 1690's has become "deadened down"; the voices are gone, but the written documents do help "us to all we seem to hear: / For how else know we save by worth of word?" Yet the legal Latin "interfilleted with Italian streaks" was not "self-sustaining" against the ravages of time; so it was necessary for Browning to construct a "fiction which makes fact alive." The poet as court reporter must become something like an examining magistrate, one of "les juges d'instruction des hommes et de leurs passions" whom Zola would recommend as the model for the novelist. Browning "assayed," weighed and judged the phenomena he had discovered; from the documents he "bit by bit . . . dug / The lingot truth." He knew now the value of his material; but that was only a "piecemeal gain."

To weld the mass of facts into a whole and give it shape and meaning, Browning needed what Zola quoting Claude Bernard called "une idée expérimentale"; he needed some way "to analyse and master the facts." An experimental idea, Zola says, is an "anticipatory interpretation of observed phenomena," a "logical structure for previsions." Neither arbitrary nor purely imaginary because it has its "basis in observed reality," an experimental idea is "quite spontaneous and completely individual in nature" and hence "constitutes the originality, the inventiveness, the genius" of the writer. Browning's moment of interpretative prevision came after he had studied the documents, closed the book, stepped onto his terrace and, with "A busy human sense beneath [his] feet," imaginatively projected himself to Arrezzo, Guido's town, Pompilia's "trap and cage and torture-place, / Also the stage where the priest played his part." In a series of striking cinematic previews, the setting for the tragedy takes form, the narrative assumes its pattern, the leading characters appear and take on their moral identities. By thus fusing his "live soul" with that "inert stuff," Browning had created a malleable alloy so that facts could take shape and be carved into form. Then he claims that by a process analogous to the goldsmith's use of acid to remove impurities, the poet "disappeared; the book grew all in all; / The lawyers' pleadings swelled back to their size, – / Doubled in two, the crease upon them yet, / For more commodity of carriage, see! –" Such purging of the author's subjective presence was important to the realists: once the spontaneous experimental idea has occurred, Zola again quoting Bernard says, "the experimenter must then disappear or rather transform himself instantly into an observer. . . ."[107] As the experimental poet, Browning now allows his characters to step forth to voice and give shape to the previously chaotic world of multiple and diverse phenomena.

In Book I Browning is the self-conscious apologist and special-pleader for realistic art. Especially in the early monologues of Half-Rome, Other Half-Rome and Tertium Quid, he is the realist artist in the Balzacian mode. In these books the narrative is slowly advanced, almost impeded, by the accumulation of "petits faits vrais," as he referred to the device in his letter to Isa Blagden in 1861.[108] The social and cultural milieu of late seventeenth-century Roman life is complexly created as these composite characters give us glimpses of street life, church interiors, the elegant gossip of salons, the salacious details of the prostitute district. If to many readers the factual detail seemed excessive, gratuitous, "un interminable dossier," others – like Henry James – found much to admire in what he called the "inordinate muchness" of these monologues packed as they were with "wonderful dreadful beautiful particulars."[109] When the major characters – Guido, Caponsacchi, Pompilia and, ultimately, Pope Innocent – are given monologues, the milieu out of which they speak has been grounded in concrete detail. Their monologues add to and expand the sense of contemporary life; however, these monologues contain greater emotional urgency and intensity, a more complex revelation of psychological states. Count Guido's clever and calculating rhetoric before his judges and his nearly melodramatic amoral posturing in his death-cell, Caponsacchi's grief for the death of Pompilia, his hatred of Guido, his sense of being a failed hero, the Pope's grand philosophic and moral soliloquy, all these remove *The*

Ring and the Book from the realistic mode. Reviewers' and subsequent commentators' preoccupation with the grandeur and intensity of the major actors' monologues and with "the sentimental splendour of the Pompilia-Caponsacchi story" has led, as Richard Altick and James Loucks complain, to an inadequate appreciation of Browning's realistic achievement of providing the reader with a "sense of concrete detail, of particular person, place, and time. . . ."[110] The dark evil of Guido, the perfect purity of Pompilia, the priestly ardour of Caponsacchi, the compassion and moral sensibility of Pope Innocent are firmly embedded within and silhouetted against the more mundane, realistic world created in the other monologues. It is just such "silhouetting and embedding effects" that Marshall Brown in his persuasive and lucid essay, "The Logic of Realism," takes to be the defining characteristic of the superior nineteenth-century realists from Balzac and Stendhal through Flaubert and Tolstoy to Galdós.[111]

9

Normandy and Haute-Savoie, 1870's and 1880's

i

Outbreak of Franco-Prussian War – RB Goes to Normandy – Watching the Débâcle of Napoleon III – A Hasty Departure from Honfleur – RB Ponders the Second Empire and the Career of Louis-Napoleon – Prince Hohenstiel-Schwangau.

ii

Fifine at the Fair *– Return to St. Aubin – Interlude at Fontainebleau – "A Capital Brand-New Subject for a Poem" – Reconciliation with Miss Anne Thackeray – The* Couronnement de Notre Dame de la Délivrande – Red Cotton Night-Cap Country *– RB's Metrical* Naturalisme.

iii

RB's Younger Contemporaries are Reminded of Balzac – A Return to St. Aubin – Summers at Mers-les-Bains, Villers-sur-Mer and Collonge – A Friend's Death in Haute-Savoie Memorialized in La Saisiaz *– Isère and a Tour of La Grande Chartreuse – A Grim Story of Murder & Suicide Near St. Pierre de Chartreuse.*

i

The rumours of war Browning had listened to in Audierne during the autumn of 1868 finally became a reality in the summer of 1870. In 1869 he had forgone, for the first time in nearly a decade, his annual French holiday and went instead to Scotland. In the early

spring of 1870 Milsand came to London for a month's visit to
Browning, so Browning also forwent his usual spring sojourn in
Paris. Sarianna, travelling with Milsand when he returned to Paris in
late March, spent April and May in Paris; Browning, however, made
only a short trip to Scotland for a funeral and then found himself
caught in London in early summer attending to Pen, who had come
down with measles. For the first time in years, Browning had begun
to think of a return to Italy: to Rome or Naples, not to Florence
which he thought "would be irritating and, on the whole, insufferable. . . ."¹ Soon, however, his thoughts of Italy turned not to a
possible return there but to the hope that Rome might soon be free
of French and Vatican oppression. On July 19, the 19th being his
normal day for writing to Isa, he read in the papers of the French
declaration of war against Prussia: "Well, Isa, here is the horrible
war, – after all the professions of peace!" he wrote, ". . . the way of
the declaration has been cynical and revolts everybody: all I trust is
that Italy will get Rome easily and naturally."² He was grimly
pleased that Napoleon III was in for "a sound beating"; yet he also
thought the Emperor was "good enough & to spare" for the "frenzied fools" in Paris who were calling for an invasion across the
Rhine. With no evident anxiety about the rapid Prussian advance in
early August, Browning decided to "go for a necessary change to 'St
Aubin-sur-mer, Calvados,' in poor France, – a little quiet bathing-
place where Milsand has a house. . . ."³ Passing through Rouen on
his way to St. Aubin, he saw in shop windows caricatures which
were evidence to him of the French folly and public ignorance of the
likely outcome of the war: there were cartoons "of a Zouave kicking
Bismark, King, and Prussia & all, leagues away over the Rhine";
another depicted a "soldier who, turning a mitrailleuse too quickly,
cleared the field before any sport could be had, – & so on. . . ." At
St. Aubin as he read the daily reports chronicling the collapse of
France, his sympathy for the French people grew strong as did his
disgust for their Emperor. After nearly two years' absence, Browning was "glad to be in France rather than elsewhere just now."⁴

At St. Aubin he took a cottage "of the most primitive kind" by the
shore. Instead of the rocky Breton coast punctuated by sandy inlets,
the Norman shore had "a good sandy stretch for miles and miles,"
and he had never been "quite so thoroughly washed by the sea air
from all quarters" as he was at St. Aubin. He planned to stay a

month before moving elsewhere, perhaps down the coast to Tréport. He and Sarianna made excursions into Caen and Bayeux and to "some out of the way châteaux," one of which was wonderfully preserved and blessedly "un-restored."[5] Although Browning enjoyed the "absolute presence of the sea" and the "solitariness of the spread of sands," he shared "the spirit of sadness [which was] over even this little out-of-the-way place," a place made more tragically solitary by the military call-up of all able-bodied men. Milsand, with whom Browning hoped to spend this holiday, was gone too. His home in Paris was near the southern fortifications; and, with the Prussians driving on Paris, he had returned to the city to arrange a safer place for his papers and library. As the extent of the war's débâcle became apparent, Browning's angry fulminations against Napoleon III temporarily subsided. He admitted that the sick Emperor was "far from his old self," that his "civil talents" had often been good for France, and he was glad that the people made "no stupid outcries against the Emperor."[6] Everyone in France, he thought, was as morally blameable as was Napoleon III; still, he could only look gloomily towards an imposition of "the Prussian system" upon France and perhaps all of Europe: it would be, he wrote, the "turning of a nation into a camp; nothing but soldiering to concern us for the next generation."[7] He could, however, find no excuse for the Emperor's "military ineptitude," the consequences of which soon caused Browning some indignity if not danger.

On September 19, the day the Prussian army invested Paris, he wrote to Isa that news from Paris had been halted and that railways leading south of Caen had been secured by invading forces. He was confident, nevertheless, that he and Sarianna could easily catch a boat from Caen to Le Havre: "so," he announced, "I think we have decided to remain until the end of the month."[8] Le Havre lay within sight across the Seine estuary; in the evenings Browning could see the setting sun shine on the city's lighthouse as he thought of the summer he and Elizabeth had spent there in 1858. But the boat he hoped to take down the Orne from Caen to Le Havre was suddenly stopped, like other boats from channel ports, by government order that no native leave France. Milsand, having returned from Paris and fearful that Browning might "be arrested as a runaway Frenchman or a Prussian spy," arranged with difficulty to get him and his sister out of the country. Though ports were closed, rails seized, and horses and diligences requisitioned, the Brownings made their way to Honfleur where, in this vivid evocation by Park Honan, "in the loud, tangily redolent, and homely company of a boatload of cattle bound for Southampton, they took leave of besieged France at midnight."[9]

Back in London Browning nursed his contempt for Napoleon III, though "in quieter moods," as Leo Hetzler has so clearly argued, "he would become gentler in his judgment. . . ."[10] Isa, whose view of the Emperor was closer to Elizabeth's than to Browning's, had been vexed by his strictures against Napoleon III. With a rather awkward attempt to apologize and mollify Isa, Browning commented that if they differed, one of them was insane for there was no person in Germany, France or England – "out of Bedlam" – who would not fully agree "that the war was unjustifiably determined upon, imprudently begun, and foolishly carried to its natural end at Sedan. . . ." He doubted that Prussian policy now would be any better than French policy, but at least Napoleon III "should simply be blotted out of the world as the greatest failure on record."[11] Shortly after the *coup d'état* of 1851, Browning had compared Louis-Napoleon to a larcenous watch-repairer; now the appropriate metaphor, he thought, was that of a fraudulent banker who for years pays extravagant interest while the principal disappears. He conceded, however, that the collapse of France was the result of "only a decline & fall of the faculties corporeal & mental" of the Emperor, who had not intended any conscious "knavery."

If Browning's attitude towards Napoleon III was mixed and ambivalent, his scorn for the Empress Eugénie remained in force. Her dynastic ambition and fanatical clericalism were, he believed, a major cause of the débâcle that had befallen the Second Empire. Browning's assessment of what had happened and was happening in France was not merely a personal and subjective one. By November he had had a long talk with Napoleon III's foreign minister, the Duc de Gramont, now exiled in London. Browning could suspend his own judgment of the Emperor, of whom he thought "more savagely *now*," to politely praise Robert Buchanan's sympathetic *Napoleon Fallen*, published in the *Athenaeum* on January 7, 1871.[12] When the communards revived the old revolutionary journal, *Le Père Duchesne*, he read it with contempt but also with care. Just "as contemptible as the Commune," however, was Thiers, whose negotiations of the peace treaty made him no less the "rascal" Browning had thought him as far back as 1850.[13] As the spring of 1871 wore on, urgent questions arose as to the form a new French government would take now that Paris had "renounced the wretched impostor [Napoleon III] and all his works." To get some answers, Browning sought out the new French Ambassador to London and soon-to-be Prime Minister under the Third Republic, the Duc de Broglie, to "hear what he says. . . ."[14]

Browning's ambivalence towards Napoleon III – that mixture of sympathy and contempt revealed in his letters – found complex expression in *Prince Hohenstiel-Schwangau*, "a sort of political satire," as he called it a few days after its publication in December of 1871.[15] In the late summer of 1871, while Sarianna went to "poor Paris," Browning travelled to Scotland. He took along a short prose outline of a poem on Louis-Napoleon he had begun in Rome in 1860 and had then abandoned when Elizabeth quickly completed her *Ode to Napoleon*.[16] Against his usual practice, Browning made this holiday an occasion for regular writing; and by October 1 the little prose sketch had grown to over eighteen hundred lines of conversational iambic pentameter in which Napoleon III, in the guise of Hohenstiel-Schwangau, reviews, examines and defends his career. The monologue, Browning later told Isa, "is just what I imagine the man might, if he pleased, say for himself."[17] At the outset of the poem the Prince promises his listener an honest "Revealment of myself," but halfway through he admits that what he has promised to tell with candour has been "Told as befits the self-apologist." As the poem closes, the reader learns with some surprise that the Prince has not been speaking to anyone at all: he has been but carrying on a "ghostly dialogue" with himself, rehearsing, perhaps, what he might say in his defence if necessity dictated. Browning told the young Edith Story, apropos the poem, that "in a soliloquy, a man makes the most of his good intentions and sees great excuse in them – far beyond what our optics discover!"[18] Throughout his soliloquy the Prince does find "great excuse" for the various practical and expedient compromises he was forced to make with his original high ideals of freedom, democracy and peace. He is not, however, an obvious casuist nor a clearly perceptible self-apologist; nor is he a transparent self-deceiver. He knows and several times insists that deception is inherent in language, that one cannot tell even oneself the truth about one's actions and motives because in trying to do so "one lies oneself." Even if one were able to summon "the armoury o' the tongue," truth would be impossible, for "somehow the words deflect / As the best cannon ever rifled will."

For nearly a quarter of a century Browning had watched the career of Louis-Napoleon with suspicion, contempt, and sometimes with hopeful sympathy. After the Emperor's surrender at Sedan, he could find no excuse for the man's policies but neither could he un-equivocally blame Napoleon III, whom he now viewed as a victim of "old age and decayed faculty" led to his folly by "the verminous people about him."[19] Browning was unable to muster a sufficiently decisive anger against the "lazy, old and worn-out voluptuary" to write effective political satire about him. He should not have been surprised – though he was – that reviewers drew contradictory mes-sages from his poem: one reviewer, he complained to Isa, took the poem to be a " 'eulogium on the Second Empire,' " while "another wiseacre" objected strenuously to Browning's " 'scandalous attack' " upon the deposed Emperor.[20] The tonal and structural ambiguity of *Prince Hohenstiel-Schwangau* continues as the focus of much of the excellent recent commentary on the poem.[21]

One source of readers' misunderstanding of Browning's intent may well have been the innovation he made in the ostensible drama-tic situation of this monologue. From the opening of the poem until near its conclusion some 2100 lines later, the Prince appears to be in a room just off Leicester Square in London. Improvising illustrative ink-sketches and watching his cigar smoke curl up to the ornate ceiling, the Prince talks with an ageing courtesan, who, like himself, has "seen better days." She is to be his confidante, his Oedipus who is at last to learn the riddle of Napoleon III, the sphinx who for over two decades has fascinated and puzzled European observers and caricaturists. The woman is an unlikely Oedipus, lurking there "Under pork-pie hat and crinoline." As another ageing voluptuary, however, she is a fit audience to learn the truth about the Prince's life. The time for such a revelation has come because he is anxious that posterity should not class his political manipulations with the "stilts and tongs of medium-ware" of Daniel Home, whose patron he had once been and to whom Browning had given his "say" in "Mr. Sludge." The Prince spins out his apologia for the decay of his early idealism, defends the *coup d'état* of 1851, rationalizes the need for censorship and manipulated plebiscites, makes a case for his excessive concern for France's material prosperity, and answers objections to his Austrian war and the annexation of Nice and Savoy. He speaks as a man who no longer wields authority, and early in the monologue he laments that as recently as "last July" he could still bid couriers scurry about Europe with important messages.

The reference to "last July," the London setting, and the implication that the Prince is no longer in power, all suggest to the reader that here is a Napoleon III after his surrender, abdication and exile to England on March 20, 1871. Were that the case, the Prince would have not only to find an excuse for his actions prior to, say, the spring of 1870, but also he would have to muster a defence for the débâcle that followed the French proclamation of war in July of 1870: the surrender at Sedan, the suffering and loss of Bazaine's army at Metz, the investment and bombardment of Paris, and the bloody war of reprisal between communard and republican forces. The Prince, however, makes no mention of these catastrophic events because within the temporal scheme of the poem they lie in the dark and forbidding future. The spatial setting is not as it had seemed, either, for the concluding lines reveal that he is in "the Residenz yet, not Leicester-square" and that he has been indulging in a lonely reverie rather than "congenial intercourse" with a London courtesan. He is, after all, in the palace at St. Cloud some time prior to the proclamation of war with Prussia. The reverie about how he might defend his action has been provoked by his deep anxiety and indecision about an "adventure" he wishes to undertake. The adventure will be initiated by a letter he has composed to his hard-headed "Cousin-Duke"; the sight of that "grey oblong" letter with its "grim seal" has led him to fancifully prefigure his apologia in exile. He knows that the adventure is a desperate gamble, and he remains indecisive to the end: "Twenty years are good gain, come what come will! / Double or quits! The letter goes! Or stays?" But Browning's readers knew that Napoleon III had undertaken the "adventure," that war was declared on July 19, 1870, and that the consequences were calamitous for France. More than most Browning poems, *Prince Hohenstiel-Schwangau*, as Philip Drew has said, "depends for its full meaning on something outside itself."[22] It depends upon the readers' knowledge of events in France between July of 1870 and May of 1871. With that knowledge they could measure the hollowness of Napoleon's claims that he was the "conservator not destroyer" of his society, that he had brought his people "the sweets of ease and safety," that he had pursued peace in Europe and engaged only in "war for the hate of war." Further, his pride in "boulevard-building" and his role as "a city-builder" were mocked by the rubble of Paris.

Napoleon's monologue ends sometime in the early summer of 1870; Browning wrote the poem in the autumn of 1871. The intervening historical events clearly make the subtitle, "Saviour of Society," scornfully ironic. The Hohenstiel-Napoleon speaker is audacious enough or blasphemous enough to develop overt analogies between himself and Christ.[23] In such casuistical passages, Browning's contempt for Napoleon III is clear enough. Even Elizabeth, when shortly after the *coup d'état* of 1851 she most enthusiastically supported Louis-Napoleon, could not accept such an exaggerated role for the man: when she heard people in Parisian salons refer to Louis-Napoleon as "the people's 'Messiah,'" she deflated such absurdity by commenting that Louis-Napoleon might also be but "Caligula's horse."[24] Elizabeth was, on the other hand, equally dubious about the extreme charges against Louis-Napoleon by radicals. "The wits go on talking . . . ," she told Miss Mitford in January of 1852, "and I heard a suggestion yesterday, that, for the effaced 'Liberté, égalité, fraternité,' should be written up, 'Infanterie, cavallerie, artillerie.' That's the last 'mot,' I believe."[25]

Karl Marx picked up this "'mot'" for his dispatch – to become *The Eighteenth Brumaire of Louis Bonaparte* – to a New York German-language newspaper. For Marx the deft rhyming inversion was not just a witty phrase but a revolutionary indictment. Neither Elizabeth nor Robert Browning could make so unqualified a judgment on Louis-Napoleon. In his February, 1852, letter to George Barrett, Browning was tortuously painstaking in his assessment of Louis-Napoleon, and he maintained a similar cautious ambivalence when he allowed Napoleon III to defend in *Prince Hohenstiel-Schwangau* the *coup*, the manipulated plebiscites, the press censorship, and the arrest and transport of opponents during the early months of his regime. Argument and counter-argument are also marshalled to both indict and defend the abbreviated war with Austria to free Northern Italy and the subsequent annexation of Nice and Savoy. Further, Browning shared Hohenstiel-Napoleon's scorn for the visionary utopianism of "Fourier, Comte, and all that ends in smoke," for the equally absurd radical individualism in which there is "Sovereignty of each Proudhon o'er himself, / And all that follows in just consequence," for the bardic posturing and futile prophetic denunciations of Victor Hugo, and for the self-serving autobiographical writings which Hohenstiel-Napoleon dubs "not the ineffective truth, / But Thiers-and-Victor-Hugo exercise." Hohenstiel-Napoleon's contempt for autobiographical apologia is, of course, but another of the many ironies Browning wove into *Prince Hohenstiel-Schwangau*. That those ironies do not consistently serve a satiric purpose should advise us to accept Browning's stated intention to write a poem in which Napoleon III is allowed to say what he "might, if he pleased, say for himself."[26] At the same time *Prince Hohenstiel-Schwangau*, in Philip Drew's concise description, "is a record as it were of Browning's own difficulty in assessing Napoleon III. . . ."[27]

ii

By the time *Prince Hohenstiel-Schwangau* was published in December of 1871, Browning was already at work on the long monologue set in Pornic and its environs, *Fifine at the Fair*. Throughout the winter and early spring of 1872 he worked steadily at the new poem, which he considered "the most metaphysical and boldest he had written since *Sordello*."[28] Joseph Milsand, to whom Browning had dedicated his new edition of *Sordello*, was his house-guest in London for the month of March. Before *Fifine* went to press in May, Milsand, displaying the careful scrutiny he had given Browning's poetry for over twenty years, read through the proofs and suggested a number of changes in syntax and diction.[29] Browning's fame in London was now sufficiently widespread that within two weeks of the poem's publication, "Fifine at the Fair was the subject of a very brief but not unimportant discussion in the House of Lords . . . ," or so *The Daily News* said on June 17, while reporting on Lord Buckhurst's proposed legislation to regulate the employment of young girls as circus acrobats.[30] London reviewers thought the Breton Don Juan's apologia for adultery "questionable, but always, when it is clear, ingenious and brilliantly illustrated."[31] London reviewers, however, lacked Milsand's patient appreciation of Browning's style; one complained that "for the ordinary reader it might as well be written in Sanskrit. There are such breaks, digressions, involutions, crabbed constructions, metaphysical hair-splitting, that reading becomes a positive fatigue."[32]

In August Browning left London for St. Aubin-sur-Mer, where he and his sister could have the "benefit of air, exercise, peace, quietness, and Milsand."[33] Browning took unusually commodious rooms: two bedrooms, "a parlour, kitchen, & room for the 'bonne'," and, he told Isa, there was in front "a little field, and then comes the sea – very wide, warm and enjoyable. . . ."[34] The Calvados coast had changed little since Browning's hurried departure two years before. No one had yet raised "an energetic thumb / And index" to remove a two-year-old poster announcing the forthcoming sale of a "chateau / With all its immobilities." Time seemed to have stopped in the sleepy village. In the voice of the genial persona Browning would adopt in his next poem, he describes another faded poster which

> . . . woe's me, still placards the Emperor,
> His confidence in war he means to wage,
> God aiding and the rural populace.

He spent a pleasant month at St. Aubin with Milsand and another French friend, Gustave Dourlans, before travelling to Fontainebleau where, for a month, he "enjoyed the quiet, the sans-façon, the air and forest-walks, extremely." And the French holiday had yielded a subject for a new poem: "I bring back with me, for winter-work in London," he wrote to Isa from Fontainebleau, "a capital brand-new subject for my next poem. . . ."[35] London was wet and foggy and darker than ever because, the "gas-men having struck," only half the street-lamps were lighted and the city took on "a sepulchral appearance."[36] Browning's "winter-work" on his new poem, however, soon sent him in imagination back to St. Aubin, that as yet "un-Murrayed bathing-place, / Best loved of sea-coast-nook-ful Normandy!"

During his holiday at St. Aubin there occurred three events which Browning combined to create *Red Cotton Night-Cap Country*. First, he renewed his friendship with Anne Thackeray, who was staying at nearby Lion-sur-Mer. Then, a few miles inland on August 22, the *Couronnement de Notre-Dame de la Délivrande* was celebrated. Finally, a civil suit had just concluded in the courts at Caen to determine the validity of the will of Antoine Mellerio, a rich Parisian jeweller's son, who had either leaped or fallen to his death from a tower on his estate at nearby Tailleville.[37] Browning had known Anne Thackeray from her childhood onward. He had often met her, her sister and her father in Paris, Rome and London. Their friendship was strained and finally broken off, however, when Browning learned that Anne was gossiping about a subject quite painful to him – rumours that he would remarry. Sometime during the previous winter, he had quite literally run into her while she talked near a staircase at a London soirée. He apparently stepped upon the hem of her gown and awkwardly jostled her while digging his elbow into her ribs, an action Anne, at least, took to be a rebuff for her gossiping.[38] At St. Aubin in August, Milsand learned that Anne was staying at a château near Lion-sur-Mer; he visited her and returned to St. Aubin to urge Browning to do likewise. His white hat and white suit shaded by a white parasol, Browning walked the five miles to Anne's house and the reconciliation was accomplished. *Red Cotton Night-Cap Country* opens with this version of the meeting:

And so, here happily we meet, fair friend!
Again once more, as if the years rolled back
And this our meeting-place were just that Rome
Out in the champaign, say, o'er-rioted
By verdure, ravage, and gay winds that war
Against strong sunshine settled to his sleep;
Or on the Paris Boulevard, might it prove,
You and I came together saunteringly,
Bound for some shop-front in the Place Vendôme –
Gold-smithy and Golconda mine, that makes
"The Firm-Miranda" blazed about the world –
Or, what if it were London, where my toe
Trespassed upon your flounce? "Small blame," you smile,
Seeing the Staircase Party in the Square
Was Small and Early, and you broke no rib.

Even as we met where we have met so oft,
Now meet we on this unpretending beach
Below the little village. . . .

Little, unassuming, out-of-the-way places like Lion or St. Aubin, he tells Anne as the poem progresses, can as much as the great capitals be the scenes of significant and instructive human experience. "If we have souls, know how to see and use," he comments; "One place performs, like any other place" to provide us with important human drama. Admittedly, the central street of St. Aubin is not as imposing as "Rome's Corso"; nor is the Sunday sailing race so grand a spectacle as "Paris assures you when she welcomes back / (When shall it be?) the Assembly from Versailles. . . ." Nevertheless, this apparently peaceful and sleepy region, too, "touches the great sea" of the world. The beach itself is a kind of "razor-edge" from which one can gain a perspective on the great and the small, the general and the particular. By standing "on this edge of things," Browning has discovered an extraordinary story of human passion, aspiration and despair in a land so apparently slumbrous that Anne wishes to call it *White* Cotton Night-Cap Country. Browning had already in the opening lines dimly hinted at the story when he imagined himself and Anne seeking out in Paris the famous goldsmithing and jewelry shop of the family of Antoine Mellerio. He drops a few other hints about the tragic life of Mellerio, but they are all but hidden in the jovial and leisurely discourse the poet provides as he conducts Anne on the tour of the region.*

---

*Fear of possible libel action caused Browning to change the names of people and places in *Red Cotton Night-Cap Country*; hence the Mellerio firm becomes in the poem "'The Firm-Miranda.'" Mrs. Orr, in *A Handbook to the Works of Robert Browning* (London, 1913, pp. 261–62), gives the equivalents and DeVane, in *Handbook*, p. 272, reproduces them. They are as follows:

In manuscript	As published
Mellerio Brothers	The Firm Miranda
Antoine Mellerio	Leonce Miranda
Anna de Beaupré	Clara de Millefleurs
St. Aubin	St. Rambert
Debacker	Muhlhausen
Lion *or* Lioness	Joyeux, Joyous-Gard
Caen	Vire
La Délivrande	La Ravissante
Tailleville	Clairvaux
Miromesnil Street	Coliseum Street

Sometimes Browning left original names; Caen in particular persists throughout the published poem. Other changes can be added: the quai Voltaire / quai Rousseau; Bayeux / Raimbaux, and its presiding Bishop Mgr. Flavien Hugonin / Morillon; Douvres / Londres; Courseulles / La Roche; Bernières / Monlieu. In my commentary I have adopted what I hope is not a confusing strategy by retaining the real names for Mellerio and La Délivrande and for Lion-sur-Mer, St. Aubin and Caen (though I do not change Clara to Anna). I do this primarily to keep before my reader a sense of the

Starting from Lion, Anne and Browning, who poses as a kind of genial poetic *avocat ficelle*, first walk along the beach. As if to exercise and sharpen the senses so necessary to see ultimately beyond the mere appearances of the area, Browning draws Anne's attention to the details of the coast: the small blue blossom on the "emerald luzern," the acrid aroma of wild mustard crushed under foot, the "pipy wreathe-work" worms make in the moist sand, the line of seaweed "Burnt cinder-black." Part way down the beach towards St. Aubin, they look back to see the old church at Lion and forward to the "brand-new stone cream-coloured masterpiece" at St. Aubin. Browning envies Anne the old church at Lion and wishes it could be exchanged for the new one at St. Aubin. Perhaps angels still famous in the region for fetching and carrying great weights through the air could accomplish the task. (Belief in such literal angelic transport, Browning later makes clear, was a crucial element in Mellerio's death.) Then, through the "learned eye" of Anne, Browning describes the pastoral inland,

> . . . its quietude, productiveness,
> Its length and breadth of grain-crop, meadow-ground,
> Its orchards in the pasture, farms a-field
> And hamlets on the road-edge, nought you missed
> Of one and all the sweet rusticities!
> From stalwart strider by the waggon-side,
> Brightening the acre with his purple blouse,
> To those dark-featured comely women-folk,
> Healthy and tall, at work, and work indeed,
> On every cottage door-step, plying brisk
> Bobbins that bob you ladies out such lace!

---

contemporary event and of the topography of Calvados. In doing so, I in part adopt the method of the reviewer of the poem in the *Athenaeum*, May 10, 1873, who commented that "it would be false delicacy in us if, being well acquainted with the facts of a story so easily accessible in the French law reports, should we follow Mr. Browning in his alteration of names." (*New Letters*, p. 217n.) In this practice I also follow the lead of Mark Siegchrist whose recently published *Rough in Brutal Print: The Legal Sources of Browning's "Red Cotton Night-Cap Country"* (Columbus: Ohio State University Press, 1981) becomes the definitive work on the documentary sources of Browning's poem. With its translations of legal documents and newspaper accounts of the Mellerio affair as well as its analysis of Browning's significant departures from the factual record, Siegchrist's book is a model of careful scholarship and intelligent criticism.

Anne then proposes a name properly symbolic of the region – *White* Cotton Night-Cap Country; such a name, Browning suggests, might well serve as title to a little guidebook or memoir of her sojourn in Normandy. Like an English Emma Bovary on holiday, she would cast a romantic haze over the countryside:

> How I foresee the cursive diamond-dints, –
> Composite pen that plays the pencil too, –
> As, touch the page and up the glamour goes,
> And filmily o'er the grain-crop, meadow-ground,
> O'er orchard in the pasture, farm a-field
> And hamlet on the road-edge, floats and forms
> And falls, at lazy last of all, the Cap
> That crowns the country!

But, Browning warns Anne, there are many kinds of night-caps, as many perhaps as there are stringed instruments now on display at the Kensington Museum, where the variety of shape, size and tone would make one wonder what a fiddle is. There must be as many night-caps as fiddles. And, from what Browning has perceived behind the seeming somnolence of Calvados, he thinks that the *red* cap of revolution and the Reign of Terror might be more appropriate. That red cap has persisted and has been donned just recently when "twelve months since, the Commune had the sway." He will call the region *Red* Cotton Night-Cap Country, though he admits ironically that the "snowy innocence" of the spire of the new church at St. Aubin does look like a white cap and thus supports Anne's argument. Still withholding his reasons for choosing red over white, Browning leads Anne inland to higher ground where, as though they stood on the face of a clock, they can see spread equidistant around them the white-night-cap-like spires of the region's churches: St. Aubin, (St. Rambert) Douvres (Londres), Courseulles (La Roche), Bernières (Monlieu), "Villeneuve, and Pons the Young, with Pons the Old"; Lion-sur-Mer is just out of sight.

At this point the sense of an almost random, leisurely reconnaissance of the countryside gives way to a stronger sense of purpose and urgency. Moving inland, Browning urges Miss Thackeray to be "Quick to the quest." Like Don Juan in *Fifine* cunningly leading his wife to the site of the dolmen and menhir, Browning has led Miss Thackeray to the most famous and important church of the area – La

Délivrande. A shrine to the Virgin had, by local tradition, existed at Délivrande prior to the Norman invasions of the ninth century; in the twelfth century a statue of the Virgin was unearthed there, and a romanesque chapel built.[39] This chapel, Louis XI was saddened to discover on his pilgrimage, had nearly fallen to ruin by 1470.[40] La Délivrande was, apparently, an unimportant site during the next five hundred years. And it did not benefit from what Browning in his poem calls "Count Alessandro Sforza's legacy," that is, Sforza's initiation of the rite of the Coronation of the Virgin at St. Peter's in 1631. By 1854 a revival of Marian worship was underway. There was renewed clerical strength under Napoleon III, and Pius IX ("Papa Nono" to Elizabeth and Robert Browning) was secure under French protection at Rome. That year Pius IX announced the dogma of the Immaculate Conception. In 1854 at La Délivrande, most of the old romanesque chapel was torn down and foundations for a new church laid. On one of the foundation stones for the new south tower was engraved: "this tower was raised . . . when Pope Pius the Ninth proclaimed the dogma of the Immaculate Conception of the Blessed Virgin Mary." (This is one of the two towers referred to by Browning in the subtitle of the poem, "Turf and Towers.")

Interest in the worship of Mary had been fuelled by Her appearance in the rue du Bac in 1830 and at La Salette in 1846. In February of 1849 Pius IX, recently restored to temporal power by French troops, asked his bishops for their advice on the question of the Immaculate Conception; in 1854 the dogma was proclaimed. Then it was, as it were, ratified, when in 1858 the Virgin appeared to Bernadette at Lourdes and announced: "Je suis l'Immaculée Conception."[41] Between 1853 and 1871 thirty-two French churches had been permitted to celebrate the Coronation of the Virgin. In 1872 the nearly completed new church at La Délivrande was granted similar permission by Pius IX. This rather neglected church now made its bid to be one of a trinity of French pilgrimage churches dedicated to the Virgin, or as Browning says upon pointing out the church to Miss Thackeray,

There is something now like a Night-Cap spire
Donned by no ordinary Notre-Dame!
For, one of the three safety-guards of France,
You front now, lady! . . .
She and her sisters Lourdes and La Salette

Are at this moment hailed the cynosure
Of poor dear France, such waves have buffeted
Since she eschewed infallibility. . . .

Browning had fully exercised his scorn of claims of Papal Infallibility
in *The Ring and the Book* and was apparently rather pleased that
many of the French bishops had joined the anti-council when it
became inevitable at the Vatican Council of 1870 that the claims
would become dogma. While "waves" of war, siege, and civil war
had "buffeted" France in 1870–71, the church at La Délivrande had
remained quite loyal to the Pope. On September 4, 1870, while
Browning was at St. Aubin, the Virgin's statue was carried in procession before some fifteen thousand people,[42] as public prayers were
made "in the chapel of La Délivrande in order to ask God for the end
of this scourge of war which holds all France in anguish." Napoleon
III had surrendered at Sedan two days earlier. By September 20,
Victor-Emmanuel had seized Rome from Pius IX, and to the prayers
at La Délivrande were added laments that "the enemy has entered
the territory of the Sovereign Pontif at the same time that the Prussians ravage our beautiful provinces."[43] The Vatican Council went
on through the political, military, and ecclesiastical turmoil. But
before it ended on October 20, 1870, the young Bishop of Bayeux
and Lisieux, Mgr. Flavien Hugonin, had successfully petitioned the
Pope for permission to celebrate the Coronation of the Virgin at La
Délivrande. In his poem, Browning has the collective voice of the
diocese urge the Bishop, whom Browning names Morillon, to seek
this great honour for La Délivrande:

"Thou hast a summons to repair to Rome,
Be efficacious at the Council there:
Now is the time or never! Right our wrong!
Hie thee away, thou valued Morillon,
And have the promise, thou who hast the vote!"
So said, so done, so followed in due course
(To cut the story short) this festival,
This famous Twenty-second, seven days since.

Browning did not go to the great festival on August 22, 1871;
instead he went, according to his poem, swimming. He did visit the
church the following week, however; and in the meantime he must
have read news accounts of the celebration, perhaps in *Semaine*

religieuse de Bayeux but more likely in the *Journal de Caen et de la Normandie*. The 22nd, he tells Miss Thackeray, was a "memorable day":

> Did not the faithful flock in pilgrimage
> By railway, diligence and steamer – nay
> On foot with staff and scrip, to see the sights
> Assured them?

The young vicar of Falaise, destined to be Cardinal Touchet, remembered the noisy bustle of the occasion:

> especially on the morning of August 22, 1872, there was, on all roads converging at La Délivrande, an avalanche of carriages, *cabriolets*, carts, fiacres, berlins, single pedestrians, monks, nuns, farmers in the midst of their folk, thickly bearded sailors decked out in necklaces, seminarians, soldiers, curés with their flocks, here in "compagnie," there in procession.

Some forty thousand in all, Touchet remembered, were there to see crowns placed on the statue of the Virgin and her Son.[44]

Although Browning and Miss Thackeray have covered two-thirds of the physical terrain of the countryside in question – after nearly six hundred lines – Browning has not yet revealed to his listener just what dark and bloody secret he has discovered. Whatever the secret, the church at La Délivrande, as a centre for a revived belief in miraculous intervention, must have played a role in the tragedy. As the poet and his companion turn their backs on La Délivrande and stroll towards Tailleville, Browning comments that the Mellerio firm had crafted the gold, jewel-encrusted crowns given to the Virgin and her Child and that Mellerio himself had given the central gem, a gem so fine that nothing like it could be found in Paris, and Mellerio "had to forage in New York" for it. Asking Miss Thackeray to "quicken pace" as they walk towards Mellerio's estate at Tailleville, Browning promises to reveal the secret. The estate, built within a "parc Anglais" upon the site of an ancient priory once dependent upon the Abbaye aux Hommes in Caen, has its own tower, "a quaint device, / Pillared and temple-treated Belvedere." Browning begins to tell of the domestic happiness of Mellerio and his "wife," but he breaks off, mockingly impatient with his own dilatory telling:

. . . how can I in conscience longer keep
My little secret that the man is dead
I, for artistic purpose, talk about
As if he lived still? No, these two years now,
Has he been dead. You ought to sympathize,
Not mock the sturdy effort to redeem
My pledge, and wring you out some tragedy
From even such a perfect commonplace!

He then tells of Mellerio's generosity to the church, of his bequest of his entire fortune to La Délivrande; he digresses to describe the "wife," whom Browning had caught sight of only yesterday, but again he promises to get on with the telling of "this old tale of town and country life, / This rise and progress" of a bourgeois family. Miss Thackeray, obviously impatient with a tale held together only by topography, gets up to leave, but Browning bids her "sit and stay!" He will now throw back the curtain hiding his secret here on the very stage where the "tragic death befell" and tell the true story as it came out in the recently concluded court case at Caen. Begging but one more "preliminary word," a digression on the need to clear away the rubbish of old ruins before one builds anew, Browning finally (at line 1150) begins a fairly straightforward account of the life of Antoine Mellerio.

Joseph Milsand, lawyer and long-time summer resident at St. Aubin, had brought to Browning's attention the case of Antoine Mellerio and had gained him access to the court records at Caen. Cousins of Mellerio, hoping to prove that Mellerio was insane and a suicide and hence to break the will in which his fortune went to La Délivrande, instituted the suit in the summer of 1870, soon after Mellerio's death. The Franco-Prussian War had interrupted the proceedings, and they were not concluded until July 9, 1872. From court testimony, letters introduced as evidence, depositions, and newspaper accounts, Browning gleaned the life story of Antoine Mellerio (Leonce Miranda),

This son and heir then of the jeweller,
Monsieur Leonce Miranda, at his birth,
Mixed the Castilian passionate blind blood
With answerable gush, his mother's gift,
Of spirit, French and critical and cold.

From the beginning, Browning makes clear that he believes "blood comes first" and that Mellerio's heredity was most important in determining the deep internal division which would wrack him throughout his life. Family training, priestly teaching, and the general temper of nineteenth-century French society, however, also went to shape his tragic fate. During his childhood summers at Tailleville, Mellerio "sucked in along with mother's-milk" tales of miraculous cures by the Virgin or of angels bearing the statue of the Virgin from the church at Douvres to her rightful place at La Délivrande.

In his early manhood, Mellerio's narrow, superstitious Catholicism was challenged by other forces in French culture, imaged by Browning as a chuckling Rabelais and a grimacing Voltaire, the old sceptic who had "Died mad and raving" in a house not far from the Mellerio mansion at 33 quai Rousseau (Voltaire). Mellerio, young and handsome and rich and in Paris, began to listen to "The Spirit of the Boulevard." In his pursuit of the pleasures of Paris, Mellerio resembled neither Voltaire nor Rabelais; he became, rather, the reimbodiment of that confused, hypocritical, easily duped comic character of Molière, Sganarelle. Playing the "Boulevard game," he had by twenty-five acquired five mistresses and deemed himself a man of the world, "realistic and illusion-proof." At the Variétés on a New Year's Eve, Mellerio saw a beautiful woman whom he pursued to her home in Coliseum Street; he announced his love and heard her tearful tale of how she "Of poor though noble parentage" had been forced to become a London actress only to be pursued by the amorous Lord N. and his competitor "The Prince of O." To save her virtue, she had fled to Paris. Mellerio believed he had found the most pure and perfect flower of womanhood. In an intrusive aside, Browning makes it clear that Mellerio here was as much a victim of illusion as he was when as a child he confused Christianity with the superstitious worship of the Virgin. The poet does, however, admit the woman's beauty: in her case "Social manure had raised a rarity." She who – in the names Browning used in the poem – called herself "Clara de Millefleurs, of the noble race, / Was Lucie Steiner, child of Dominique / And Magdalen Commercy; born at Sierck, / About the bottom of the Social Couch." Married early to a tailor named Muhlhausen, Clara worked in her husband's London milliner's shop until it failed and her husband decided she should earn their way on the streets. She fled to Paris to become the mistress of a certain Carlino Centofanti. When Mellerio appeared upon the scene, Centofanti left Clara and his debts behind. Mellerio paid the debts with jewelry found by "rummaging / Of old Papa's shop in the Place Vendôme."

Heritage and religious and social influences have created in Mellerio an unstable mixture of *homme sensuel* and religious naïf. The deaths of his brother and father brought him the family fortune and further freed him to pursue his illicit liaison; Clara, too, was partially freed by official separation from her husband, who, in the company of legal functionaries, caught Mellerio and Clara *in flagrante delicto* in her rooms in Coliseum Street. Mellerio's mother, "a daughter of the Church, / Duteous, exemplary, severe," hypocritically acquiesced to the liaison and even encouraged the couple to make the family estate at Tailleville their home. There they led the pleasant life of musical and artistic dilettantes, entertaining Parisian music publishers and receiving as guest that great patron and debtor of Parisian jewellers, Dumas *père*. Extravagant expenditures, however, soon caused Mellerio to be summoned to Paris for an accounting. Encouraged by priests and cousins in charge of the family business, Madame Mellerio berated him for his improvidence in remodelling the old Tailleville estate into a "gilt-ginger-bread big baby-house," for his disloyalty to her and for his sinful liaison. Torn by remorse and guilt, Mellerio threw himself into the Seine. Hoping to find death, he only caught something like pneumonia. The materialistic and brusquely anti-clerical physician Beaumont attributed the suicide attempt to religious mania, but all he could do was "blister and phlebotomize" the body.

Soon after Mellerio had recovered strength and returned to Tailleville and Clara, he received a telegraphic message – "just a spark / From Paris, answered by a snap at Caen" – to return to Paris. His mother had died, her heart broken, a priest sternly informed Mellerio, by his sinful life. His guilt and remorse deepened, and he determined to purge himself according to the teachings of the priests: "The doctrine he was dosed with from his youth – / 'Pain to the body – profit to the soul.'" Calmly, while calling out "'Burn, burn, and purify my past!'" Mellerio held a box of Clara's loveletters over the fire and kept it there until he was pulled away by cousins. His hands were but "Two horrible remains of right and left,

/ 'Whereof the bones, phalanges formerly, / Carbonized, were still crackling with the flame,' / Said Beaumont." Dr. Beaumont berated the priests and warned them that the next Republic would bar them from practising such "'Spiritual terrors.'" (Browning comments parenthetically that Beaumont's hopes for the Republic were premature, "for the Commune ruled / Next year, and ere they shot his priests, shot him.") Mellerio recovered sufficiently to sell, in a businesslike manner, the jewelry firm to his cousins; then with Clara he returned to "the land of miracles," La Délivrande and Tailleville. There, his union with Clara condoned by local priests who greatly benefited from his charity, he lived quietly for nearly two years. His hands charred to stumps, he painted with brush in mouth and played Bach with his feet on a pedal-keyed piano. Often he stood atop his belvedere musing upon the miraculous cures "Of ploughman Claude, rheumatic in the joints, / And spinster Jeanne, with megrim troubled sore" – cures attributed to the Virgin of La Délivrande.

At this point in his poem, Browning asks Miss Thackeray to once again note that the belvedere beneath which they are sitting is at one point of an equilateral triangle, La Délivrande and St. Aubin occupying the other points. As a source of remedy for Mellerio's spiritual disease, scientific medicine has already been rejected by Browning in a number of overt analogies and in extended imagistic conceits. In his isolation atop the tower, Mellerio must look for cure to La Délivrande – or to St. Aubin. Imagining Mellerio still alive, poised on the tower, Browning urges him not to choose La Délivrande but to go instead to St. Aubin. At St. Aubin lives that "man of men," Joseph Milsand, who had himself fought through such a spiritual crisis. Milsand would listen quietly and patiently to casual conversation and gradually come to understand Mellerio. With his knowledge and generosity, Milsand would sound "to the bottom ignorance / Historical and philosophical / And moral and religious," ignorance which has so afflicted Mellerio. In addition to practical advice, such as how Mellerio might acquire artificial hands, Milsand could supply his "crippled soul / With crutches." But he was ignorant alike of Milsand's presence and of the reasonable Christianity Milsand held to. Mellerio turned solely to the Virgin for relief, even to the extremity of travelling from Tailleville to her shrine at La Délivrande on his knees. Then, on a delightful spring day, "the

Twentieth Day / Of April, 'Seventy, – folly's year in France," Mellerio mounted the tower for the last time. Browning directs Miss Thackeray's attention to the platform of the tower; then rather wearily requests: "Look at it for a moment while I breathe."

After a pause, Miss Thackeray politely consents to hear Browning's story to its end. The remaining thousand lines are given over to an internal monologue by Mellerio just before his fall, to a similar monologue by Clara who responds to the cousins, to interpretative intrusions by Browning, to full quoting of the opinion on the case recently handed down by the court at Caen, and finally to an envoi to Miss Thackeray. Cultural forces at work in contemporary France are frequently integrated into this concluding section to imply that Mellerio was indeed a product of his milieu. To render his final thoughts before his leap, Browning must turn away from the documents and newspaper accounts he has so far relied upon: "Speech," he comments, "is reported in the newspaper"; but a poet must blend speech with the "thoughts which give the act significance." So Mellerio thinks over his life and present condition. He calls upon the Virgin of la Délivrande to cure that continued division within him, loyalty to Her opposed to "Lust of the flesh," reminding Her that he has sacrificed his hands and been generous with his fortune. He notes that the Virgin's "miracles are grown our commonplace," not only at La Délivrande but at Lourdes and La Salette. He reviews the gifts of royal donors to La Délivrande – Louis XI, Marie-Antoinette's gift of a robe in thanks for the birth of the Dauphin, the Duchess de Berry's gift of thanks for the birth of "Henri V," Comte de Chambord. Ominously, Mellerio remembers that the Dauphin was martyred at the Temple and that the Comte de Chamfort's hopes of restoring the Bourbon monarchy are remote even during the chaos of 1870. Still, citing his own greater generosity to Her, Mellerio urges the Virgin to become the healing surgeon of his soul: "I bid you cut, hack, slash, anatomize, / Till peccant part be found and flung away," he demands while extending a metaphor of spiritual cancer. Recalling the legend that angels had once carried the Virgin's image from Douvres to La Délivrande, he now calls upon Her to send those angels to bear him through the air from his tower to Her shrine. In keeping with the scientific imagery pervasive in the poem, Mellerio prays for the Virgin to suspend one physical law and to activate the principles of aerodynamics:

278

. . . suspend the law of gravity,
And, while at back, permitted to propel,
The air helps onward, let the air in front
Cease to oppose my passage through the midst!

News of such miraculous demonstration of the Virgin's powers
would spread, he thinks, "like wild-fire" across France. Telegraphic
messages describing Mellerio's "flight" would set the boulevards
a-buzz and moral regeneration of France would be instantaneous.
The Empress Eugénie would convince Napoleon III first to restore
Pius IX to temporal power and then to resign so that Henri V could
ascend the throne. The quai Rousseau would be renamed after
Sainte Marguerite Marie Alacoque, the seventeenth-century visionary French nun whose rheumatic paralysis had been cured by the
Virgin and whose *La Dévotion au coeur de Jésus* became the basis of
the observance of the Sacred Heart.[45] On the newly-named quai,
Renan, after burning his books, would himself be burned by the
vitriolic and militant Catholic editor, Louis Veuillot. Veuillot's
newspaper, *L'Univers*, banned for a decade by Napoleon III, would
once again be freely published. The restoration of the Virgin's
authority throughout French society would also bring sanctification
to the "marriage" of Mellerio and Clara. With that final hope, Mellerio leaps from the tower:

. . . A sublime spring from the balustrade
About the tower so often talked about,
A flash in middle air, and stone-dead lay
Monsieur [Antoine Mellerio] on the turf.

The dry, matter-of-fact tone in which Browning reports the fall
provides a fitting anti-climax to the frenzied sublimity of Mellerio's
hopes. The man's spiritual aspirations and hopes of national moral
regeneration are further undercut by the testimony of a gardener
who witnessed the fall and who, coming to the body, raised the
bloody "Red Night-Cap" shrouding Mellerio's crushed head and
pronounced his employer " 'Mad!' " Browning disagrees with the
gardener's verdict just as he disagreed with the cousins' charge in
court that Mellerio was insane. Resorting once again to the metaphor
of medical science, Browning claims that Mellerio was surgeon to his

own diseased soul:

> . . . No! sane, I say,
> Such being the conditions of his life,
> Such end of life was not irrational.
> Hold a belief, you only half-believe,
> With all-momentous issues either way, –
> And I advise you imitate this leap,
> Put faith to proof, be cured or killed at once!
> Call you men, killed through cutting cancer out,
> The worse for such an act of bravery?
> That's more than *I* know.

Blood heritage and cultural milieu had brought Mellerio to the extremity where such a desperate leap of faith was both necessary and reasonable and, to Browning, even admirable. It had been a leap of faith which, at least, had ended an illusion of miraculous intervention into the physical world.

Before his story ends, Browning must deal with Clara, of whom he had caught a glimpse during his visit to Tailleville the previous day. Then he had found her physiognomy strangely "blank"; her face was "colourless, featureless," "a set of wax-like features," much like, one is tempted to say, the faces of those women in Manet's *Le Déjeuner sur l'herbe* and *Olympia*, faces still creating controversy in Paris when Browning went over for the Great Exhibition of 1867. Now Browning allows Clara to speak in her defence against charges by the cousins that she was a "Jezebel," a "Queen of the Camellias." When Mellerio had "emerged all dripping with slime" after his earlier excesses in the Parisian "cesspool of debauchery," Clara had, the cousins said, attached herself to him as does some sucking insect to a "heap grotesque / Of fungous flourishing excrescence." She retorts angrily that it is the cousins, not she, who are guilty of "hypocritical rapacity." It was she who encouraged Mellerio to remain faithful to the Church while the cousins turned Voltairian mockers. After he had charred his hands to stumps, it was she who urged Mellerio to " 'Live, not die' ": to find ways to write, play the piano, even to paint. The "last Exposition" in Paris, Clara says with sardonic scorn, convinces her that "Plenty of people must ply brush with toes." She ends her monologue, as had Mellerio, by appeal to the Virgin of La Délivrande and by promise of yet another gift to

Her: the lace of Clara's gown " 'must go to trim Her gown!' " Browning now intrudes to offer his assessment of Clara's character. He accepts the cousins' image of her as a sucking insect, but he does not endorse their moral condemnation. Browning studies Clara as might "entomologists." She was, he says, "caterpillar-like" and fed only by instinct: she fed first on her husband; then she "settled on [Mellerio] . . . sucked, / Assimilated juices, took the tint, / Mimicked the form and texture of her food!"[46] Browning accepts without moral judgment Clara's natural instinct, her "self's own birthright to sustain / Existence, grow from grub to butterfly" by feeding on Mellerio. He even praises her for sufficiently devouring Mellerio to prevent the insect-cousins, "earwig and blackbeetle," from feeding on the Mellerio fortune. He then quotes at length the judgment handed down by the court at Caen, a judgment which supports Clara and denies the charges of the cousins.

In *Red Cotton Night-Cap Country* Browning had extended his earlier realistic mode to bring his art quite close to an emerging naturalistic one. Here he has redeemed his pledge to Miss Thackeray to wring a tragedy out of the commonplace. Seizing for his subject a contemporary event, he sought and analysed documentary evidence and investigated the principal sites of the actions. He studied the history of the region and traced the religious, social and intellectual forces at work in contemporary France. Much of what he found was brutal, sordid and ugly, and the language he uses reflects those qualities. Posing often as a chemical analyst, a physician or surgeon, or an entomologist trying to "distinguish grade and grade" of variations in insects, Browning analysed his subject and decided that heredity and environment had determined the course of Antoine Mellerio's life, and – given the man and the milieu – those forces had determined the apparently irrational nature of his death. The metaphorical matrix of *Red Cotton Night-Cap Country* is built by pervasive reliance upon botany, physics, new technologies, zoology and especially physiology and medical science. It is difficult to believe that while he wrote the poem Browning was unaware of the theories of Hippolyte Taine or of the claims Émile Zola was making in his prefaces: claims that his characters, like those in *Thérèse Raquin* (1867; preface added 1868), were "human brutes, nothing more"; and claims that he had merely applied "on two living bodies the kind of analytical task that surgeons perform on cadavers."[47]

Zola articulated the theory more closely in his 1871 preface to *La Fortune des Rougon*: "Physiologically, the Rougon-Macquart family members are the result of a succession of accidents within the nerves and blood which . . . according to the environments, determine within each individual of this race, sentiments, desires, passions, all natural and instinctive human manifestations. . . ."[48]

Near St. Aubin, Browning had discovered a story Zola himself might have envied when, three years later, flush with an unexpected 20,000 francs the early volumes of his *Rougon-Macquart* series had brought him, Zola too took a long-delayed summer holiday at St. Aubin. Browning left no record in his letters that he was aware of Zola's work; nor is there any record of what he thought of naturalism in general. Milsand, by his daughter's testimony, often raged against "les naturalistes." She recounts that her father was given to

> bursts of indignation against the so-called *naturalistes* of France. "When I hear them speak," he said, "of pathological studies and social anatomy, I shrug my shoulders. The fact is that they are a sort of drunkards who only dream of Cupid's bottle, and who can only employ their minds in new tricks to rob their neighbours' cellar. A sensual obsession prevents them from taking a real interest in character, in the development of affection, or to see what is noble near what is ignoble."[49]

Browning admired Milsand's taste and intellect, and he shared many of the same attitudes. But Milsand had also criticized Browning, in the *Revue des Deux Mondes* and *Revue contemporaine* essays, for his penchant for the morbid, the ugly and the grotesque, qualities for which the naturalists were severely criticized. In *Red Cotton Night-Cap Country* Browning certainly gave full rein to that particular predilection of his. At the same time, in choice of subject, mode of analysis, attribution of motive, and characterization, Browning had created a kind of metrical naturalistic novel. That it is written in meter and in often densely imagistic language, cannot obscure the fundamental naturalism of the poem. Other features, of course, do distinguish it from the naturalist mode. Most important of these is the intrusive, genial, sometimes darkly humorous persona Browning adopts in the poem. This persona, as it were, mocks the naturalistic methodology he seems to pursue. And, by his joking dismissal of the materialistic physician Beaumont and by occasional statements, *in propria persona*, that useful as it is the scientific analogy is an inadequate one for the artist, Browning places himself at a remove from – or beyond – naturalism. Whatever *Red Cotton Night-Cap Country* may represent in terms of Browning's search for new forms in his art, it clearly reveals his knowledge of and deep concern about contemporary French culture. In this poem, as Philip Drew and more recently Brendan Kenny have argued, Browning most fully exercised his role as commentator on nineteenth-century European society by analysing an obscure action in Normandy. And he was able to give us, in Kenny's phrase, a critique of "the entire socio-religious system of France as a system."[50]

iii

The trilogy of long poems about contemporary France – *Prince Hohenstiel-Schwangau* (December, 1871), *Fifine at the Fair* (June, 1872), and *Red Cotton Night-Cap Country* (May, 1873) – occupied Browning for over two years. The publication of the last of these poems marks the end of his attempt to assess and analyse French culture in his poetry. French subjects or themes henceforth are only sprinkled among the many and varied volumes Browning published after 1873. His manner, however, more and more began to remind some of an author whom British readers discovered rather late – Balzac. Thus Swinburne in his *Essays and Studies* found Browning's characterization of Guido in *The Ring and the Book* to be a "model of intense and punctilious realism. . . . so triumphant a thing that on its own ground can be matched by no poet; to match it we must look back to Balzac."[51] Robert Louis Stevenson thought Browning's *The Inn Album* (1875) bore "a remarkable resemblance to some of Balzac's shorter tales, and might very well have been a transcript in verse from the author of *Le Colonel Chabert* or *La Duchesse de Langeais*." Stevenson, however, was unsure whether, as a poet, Browning was "Apollo or Quasimodo"; and he thought Balzac the more careful artist. Still, he commented that *The Inn Album* had "the same purely human import and the same fundamental cruelty that we find in the great world of the *Comédie humaine*."[52] Gerard Manley Hopkins read only a bit of *The Ring and the Book* when it came out and was warned by a Jesuit colleague that "further on it was coarser"; but in 1881, Hopkins could still remember Browning's opening description of the Florentine flea-market: "a pointless photograph of still life, such as I remember in Balzac, minute upholstery description. . . ."[53]

French settings and historical anecdotes continued in Browning's poetry. In *La Saisiaz* (1878), the mountain landscape of Haute-Savoie provides the setting for his meditations on human immortality; both setting and theme naturally evoke thoughts of Voltaire and Rousseau. *The Two Poets of Croisic* (1878), which took Browning in imagination back to his Breton holidays of a decade before, is rich in comic detail drawn from Breton and French history. Seventeenth-century Fontainebleau provided a darker anecdote of vengeance and murder in "Cristina and Monaldeschi" (1883). In "Parleying with Daniel Bartoli" (1886), that Italian chronicler of fantastical history is challenged by a realistic historical tale drawn from the Marquis de Lassay's *Mémoires* and from, perhaps, one of Sainte-Beuve's *Causeries*.[54] In Browning's final volume, *Asolando* (1889), the short ballad "Rosny" takes its title from a château near Mantes and obliquely celebrates the Huguenot soldier, statesman, and lover, Maximilian de Béthune. Except for *The Two Poets of Croisic*, none of these poems has the rich and detailed allusion to French culture so prominent in the trilogy. After 1873 Browning no longer looked to France as an important source of theme and subject for his art. For yet another decade, however, French coastal and mountain villages offered him relief from what he calls in the envoi to *Red Cotton Night-Cap Country* "the Dark Winter-gloom" of London.

Browning returned to the "quiet, simplicity, and the exceeding freshness" of St. Aubin in August of 1873. He went almost immediately, as he said, "to review my old property – Tailleville; walked all round it, but found nothing material to alter in the poem."[55] His sense of proprietorship in the region took an interesting turn after an excursion to the nearby châteaux of Fontaine-Henri and Creully and to the old priory at St. Gabriel. He noted that the "delicious relic" near Creully had a few years ago sold for only £400, a price it "would be too absurd even to dream about" in England. Attracted to the old priory at St. Gabriel, he calculated that "one might buy [it] for a trifle, and, for a moderate sum, repair and complete [it] as a wonderful dwelling." Browning's earlier desire to live out his life at Sainte Marie or Le Croisic echoes faintly in his letter to Annie Egerton Smith. He quickly dismissed the notion, however; "who," he asks rhetorically, "could comfortably build, live and die in the middle of aliens?" He was content to share Milsand's companionship, ramble about the countryside, and swim in "the sea warm as new milk." St. Aubin was restorative, and Browning thought he had done "well to get away early from London" before he had become too "run down" physically.[56]

This would be his final holiday at St. Aubin. He found no new French subject for his winter work in London; instead, he read Aristophanes and added to the immense learning he would pour into *Aristophanes' Apology*, a poem Park Honan has called "a theoretical defence of his excursion among naturalistic horrors" in *Red Cotton Night-Cap Country*.[57] Browning's note on the manuscript of this poem provides us with one of the few hints we have about where he spent his holiday in 1874: "Begun about August 11 – ended Saturday, Nov. 7, '74. Mers, Picardy."[58] He and Sarianna had apparently taken a long holiday at Mers-les-Bains before journeying to Antwerp to visit Pen, who had begun to study painting there under Jean-Arnould Heyermans. The following summer, 1875, Browning and his sister again visited Pen, this time at Heyermans' summer retreat at Dinant in Belgium. Sarianna then went on to Paris to be with the Milsands, while Browning proceeded on to the Côte Fleurie to the village of Villers-sur-Mer. After the simplicity and solitude of the Calvados sands, he was apprehensive about the "publicity" of the beach at Villers, not far from the fashionable and crowded beaches at Deauville. But he was soon swimming regularly if not comfortably in water that was "*hot* rather than warm."[59] In a "trial of novelty" the following year, 1876, Browning went to the cooler Scottish coast on the Isle of Arran. Then the sixty-three-year-old poet gave up his annual regimen of sea-bathing; from 1877 onward he sought the mountain coolness and Alpine streams of Haute-Savoie, Isère, and Switzerland.

"How lovely is this place in its solitude and seclusion," Browning wrote from a chalet he had taken at Collonge near the Swiss border south-west of Geneva in August of 1877. The chalet, La Saisiaz, delighted him with "its trees and shrubs and flowers, and above all its live mountain stream which supplies three fountains, and two delightful baths, a marvel of delicate delight framed in with trees. . . ." Below, to the north-east, he could see Geneva and its lake, while across the plain of the Rhône and Arve rose the Jura. The

Grande Salève seemed to loom right behind the chalet, though, as he noted, it took "a hard hour and a half to ascend."[60] In many ways La Saisiaz was, as Clyde de L. Ryals comments, "the setting for a pastoral idyll."[61] However, it was marred in places by the "over cultivated country" and by the peasantry, whose "money grubbing" repelled Browning and led him to dismiss the foolish illusion of a " 'universal presence of Love' " which Byron's Childe Harold had discovered in the region. At nearby Bossey, he found Rousseau's *pension* turned into a cattle-shed, cracked and open to the sky, dung stacked in the doorway. Enquiries into the history of the wedge of land on which La Saisiaz was built turned up stories of "perpetual feuds and fighting" among peasant owners who "disputed the right to this and the other inch of the border." But the fresh mountain stream in which he bathed twice daily was a compensation. If it was not a lotus-land, it was a "lettuce-eating land – there being sleepiness and satisfaction in θριδαξ [lettuce], as in the nobler herb."[62] There was Voltaire's Ferney to visit; here were friends – Gustave Dourlans and Annie Egerton Smith – with whom he could talk, especially about a subject recently raised in issues of *The Nineteenth Century* magazine – the immortality of the soul. The three friends planned for September 14 an ascent of Salève. On the morning they were to make the climb, however, Browning returned from bathing to discover Miss Smith dead in her room. Arrangements – notification of Miss Smith's sister in Paris and her solicitor, a death certificate and burial in Collonge's churchyard – were made by Browning. The shock of his friend's sudden death and the "precise and trouble-some" formalities of the arrangements, made La Saisiaz so "detest-able" to Browning that he determined to leave as quickly as possible. But before he left, he ascended Salève alone; then, back in the dark "mid-November" of London, he memorialized Miss Smith and the experience in *La Saisiaz*.

Browning's solitary ascent of the Grande Salève gives rise to a different kind of poem than had the excursion of Don Juan and his wife in the environs of Pornic in *Fifine at the Fair* or Browning's perambulation with Miss Thackeray around St. Aubin in *Red Cotton Night-Cap Country*. Dramatic monologue gives way to soliloquy; the calculated search for metaphor and meaning in the landscape gives way to more abstract speculation. *La Saisiaz* opens with Browning having already attained the mountain's summit, "stationed face to face" not with nature but with "Infinitude." Below, he can see the low-walled churchyard of Collonge where Miss Smith had been buried. He recalls that a brief five days before, he and Miss Smith had taken an evening stroll about the base of Salève; they had talked of the proposed climb to the summit on the morrow, and Miss Smith had anticipated watching the gathering dusk on Lake Léman and the lights of Geneva coming on. Their ascent was to be leisurely enough to allow for a stop at an inn "Three-parts up the mountain," a visit to a convent, and time to contemplate Mont Blanc: "supreme above his earth-brood, needles red and white and green, / Horns of silver, fangs of crystal set on edge in his demesne." After some light talk of their delight in the unspoiled Collonge – "Yet untroubled by the tourist, touched on by no travel-book" – and of Gambetta's political troubles, the party retired for the night. At dawn Browning had bathed in the nearby stream and watched the Jura grow golden in the morning light. Below him he could see the meeting of the Arve and Rhône. The pulsating sounds of steamboats, the houses of Geneva and the city's "pomp of spires" appeared to him to be "Man's mild protest that there's something more than Nature, man requires. . . ." Lake and mountain cannot bring comfort to the spirit as can "the texts whence Calvin preached." Returning to the chalet, he had found Miss Smith dead. Now, five days later standing atop the Grande Salève, he recalls the shock of his friend's death; and though he finds some comfort in the peaceful quiet of her grave site, the scene now spread about him makes him "wince." He intends to leave the painful scene tomorrow, but first he must muse upon the question he and Miss Smith had so recently discussed: "'Does the soul survive the body? Is there God's self, no or yes?'"

The physical scene so carefully detailed in the opening section of *La Saisiaz* dissolves as Browning opens an internal debate upon the question of the soul's immortality. The debate begins with assumptions that the poet claims experience has proved "fact": the existence of "soul" and "God," the created and the creator, the subject and the object. Then argument and counter-argument are evolved to determine the reasonableness of belief in human immortality. The verbal fencing over questions of good and evil, fate and free will, heaven and hell is given over to personifications of the opposing points of view, Fancy and Reason. Throughout, Browning emphasizes the uncertainty of human knowledge; at the same time he insists that he can but speak for himself and can in "Nowise dare to play the spokesman" for others. The result is that the argument comes "back full circle": belief in immortality rests only on "hope." He still holds, however, to the original theistic assumptions that God and soul exist.

This reaffirmation of theism originates in part when Browning turns away from abstract argumentation and focuses once more on the particular landscape which surrounds the Grande Salève. From his station at the summit, he is but a stone's throw from the village of Bossey. He had gone to the village that morning to look at a broken-down house turned cattle-shed, its door blocked by a dung-heap: "In that squalid Bossex [*sic*]," Browning reminds himself, "under that obscene red roof, arose, / Like a fiery flying serpent from its egg, a soul – Rousseau's." Turning to look at Geneva, he is reminded by its glimmering lake that here lived the careful student and translator of Christian scripture, Giovanni Diodati. But Diodati's "gospel-news" was drowned by the scoffing misanthropy of one whose memory is evoked by the Rhône gorge, Mont Blanc and the Isle of Chillon – Byron. Poetic power and fame gave Byron's doctrine an authority Diodati's could not claim. Authority also flowed from the wit and learning of Voltaire and Gibbon and from the "all explosive Eloquence" of Rousseau. Recognizing that men will believe the words of the famous even though the famous may reach the "sorriest of conclusions" about man and God, Browning rather grandiloquently challenges Voltaire and Rousseau, Byron and Gibbon. He will brandish a burning torch from the lonely summit of the Grande Salève. In lines that Ryals describes as "scornful, sardonic, mocking, self-pitying, and playful,"[63] Browning asserts that he can match the scoffers in learning, wit, and eloquence. He, too, has fame and therefore the power to convince. Men will look at Robert Browning and say "he at least believed in Soul, was very sure of God." However self-mocking he may be about the importance his testimony will have for mankind, he did momentarily achieve a personal certainty about the soul and God while he was at the summit of the Grande Salève. The certainty remained with him while at sunset he descended the mountain, and lasted until he re-entered Collonge and was confronted by his friend's grave. Back in "London's mid-November," the chain of thoughts that had brought him to his confident assertion of faith on the Grande Salève became weak and tangled. *La Saisiaz* was an attempt to re-forge "link by link" and to unravel "any tangle of the chain" of his recent experience of death in Haute-Savoie.

The summer after Miss Smith's sudden death at Collonge, Browning, after nearly two decades of absence, returned to Italy. In early August of 1878 he and Sarianna left London for Paris, where they spent but a few days, perhaps to see Pen, who about this time changed masters – the Belgian Heyermans for the newly prominent Parisian sculptor, Auguste Rodin. Browning and his sister then travelled on to Splügen above Lake Como, where they stayed some five weeks while the late summer heat of the Italian plain moderated. This journey set a pattern Browning would follow the rest of his life: a trip by rail via Paris to some spot in the Swiss, Italian, or French mountains; a month in the mountains, followed by a sojourn in Northern Italy, usually with several weeks in Venice; then a quick return across France to London; stays in Paris were brief and intermittent. His reading of new French books now seems limited to memoirs and letters. The mixture of fiction and autobiography of Alphonse Karr's four-volume *Le Livre de Bord* (1879) interested him. Although the volumes provoked in Browning "a very mixed feeling for the author, and not too much belief in his veracity," he enjoyed Karr's jocular high spirits. He was particularly pleased by the manner in which his "narrator" displayed a distrust of the characters, such as Stephen, whom Browning took to be Karr himself.[64]

His interest in and dislike of François Guizot was renewed by an 1880 review of a volume of Guizot's personal letters. Whether or not he did so, he wrote to that "learned lady" who had become a frequent correspondent, Mrs. Thomas FitzGerald, that he was "greatly interested in reading Guizot's Memoirs," referring probably to the recently published letters, *Monsieur Guizot dans Sa Famille et avec Ses Amis*, but perhaps to Guizot's nine-volume *Mémoires pour servir a l'histoire de mon temps* (1858–68). The review stirred up Browning's old anger against Guizot. He had been amused by Karr's playful lying, but Guizot's claims to truthfulness reminded Browning how the French politician's lies in 1846 had strained Anglo-French relations and had "effectually destroyed all faith in the character of Louis Philippe, and was the main cause of his downfall." With a fair recollection of events now thirty-five years in the past, Browning reminded Mrs. FitzGerald of Guizot's hypocritical defence of public lying: "I remember the very words of Guizot in the French Chambers in excuse for his having told a direct falsehood to our Ambassador: 'Quand je reçois un ministre je ne subis pas un interrogatoire' (When I receive a minister, I do not undergo interrogation) – a good reason for holding the tongue but not for uttering a lie." He recalled also the political and religious hypocrisy of the Protestant Guizot welcoming the ultramontanist Montalembert into the Académie in 1852: "the strenuous protestant (I heard him say proudly in a speech 'Protestant comme mes pères) – he was a vehement opposer of any attempt on the part of the Italians to get rid of the Pope's rule." Browning ended this rather tetchy commentary by saying "The publication of such letters is repugnant to me."[65] Still, when the first volume of George Sand's *Correspondance* (1881) came out the following year, Browning read her intimate revelations of domestic life with apparent pleasure: "Thank you very much for George Sand's very characteristic letters," he wrote to Mrs. FitzGerald, "the sudden change from 'Casimir who is incapable of falsehood' to Casimir the brute &c. &c. is very significant: and I suspect all signs of 'motherliness' in George Sand. Maurice I remember as a 'pas grande chose' – Solange as a handsome well-behaved woman. George herself was exactly as I had long expected she would be."[66]

Beginning in the summer of 1880, Browning spent a month of each of the next three years in the vicinity of Grande Chartreuse. On their first journey to this region, he and Sarianna stopped first in Paris to visit Milsand and Gustave Dourlans. They went on to Grenoble, visited Grande Chartreuse, and, after failing to find suitable accommodation at Villard-de-Lans, settled in the tiny hamlet of Lans. As so often at other French coastal or mountain villages, Browning was immediately delighted with "this little rural quiet unspoiled Lans. . . ." At the tiny inn, rather grandiloquently named Hôtel Colomb, he found "the simplest possible lodging – of perfect cleanliness and *sufficient* comfort – with a capital *cuisine bourgeoise* . . . and the kindest simplest people we ever met. . . ." The scenery surrounding the village was so various that on each day's walk Browning discovered something novel in "the fine air, the beautiful country, the grand mountains which frame in a wonderful vale or plain of pasturage and cornfields. . . ."[67] The beauty, simplicity and kindness of Lans was something of a contrast to what he had found at Grande Chartreuse. When Mrs. FitzGerald wrote asking for his impressions of the monastery, Browning referred her to the "Guide to Grenoble," but warned her against the "high-flown paragraphs." His own expectations about what one might find at the famed home of the Carthusian monks were not, as he said, "gratified." Assuredly, he did not find at Grande Chartreuse anything resembling the simple, severe piety of ancient Christian faith Matthew Arnold celebrated in his nostalgic and elegiac "Stanzas from the Grande Chartreuse." Browning's account of his visit there seems not only an attempt to correct misleading guidebooks but to refute the sentiments found in Arnold's poem.

He begins his account of his tour of Grande Chartreuse by informing Mrs. FitzGerald that his sister had to dine alone in a separate building and was not allowed to tour the main building. Although he found the food, wine and especially the liqueur quite excellent, the dining itself struck him as rowdy and commercial:

> The acceptance of the Hospitality of the Convent means that you dine there at your own expence (very moderate indeed, but still exacted:) and the consequence is anything but a *conventual* behaviour on the part of the multifarious guests, who make merry as at an eating house, in a mean-looking room: the lower classes, still more uproarious, getting their meal in a downright pot-house style. The fare, – all *meagre*, though you would hardly guess it, – is excellent, and the wine capital: the convent's single dole to a visitor, on his entry, is the traditional bumper of "Liqueur": after dinner, there is an extra charge for another, if you incline to take it.

When finally "Reflection ended," the too-numerous crowd of tourists was conducted on a quick tour of the building. The crowd pushed here and there while a lay assistant explained to those who could make their way to the front of the crowd "what this corridor is called, when that wing was built, and so forth." Browning apparently pushed close enough to the front of the tour to inspect rather closely a monk's cell:

> a clean chamber of the size of this in which I write, with a compartment wherein is a bed – the covering for which is deposited on

a shelf above it: a little oratory is continuous to the cell, with a prie-dieu, crucifix and religious prints. Each monk has a little bit of garden, – not much cultivated, but with a flower or two. There is an under-cell, furnished with turning-lathe, and other implements of manual labour – "for they all *work*," said our Guide.

The simplicity of the cell and the surprisingly large library of books, manuscripts and maps were attractive to Browning. He thought his father would have enjoyed the simple, scholarly routine; and he himself might, "in one *mood* possible," desire such a life. Even the burial-ground was impressive to him, although it roused his distaste for hierarchy: it was an oblong divided by a path, he noted, "on your left as you enter – the *Fathers* – distinguished by a cross of stone, with (I think) the name: on your right, the simple graves of the Brothers marked merely by a wooden cross." Browning was shown the chapel in which was celebrated the ritual Arnold had described with rather envious solemnity. Browning dismisses it as a "spectacle as monks prostrate themselves at the midnight mass." To witness this spectacle, he would have had to stay at the monastery two days, but he "had not the least mind to do so." Arnold had sought at Chartreuse the vestiges of simple piety and unquestioning Christian faith; having discovered such a survival, he lamented that as a nineteenth-century Englishman he could not share that faith. Browning, too, toyed with the change history had wrought upon such simple faith: "Had I arrived alone, three centuries ago, – been gratified by a crust & water, and shown the mysteries by an intelligent recluse, – well, who knows whether a wish for that vegetative life might not have arisen?" But Browning acknowledged quite cheerfully that he was a tourist, not a religious seeker. He had, he said, no more vocation to turn Carthusian monk "than a holiday explorer of the Tower has to turn Beef-Eater." If the excursion to the monastery had not altered his religious bias, it had at least dispelled his prejudice against the Carthusians' famed liqueur: "I shall not refuse so constantly as has been my wont," he told Mrs. FitzGerald, "a *petit-verre* of Chartreuse after coffee!"[68]

Browning's epistolary account of his tour of Grande Chartreuse is a witty, allusive, high-spirited description of the famed and much-visited French monastery. The carefully observed realistic detail builds a vignette of contemporary life quite in contrast to his rendering into poetry of the story of Queen Cristina's execution of Monaldeschi at the Palace at Fontainebleau in 1657. Browning was, perhaps, reminded of this tale as he passed through Fontainebleau on his way to St. Pierre de Chartreuse in the summer of either 1881 or 1882. He returned to the little village below the monastery for both of those years. It was probably there that he wrote "Cristina and Monaldeschi," a poem nearly devoid of a sense of time and place as Browning focused more upon the careful cunning of Cristina as she leads Monaldeschi to his place of execution.[69] In his letters, however, Browning did portray vividly the life he found around him. In 1881 he spent five weeks at St. Pierre de Chartreuse, then travelled towards Italy via Chambéry with an excursion to revisit Rousseau's Les Charmettes. His departure from St. Pierre had been interrupted by a curious incident. He and Sarianna had taken daily walks to a nearby summit where they could look "down upon the minute hamlet of St. Pierre d'Entremont," a "paradisiac place," more delightful and secluded than their own village. About a week before their departure, Browning wrote to Mrs. FitzGerald, while he and Sarianna "were looking at the utter solitude, I had the fancy 'What should I do if I suddenly came upon a dead body in this field? Go and proclaim it – and subject myself to all the vexations inflicted by the French way of procedure (which begins by assuming that *you* may be the criminal) – or neglect an obvious duty, and return silently?'" He did not have to choose his course of action in this imagined ethical dilemma. However, either on the very day or the day after he had imagined such a dilemma, a body was found in "this Paradisiac place." It was, he wrote, the body of

a murdered man – frightfully mutilated – who had been caught apparently in the act of stealing potatoes in a field: such a crime had never occurred within the memory of the oldest of our folk. Who was the murderer is the mystery: whether the field's owner – in his irritation at discovering the robber, – or one of a band of similar *charbonniers* (for they suppose the man to be a Piedmontese of that occupation) remains to be proved: they began by imprisoning the owner, who denies his guilt energetically.

The Brownings' departure from St. Pierre de Chartreuse was delayed several hours because the "Juge d'Instruction" from Grenoble investigating the murder had requisitioned the only mule available to carry luggage down to Grenoble.[70] When Browning returned to St. Pierre the following summer (1882), the oddity of the coincidence remained with him. He repeated to Mrs. FitzGerald his strange fancy of coming suddenly upon a corpse in a solitary field "of great beauty and peacefulness." Clearly the juxtaposition of a hidden mutilated corpse with an apparent paradise interested Browning. So, too, did the risk to the discoverer of the body: a risk of either being suspected himself or of casting suspicion upon someone who might be innocent. During his walks about the countryside in the summer of 1882, he made enquiries about the case:

> They said the accused man, a simple person, had been locked up in a high chamber, – protesting his innocence strongly, – and, troubled in his mind by the affair altogether and the turn it was taking, had profited by the gens d'armes negligence, and thrown himself out of the window – and so died, continuing to the last to protest as before. My presentiment of what such a person might have to undergo was justified, you see: tho' I should not have in any case taken *that* way of getting out of a difficulty. The man added "It was not he who committed the murder, but the companions of the man, an Italian charcoal-burner, who owed him a grudge, killed him, and dragged him to the field, – filling his sack with potatoes as if stolen, to give a likelihood that the field's owner had caught him stealing and killed him, – so M. Perrier, the greffier told me."

"Enough of this grim story," Browning writes before turning to news of recent Browning Society activities and quoting a bit of "grotesque rhyme." To close his letter to Mrs. FitzGerald, however, he returns to the experience which had so intrigued him. Sarianna had been "anxious to know exactly where the body was found." Browning enquired and was told: " *'Vous savez la croix au sommet de la colline? A cette distance de cela!'* (You know the cross at the summit of the hill? At this [short] distance from that!) That is precisely where I was standing when the thought came over me."[71]

This tale of violent murder, vengeance, and suicide set amid the illusory idyllic peace of the mountain meadows surrounding Grande Chartreuse might a decade earlier have become the germ of a poem like that in which Browning investigated and analysed the death of Antoine Mellerio near St. Aubin. The poet's own "presentiment" of discovering a corpse, his ambivalence towards the duty of reporting the corpse and becoming entangled in the reasonable but ultimately unjust mode of French criminal investigation, the suicidal leap of the innocent landowner, the eventual unravelling of the mystery and the poet's local enquiries about the curious case, all these elements might have provided Browning with a "capital brand-new subject" such as he had rendered in *Red Cotton Night-Cap Country*. But it did not. He was seventy years old in the summer of 1882. In his poetry, beginning with the first series of *Dramatic Idyls* in 1879, Browning more and more was turning to simpler narratives, anecdotes, legends, moral tales drawn from English, Greek, Italian, Russian, Hebrew, or Persian folklore, myth and history. The crowded and often ambiguous contemporary world that he observed on his travels or read about in the newspapers continued to interest him, but it did not enter his poetry. This two-month holiday at St. Pierre de Chartreuse in 1882 was his last extended stay in France. The following year he travelled quickly by rail across France; and then, by diligence, muleback and foot, he made his way to the little Italian village of Gressoney St. Jean below the Monte Rosa glacier, where he waited several weeks for cooler weather before going on to Venice. In the six years remaining to him he sought similar retreats at St. Moritz and Primiero in the Tyrol.

Browning's long intimacy with France was over. In his surviving letters we catch glimpses of him sporadically interested in things French: he quibbles over the rendering into French of certain lines from *Hervé Riel*; he quotes from an early Stendhal novel a phrase that seems apposite to him or cites a French source to defend his son's nude painting of Jeanne d'Arc. A M. Thurat remembered that Browning had taken the time while in Paris to entertain Auguste Rodin at dinner "in a restaurant in the Place de Rennes"; later, Rodin was unable to remember the occasion.[72] The stiffly polite notes exchanged between Browning and Rodin in January of 1883 suggest that the only shared interest between sculptor and poet was the poet's son's progress in his artistic studies. A few months before his death in 1889, Browning accepted the French ambassador's invitation to lunch with Hippolyte Taine at the Bristol Hotel; if they met, perhaps Taine cheered Browning by repeating what he had told George Sand years ago when he sent her a copy of *Aurora Leigh*: "I hope *Aurora Leigh* pleases you. . . . I love it too much; like Flaubert who regretted not having seen Balzac, I have a sense of loss in my life: not having listened to and looked upon for an hour Elizabeth Browning."[73] Browning, however, left no record of a meeting with Taine. He did record two months later a French dialogue between himself and the Shah of Persia: "Vous êtes poète?" asked the Shah of the author whose thirtieth volume had been a collection of versified Persian moral anecdotes. Browning replied:

> "On s'est permis de me le dire quelquefois."
> "Et vous avez fait des livres?"
> "Trop de livres."
> "Voulez-vous m'en donner un, afin que je puisse me ressouvenir de vous?"
> "Avec plaisir."[74]

If Browning's interest in France had waned during his last few years, his facility with her language had not. Since adolescence that language had served him well and had given him access to a culture that had enriched many of those volumes of which the Shah enquired.

Notes

1 An Early Acquaintance with Things French

1 *Elizabeth Barrett Browning: Hitherto Unpublished Poems and Stories with an Inedited Autobiography* (Boston: Bibliophile Society, 1914), I, 165.

2 *Ibid.*, I, 165–73.

3 Quoted by Gardner B. Taplin, *The Life of Elizabeth Barrett Browning* (New Haven: Yale University Press, 1957), p. 16 (Friday, March, 1844).

4 *Elizabeth Barrett to Mr. Boyd: Unpublished Letters of Elizabeth Barrett Barrett to Hugh Stuart Boyd*, ed. Barbara P. McCarthy (New Haven: Yale University Press, 1955), p. 174 (May 26, 1832).

5 Elizabeth Barrett Browning, *Complete Works*, eds Charlotte Porter and Helen A. Clarke (New York: George D. Sproul, 1901), I, 151–52.

6 *Diary by E.B.B.: The Unpublished Diary of Elizabeth Barrett Browning, 1831–1832*, eds Philip Kelley and Ronald Hudson (Athens: Ohio University Press, 1969), p. 202 (January 6, 1832).

7 *Hitherto Unpublished Poems*, I, 110–23.

8 In Hewlett Collection and generously described in Dorothy Hewlett, *Elizabeth Barrett Browning* (New York: Knopf, 1952), pp. 35–36.

9 *EB to Mr. Boyd*, pp. 14, 13 (December 1, 1827); p. 22 (March 3, 1828).

10 *Complete Works*, I, 261.

11 *Ibid.*, I, p. 71, lines 369–71.

12 Bennett Weaver, "Twenty Unpublished Letters of Elizabeth Barrett Browning to Hugh Stuart Boyd," *PMLA*, 65 (1950), 400 (August 8, 1829?).

13 *Letters of Elizabeth Barrett Browning Addressed to Richard Hengist Horne*, ed. S. R. T. Mayer (London: Richard Bentley and Son, 1877), I, 244, 248 (February 20, 1844).

14 *The Letters of Elizabeth Barrett Browning*, ed. Frederic G. Kenyon (New York: Macmillan, 1897), II, 100 (to Miss Mitford, February [1853]).

15 *Ibid.*, II, 100.

16 *EB to Mr. Boyd*, p. 176 (June 9, 1832).

17 *Ibid.*, p. 176.

18. *Diary by EBB*, p. 54 (July 11, 1831).

19 *Ibid.*, pp. 220–21 (March 3, 1832).
20 *Ibid.*, p. 136 (September 21, 1831).
21 *Ibid.*, p. 138 (September 24, 1831).
22 *EB to Mr. Boyd*, p. 104 (August 2 [1830]).
23 *Ibid.*, p. 104.
24 *Ibid.*, p. 176 (June 9, 1832).
25 John Maynard, *Browning's Youth* (Cambridge: Harvard University Press, 1977), p. 256.
26 *Ibid.*, pp. 86, 255.
27 Griffin's "surmise" that the *Biographie* was in the library of Browning's home comes on p. 25 of *The Life of Robert Browning* (London: Methuen & Co., 1911, rev. edn 1938). In his biographical sketch in *A Browning Handbook* (New Haven: Yale University Press, 1935, rev. edn 1955) DeVane accepts Griffin; then, in discussions of the sources for *Paracelsus* (p. 53), for *King Victor and King Charles* (p. 99), and for *The Return of the Druses* (p. 133), DeVane transforms the original "surmise" into actuality. William Irvine and Park Honan in *The Book, the Ring, and the Poet* (New York: McGraw-Hill, 1974), p. 7, make no direct claim that the *Biographie* was in the Browning library, although they list it while describing the library, as does Maynard, p. 86. Roma A. King, Jr., in his annotations to *Sordello* in *The Complete Works of Robert Browning* (Athens: Ohio University Press, 1970), II, 361 ff., politely but firmly demonstrates that "there is no concrete evidence" that the *Biographie* was in the Browning library.
28 Maynard, p. 121.
29 Morse Peckham, "Browning and Romanticism" in *Robert Browning*, ed. Isobel Armstrong (Athens: Ohio University Press, 1975), p. 49.
30 Henri-Léon Hovelaque, *La Jeunesse de Robert Browning* (Paris: Les Presses Modernes, 1932), p. 126.
31 *Ibid.*, p. 127.
32 *Amiel's Jounal: The Journal Intime of Henri-Frédéric Amiel*, trans. Mrs. Humphrey Ward (London: Macmillan, 1885, 1922), pp. 8–9.
33 Peckham, p. 71.
34 Maynard, p. 219.
35 Hovelaque, p. 125.
36 Honoré de Balzac, *La Peau de chagrin*, "Préface de la première édition" (1831); reprinted in *La Comédie Humaine*, ed. Marcel Bouteron (Paris: Gallimard, Pléiade, 1949–65), XI, 169–77.
37 Trans. from *The Works of Honoré de Balzac*, introduction by George Saintsbury (London and New York: Harper and Brothers, n.d.), I, 261–62.
38 *Elizabeth Barrett to Miss Mitford: The Unpublished Letters of Elizabeth Barrett to Mary Russell Mitford* (London: John Murray, 1954), p. 47 (April, 1839).

39 *Letters*, ed. Kenyon, I, 234 (to Mr. Chorley, 1845).

40 *EB to Miss Mitford*, p. 148 (November 27, 1842).

41 EBB's use of the term "La Jeune France" follows that of Mrs. Trollope in her *La Jeune France* (London, 1835), and hence refers not only to young men around Gautier but also to Hugo, Balzac, Dumas, Lamartine, and other contemporaries.

42 *Letters*, ed. Kenyon, I, 206 (to Mrs. Martin, October 15, 1844).

43 *Ibid.*, I, 253 (to Mrs. Martin, April 3, 1845); *EB to Miss Mitford*, p. 208 (December 7, 1843) and pp. 263, 237.

44 *Letters*, ed. Kenyon, I, 59 (to Kenyon [1838?]).

45 *EB to Miss Mitford*, pp. 224–25 (September 28, 1844).

46 *Ibid.*, p. 205 (November, 1843); EBB's ellipses.

47 *Letters*, ed. Kenyon, I, 234 (to Mr. Chorley [1845]).

48 *Ibid.*, I, 234 (to Mr. Chorley [1845]).

49 *EB to Miss Mitford*, p. 144 (November 21, 1842).

50 *Letters to Horne*, I, 243.

51 *EB to Miss Mitford*, p. 155 (December 17, 1842) and p. 233 (January 15, 1845).

52 *Ibid.*, pp. 147–8 (November 27, 1842).

53 *Letters of Robert Browning Collected by Thomas J. Wise*, ed. Thurman L. Hood (New Haven: Yale University Press, 1933), p. 5 (to Macready [*ca.* 1840]).

54 *EB to Miss Mitford*, p. 145 (November 21, 1842).

55 *Ibid.*, p. 144.

56 *Letters to Horne*, I, 243.

57 *EB to Miss Mitford*, p. 147 (November 27, 1842); *Letters*, ed. Kenyon, I, 124 (to James Martin, February 6, 1843).

58 *EB to Miss Mitford*, p. 147 (November 27, 1842).

59 *Ibid.*, p. 157 (December 21, 1842).

60 *Ibid.*, p. 229 (December 30, 1844).

61 *Ibid.*, p. 146 (November 27, 1842).

62 *Letters*, ed. Kenyon, I, 232–33 (to Mr. Chorley, January 7, 1845).

63 Howard Foster Lowry, *The Letters of Matthew Arnold to Arthur Hugh Clough* (New York: Oxford University Press, 1932), p. 20. See Paul G. Blount, *George Sand and the Victorian World* (Athens: University of Georgia Press, 1979) for a quite full and intelligent description of Sand's English admirers and critics.

64 Quoted by Curtis Cate, *George Sand: A Biography* (Boston: Houghton, Mifflin, 1975), p. x.

65 *Correspondance*, ed. Georges Lubin (Paris: Garnier, 1969), VI, 745–46 (December 30, 1844).

66 *EB to Miss Mitford*, p. 227 (October 1, 1844); see also the excellent commentary by Patricia Thomson in *George Sand and the Victorians* (London: Macmillan, 1977), pp. 43–60.

67 *Ibid.*, p. 212 (January 11, 1844).

68 *Ibid.*, p. 147 (November 27, 1842).

69 *Ibid.*, p. 147.
70 *Ibid.*, p. 156 (December 21, 1842).
71 Cate, p. 201.
72 *EB to Miss Mitford*, p. 156 (December 21, 1842).
73 *Ibid.*, p. 157.
74 *Oeuvres autobiographiques*, ed. Georges Lubin (Paris: Gallimard, Pléiade, 1971) II, 173–74, 1342–43. See also André Maurois, *Lélia: The Life of George Sand*, trans. Gerard Hopkins (New York: Harper and Brothers, 1954), p. 9.
75 *EB to Miss Mitford*, p. 228 (October 1, 1844).
76 *Ibid.*, p. 155 (December 17, 1842).
77 *Ibid.*, p. 158.
78 *Ibid.*, p. 217 (May 20, 1844).
79 *Ibid.*, p. 237 (March 2, 1845).
80 *Ibid.*, p. 241 (April, 1845).

2 *A Mutual Admiration for* La Jeune France

1 Maynard, p. 446, note 32.
2 *The Letters of Robert Browning and Elizabeth Barrett Barrett, 1845–1846*, ed. Elvan Kintner (Cambridge: Harvard University Press, 1969), II, 658 (April 27, 1846).
3 Lionel Stevenson, "A French Text-book by Browning," *Modern Language Notes*, 42 (May, 1927), 299–305.
4 Maynard, p. 124.
5 *RB and EBB*, II, 658 (April 27, 1846).
6 Maynard, p. 124.
7 *New Letters of Robert Browning*, ed. William C. DeVane and Kenneth L. Knickerbocker (London: John Murray, 1951), p. 16 (to Miss Haworth [April, 1839]).
8 *RB and EBB*, II, 658 (April 27, 1846).
9 *Ibid.*, II, 663 (April 28, 1846).
10 Maynard, p. 304.
11 E. J. Oliver, *Honoré de Balzac* (London: Macmillan, 1964), p. 117.
12 [John Forster], "Evidence of a New Genius for Dramatic Poetry," *The New Monthly Magazine and Literary Journal*, 47 (March 1836), 289–308; reproduced in *Browning: The Critical Heritage* eds Boyd Litzinger and Donald Smalley (London and New York: Routledge & Kegan Paul, 1970), p. 47.
13 Trans. from *The Works of Honoré de Balzac*, intoduction by George Saintsbury, XVII, 1.
14 Philarète Chasles, "De l'art dramatique et du théâtre actuel en Angleterre," *Revue des Deux Mondes*, 23 (April, 1840), 127, 133, 128.
15 *EB to Miss Mitford*, p. 240 (April, 1845).
16 *Letters*, ed. Kenyon, I, 319 (February 8, 1847).
17 *Vie de Henri Brulard*, ed. Henri Martineau (Paris: Garnier, 1961), p. 205.

18 *Journal of "The Counterfeiters,"* trans. Justin O'Brien (New York: Knopf, 1951), p. 382.

19 *Letters*, ed. Kenyon, I, 442 (to Mrs. Jameson, April 2 [1850]).

20 *The Gates of Horn: A Study of Five French Realists* (New York: Oxford University Press, 1966), p. 105.

21 *Le Rouge et le noir*, ed. Pierre-Georges Castex (Paris: Garnier, 1973), pp. 172, 339, 228.

22 "Liking Julien Sorel" in *Red and Black*, trans. and ed. Robert M. Adams (New York: Norton, 1969), p. 549.

23 See Paul Hooreman, "Promenades romaines: la rencontre inopinée de Stendhal et de Robert Browning," *Stendhal Club*, 6 (1964), 185–200. Hooreman gives March 28, 1833, for Stendhal's letter to Domenico Fiore describing the documents; in *Stendhal: Correspondance*, eds Henri Martineau and V. de Litto (Paris: Pléiade, 1968), III, 18–21, the letter is dated March 18, 1835.

24 Oscar Maurer, "Bishop Blougram's French Book," *Victorian Poetry*, 6 (Summer 1968), 177–79.

25 *Dearest Isa: Robert Browning's Letters to Isabella Blagden*, ed. Edward C. McAleer (Austin: University of Texas Press, 1951), p. 76 (May 13, 1861).

26 *Learned Lady: Letters from Robert Browning to Mrs. Thomas FitzGerald, 1876–1879*, ed. Edward C. McAleer (Cambridge: Harvard University Press, 1966), p. 187 (November 5, 1885).

27 *RB and EBB*, I, 248 (October 24, 1845); 145 (August 8, 1845); 164 (August 20, 1845).

28 *Ibid.*, II, 887 (July 19, 1846).

29 *Ibid.*, I, 396 (January 17, 1846).

30 *Ibid.*, I, 248 (October 24, 1845).

31 *Ibid.*, II, 818 (June 26, 1846).

32 *Ibid.*, II, 853 (July 6, 1846).

33 *Ibid.*, I, 325, 326 (December 18, 1845); 337 (December 21, 1845).

34 *Ibid.*, II, 653, 654 (April 26, 1846).

35 *Ibid.*, II, 763 (June 7, 1846).

36 *Ibid.*, II, 642 (April 21, 1846).

37 *Ibid.*, I, 254 (October 31, 1845).

38 *Ibid.*, I, 250 (October 27, 1845).

39 *Ibid.*, I, 566 (March 27, 1846).

40 *Ibid.*, II, 588 (April 4, 1846).

41 *Ibid.*, II, 590 (April 5, 1846).

42 *Ibid.*, I, 537 (March 15, 1846).

43 *Ibid.*, I, 96 (June 16, 1845).

44 *Ibid.*, I, 113–14 (July 2–3, 1845).

45 *Ibid.*, I, 110 (July 1, 1845).

46 *Ibid.*, I, 150 (August 10, 1845).

47 *Ibid.*, I, 157–58 (August 15, 1845).

48 *Ibid.*, I, 159–60 (August 16, 1845).

49 *Ibid.*, II, 657 (April 27, 1846).

50 *Ibid.*, II, 774n. (June 12, 1846).
51 *Ibid.*, II, 893 (July 22, 1846).
52 *Ibid.*, I, 194 (September 13, 1845).
53 *EB to Mr. Boyd*, p. 238 (July 8, 1840).
54 *Ibid.*, p. 238.
55 *Letters*, ed. Kenyon, I, 233 (to Mr. Chorley, January 7, 1845).
56 *RB and EBB*, I, 24 (February 17, 1845); 296 (November 28, 1845).
57 *Ibid.*, I, 230 (October 12, 1845).
58 *Ibid.*, I, 404 (January 19, 1846).
59 *Letters to Horne*, II, 26–27; *RB to EBB*, I, 447 (February 10, 1846).
60 *Ibid.*, I, 130.
61 Ibid., II, 28.
62 *RB and EBB*, II, 861 (July 9, 1846); 859 (July 8, 1846).
63 *Letters*, ed. Kenyon, I, 177 (to Mr. Boyd, August 1, 1844).
64 *Ibid.*, I, 204 (to Kenyon, October 8, 1844).
65 *RB and EBB*, I, 31 (February 27, 1845).
66 William C. DeVane, *A Browning Handbook* (New York: Appleton-Century-Crofts, 1955), pp. 134–35.
67 Browning's interest in Rabelais seems to date from about 1844. It was an interest he shared with his friend Joseph Arnould (see *Robert Browning and Alfred Domett*, ed. F. G. Kenyon (London: Smith, Elder & Co., 1906), p. 110 (February 23, 1845).
68 DeVane, *Handbook*, pp. 181 ff.
69 *RB and EBB*, I, 252 (October 29, 1845).

3 Watching France from Italy, 1846–51

1 *RB and EBB*, II, 917 (July 30, 1846).
2 *Letters*, ed. Kenyon, I, 59 (to Kenyon [1839]).
3 *RB and EBB*, II, 1008 (August 26, 1846).
4 *Ibid.*, II, 1015 (August 28, 1846).
5 *Ibid.*, II, 1024 (August 30, 1846).
6 Quoted by Taplin, p. 181.
7 George K. Boyce, "From Paris to Pisa with the Brownings," *New Colophon*, 3 (1950), 112 (Anna Jameson to Lady Byron, September 22–23 [1846]).
8 Quoted in Irvine and Honan, p. 217.
9 *Letters*, ed. Kenyon, I, 299 (to Miss Mitford, November 5 [1846]).
10 *Ibid.*, II, 108 (to Mrs. Jameson, March 17 [1853]).
11 *Aurora Leigh*, Book VI, 11, 81 ff.
12 *New Colophon*, 115 (September 28 [1846]).
13 *Twenty-two Unpublished Letters of Elizabeth Barrett Browning and Robert Browning Addressed to Henrietta and Arabella Moulton-Barrett* (New York: The United Feature Syndicate, 1935), p. 7 (October 2, 1846).

14 *Ibid.*, p. 10.
15 Charles Dickens, "Pictures from Italy," *The Works of Charles Dickens*, Gadshill Edition (London: Chapman and Hall, 1898), XXVIII, p. 316.
16 *New Colophon*, 116 (October 7 [1846]).
17 *Murray's Handbook: France* (London, 1854), p. 339.
18 Quoted by Taplin, p. 184.
19 *Twenty-two Letters*, p. 10 (October 2, 1846).
20 Murray, p. 411.
21 *Ibid.*, p. 370.
22 Dickens, pp. 322, 321.
23 Murray, p. 370.
24 Dickens, pp. 321–22.
25 Murray, p. 425.
26 *Ibid.*, p. 433.
27 Dickens, p. 324.
28 Quoted in Taplin, p. 185.
29 Murray, p. 437.
30 *Anna Jameson, Letters and Friendships*, ed. Mrs. Stewart Erskine (London: T. Fisher Unwin, 1915), p. 234.
31 Dickens, p. 327.
32 *New Colophon*, 116 (October 7 [1846]).
33 Murray, p. 443.
34 *New Colophon*, 117 (October 7 [1846]).
35 Taplin, p. 185.
36 Frances Winwar, *Immortal Lovers* (New York: Harper and Brothers, 1950), p. 191.
37 Virginia Woolf, *Flush: A Biography* (New York: Harcourt, Brace and Co., 1933), p. 118.
38 *New Colophon*, 117 (October 7 [1846]).
39 Dickens, p. 335.
40 Murray, p. 466.
41 Ronald Hudson, "Elizabeth Barrett Browning and Her Brother Alfred: Some Unpublished Letters," *Browning Institute Studies*, 2 (1974), 143.
42 *Letters*, ed. Kenyon, I, 324 (to Mr. Westwood, March 10, 1847).
43 *Ibid.*, I, 369 (to Miss Browning [June 1848]).
44 Barbara Melchiori, "Browning in Italy," in *Robert Browning*, ed. Armstrong, p. 171.
45 *Letters*, ed. Kenyon, I, 387 (to Miss Mitford, October 10, 1848); *Elizabeth Barrett Browning: Letters to her Sister, 1846–1859*, ed. Leonard Huxley (London: John Murray, 1929), pp. 117–18 (February 20, 1850).
46 *Letters*, ed. Kenyon, I, 302–3 (to Mrs. Martin, November 5, 1846).
47 Taplin, pp. 192–3.

48 G. M. Carsaniga, "Realism in Italy" in *The Age of Realism*, ed. F. W. J. Hemmings (London: Penguin Books, 1974), p. 329.
49 *Letters*, ed. Huxley, p. 5 (November 24, 1846).
50 *Letters*, ed. Kenyon, I, 309 (to Mrs. Jameson, November 23, 1846).
51 *Ibid.*, I, 309–10.
52 *Ibid.*, I, 313 (to Miss Mitford, December 19, 1846).
53 Taplin, p. 193.
54 *Letters*, ed. Kenyon, I, 312 (to Miss Mitford, December 19 [1846]).
55 *Ibid.*, I, 318 (to Miss Mitford, February 8, 1847).
56 *Ibid.*, I, 375 (to Miss Mitford, July 4 [1848]).
57 *Ibid.*, I, 377–78 (to Mrs. Jameson, July 15 [1848]).
58 *Ibid.*, I, 442 (to Mrs. Jameson, April 2 [1850]).
59 *Ibid.*, I, 318–19 (to Miss Mitford, February 8 [1847]).
60 *New Letters*, p. 16 (to Miss Haworth [April, 1839]).
61 *Dearest Isa*, p. 178 (November 19, 1863).
62 *Letters*, ed. Kenyon, I, 375 (to Miss Mitford, July 4 [1848]).
63 Henry James, *Notes on Novelists* (New York: Scribner's, 1914), p. 112
64 *Letters*, ed. Kenyon, I, 401 (to Miss Mitford, April 30 [1849]).
65 *Ibid.*, I, 420 (to Miss Mitford, August 31 [1849]).
66 *Ibid.*, I, 324 (to Mr. Westwood, March 10 [1847]).
67 *Ibid.*, I, 329 (to Mrs Jameson, May 12 [1847]).
68 *Ibid.*, I, 428 (to Miss Mitford, December 1 [1849]).
69 *Ibid.*, I, 357 (to Miss Mitford, February 22 [1848]).
70 *Ibid.*, I, 457 (to Miss Blagden, September [1850]).
71 *Ibid.*, I, 413 (to Miss Mitford [July, 1849]); 420 (to Miss Mitford, August 31 [1849]).
72 *Ibid.*, I, 363 (to Kenyon, May 1 [1848]).
73 George Sand, *Mauprat* (Paris: Michel Lévy Frères, 1899), chapter X, p. 141.
74 *Browning: The Critical Heritage*, eds Litzinger and Smalley, p. 12.
75 *Letters*, ed. Kenyon, I, 419 (to Miss Mitford, August 31 [1849]).
76 *Ibid.*, I, 462 (to Miss Mitford, September 24 [1850]).
77 *Ibid.*, I, 425 (to Miss Mitford, October 2 [1849]).
78 *Ibid.*, I, 466 (to Miss Mitford, November 13 [1850]).
79 *Ibid.*, I, 452 (to Miss Mitford, June 15 [1850]).
80 *Letters*, ed. Huxley, p. 44 (September 13, 1847).
81 *Letters*, ed. Kenyon, I, 350 (to Miss Mitford, December 8 [1847]).
82 *Ibid.*, I, 386 (to Miss Mitford, October 10 [1848]).
83 *Ibid.*, I, 406 (to Mrs. Martin, May 14 [1849]).
84 *Ibid.*, I, 405.
85 *Ibid.*, I, 424 (to Miss Mitford, October 2 [1849]).
86 *Ibid.*, I, 442 (to Mrs. Jameson, April 2 [1850]).
87 *Letters*, ed. Huxley, p. 83 (April 22, 1848).

88 *Ibid.*, p. 81 (March 7 – April 1, 1848).
89 *Letters*, ed. Kenyon, I, 359 (to Miss Mitford, April 15 [1848]).
90 Pierre-Joseph Proudhon, *Sa Vie et sa correspondance* (Paris: Librairie Internationale, 1866), II, 284 (February 25, 1848). Trans. in *Selected Writings of Pierre-Joseph Proudhon*, ed. Stewart Edwards (London: Macmillan, 1969), p. 154.
91 Alexis de Tocqueville, *Oeuvres complètes: Souvenirs*, ed. Luc Monnier (Paris: Gallimard, 1964), XII, 75.
92 *Letters*, ed. Kenyon, I, 425 (to Miss Mitford, October 2 [1849]).
93 *Ibid.*, I, 361 (to Miss Mitford, April 15 [1848]).
94 George Sand, "Revue politique de la Semaine," *La Vraie République* (May 7, 1848); trans. in Maurois, *Léila*, p. 338.
95 *Letters*, ed. Huxley, p. 83 (April 22, 1848).
96 Percy Lubbock, *Elizabeth Barrett Browning in Her Letters* (London: Smith, Elder and Co., 1906), p. 243.
97 *Letters*, ed. Kenyon, I, 362–63 (to Kenyon, May 1 [1848]).
98 Printed in Th. Bentzon (Mdme. Blanc), "A French Friend of Browning – Joseph Milsand," *Scribner's Magazine*, 20 (July 1896), 110.
99 Pierre-Joseph Proudhon, *Confessions d'un révolutionnaire* (Paris: *La Voix du peuple*, 1849), p. 81. Trans. in *Selected Writings*, ed. Edwards, p. 156.
100 Quoted in Vladimir Karénine, *George Sand: Sa Vie et ses oeuvres* (Paris: Plon, 1926), IV, 481–84.
101 *Letters*, ed. Kenyon, I, 368 (to Miss Mitford, May 28, 1848).
102 *Ibid.*, I, 467 (to Miss Blagden [1850]).
103 George Sand, *Correspondance*, ed. Lubin (1963–64), VIII, 469–78. Trans. in Cate, pp. 602–3.
104 *Letters*, ed. Kenyon, I, 374–75 (to Miss Mitford, July 4 [1848]).
105 *Ibid.*, I, 386–87 (to Miss Mitford, October 10 [1848]).
106 *Ibid.*, I, 389–90 (to Mrs. Martin, December 3 [1848]).
107 *Ibid.*, I, 400 (to Miss Mitford, April 30 [1849]).
108 *Ibid.*, I, 406 (to Mrs. Martin, May 14 [1849]).
109 *Ibid.*, I, 419–20 (to Miss Mitford, August 31 [1849]).
110 *Ibid.*, I, 425–26 (to Miss Mitford, October 2 [1849]).
111 *Ibid.*, I, 428–9 (to Miss Mitford, December 1 [1849]).
112 *Ibid.*, I, 452 (to Miss Mitford, June 15 [1850]).

4 Paris and Politics, 1851–52

1 *Letters*, ed. Kenyon, I, 361 (to Miss Mitford, April 15 [1848]).
2 *Letters*, ed. Huxley, pp. 105–6 (May 2, 3, 4, 5, 1849).
3 *Ibid.*, pp. 117–18 (February 20, 1850).
4 *Ibid.*, p. 118.

5 *Ibid.*, pp. 121–22 (May 25, 1850).

6 *Ibid.*, p. 125 (July 7, 1850).

7 *Letters*, ed. Kenyon, II, 7 (to Miss Mitford, June 4 [1851]).

8 *Ibid.*, II, 10–11 (to Kenyon, July 7 [1851]).

9 *Elizabeth Barrett Browning's Letters to Mrs. David Ogilvy*, eds Peter N. Heydon and Philip Kelley (New York: The New York Times Book Co. and The Browning Institute, 1973), p. 42 (July 2 [1851]).

10 *Letters*, ed. Kenyon, II, 13 (to Kenyon, July 7 [1851]).

11 *Letters to Ogilvy*, p. 45 ([July 25 – August 1, 1851]).

12 *Ibid.*, p. 46.

13 Quoted in Maisie Ward, *Robert Browning and His World: The Private Face* (New York: Holt, Rinehart, and Winston, 1967), p. 191.

14 *Letters*, ed. Kenyon, II, 6 (to Miss Mitford, June 4 [1851]).

15 *Letters to Ogilvy*, p. 46.

16 *Letters*, ed. Kenyon, II, 17 (to Mrs. Martin [August, 1851]).

17 *Last Words of Thomas Carlyle* (London: Longmans, Green, 1892), p. 151.

18 *Ibid.*, pp. 154 ff.

19 *Ibid.*, pp. 161 ff.

20 *Ibid.*, pp. 163–64.

21 *Ibid.*, p. 177.

22 *Ibid.*, p. 168.

23 *Ibid.*, p. 184.

24 *Letters of Thomas Carlyle to John Stuart Mill, John Sterling and Robert Browning*, ed. Alexander Carlyle (New York: T. F. Unwin, 1923), pp. 287–88.

25 *Letters*, ed. Kenyon, II, 23 (to Mrs. Jameson, October 21 [1851]).

26 *Ibid.*, II, 29 (to Miss Mitford, November 12, 1851).

27 *Letters to Ogilvy*, p. 53 (October 17, 1851).

28 *Letters*, ed. Kenyon, II, 28 (to Miss Mitford, October 22 [1851]).

29 *Ibid.*, II, 30 (to Miss Mitford, November 12, 1851).

30 *Letters*, ed. Huxley, pp. 148–49 (December 1, 1851).

31 George Sand, *Oeuvres autobiographiques*, ed. Georges Lubin (Paris: Gallimard, Pléiade, 1970–71), II, 1195–1222. Trans. Cate, p. 624.

32 *Letters to Ogilvy*, pp. 58–59 (December 30 [1851]).

33 *Letters*, ed. Huxley, p. 150 (December 13, 14, 1851).

34 *Letters to Ogilvy*, p. 59.

35 *Letters of the Brownings to George Barrett*, ed. Paul Landis (Urbana: University of Illinois Press, 1958), pp. 156–59 (December 4–5, 1851).

36 *Letters*, ed. Huxley, p. 149 (December 13, 14, 1851).

37 *Letters to Ogilvy*, p. 65 (December 30 [1851]).

38 *Letters*, ed. Kenyon, II, 35 (to Mrs. Martin, December 11 [1851]).

39 Victor Hugo, *Oeuvres politiques complètes*, ed. Francis Bouvet (Paris: Jean-Jacques Pauvert, 1964), p. 301.

40 *Letters to Ogilvy*, p. 40 (July 2 [1851]).
41 *Ibid.*, p. 59 (December 30 [1851]).
42 *Ibid.*, p. 61.
43 *Letters*, ed. Kenyon, II, 37 (to Mrs. Martin, December 11 [1851]).
44 *Ibid.*, II, 78 (to Miss Mitford, July 31, 1852).
45 *Letters to Ogilvy*, p. 60 (December 30 [1851]).
46 *Letters*, ed. Kenyon, II, 36 (to Mrs. Martin, December 11 [1851]).
47 *Ibid.*, II, 51 (to Miss Mitford, February 15 [1852]).
48 *Ibid.*, II, 55 (to Kenyon, February 15, 1852).
49 *Ibid.*, II, 53.
50 *Ibid.*, II, 48 (to Miss Mitford [January-February, 1852]).
51 *Letters to Ogilvy*, p. 71 (March 18 [1852]).
52 *Letters*, ed. Kenyon, II, 52 (to Miss Mitford, February 15 [1852]).
53 *Ibid.*, II, 54 (to Kenyon, February 15, 1852).
54 *Ibid.*, II, 70 (to Miss Mitford, May 9 [1852]).
55 *Ibid.*, II, 47 (to Miss Mitford [January-February, 1852]).
56 *Ibid.*, II, 70 (to Miss Mitford, May 9 [1852]).
57 *Ibid.*, II, 53 (to Kenyon, February 15, 1852).
58 *Ibid.*, II, 53.
59 *Letters to George*, p. 168 (February 4, 1852).
60 *Letters to Ogilvy*, p. 62 (December 30 [1851]).
61 *Ibid.*, p. 73 (March 18 [1852]).
62 *Letters*, ed. Kenyon, II, 67 (to Mrs. Jameson, April 12, 1852).
63 *Ibid.*, II, 71–72 (to Miss Mitford, May 9 [1852]).
64 *Letters to George*, p. 164 (February 2 [1852]).
65 *Dearest Isa*, p. 372 (January 19–25, 1872).
66 *Ibid.*, p. 371 (December 29, 1871).
67 *Ibid.*, p. 372 (January 19–25, 1872).

5 *Paris and Literature, 1851—52*

1 *Letters*, ed. Huxley, p. 125 (July 7, 1850).
2 *Ibid.*, p. 145 (November 2, 1851).
3 *Letters*, ed. Kenyon, II, 29 (to Miss Mitford, November 12, 1851).
4 *Ibid.*, II, 31.
5 *Letters*, ed. Huxley, p. 158 (April 1, 1852).
6 *Letters*, ed. Kenyon, II, 89 (to Kenyon [November, 1852]).
7 *Letters*, ed. Huxley, p. 148 (December 1, 1851); p. 160 (April 1, 1852).
8 *Letters*, ed. Kenyon, II, 50 (to Miss Mitford, February 11 [1852]).
9 *Letters of Robert Browning Collected by Thomas J. Wise*, ed. Thurman L. Hood (New Haven: Yale University Press, 1933), p. 36 (to Carlyle [October, 1851]).
10 De Tocqueville, XII, 149–50.
11 *Letters*, ed. Kenyon, II, 29 (to Miss Mitford, November 12, 1851).

12 *Ibid.*, II, 40 (to Miss Mitford, Christmas Eve [1851]).

13 *Ibid.*, II, 70 (to Miss Mitford, May 9 [1852]).

14 *Ibid.*, II, 50 (to Miss Mitford, February 15 [1852]).

15 *Ibid.*, II, 55–56 (to Kenyon, February 15, 1852).

16 *Letters*, ed. Huxley, p. 155 (March 3, 1852).

17 *Letters*, ed. Kenyon, II, 63–64 (to Miss Mitford, April 7, 1852).

18 *Letters*, ed. Huxley, p. 163 (June 10–18, 1852).

19 *Letters to George*, p. 158 ([December 4–5, 1851]).

20 *Letters*, ed. Huxley, p. 144 (October 29, 1851).

21 *Letters*, ed. Kenyon, II, 26 (to Miss Mitford, October 22 [1851]).

22 *Letters to Ogilvy*, pp. 64–65 (December 30 [1851]).

23 *Letters*, ed. Huxley, p. 148 (December 1, 1851).

24 *Letters to George*, p. 165 (February 2 [1852]).

25 *Ibid.*, p. 18 (May 13–14 [1852]).

26 Henri Dabot, *Souvenirs et impressions d'un bourgeois du Quartier Latin* (Paris: Péronne, 1899), p. 26.

27 *Letters*, ed. Huxley, p. 156 (March 3, 1852).

28 *Ibid.*, p. 158 (April 1, 1852).

29 *Letters*, ed. Kenyon, II, 49 (to Miss Mitford, February 15 [1852]).

30 *Ibid.*, II, 64 (to Miss Mitford, April 7, 1852).

31 *Ibid.*, II, 41 (to Miss Mitford, Christmas Eve [1851]).

32 *Letters to Ogilvy*, p. 79 (June 18 [1852]).

33 *Letters*, ed. Kenyon, II, 71 (to Miss Mitford, May 9 [1852]); Victor Hugo's anecdote about Balzac's walnut tree is amusingly retold by André Maurois in *Prometheus* (London: The Bodley Head, 1965), p. 396.

34 *Ibid.*, II, 90 (to Kenyon [November 1852]).

35 *Ibid.*, II, 40 (to Miss Mitford, Christmas Eve [1851]).

36 *Ibid.*, II, 86 (to Miss Mitford, September 14 [1852]).

37 *Letters to George*, p. 181 (May 13–14 [1852]).

38 *Ibid.*, p. 181.

39 *Letters*, ed. Kenyon, II, 66 (to Mrs. Jameson, April 12, 1852).

40 *Letters to George*, p. 181 (May 13–14 [1852]).

41 *Letters*, ed. Kenyon, II, 66 (to Mrs. Jameson, April 12, 1852).

42 *Letters to George*, p. 181 (May 13–14 [1852]).

43 [Anon.], *The Leader* (April 27, 1850) in *Browning: The Critical Heritage*, eds Litzinger and Smalley, p. 140.

44 Trans. in Marjorie Bowden, *Tennyson in France* (Manchester: University of Manchester Press, 1930), p. 19.

45 Joseph Milsand, "La Poésie anglaise depuis Byron: Robert Browning," *Revue des Deux Mondes*, XI (August 15, 1851), 688–89.

46 *New Letters*, p. 92 (to Edward Chapman, April 21, 1856).

47 *Letters*, ed. Kenyon, II, 29–30 (to Miss Mitford, November 12, 1851).

48 *Letters to George*, p. 158 (December 4–5, 1851).
49 *Letters*, ed. Kenyon, II, 43 (to Mrs. Martin, January 17 [1852]).
50 *Letters to Ogilvy*, pp. 68–69 (March 18 [1852]).
51 *Letters to George*, p. 180 (May 13–14 [1852]); *Letters to Ogilvy*, p. 69.
52 *Ibid.*, p. 166 (February 2 [1852]).
53 *Ibid.*, p. 166.
54 *Letters*, ed. Kenyon, II, 52 (to Miss Mitford, February 15 [1852]).
55 Bentzon, "A French Friend of Browning," p. 109.
56 V[erdun]-L. Saulnier, *La Littérature du siècle romantique* (Paris: Presses universitaires de France, 1948), pp. 70 ff.; Henri Lemaître, *La Littérature française: Les Évolutions du XIXe siècle* (Paris: Éditions Bordas, 1970), pp. 499–500.
57 Quoted in Lewis Mott, *Ernest Renan* (New York: D. Appleton and Co., 1921), p. 79.
58 *Ibid.*, p. 147.
59 *Letters to Ogilvy*, p. 68 (March 18 [1852]); *Letters to George*, p. 163 (February 2 [1852]); *Letters*, ed. Huxley, pp. 289 ff. (March 4, 1858).
60 Théophile Gautier, *Mademoiselle de Maupin*, ed. Adolphe Boschot (Paris: Garnier, 1968), p. 135.
61 Théophile Gautier, *Spirite – Nouvelle Fantastique* (Paris: Charpentier, 16th edn 1886), p. 111.
62 Charles Baudelaire, *Oeuvres complètes* (Paris: Gallimard, Pléiade, 1961), p. 749.
63 Leconte de Lisle, "Préface" to *Poèmes antiques, Oeuvres de Leconte de Lisle* (Paris: A Lemerre, n.d.), IV, 216.
64 "Essay on Shelley," ed. Donald Smalley, in *The Complete Works of Robert Browning*, eds. Roma A. King, Jr. *et al* (Athens: Ohio University Press, 1969–81), V, 140.
65 Philip Drew, *The Poetry of Browning: A Critical Introduction* (London: Methuen, 1970), pp. 5–6.
66 *New Letters*, p. 54 (to Edward Chapman, January 16, 1852).
67 "Essay on Shelley," p. 137.
68 Quoted in F. W. J. Hemmings, *Culture and Society in France, 1848–1898* (London: Batsford, 1971), p. 119n.
69 Thomas J. Collins, *Robert Browning's Moral-Aesthetic Theory 1833–1855* (Lincoln: University of Nebraska Press, 1967), p. 115.
70 Ernest Renan, *Oeuvres complètes*, ed. Henriette Psichari (Paris: Calmann-Lévy, 1947–61), II, 937–38.
71 "Préface" to *La Peau de chagrin*, p. 554; see above, Chapter 1, note 36.
72 Edgar Allan Poe, "The Philosophy of Composition," *The Complete Works*, ed. James A. Harrison (New York, 1902, 1965), XIV, 194.
73 "Essay on Shelley," p. 140.
74 Leconte de Lisle, "Préface" to *Poèmes antiques*, IV, 216.

75 "Essay on Shelley," p. 140.
76 [Charles Kingsley], "Mr. and Mrs. Browning," *Fraser's Magazine*, 43 (February 1851), 170–82 in *Browning: The Critical Heritage*, eds Litzinger and Smalley, p. 148.
77 *Oeuvres complètes de Charles Baudelaire: Correspondance générale*, ed. M. Jacques Crepet (Paris: L. Conard, 1947), I, 152 (to Ancille, March 5, 1852).
78 Bentzon, "A French Friend of Browning," p. 115.
79 Ezra Pound, *How to Read* (London: Harmsworth, 1931), p. 42.
80 *Dearest Isa*, pp. 48–49 (November 30, 1859).
81 E. D. H. Johnson, *The Alien Vision in Victorian Poetry* (Princeton: Princeton University Press, 1952), p. 115; Charline Kvapil, " 'How It Strikes a Contemporary,' A Dramatic Monologue," *Victorian Poetry*, 4 (Autumn 1966), 279–83; Mary W. Schneider," Browning's Spy," *Victorian Poetry*, 17 (Winter 1979), 384–88.
82 For a discussion of the sexual imagery see Barbara Melchiori, *Browning's Poetry of Reticence* (London: Oliver and Boyd, 1968), pp. 50–51; for dating see John Huebenthal, "The Dating of Browning's 'Love Among the Ruins', 'Women and Roses,' and 'Childe Roland,' " *Victorian Poetry*, 4 (Summer 1966), 51–54.
83 Isobel Armstrong, "Browning and Victorian Poetry of Sexual Love," in *Robert Browning*, p. 284.
84 Henri Peyre, *French Literary Imagination and Dostoevsky and other Essays* (Birmingham: University of Alabama Press, 1975), p. 107.
85 Swinburne, "Notes on the Text of Shelley," *Fortnightly Review* (May 1, 1869), 560–61; reprinted in *Essays and Studies* (London: Chatto and Windus, 1875, 5th edn 1901), p. 220.
86 *Letters*, ed. Kenyon, II, 88 (to Miss Mitford [October 6, 1852]).
87 Henrietta Corkran, *Celebrities and I* (London: Hutchinson, 1902), p. 34.
88 *Letters*, ed. Kenyon, II, 89–90 (to Kenyon [November, 1852]).
89 *Ibid.*, II, 92–93 (to Miss Browning, November 4, 1852).

6 Back to Paris after an Italian Interlude, 1853–55

1 *Letters*, ed. Kenyon, II, 96–97 (to Kenyon, November 23, 1852).
2 *Letters to Ogilvy*, p. 91 (January 24 [1853]).
3 *Letters*, ed. Kenyon, II, 119 (to Miss Haworth, June [1853]).
4 *Ibid.*, II, 123 (to Miss Mitford [July 15, 1853]).
5 *Ibid.*, II, 96 (to Kenyon, November 24, 1852).
6 *Ibid.*, II, 109 (to Mrs. Jameson [March 17, 1853]).
7 Bentzon, "A French Friend of Browning," p. 110.
8 *Letters*, ed. Kenyon, II, 124 (to Miss Mitford, July 15, 1853).

9 *Letters to Ogilvy*, p. 123 (June 8 [1854]).
10 *Letters*, ed. Kenyon, II, 203 (to Miss Browning, June 15, 1855). Italics mine.
11 *Ibid.*, II, 204.
12 *Ibid.*, II, 190 (to Mrs. Jameson, February 24, 1855).
13 *Ibid.*, II, 203 (to Miss Browning, June 15, 1855).
14 *Ibid.*, II, 110 (to Mrs. Jameson, April 12 [1853]).
15 *Ibid.*, II, 108 (to Mrs. Jameson, March 17 [1853]).
16 Quoted in Hemmings, *Culture and Society in France, 1848–1898*, p. 53.
17 *Letters*, ed. Kenyon, II, 182 (to Mrs. Martin, November, 1854); 99 (to Miss Blagden [Winter 1852–53]); 106 (to Miss Mitford, March 15 [1853]).
18 *Ibid.*, II, 100 (to Miss Mitford, February [1853]).
19 *Dearest Isa*, p. 173 (August 19, 1863).
20 "Browning and Sainte-Beuve," *North American Review*, CXCI (1910), 498.
21 *Letters*, ed. Kenyon, II, 101 (to Miss Mitford, February [1853]).
22 *Ibid.*, II, 100.
23 *Ibid.*, II, 139 (to Mr. Westwood, September [1853]).
24 *Ibid.*, II, 108 (to Mrs. Jameson, March 17 [1853]); 128 (to Mr. Chorley, August [1853]); 170 (to Miss Mitford, June 6, 1854); *Letters to Ogilvy*, p. 108 (September 9 [1853]).
25 *Ibid.*, II, 165 (to Miss Mitford, May 10, 1854).
26 *New Letters*, p. 69 (to Miss Browning, December 19, 1853).
27 *Ibid.*, pp. 76–77 (to Forster, June 5, 1854).
28 *Letters*, ed. Kenyon, II, 162 (to Miss Browning [March, 1854]).
29 *New Letters*, p. 77 (to Forster, June 5, 1854).
30 *Letters*, ed. Hood, p. 39 (to Kenyon, January 16, 1853).
31 *Letters to George*, p. 194 (July 16–18 [1853]).
32 *Letters*, ed. Kenyon, II, 121 (to Miss Haworth, June [1853]).
33 *Ibid.*, II, 133 (to Miss Mitford, August 20–21, 1853).
34 See Paul Turner's note to "Instans Tyrannus" in his edition of *Men and Women* (London: Oxford University Press, 1972), p. 326.
35 *Letters*, ed. Kenyon, II, 121 (to Miss Haworth, July 3 [1853]); *New Letters*, p. 77 (to Forster, June 5, 1854).
36 *Ibid.*, II, 112 (to Mrs. Jameson, April 12 [1853]).
37 Scott to William Rossetti (December 22, 1856), in *Ruskin: Rossetti: Pre-Raphaelitism*, ed. William Michael Rossetti (London: G. Allen, 1899), p. 147.
38 *New Letters*, p. 77 (to Forster, June 5, 1854).
39 *Letters*, ed. Kenyon, I, 380–81 (to Miss Mitford, August 24, 1848).
40 Maurer, "Bishop Blougram's French Book," p. 178. See above, Chapter 1, note 19.

41 "Une Nouvelle Forme de poésie dramatique," *Revue des Deux Mondes*, 85 (February 1, 1870), 723.

42 Barbara Melchiori, "Browning's 'Andrea del Sarto': A French Source in De Musset," *Victorian Poetry*, 4 (Spring 1966), 132–36.

43 Rose M. Bachem, "Musset's and Browning's *Andrea del Sarto*," *Revue de Littérature Comparée*, 38 (1963), 254.

44 Geoffrey Tillotson "Victorian Novelists and Near Novelists," *Sewanee Review*, 64 (Autumn 1956), 665.

45 T. McNicoll, *London Quarterly Review*, 6 (July 1856), 493–501; in *Browning: The Critical Heritage*, eds Litzinger and Smalley, p. 192.

46 *Ibid.*, p 177.

47 *Ibid.*, pp. 171–72.

48 W. G. Collingwood, *Life and Work of John Ruskin* (Boston: Houghton, Mifflin, 1902), pp. 232 ff.

49 *New Letters*, p. 77 (to Forster, June 5, 1854).

50 *Letters to Ogilvy*, p. 98 (June 2 [1853]).

51 *Ibid.*, p. 127 (August 28 [1854]).

52 *Letters*, ed. Kenyon, II, 196 (to Mrs. Braun, May 13 [1855]).

53 *Murray's Handbook: France*, p. 466.

54 Rossetti was present when Tennyson came in September to the Brownings' at 13 Devonshire Place and read *Maud*, after which Browning read "Fra Lippo Lippi." When Rossetti had hastily read *Maud* in July he thought the poem "an odd *De Balzacish* sort of story for an Englishman at Tennyson's age" (*Letters of Dante Gabriel Rossetti*, eds Oswald Doughty and John Wahl (Oxford: Clarendon Press, 1965), I, 265). Though later, as his brother William Michael would testify, Rossetti rated Balzac "as one of the most intellectual and deep-probing men of our age," at this time he associated him with the kind of melodramatic plotting found in *Maud*. That quality and the intensity of the style, as well perhaps as its contemporary setting, made Rossetti think that *Maud* was "quite overloaded and sometimes almost as bad as *Lady Geraldine's Courtship*," which Elizabeth had published a decade before. "Fra Lippo Lippi," Rossetti told Ruskin, was "perfection" (*Letters*, eds. Doughty and Wahl, I, 267, 277).

55 *Letters* ed. Kenyon, I, 280.

56 *Ibid.*, I, 281, 280.

57 Eugène Delacroix, *Journal*, ed. André Joubin (Paris: Plon, 1932), II, 339.

58 *Letters*, ed. Kenyon, II, 219 (to Ruskin, November 5 [1855]); 221 (to Mrs. Jameson, December 17, 1855).

59 *Ibid.*, II, 221.

60 *Ibid.*, II, 222.

61 *Letters*, ed. Hood, pp. 43–44 (to Carlyle, January 23, 1856).

62 *Letters*, ed. Huxley, p. 245 (April 11, 1856); *Letters*, ed. Kenyon, II, 229 (to Mrs. Jameson, May 2, 1856).
63 *New Letters*, p. 90 (to Chapman, April 12 [1856]); *Letters*, ed. Kenyon, II, 230 (to Mrs. Jameson, May 2, 1856).
64 *Ibid.*, p. 87 (to Chapman, January 17 [1856]).
65 *Ibid.*, p. 85 (to Chapman, December 17, 1855).
66 *Ibid.*, pp. 92–93 (to Chapman, April 21, 1856).
67 *Letters of Carlyle*, ed. A. Carlyle, p. 300.
68 *Letters of Dante Gabriel Rossetti*, eds Doughty and Wahl, I, 278.
69 *Letters*, ed. Huxley, p. 233 (November 15, 1855).
70 Joseph Milsand, "La Poésie expressive et dramatique en Angleterre: M. Robert Browning," *Revue contemporaine*, 27 (September 15, 1856), 516.
71 Bentzon, "A French Friend of Browning," p. 118.

7 *The Brownings and* le Réalisme, *1856–61*

1 Théophile Gautier, "De l'art moderne," *Artiste*, 10 (June 1, 1853), 129–33. See Bernard Weinberg, *French Realism: The Critical Reaction, 1830–1870* (New York: Modern Language Association of America, 1937), pp. 98–102.
2 Quoted in Hemmings, *Culture and Society in France*, p. 96.
3 Louis de Geofroy, "Le Salon de 1850," *Revue des Deux Mondes*, 1 (March 1, 1851), 928–31; Étienne Delécluze, "Exposition de 1850," *Journal des Débats* (January 7, 1851); see Weinberg, *French Realism*, pp. 99, 232; and Hemmings, *Culture and Society in France*, p. 97.
4 Champfleury, "Movement des arts," *L'Ordre* (September 21, 1850); see Weinberg, pp. 98, 232; and Hemmings, *Culture and Society in France*, p. 105.
5 Champfleury, *Les Aventures de Mlle Mariette* (Paris: V. Lecou, 1853), "Preface." Philarète Chasles commented of the novel: "this system of exact reproduction is to art what photography is to painting . . . the single soul of the artist must preside over the work by which souls are studied." (quoted in Émile Bouvier, *La Bataille Réaliste (1844–1857)* (Paris: Fontemoing, 1913), p. 293. Chasles lecturing Champfleury sounds a little like the prior lecturing Fra Lippo Lippi: "Your business is to paint the souls of men."
6 G. Brimley-T. C. C., *Fraser's Magazine*, 53 (January, 1856), 105–16; in *Browning: The Critical Heritage*, eds Litzinger and Smalley, p. 172.
7 Champfleury, "Du réalisme. Lettre à madame Sand," *Artiste*, 16 (September 2, 1855), 1–5. Reprinted in Champfleury, *Le Réalisme* (Geneva: Slatkine Reprints, 1967), pp. 270–85.
8 *Letters*, ed. Kenyon, II, 214–15 (to Ruskin, October 17, 1855).

9 Quoted in Hemmings, *Culture and Society in France*, p. 105.
10 [George Eliot], *Westminster Review*, 65 (January, 1856), 290–96; in *Browning: The Critical Heritage*, pp. 175, 177.
11 *Les Fleurs du mal, précédé du dossier des fleurs du mal*, ed. Claude Bonnefoy (Paris: Éditions P. Belfond, 1965), p. 146.
12 Georg Lukács, *Studies in European Realism* (New York: Grosset & Dunlap, 1964), p. 22.
13 Barbara Smalley, *George Eliot and Flaubert: Pioneers of the Modern Novel* (Athens: Ohio University Press, 1974), p. v.
14 *Dearest Isa*, p. 173 (August 19, 1863); p. 295 (March 19, 1868).
15 Quoted in Enid Starkie, *Flaubert: The Making of the Master* (New York: Atheneum, 1967), p. 246.
16 *Ibid.*, pp. 248–51.
17 Flaubert, *Oeuvres complètes: Madame Bovary* (Paris: L. Conard, 1930), XII, 577–78.
18 Émile Montégut, "Un Poème de la vie moderne en Angleterre," *Revue des Deux Mondes*, 8 (March 15, 1857), 326–27.
19 *Letters of Carlyle*, ed. A. Carlyle, p. 293.
20 Émile Montégut, "Le Roman intime de la littérature réaliste," *Revue des Deux Mondes*, 18 (November 1, 1858), 200.
21 *Letters*, ed. Kenyon, II, 245 (to Mrs. Jameson, December 25 [1856]).
22 Taplin, pp. 322–23; see also Ellen Moers, *Literary Women: The Great Writers* (New York: Doubleday, 1976), pp. 59–62, and Thomson, *George Sand and the Victorians*, pp. 43–60.
23 Alethea Hayter, *Mrs. Browning: A Poet's Work and Its Setting* (New York: Barnes and Noble, 1963), p. 160.
24 *Aurora Leigh*, Autograph Edition, eds Charlotte Porter and Helen A. Clarke (New York: George D. Sproul, 1901), I, 212.
25 *Ibid.*, I, 219.
26 Flaubert, *Oeuvres complètes: Correspondance*, V, 138.
27 *Ibid.*, II, 316.
28 Scott to W. M. Rossetti in *Ruskin: Rossetti: Pre-Raphaelitism*, ed. Rossetti, p. 147. See above, Chapter 6, note 37.
29 Walter Bagehot, "Wordsworth, Tennyson, and Browning," *The National Review*, 19 (November, 1864), 27–67; and Swinburne's letter to John Nichol (June 19, 1864) in *The Swinburne Letters*, ed. Cecil Lang (New Haven: Yale University Press, 1959–62), I, 102.
30 *Les Fleurs du mal*, ed. Bonnefoy; above, note 11 to this chapter.
31 For Elizabeth's reaction to Poe's dedication see *Letters of RB and EBB*, I, 297 ff.
32 *Letters*, ed. Kenyon, II, 226 (to Mrs. Martin, February 21 [1856]).
33 *Ibid.*, II, 231 (to Mrs. Jameson, May 2 [1856]). EBB's italics.
34 Daniel D. Home, *Incidents in My Life* (London: Longman, 1872), p. 107.

35 Lubbock, *EBB in Her Letters*, p. 356.
36 *Letters*, ed. Huxley, pp. 248–49 (June 12, 1856).
37 Madame Jules Baroche, *Le Second Empire* (Paris: G. Crès, 1921), p. 64. My translation.
38 *Letters*, ed. Kenyon, II, 266 (to Miss Haworth [July, 1857]).
39 *Letters to George*, p. 220 (October 27, 1856).
40 *Ibid.*, p. 336 (to "Grandmama", July 27, 1816); *EB to Miss Mitford*, p. 236 (March 5, 1845).
41 *Murray's Handbook: France*, p. 475.
42 *Letters*, ed. Huxley, p. 266 (January 10, 1857).
43 *Ibid.*, p. 262 (November 18, 1856).
44 *Ibid.*, p. 279 (August 15, 1857); p. 274 (June 2, 1857).
45 *New Letters*, p. 97 (to Chapman, December 2, 1856).
46 *Ibid.*, p. 103 (to Chapman, September 1, 1857).
47 *Letters*, ed. Kenyon, II, 275 (to Miss Haworth, September 28 [1857]); 279 (to Mrs. Martin, March 27 [1858]); *Letters*, ed. Huxley, p. 289 (March 4, 1858).
48 Quoted in Taplin, p. 354.
49 *Letters*, ed. Kenyon, II, 257 (to Miss Browning [February, 1857]).
50 *Letters*, ed. Huxley, p. 277 (August 4, 1857).
51 *Letters to Ogilvy*, p. 140 ([January 29, 1859]); p. 141 ([January 30, 1859]).
52 Hugo to Paul Meurice (February 21, 1856) quoted in *La Littérature française: Les Évolutions du XIXᵉ siècle*, eds André Lagarde and Laurent Michard (Paris: Éditions Bordas, 1970), p. 141.
53 *Letters*, ed. Kenyon, II, 260 (to Mrs. Jameson, April 9 [1857]).
54 *Ibid.*, II, 261–62 ([April, 1857]).
55 *Dearest Isa*, pp. 48–49 (November 30, 1859).
56 Ernest Renan, *Oeuvres complètes: "La théologie de Béranger,"* I, 315.
57 *New Letters*, pp. 106–7 (to Chapman, June 5, 1858); *Letters*, ed. Huxley, p. 280 (August 15, 1857).
58 *Dearest Isa*, p. 6 (July 3 [1858]).
59 *Letters*, ed. Kenyon, II, 282–83 (to Miss Haworth, July 8 [1858]); II, 283 (to Miss Blagden, July 8 [1858]).
60 *Ibid.*, II, 284.
61 *Dearest Isa*, p. 11 (July 8, 1858); *Letters*, ed. Kenyon, II, 285 (to Miss Haworth, July 23, 1858); II, 283 (to Miss Haworth, July 8, 1858).
62 William Allingham, *A Diary*, eds H. Allingham and D. Radford (London: Macmillan, 1907), pp. 76–77.
63 *Dearest Isa*, p. 17 (September 4, 1858).
64 *Murray's Handbook: France*, p. 65.
65 *Letters*, ed. Kenyon, II, 287–88 (to Mrs. Jameson, July 24, 1858).
66 *Dearest Isa*, p. 12 (August 1, 1858).
67 *Ibid.*, p. 13.

68 *Ibid.*, p. 12; *New Letters*, p. 108 (to Chapman, August 8, 1858).
69 *Dearest Isa*, p. 13; p. 18 (September 4, 1858).
70 *Letters*, ed. Kenyon, II, 293 (to Miss Haworth [October, 1858]).
71 *Ibid.*, II, 151 (to Miss Haworth, December 27 [1853, *sic*]).
72 *Ibid.*, II, 304 (to Miss Blagden, January 7 [1859]).
73 *Letters*, ed. Kenyon, II, 343–44 (to Miss Browning [September–October, 1859]).
74 *Letters*, ed. Kenyon, II, 368 (to Miss Browning [March, 1860]).
75 *Ibid.*, II, 361 (to Mrs. Jameson, February 22 [1860]).
76 *Poems Before Congress* (London: Chapman and Hall, 1860), p. vi. When the volume was reissued, Browning removed this preface.
77 *Letters*, ed. Kenyon, II, 286 (to Miss Haworth, July 23 [1858]).
78 *Ibid.*, II, 385 (to Forster [May, 1860]).
79 *Ibid.*, II, 403 (to Mrs. Martin, August 21 [1860]).
80 *Ibid.*, II, 403.
81 *Ibid.*, II, 436 (to Miss Browning [March] 1861).
82 *Ibid.*, II, 441 (to Miss Browning, May 11, 1861).

8 Breton Holidays, 1861–68

1 *Browning to His American Friends: Letters Between the Brownings, the Storys and James Russell Lowell, 1841–1890*, ed. Gertrude Reese Hudson (New York: Barnes and Noble, 1965), pp. 75–76 (August 20, 1861).
2 *Dearest Isa*, p. 82 (August 22, 1861).
3 *American Friends*, p. 76.
4 *Dearest Isa*, p. 83.
5 *Ibid.*, pp. 88–89 (September 9, 1861).
6 *American Friends*, p. 83; *Letters to George*, pp. 274–75 ([September 30, 1861]).
7 *Dearest Isa*, pp. 94–95 (February 6, 1862). Browning's italics.
8 *American Friends*, pp. 100–1 (March 19, 1862).
9 *Dearest Isa*, pp. 106–7 (June 19, 1862).
10 *Ibid.*, p. 110 (July 19, 1862); p. 114 (July 26, 1862); p. 115 (August 1, 1862).
11 *American Friends*, p. 109 (September 13 [1862]).
12 *Ibid.*, pp. 109–10; *Dearest Isa*, p. 123 (September 19, 1862).
13 *Dearest Isa*, p. 119 (August 18, 1862).
14 *Ibid.*, pp. 122–23 (September 19, 1862).
15 *Robert Browning and Julia Wedgwood: A Broken Friendship as Revealed by Their Letters*, ed. Richard Curle (New York: Frederick A. Stokes Co., 1937), p. 107 (Christmas Day, 1864).
16 *Ibid.*, p. 109 (December 31, 1864).

17 Flaubert, *Oeuvres complètes: Correspondance*, I, 208.
18 *Dearest Isa*, p. 127 (October 18, 1862); pp. 145, 150 (January 19, 1863).
19 *Ibid.*, pp. 156–57 (March 19, 1863).
20 *Ibid.*, p. 172 (August 19, 1863).
21 *Ibid.*, p. 173.
22 *American Friends*, p. 125 (July 17, 1863); p. 128 (September 5, 1863).
23 *Dearest Isa*, p. 177 (September 19, 1863).
24 *Ibid.*, pp. 173–74 (August 19, 1863); pp. 176–77 (September 19, 1863).
25 *Ibid.*, p. 173.
26 *Ibid.*, p. 173.
27 *Ibid.*, p. 178 (November 19, 1863).
28 *Ibid.*, p. 173.
29 Flaubert, *Oeuvres complètes: Correspondance*, VI, 56, 58.
30 Quoted in René Dumesnil, *Gustave Flaubert: L'homme et l'oeuvre* (Paris: Desclée de Bouwer, 3rd edn, 1947), p. 236.
31 *Dearest Isa*, p. 176 (September 19, 1863).
32 Quoted in Mott, *Ernest Renan*, p. 236.
33 The translator's preface to the 1863 English edition of *The Life of Jesus* is reprinted in Ernest Renan, *The Life of Jesus* (New York: Modern Library, 1927), p. v.
34 *Dearest Isa*, p. 152 (February 19, 1863).
35 *Ibid.*, p. 180 (November 19, 1863).
36 Renan, *The Life of Jesus*, p. 251.
37 *Dearest Isa*, p. 180.
38 Cited by Mott, *Ernest Renan*, p. 237.
39 *Dearest Isa*, p. 180.
40 Irvine and Honan, p. 391.
41 *Dearest Isa*, p. 180.
42 Ernest Renan, *Vie de Jésus* (Paris: Calmann-Lévy, 20th edn, 1891), p. 461.
43 *Ibid.*, p. 465.
44 *American Friends*, p. 146 ([August 22, 1864]).
45 *Dearest Isa*, p. 190 (August 19, 1864).
46 *RB and Julia Wedgwood*, p. 40 (August 19, 1864).
47 *American Friends*, p. 145 (August 22, 1864).
48 *RB and Julia Wedgwood*, pp. 42–43 (August 19, 1864).
49 *American Friends*, pp. 145–46.
50 *Ibid.*, p. 146.
51 *RB and Julia Wedgwood*, p. 43.
52 *American Friends*, p. 146.
53 *RB and Julia Wedgwood*, p. 43.

54 *Ibid.*, p. 42.
55 *Rossetti Papers, 1862 to 1870*, ed. William Michael Rossetti (London: Sands and Co., 1903), p. 302.
56 Irvine and Honan, p. 406.
57 *RB and Julia Wedgwood*, p. 53 (September 2, 1864).
58 *Dearest Isa*, p. 193 (September 18, 1864).
59 *RB and Julia Wedgwood*, p. 69 (September 19, 1864).
60 *Dearest Isa*, p. 193.
61 *RB and Julia Wedgwood*, p. 76 (October 3, 1864).
62 *Dearest Isa*, p. 212 (March 18, 1865).
63 *Ibid.*, p. 216 (May 19 [1865]).
64 *RB and Julia Wedgwood*, p. 76 (October 3, 1864).
65 *Dearest Isa*, p. 217 (May 19 [1865]).
66 *American Friends*, p. 154 (July 8, 1865).
67 *Dearest Isa*, p. 218 (August 19, 1865).
68 *Ibid.*, pp. 227–28 (October 19, 1865).
69 *Ibid.*, p. 223 (September 19, 1865).
70 *Ibid.*, p. 219 (August 19, 1865).
71 *Ibid.*, pp. 222–23 (September 19, 1865).
72 *The Diary of Alfred Domett, 1872–1885*, ed. E. A. Horsman (London: Oxford University Press, 1953), p. 5.
73 Samuel B. Southwell in his new book *Quest for Eros: Browning and 'Fifine'* (Lexington: University of Kentucky Press, 1980) suggests on p. 244 that it is possible that "Browning knew *Recherches sur l'origine, l'esprit, et le progrès des arts de la Grèce* (1785) by Pierre d'Hancarville. . . . Hancarville could be the somebody 'pert from Paris.'" Hancarville speculated upon the development of phallic symbolism. Southwell's book is a wide-ranging and interesting analysis of Browning's exploration of sexual repression in *Fifine*. Southwell discusses the dolmen and menhir section of the poem on pp. 153–72; on p. 154 he transports the Breton megaliths to Normandy.
74 *Dearest Isa*, pp. 231–32 (March 19, 1866).
75 *Letters*, ed. Hood, p. 106 (to Seymour Kirkup, February 19, 1867).
76 Mrs. Sutherland Orr, *Life and Letters of Robert Browning* (London: Smith, Elder and Co., 1891), p. 179.
77 *New Letters* p. 177 (to Richard Monckton Milnes, July 24, 1866).
78 *Dearest Isa*, p. 244 (August 7 [1866]).
79 *Ibid.*, p. 243.
80 *Letters*, ed. Hood, p. 107 (to Seymour Kirkup, February 19, 1867).
81 *Ibid.*, p. 106
82 *New Letters*, p. 16 (to Fanny Haworth [April, 1839]).
83 *Letters*, ed. Hood, pp. 106–7.
84 *Dearest Isa*, p. 247 (September 24, 1866).

85 Paul Joanne, *La Loire* (Paris: Joanne, 1888), p. 276.

86 *Letters*, ed. Hood, p. 106 (to Seymour Kirkup, February 19, 1867).

87 *Dearest Isa*, p. 249 (October 19, 1866).

88 *Ibid.*, p. 266 (May 22, 1867).

89 *Ibid.*, pp. 277–78 (August 19, 1867).

90 *Ibid.*, p. 282 (September 19, 1867).

91 See De Vane, *Handbook*, p. 408, and Irvine and Honan, p. 420. For Browning's use of Carou's *Histoire de Pornic* see Michael E. Darling, "Notes on Browning's 'Gold Hair' and 'Apparent Failure,'" *Studies in Browning and His Circle*, 7 (Spring 1979), 70–84.

92 *Bretagne* (Paris: Michelin, 1968), p. 83.

93 *Dearest Isa*, p. 290 (January 19, 1868).

94 *Ibid.*, p. 290.

95 *Ibid.*, p. 299 (August 28 [1868]).

96 *Ibid.*, p. 300.

97 *New Letters*, p. 182 (to Lily Benzon, September 2, 1868).

98 *Dearest Isa*, p. 302 (October 19, 1868).

99 *Ibid.*, p. 315 (April 19, 1869); p. 317 (May 16, 1869).

100 Louis Étienne, "Une Nouvelle forme de poésie dramatique," *Revue des Deux Mondes*, 85 (February 1, 1870), 704–35.

101 Georges Connes, "Étude documentaire," *L'Anneau et le livre* (Paris: Gallimard, 1959), p. 14.

102 Isobel Armstrong, *Victorian Scrutinies: Reviews of Poetry 1830–1870* (London: Athlone Press, 1972), pp. 57 ff.

103 Quoted by Armstrong, *Victorian Scrutinies*, p. 58.

104 *Browning: The Critical Heritage*, eds Litzinger and Smalley, p. 309. For other contemporary comparisons of Browning to Balzac see below, Chapter 9, section iii and also Joseph Solomine's recent note, "Balzac and Browning: Context, Culture, History in *The Ring and the Book*," *Studies in Browning*, 8 (Fall 1980), 94–96.

105 Simpson's essay in *North British Review*, I (October 1869), 97–126, is reprinted in Armstrong, *Victorian Scrutinies*, pp. 259–87. My citations are to pp. 286, 269, 277 and 279.

106 Flaubert, *Oeuvres Complètes: Correspondance*, III, 249 (to Louise Colet, June 25–26, 1853).

107 Émile Zola, *Le Roman expérimental* (Paris: Charpentier, 1880), pp. 10, 12, 6, 11, and 7.

108 *Dearest Isa*, p. 76 (May 13, 1861).

109 Henry James, *Notes on Novelists*, pp. 385, 402.

110 Richard Altick and James Loucks, *Browning's Roman Murder Story* (Chicago: University of Chicago Press, 1968), pp. 5–7.

111 Marshall Brown, "The Logic of Realism: A Hegelian Approach," *PMLA*, 96 (March 1981), 232–33.

Notes to pp. 258–64

9 Normandy and Haute-Savoie, 1870's and 1880's

1 *Dearest Isa*, p. 330 (February 24, 1870).
2 *Ibid.*, p. 340 (July 19, 1870).
3 *Ibid.*, p. 342 (August 9, 1870).
4 *Ibid.*, p. 344 (August 19, 1870). Park Honan gives an excellent account of this episode in chapter 24 of *The Book, the Ring, and the Poet*. Honan suggests that Browning may have been a little foolhardy and naive to visit at this time what Honan calls "embattled France!" Browning's hurried and somewhat inglorious return to England aboard a cattle-boat does suggest that he underestimated the seriousness of the conflict. French statesmen and generals, of course, also seriously underestimated the suddenness of the Prussian onslaught. So, too, had French men-of-letters such as Taine, who was caught doing scholarly research in the Rhineland, and Renan, who, in the company of Prince Jerome, was on a pleasure cruise to Spitzbergen.
5 *Dearest Isa*, pp. 342–44 (August 19, 1870).
6 *Ibid.*, pp. 342–43.
7 *Ibid.*, p. 344.
8 *Ibid.*, p. 345 (September 19, 1870).
9 Irvine and Honan, p. 456; see also Orr, *Life and Letters of Robert Browning*, p. 289.
10 Leo Hetzler, "The Case of Prince Hohenstiel-Schwangau: Browning and Napoleon III," *Victorian Poetry*, 15 (Winter 1977), 341.
11 *Dearest Isa*, pp. 347–48 (October 19, 1870).
12 *Letters*, ed. Hood, p. 145 (to Robert Buchanan, January 25, 1871).
13 *Dearest Isa*, p. 360 (May 21, 1871).
14 *Ibid.*, p. 356 (January 23, 1871); p. 360.
15 *American Friends*, p. 166 (December 20, 1871).
16 See above, Chapter 7, section iv.
17 *Dearest Isa*, p. 372 (January 19, 25, 1872).
18 *American Friends*, p. 167 (January 1, 1872).
19 *Dearest Isa*, p. 357 (April 25, 1871); p. 348 (October 19, 1870).
20 *Ibid.*, p. 372 (January 19, 25, 1872).
21 In addition to Leo Hetzler's essay (note 10), see Clyde de L. Ryals, *Browning's Later Poetry: 1871–1889* (Ithaca and London: Cornell University Press, 1975), pp. 42–58, and Philip Drew, *The Poetry of Browning*, pp. 291–303.
22 Drew, *The Poetry of Browning*, p. 299.
23 See above, Chapter 4, section iii.
24 *Letters*, ed. Kenyon, II, 55 (to Kenyon, February 15, 1852); see above, Chapter 4, section ii.
25 *Ibid.*, II, 48 (to Miss Mitford [January–February 1852]).

26 *Dearest Isa*, p. 372 (January 19, 25, 1872).
27 Drew, p. 297.
28 Horsman, *The Diary of Alfred Domett*, p. 5. For discussion of *Fifine*, see above, Chapter 8, sections ii and iii.
29 Bentzon, "A French Friend of Browning," p. 111.
30 *The Daily News* (London), June 17, 1872, p. 5.
31 [Anon.] *The Spectator*, 45 (July 6, 1872), 853–55; in *Browning: The Critical Heritage*, eds Litzinger and Smalley, p. 375.
32 [Anon.], *Westminster Review*, NS 42 (October 1, 1872), 545–46; in *Browning: The Critical Heritage*, p. 377.
33 *Letters*, ed. Hood, p. 156 (to Miss Smith, August 27, 1872).
34 *Dearest Isa*, p. 383 (August 27, 1872).
35 *Ibid.*, p. 385 (September 19, 1872).
36 *Letters*, ed. Hood, p. 157 (to Miss Smith, December 6 [1872]).
37 Those interested in Miss Thackeray's own writing and its relation to Browning's poem should see Malcolm Hicks, "Anne Thackeray's Novels and Robert Browning's *Red Cotton Night-Cap Country*," *Studies in Browning*, 8 (Fall 1980), 17–32.
38 Irvine and Honan, p. 471.
39 Père Fossard, *L'Ancienne fondation de la chapelle de N.-D. de la Délivrande* (Caen: P. Dumesnil, 1642), pp. 6 ff. That Browning knew this legend is clear in lines 1190 ff.
40 *Livre de Millenaire de la Normandie* (Paris: Librairie Ficker, 1911), pp. 61–62.
41 Quoted from G. Burnel, *Notre-Dame de la Dell 'Yvrande* (Bayeux: M. Chatillon, 1971), p. 7.
42 *Ibid.*, p. 21, note 23.
43 *Semaine religieuse de Bayeux*, Année 1870 (September 25, 1870), pp. 618–19.
44 *Ibid.*, Année 1922, pp. 353–54. Quoted in Burnel, p. 16.
45 *Biographie universelle, ancienne et moderne* (Paris, 1811), I, 369.
46 "L'Instinct chez les insectes" was the subject of a long review-essay by Georges Pouchet, published next to Louis Étienne's review of *The Ring and the Book* in the February 1, 1870 issue of the *Revue des Deux Mondes* (vol. 85, pp. 682–703). Pouchet includes in the essay a review of the recent French translation of *The Origin of Species*. See also Browning's letter about Darwin and insects, *Letters*, ed. Hood, p. 200.
47 Reprinted in *Anthologie des préfaces de romans français du XIXᵉ siècle*, eds Herbert S. Gershman and Kernan B. Whitworth (Paris: Julliard, 1964), p. 248.
48 *Ibid.*, p. 254.
49 Bentzon, "A French Friend of Browning," p. 118.
50 Brendan Kenny, "Browning as a Cultural Critic: *Red Cotton Night-Cap*

Country," Browning Institute Studies, 6 (1978), p. 148. See also Drew, pp. 321–32 and Ryals, pp. 83–100. A recent study is Walter M. Kendrick, "Facts and Figures: Browning's *Red Cotton Night-Cap Country,"* Victorian Poetry, 17 (Winter 1979), 343–63.

51 Swinburne, *Essays and Studies,* p. 220; see above, Chapter 5, note 85.

52 [Robert Louis Stevenson], *Vanity Fair,* 180 (December 11, 1875), 332; in *Browning: The Critical Heritage,* pp. 411–12.

53 *The Correspondence of Gerard Manley Hopkins and Richard Watson Dixon,* ed. C. C. Abbott (London: Oxford University Press, 1955), pp. 74–75; in *Browning: The Critical Heritage,* p. 472.

54 DeVane, *Handbook,* p. 502; Viola Cook, "Browning's *Parley* and DeLassay's *Mémoire,"* Modern Language Notes, 59 (December, 1944), 553–56. For a comment on the general similarities between Browning and Sainte-Beuve see Gamaliel Bradford, Jr., "Browning and Sainte-Beuve," *North American Review,* 191 (1910), 488–500.

55 *Letters,* ed. Hood, p. 159 (to Miss Smith, August 16, 1873); p. 158 (to Miss Smith, August 3, 1873).

56 *Ibid.,* pp. 159–60.

57 Irvine and Honan, p. 475.

58 DeVane, *Handbook,* p. 376.

59 *New Letters,* p. 228 (to Miss Browning [August or September, 1875]).

60 *Learned Lady,* pp. 44–45 (August 17, 1877).

61 Ryals, p. 147.

62 *Learned Lady,* pp. 46–47 (August 30, 1877).

63 Ryals, p. 156.

64 *Learned Lady,* p. 84 (July 13, 1880).

65 *Ibid.,* p. 92 (September 19, 1880); see McAleer's excellent notes; for Browning's earlier response to Guizot and Montalembert, see above, Chapter 4, section iii.

66 *Learned Lady,* p. 112 (February 5, 1881).

67 *Ibid.,* pp. 85–86 (August 17, 1880).

68 *Ibid.,* 87–88 (September 4, 1880).

69 DeVane, *Handbook,* p. 464.

70 *Learned Lady,* pp. 127–8 (September 24, 1881).

71 *Ibid.,* pp. 147–48 (August 16, 1882).

72 Frederick Lawton, *The Life and Work of Auguste Rodin* (New York: Scribner's, 1907), p. 243.

73 "Lettres de George Sand et Hippolyte Taine," *Revue des Deux Mondes,* Series 8, vol. 13 (January 1, 1933), 336. Browning indicated his intention of meeting Taine on the back of the envelope containing the invitation from the Ambassador; see *Baylor Browning Interests,* 8 (September, 1934), 130.

74 *Letters*, ed. Hood, p. 310 (to Miss Lehmann, July 6, 1889). Browning follows his transcript of his conversation with the Shah with this statement: "I have been accordingly this morning to town, where the thing [a volume of his poems] is procurable, and as I chose a volume of which I judged the binding might take the imperial eye, I said to myself, 'Here do I present my poetry to a personage for whom I do not care three straws. . . .'" The conversation may be rendered this way: to the Shah's question, "Are you a poet?" Browning replied, "It is sometimes said that I am." "And have you written some books? "Too many books." "Would you give me one of them, so that I may remind myself of you?" "With pleasure."

Index

This index is supplementary to the detailed contents listings given at the head of each chapter.

Index

Tremorne, 41; *Nora and Archibald*, 242
Blake, William, 52
Blanc, Louis, 74, 77, 83; *Histoire de la Révolution en 1848*, 155; *L'Organisation du travail*, 77
Bodin, Camille, 19–20
Bonheur, Rosa, 169, 218
Boyd, Hugh Stuart, 3, 5, 12, *passim*
Bracken, Mrs. Mary, 219, *passim*
Braun, Madame Émile, 168
Brimley, T. C. C., 167, 176–77
Brizeux, Auguste, 160–61
Broglie, Duc de, 261
Browning, Elizabeth Barrett, "An August Voice," 203; *Aurora Leigh*, 48, 53, 60, 82–83, 128, 162, 164, 180–87, 194, 295; *Casa Guidi Windows*, 73, 74, 86–87, 93, 105, 132; "Crowned and Buried," 50; *The Cry of the Children*, 73, 184; *The Dance*, 203; "A Desire," 25; *A Drama of Exile*, 132; *An Essay on Mind*, 5–6; "Lady Geraldine's Courtship," 53; *Last Poems*, 211; *Napoleon III in Italy*, 204; *Ode to Napoleon*, 261; *Poems* (1844), 132; *Poems Before Congress*, 204–05; *The Poet's Vow*, 132; "A Recognition," 25–26; *Régulus*, 4–5; "To Victoire, on Her Marriage," 3; "A Vision of Poets," 53
Browning, Reuben, 11
Browning, Robert, Sr., 11–12, 116, 239, *passim*
Browning, Robert, "Andrea del Sarto," 166, 249; "Another Way of Love," 165; "Any Wife to Any Husband," 165; "Apparent Failure,' 41, 187–90; *Aristophanes' Apology*, 285; *Bells and Pomegranates*, 129, 143; "Bishop Blougram's Apology," 41, 52, 68, 127, 156, 165–66; *Childe Roland to the Dark Tower Came*, 135–36, 149–50; *Christmas Eve and Easter Day*, 73, 82,

128–129, 130, 134, 139, 149; "Cleon," 165, 229; "Count Gismond," 54; "Cristina and Monaldeschi," 284, 292–93; "Dance of Death," 11; "A Death in the Desert," 229–30; "Dis aliter visum," 199, 201–02; *Dramatic Lyrics*, 20, 143; *Dramatic Romances*, 143; *Dramatis Personae*, 187, 201, 210; "Epilogue" to *Dramatis Personae*, 227–29; "An Epistle . . . of Karshish," 165, 179, 229; *Essay on Shelley*, 137–43; *Fifine at the Fair*, 133, 210, 216, 219, 233–38, 241, 265–66; "The Flight of the Duchess," 54; "Fra Lippo Lippi," 140, 147–48, 178; "The Glove," 55–56; "Gold Hair," 223–24, 235; "The Guardian Angel," 148; "A Heretic's Tragedy," 149; *Hervé Riel*, 122, 210, 243–45, 295; "How It Strikes a Contemporary," 146–48; "Incident in the French Camp," 50–51; *The Inn Album*, 283; "Instans Tyrannus," 164; "In Three Days," 150; "James Lee's Wife," 214–17; *King Victor and King Charles*, 53; "The Laboratory," 54; "A Light Woman," 149; "A Likeness," 222–23; "Love Among the Ruins," 149–50; "A Lovers' Quarrel," 164; "Memorabilia," 144–45; *Men and Women*, 165–67, 170, 172–74, 178–79, 194; "Mr. Sludge, 'The Medium,' " 187, 191–93, 262; "Nationality in Drinks," 52–53; "One Way of Love," 165; "On Napoleon," 11; *Paracelsus*, 19, 35–36, 129; "Parleying with Daniel Bartoli," 284; *Pauline*, 12–19, 170; *Pippa Passes*, 138; "Popularity," 142, 145; *Prince Hohenstiel-Schwangau*, 111–14, 196–97, 205–06, 210, 261–65; *Red Cotton Night-Cap Country*,

Index

Diodati, Giovanni, 288
Domett, Alfred, 33
Doré, Gustave, 211, 218, 236, 249, 251
Dorval, Marie, 118
Dostoievski, Feodor, 25
Dourlans, Gustave, 266, 286, 290
Du Camp, Maxime, 159, 180
Dudevant, Maurice, 118, 290
Dudevant, Solange, 118, 290
Dumas *fils*, Alexandre, 71, 126–27, 160, 252; *L'Affaire Clemenceau*, 242; *La Dame aux camélias*, 126–28, 179, 280
Dumas *père*, Alexandre, 21, 43–44, 45, 73, 125–26, 185, 276; *Ange Pitou*, 160; *Le Comte de Monte-Cristo*, 33, 44, 71, 202–03; *Fronde*, 73; *La Guerre des femmes*, 43; *Mes Mémoires*, 126, 135, 160; *Speronare*, 126; *Vingt ans après*, 73
Duranty, Edmond, 178

Edinburgh Review, 37
Elgin, Lady, 117, 122–23
Eliot, George, 177–78; *Adam Bede*, 178; *Romola*, 70, 221
Emerson, Ralph Waldo, 243
Époque, L', 68
Essays and Reviews, 224
Étienne, Louis, 166, 249–51
Eugénie, Empress of France, 163, 231, 260, 279
Examiner (London), 103, 151, 156
Exposition Universelle (1855), 168–69, 170, 177

Faraday, Michael, 163
Fauveau, Félicie de, 200
Ferucci, Professor, 67
Feuerbach, Ludwig, 134
Feuillet, Octave, *La Petite Comtesse*, 190
Féval, Paul, *Les Amours de Paris*, 220; *Annette Laïs*, 220; *Les Mystères de Londres*, 220

Feydeau, Ernest, *Fanny*, 160, 180, 182, 202
Flaubert, Gustave, 179, 217, 253; *L'Éducation Sentimentale*, 222; *Madame Bovary*, 19, 159, 160, 178, 179–80, 186–87, 196, 202–03, 220; *Salammbô*, 220–22
Forster, John, 35, 103, 151
Fortnightly Review, 251
Fourier, Charles, 74, 82, 113, 265
Fraser's Magazine, 167, 177
Fuller, Margaret, 71
Furnivall, Dr. F. J., 244

Galdós, Benito Pérez, 256
Gambetta, Léon, 287
Gautier, Théophile, 136–37, 176; *Albertus*, 136; *Émaux et Camées*, 136–37, 142; *La Fausse Conversion*, 136; *Les Jeunes-France*, 136; *Spirite*, 136
Gavarni (Sulpice Chevalier), 101, 159, 218
Gay, Delphine, *L'École des journalistes*, 20
Genlis, Comtesse de, *Mémoires*, 7
Gentilhomme, René, 245
Gérôme, Jean Léon, 211, 219, 236, 249
Gibbon, Edward, 288
Gide, André, 38
Gil Blas, 10, 33
Ginsberg, Allen, 29
Girardin, Émile de, 91, 101–02, 117
Goncourt, Edmond and Jules, 159, 252
Gramont, Duc de, 260
Guérin, Maurice de, *Reliquiae*, 220
Guides-Joanne, 241
Guizot, François, 102, 108, 111, 149, 289–90; *Mémoires*, 289; *Monsieur Guizot dans sa famille*, 289

Haussmann, Georges Eugène, Baron, 168
Haworth, Fanny, 160, *passim*

327